ALSO AVAILABLE FROM 🐱TOKYOPOP®

MANGA

*INDICATES 100% AUTHENTIC MANGA (RIGHT-TO-LEFT FORMAT)

6-5-03

Under the Glass Moon

Volume 2

By

Ko Ya-Seong

TOKYOPOP®

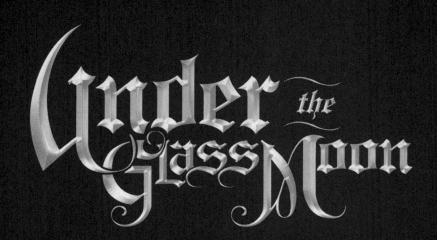

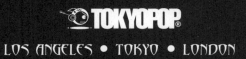

Los Angeles • Tokyo • London

Translator - Lauren Na
English Adaptation - Paul Morrissey
Retouch & Lettering - Alex SantaClara
Cover Layout & Graphic Design - Patrick Hook

Senior Editor - Rob Tokar
Managing Editor - Jill Freshney
Production Coordinator - Antonio DePietro
Production Manager - Jennifer Miller
Art Director - Matthew Alford
Director of Editorial - Jeremy Ross
VP of Production - Ron Klamert
President & C.O.O. - John Parker
Publisher & C.E.O. - Stuart Levy

Email: editor@TOKYOPOP.com
Come visit us online at www.TOKYOPOP.com

A ⊙ **TOKYOPOP**® Manga
TOKYOPOP
5900 Wilshire Blvd., Suite 2000,
Los Angeles, CA 90036

ISBN: 1-59182-241-6

First TOKYOPOP printing: Septemeber 2003

10 9 8 7 6 5 4 3 2 1
Printed in Canada

Under the Glass Moon

Meet the Reinhardt brothers—Luka and Luel. Yes, they are pretty boys, but they are also quite adept in the arcane black arts! The sassy Luka and the nebbish Luel have two gothically gorgeous witches as neighbors—Madame Batolli and her witch-apprentice daughter, Nell. Shy Luel and boisterous Nell are on the verge of a syrupy romance, much to the annoyed chagrin of Luka and Madame Batolli.

A young man named Neo pleaded to be Luka's apprentice. The misanthropic Luka refused. But, after Neo single-handedly defeated a wrathful fire spirit named Efreet, Luka theorized that Neo might have the potential to be a powerful spirit master. Luka's duplicitous mind concluded that Neo might just be handy to have around after all—if Luka can control Neo's abilities!

The supremely spoiled Sage, Luel's former lover, has concocted a sinister plot to force Luel to wed her! Rendered powerless, will Luel be able to say "I don't" at the altar? Luka, Madame Batolli and a fiercely jealous Nell fly to the rescue, but they are confronted by Fuan, a powerful sorcerer with his own hidden agenda...

유리달 아래서

Under the Glass Moon

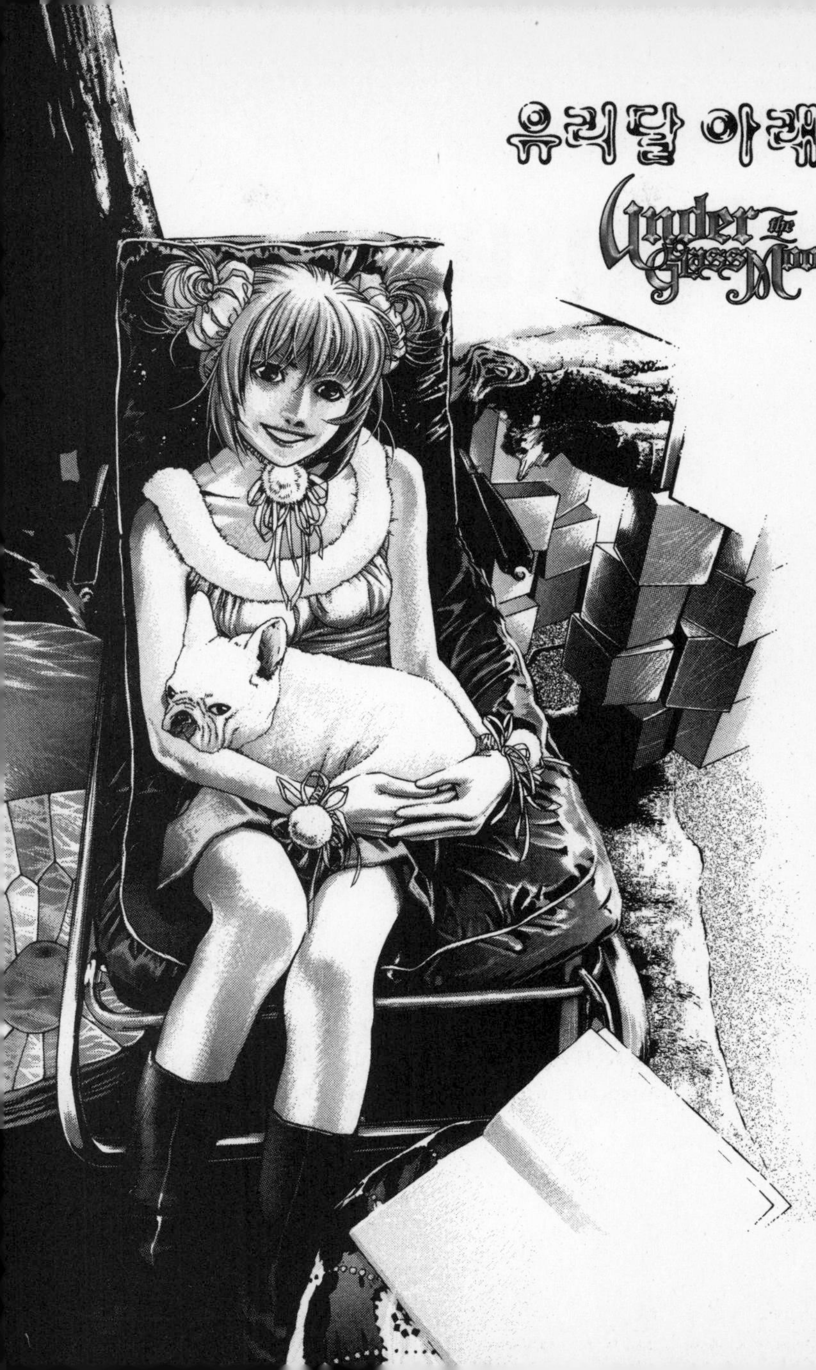

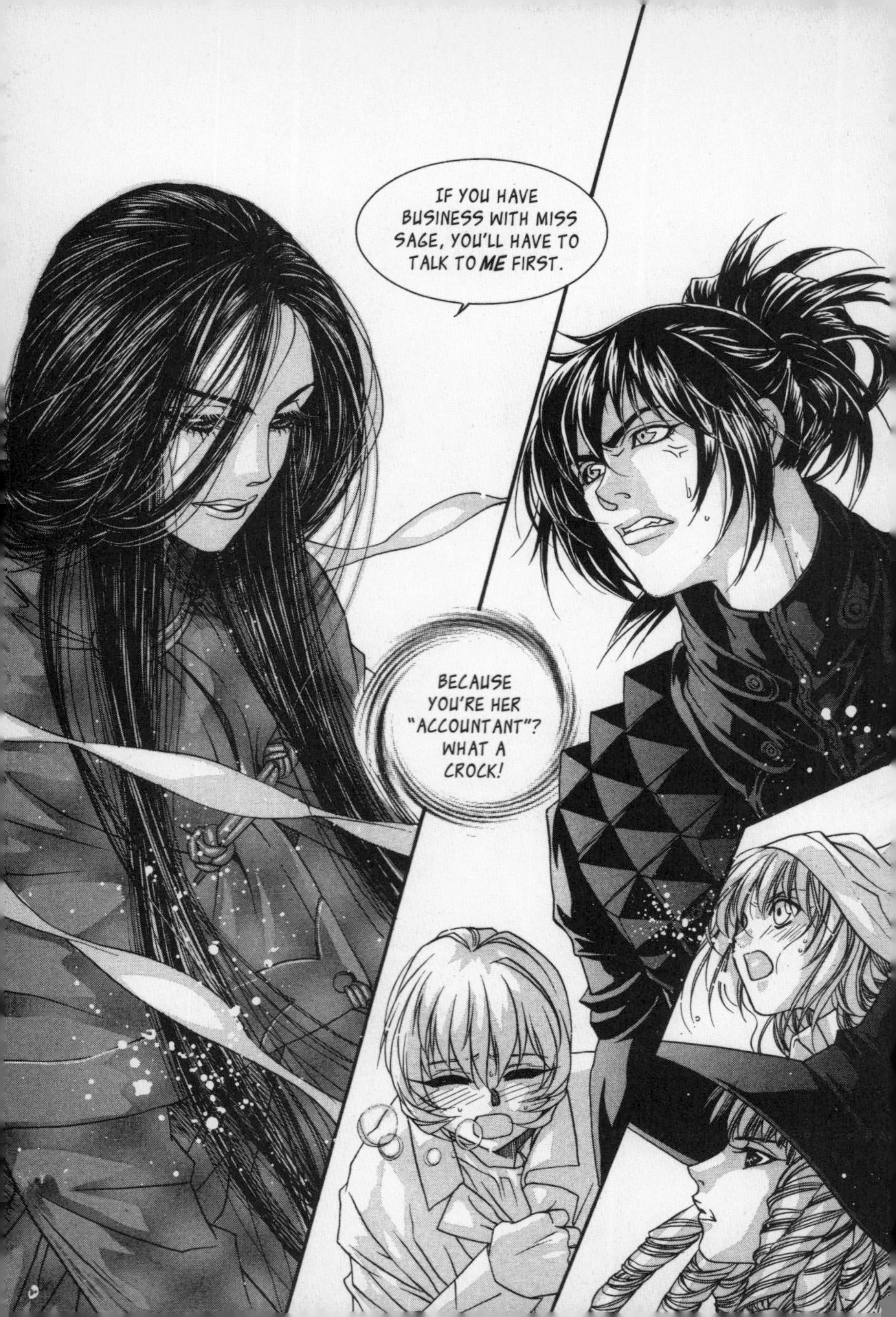
IF YOU HAVE BUSINESS WITH MISS SAGE, YOU'LL HAVE TO TALK TO *ME* FIRST.
BECAUSE YOU'RE HER "ACCOUNTANT"? WHAT A CROCK!

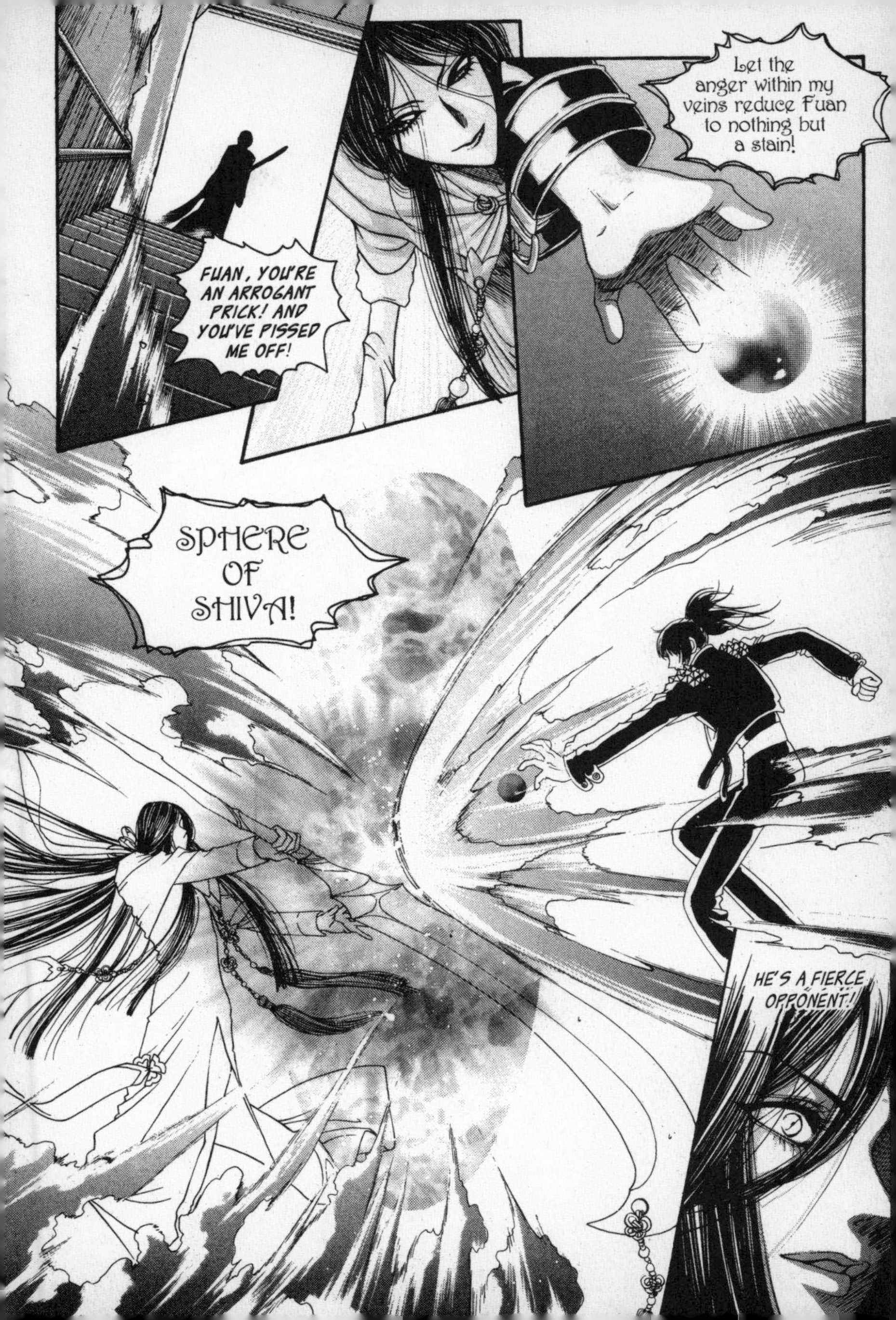
FUAN, YOU'RE AN ARROGANT PRICK! AND YOU'VE PISSED ME OFF!
Let the anger within my veins reduce Fuan to nothing but a stain!
SPHERE OF SHIVA!
HE'S A FIERCE OPPONENT!

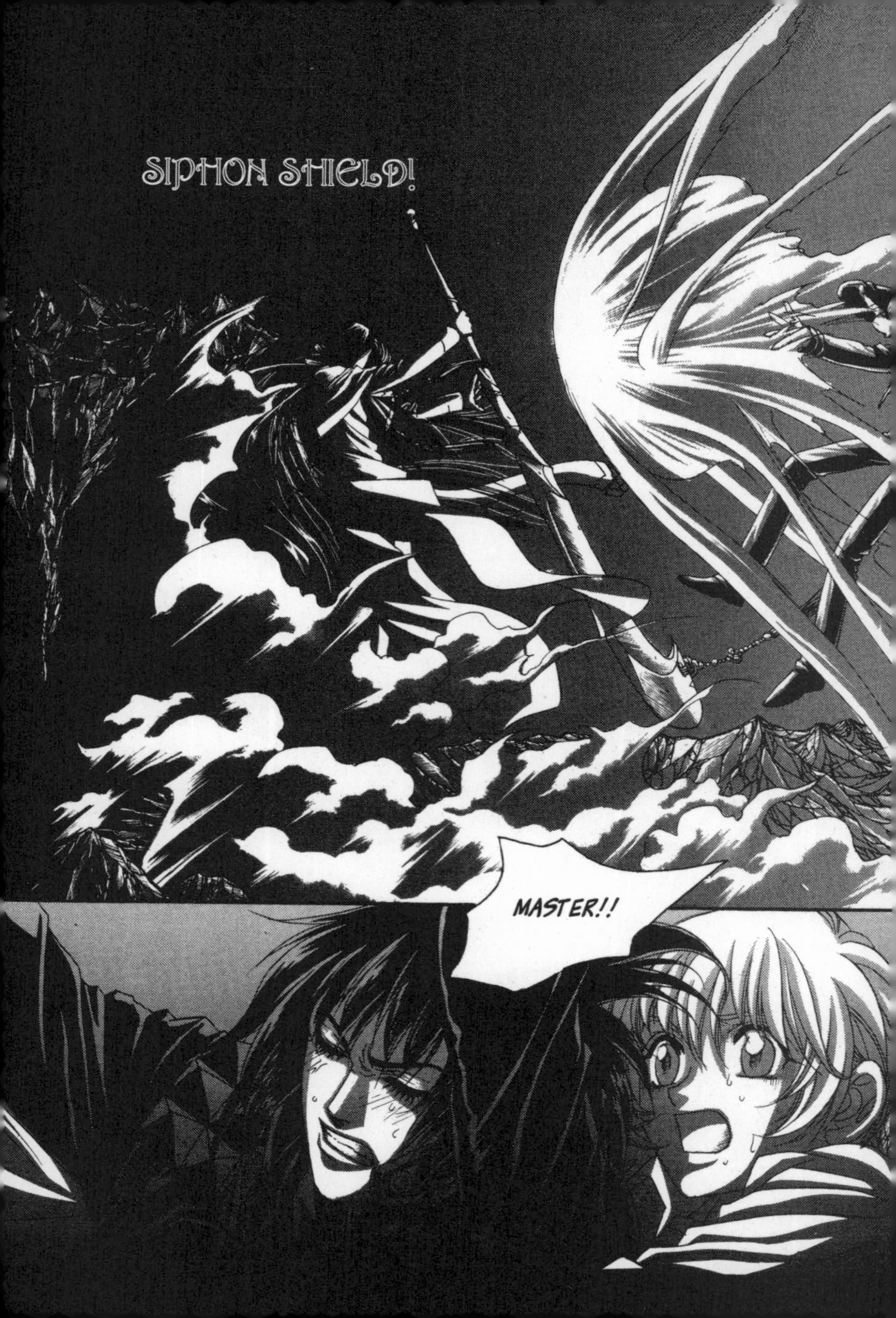
SIPHON SHIELD!
MASTER!!

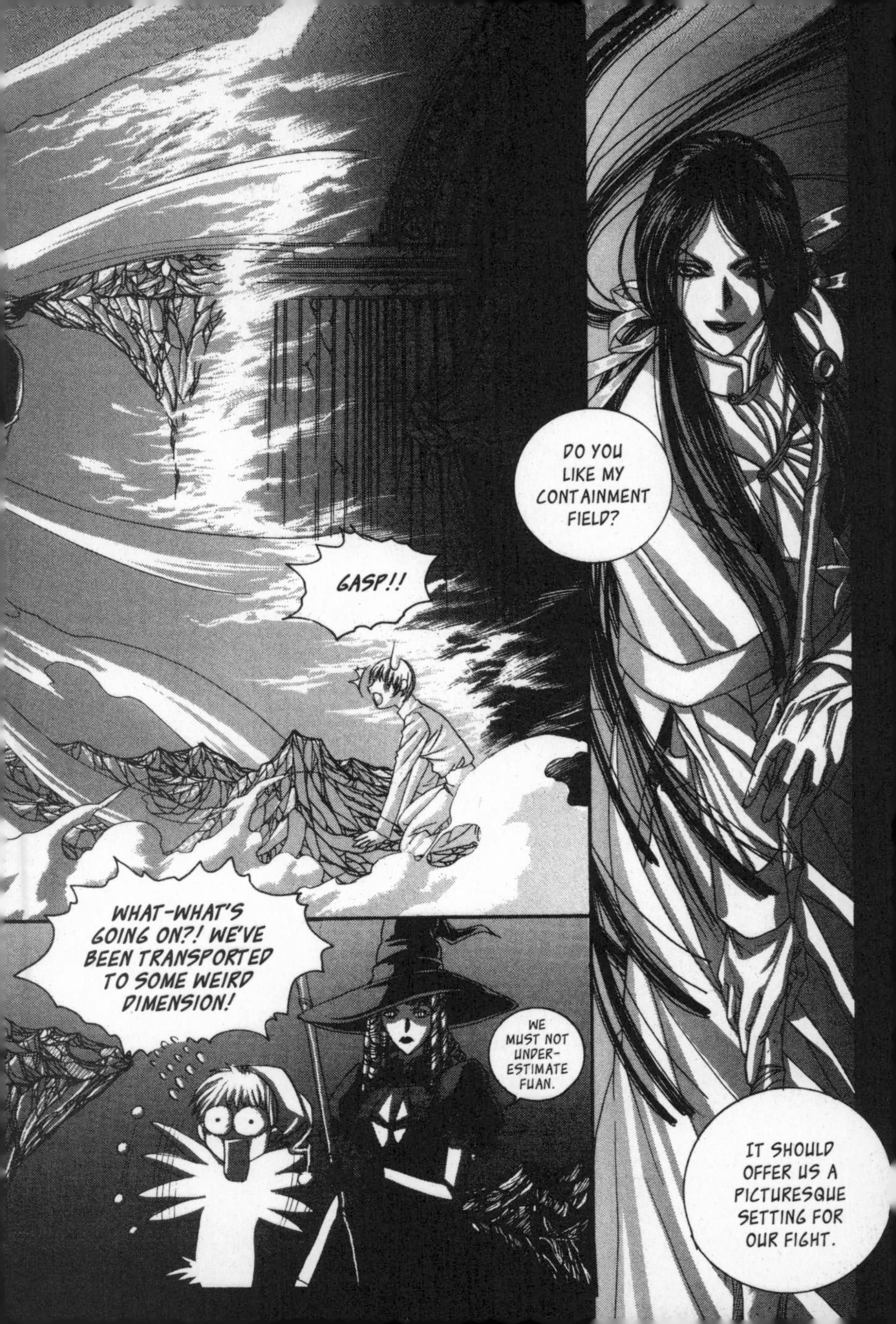
GASP!!
WHAT-WHAT'S GOING ON?! WE'VE BEEN TRANSPORTED TO SOME WEIRD DIMENSION!
WE MUST NOT UNDER-ESTIMATE FUAN.
DO YOU LIKE MY CONTAINMENT FIELD?
IT SHOULD OFFER US A PICTURESQUE SETTING FOR OUR FIGHT.

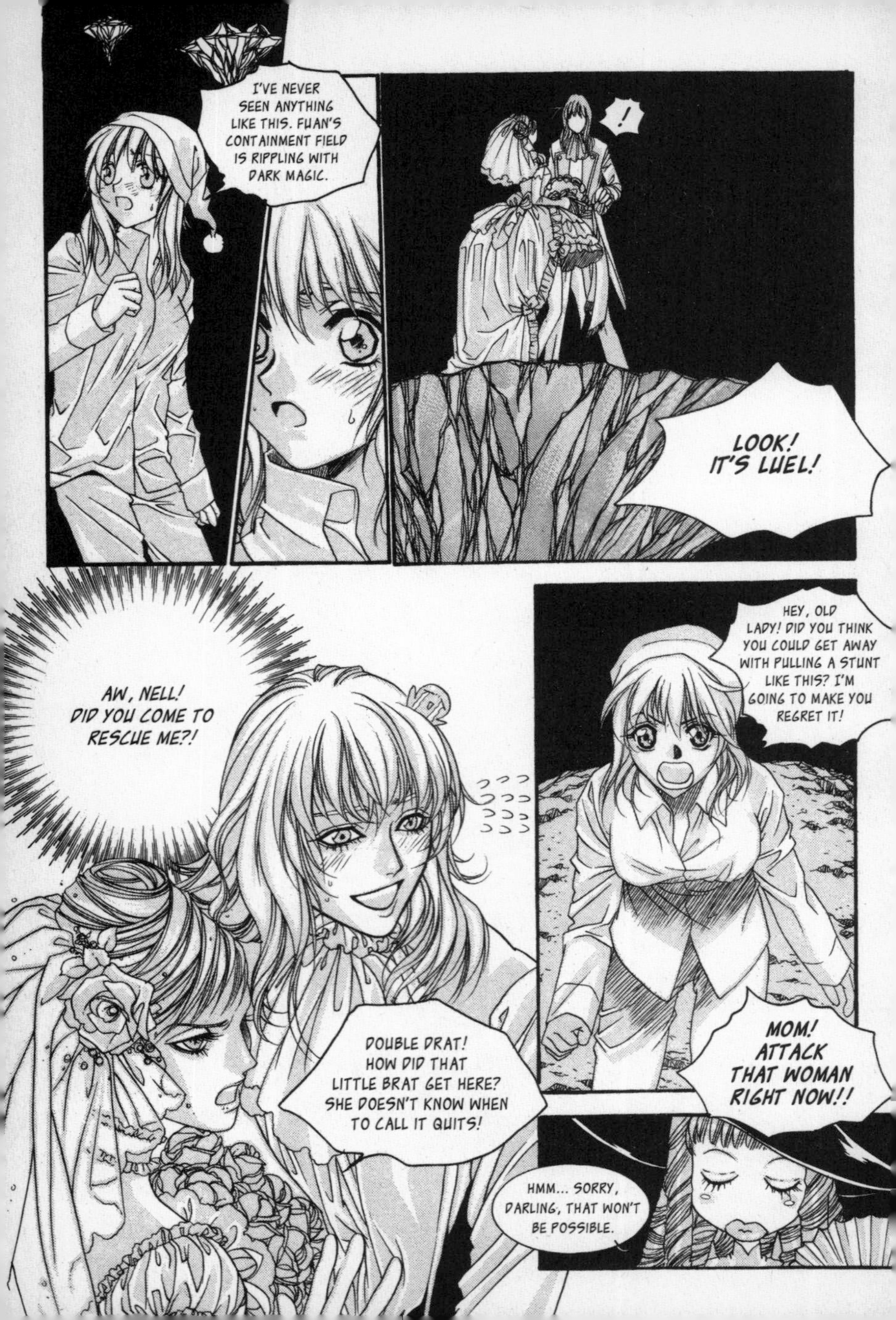
I'VE NEVER SEEN ANYTHING LIKE THIS. FUAN'S CONTAINMENT FIELD IS RIPPLING WITH DARK MAGIC.
!
LOOK! IT'S LUEL!
AW, NELL! DID YOU COME TO RESCUE ME?!
DOUBLE DRAT! HOW DID THAT LITTLE BRAT GET HERE? SHE DOESN'T KNOW WHEN TO CALL IT QUITS!
HEY, OLD LADY! DID YOU THINK YOU COULD GET AWAY WITH PULLING A STUNT LIKE THIS? I'M GOING TO MAKE YOU REGRET IT!
MOM! ATTACK THAT WOMAN RIGHT NOW!!
HMM... SORRY, DARLING, THAT WON'T BE POSSIBLE.

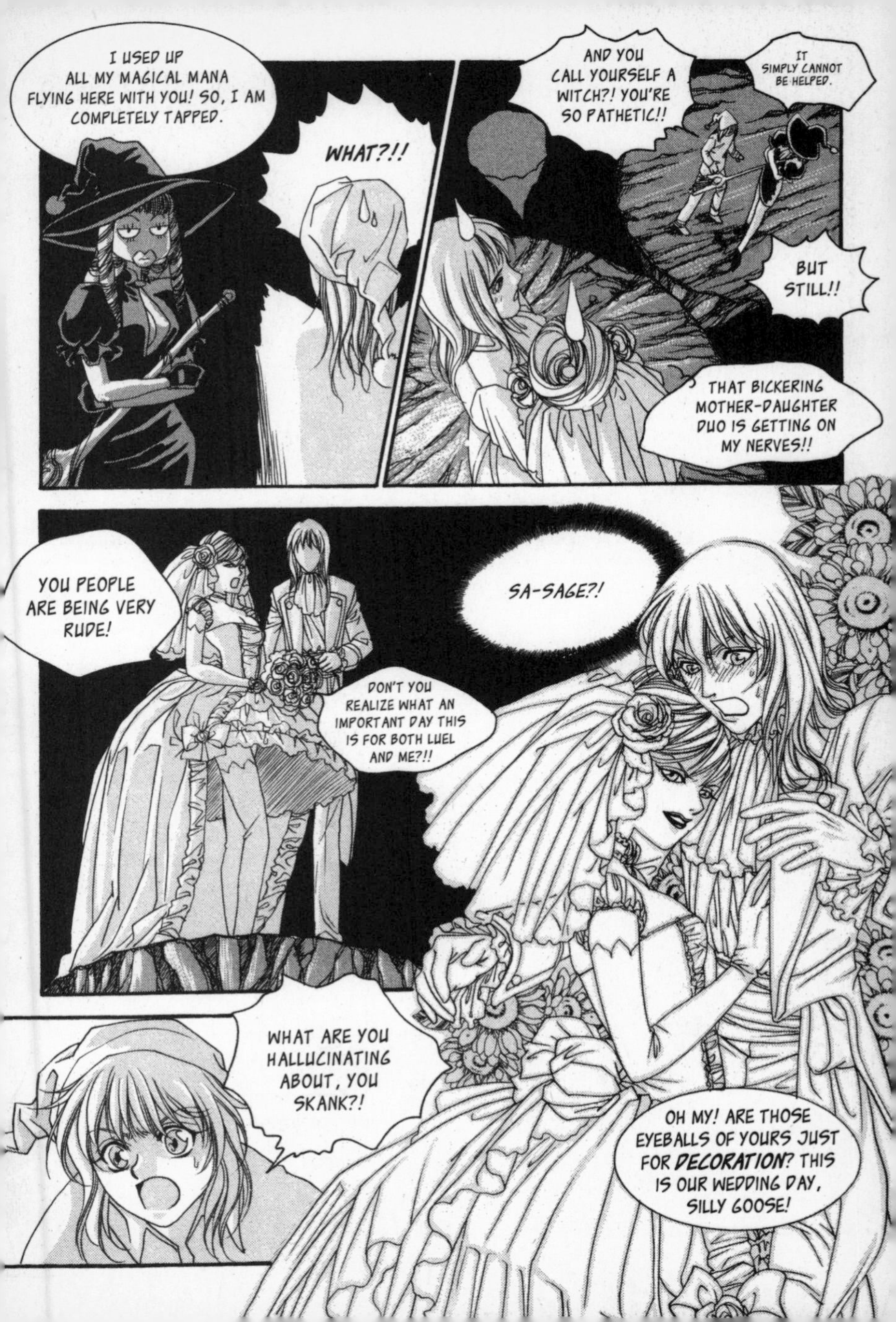
I USED UP ALL MY MAGICAL MANA FLYING HERE WITH YOU! SO, I AM COMPLETELY TAPPED.
WHAT?!!
AND YOU CALL YOURSELF A WITCH?! YOU'RE SO PATHETIC!!
IT SIMPLY CANNOT BE HELPED.
BUT STILL!!
THAT BICKERING MOTHER-DAUGHTER DUO IS GETTING ON MY NERVES!!
YOU PEOPLE ARE BEING VERY RUDE!
DON'T YOU REALIZE WHAT AN IMPORTANT DAY THIS IS FOR BOTH LUEL AND ME?!!
SA-SAGE?!
WHAT ARE YOU HALLUCINATING ABOUT, YOU SKANK?!
OH MY! ARE THOSE EYEBALLS OF YOURS JUST FOR DECORATION? THIS IS OUR WEDDING DAY, SILLY GOOSE!

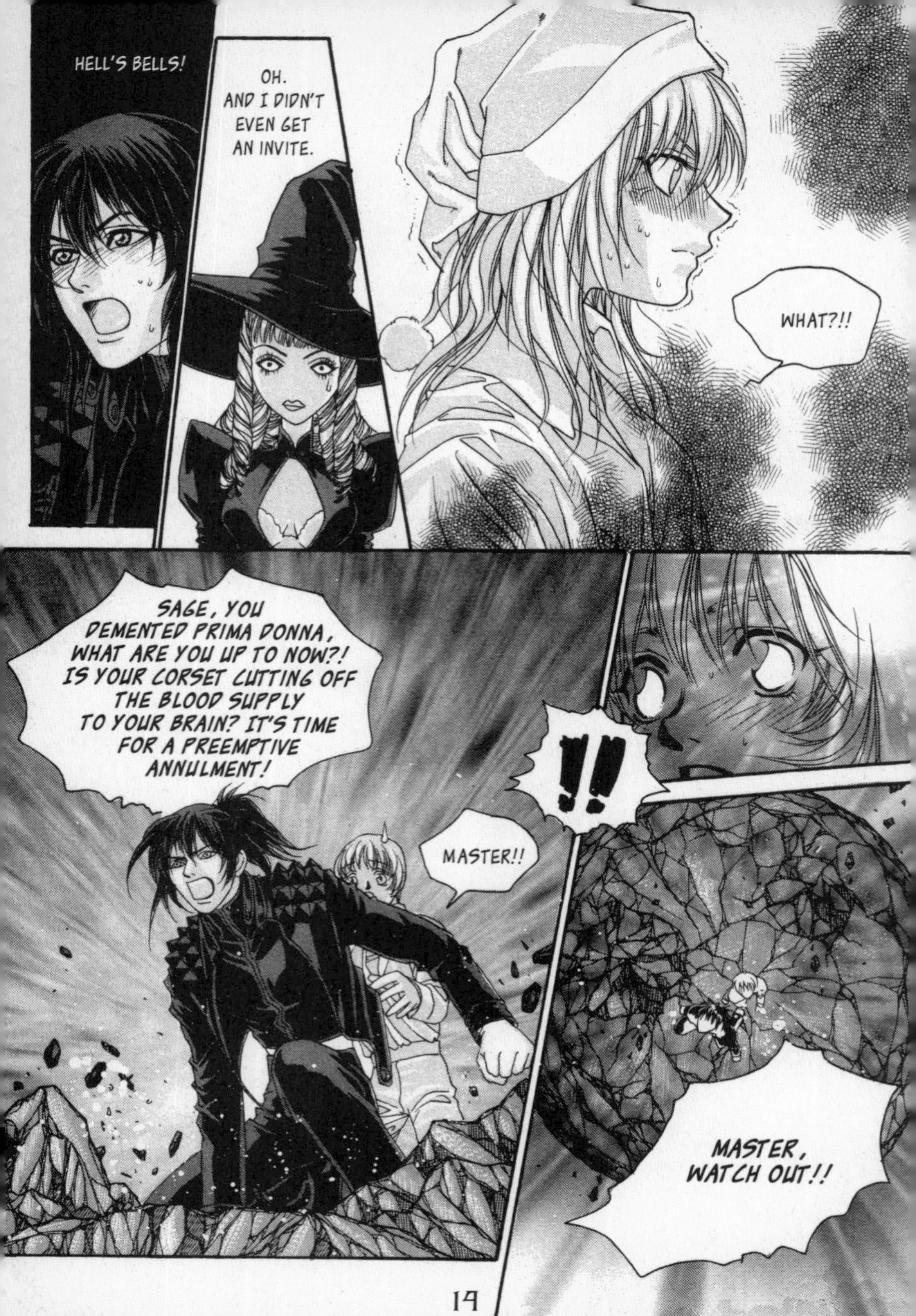
HELL'S BELLS!
OH. AND I DIDN'T EVEN GET AN INVITE.
WHAT?!!
SAGE, YOU DEMENTED PRIMA DONNA, WHAT ARE YOU UP TO NOW?! IS YOUR CORSET CUTTING OFF THE BLOOD SUPPLY TO YOUR BRAIN? IT'S TIME FOR A PREEMPTIVE ANNULMENT!
MASTER!!
!!
MASTER, WATCH OUT!!

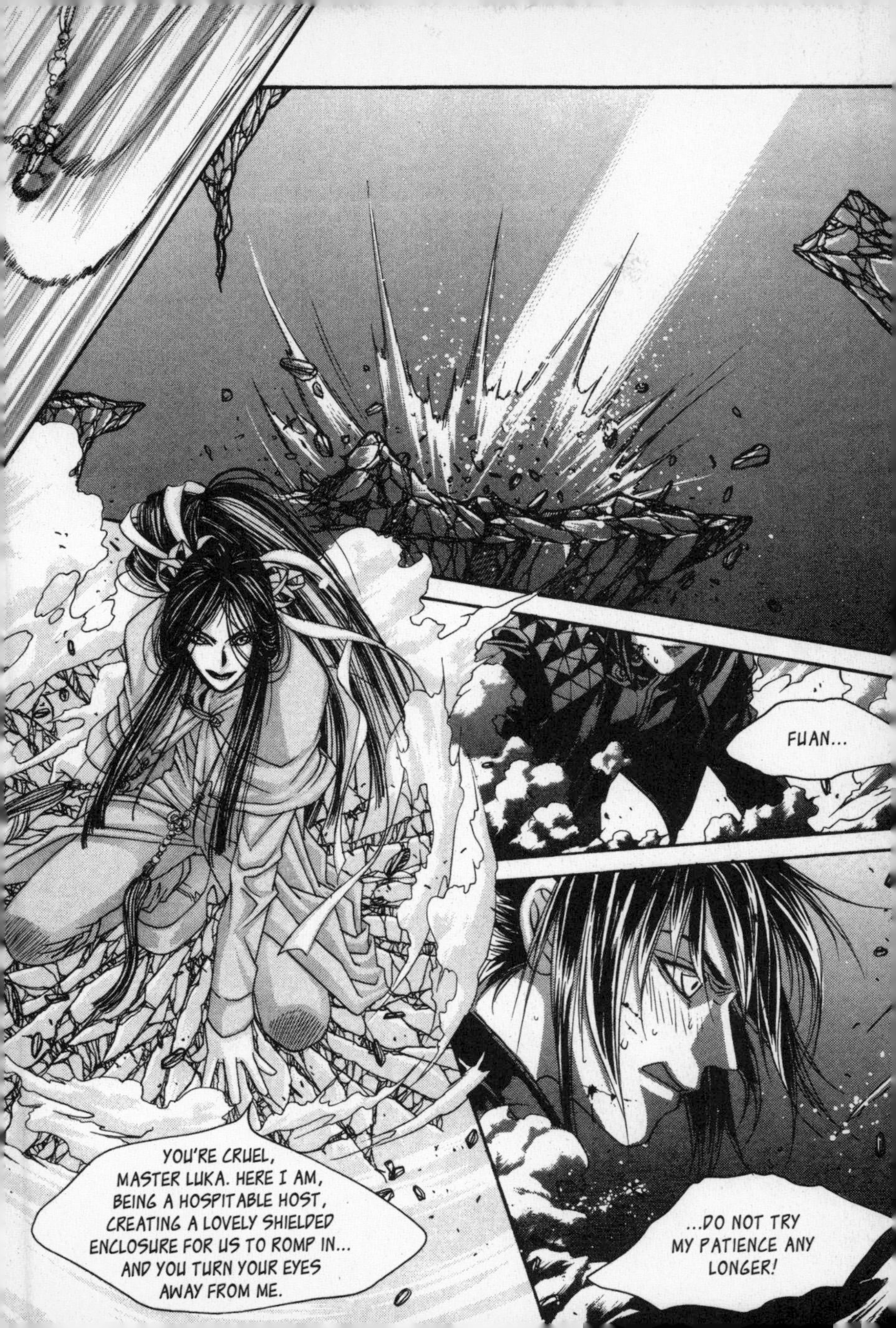
YOU'RE CRUEL, MASTER LUKA. HERE I AM, BEING A HOSPITABLE HOST, CREATING A LOVELY SHIELDED ENCLOSURE FOR US TO ROMP IN... AND YOU TURN YOUR EYES AWAY FROM ME.
FUAN...
...DO NOT TRY MY PATIENCE ANY LONGER!

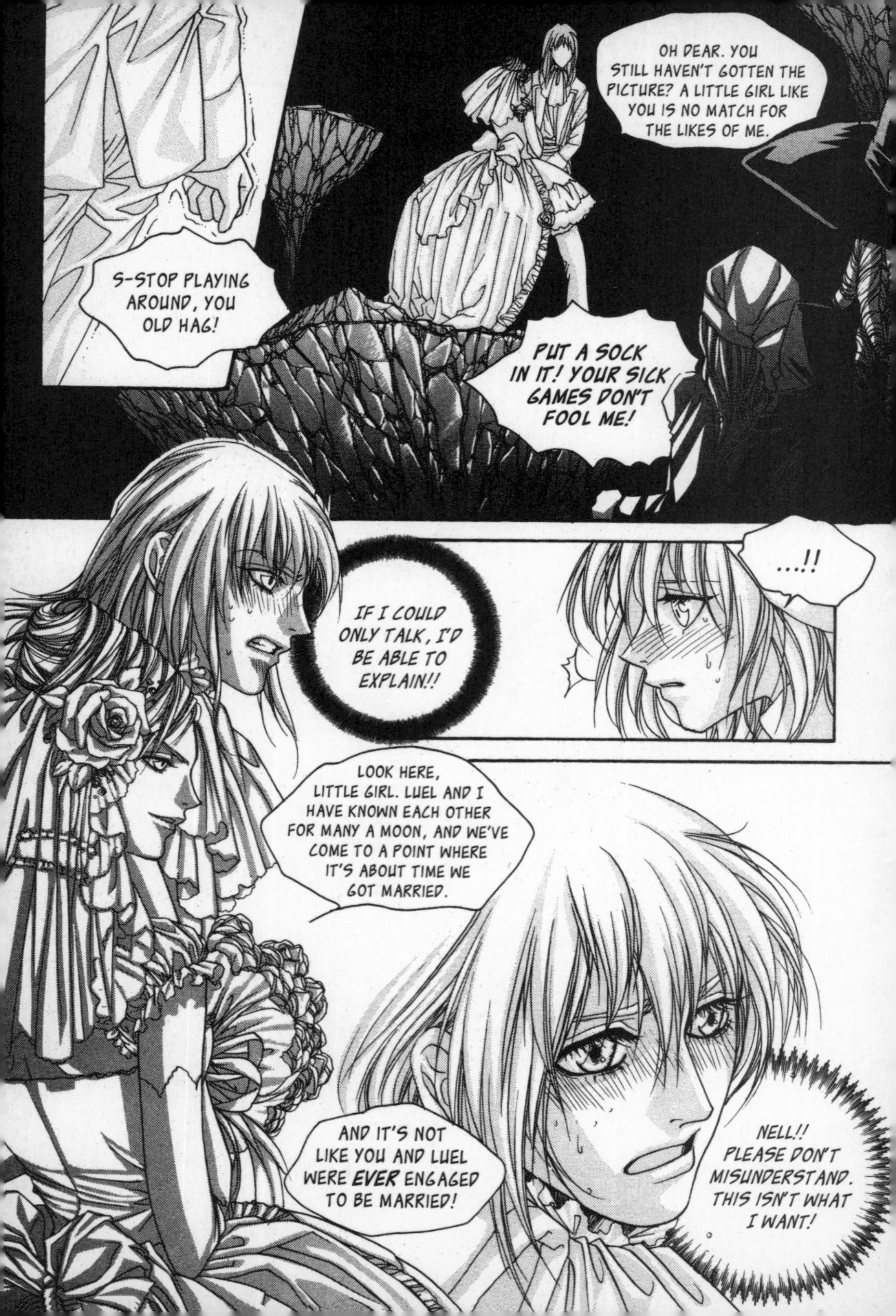
OH DEAR. YOU STILL HAVEN'T GOTTEN THE PICTURE? A LITTLE GIRL LIKE YOU IS NO MATCH FOR THE LIKES OF ME.
S-STOP PLAYING AROUND, YOU OLD HAG!
PUT A SOCK IN IT! YOUR SICK GAMES DON'T FOOL ME!
IF I COULD ONLY TALK, I'D BE ABLE TO EXPLAIN!!
...!!
LOOK HERE, LITTLE GIRL. LUEL AND I HAVE KNOWN EACH OTHER FOR MANY A MOON, AND WE'VE COME TO A POINT WHERE IT'S ABOUT TIME WE GOT MARRIED.
AND IT'S NOT LIKE YOU AND LUEL WERE EVER ENGAGED TO BE MARRIED!
NELL!! PLEASE DON'T MISUNDERSTAND. THIS ISN'T WHAT I WANT!

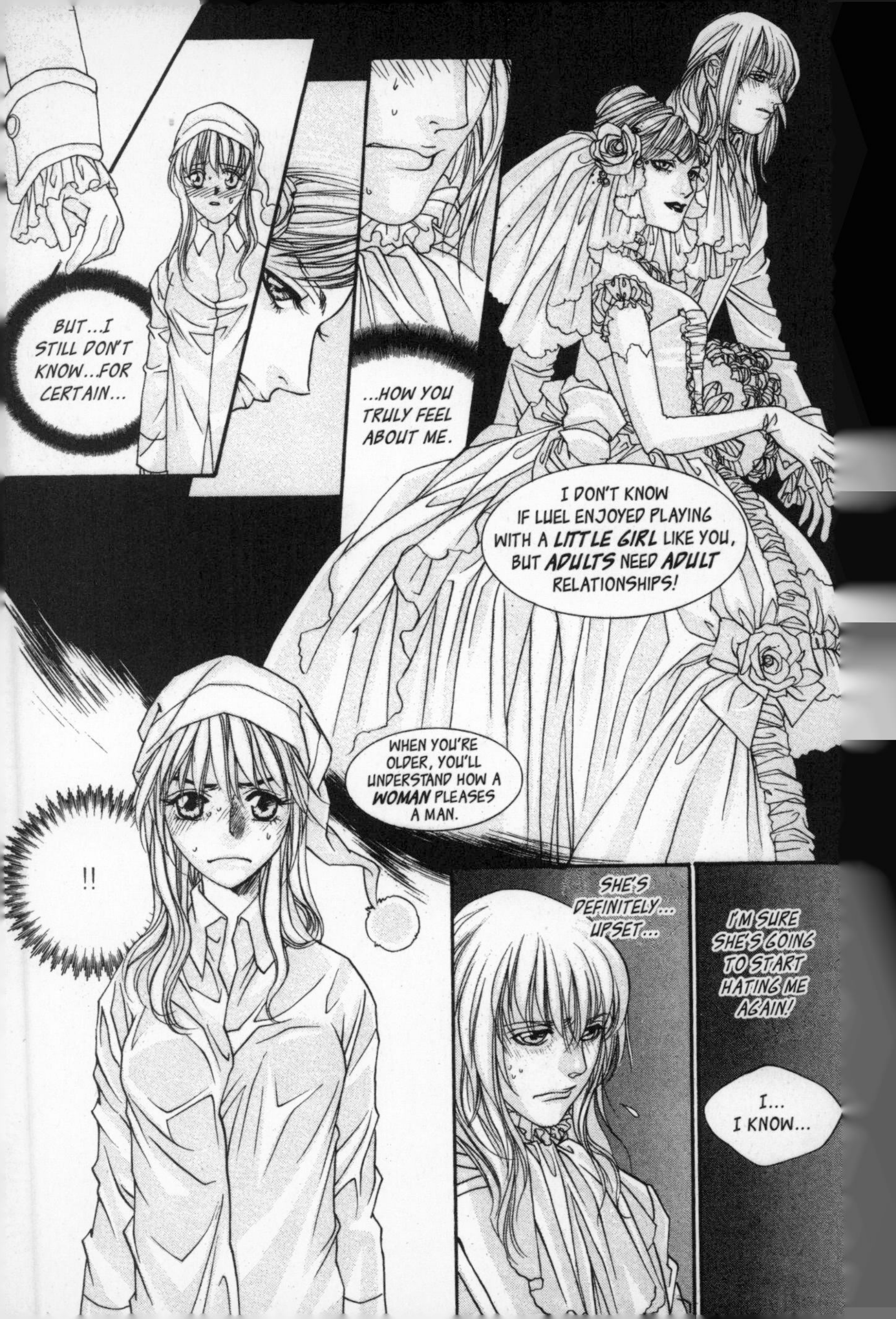
BUT...I STILL DON'T KNOW...FOR CERTAIN...
...HOW YOU TRULY FEEL ABOUT ME.
I DON'T KNOW IF LUEL ENJOYED PLAYING WITH A LITTLE GIRL LIKE YOU, BUT ADULTS NEED ADULT RELATIONSHIPS!
WHEN YOU'RE OLDER, YOU'LL UNDERSTAND HOW A WOMAN PLEASES A MAN.
!!
SHE'S DEFINITELY... UPSET...
I'M SURE SHE'S GOING TO START HATING ME AGAIN!
I... I KNOW...

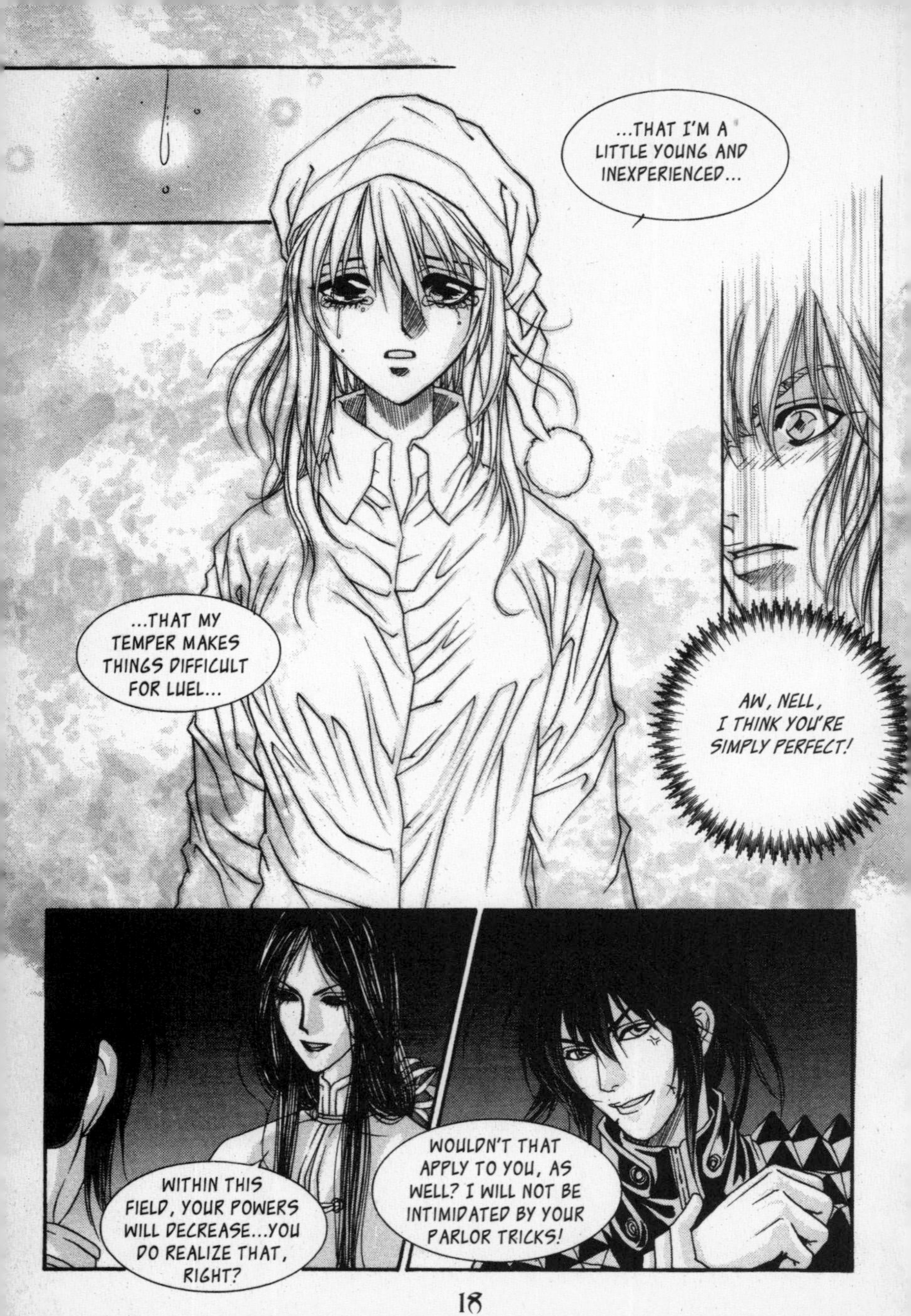
...THAT I'M A LITTLE YOUNG AND INEXPERIENCED...
...THAT MY TEMPER MAKES THINGS DIFFICULT FOR LUEL...
AW, NELL, I THINK YOU'RE SIMPLY PERFECT!
WITHIN THIS FIELD, YOUR POWERS WILL DECREASE...YOU DO REALIZE THAT, RIGHT?
WOULDN'T THAT APPLY TO YOU, AS WELL? I WILL NOT BE INTIMIDATED BY YOUR PARLOR TRICKS!

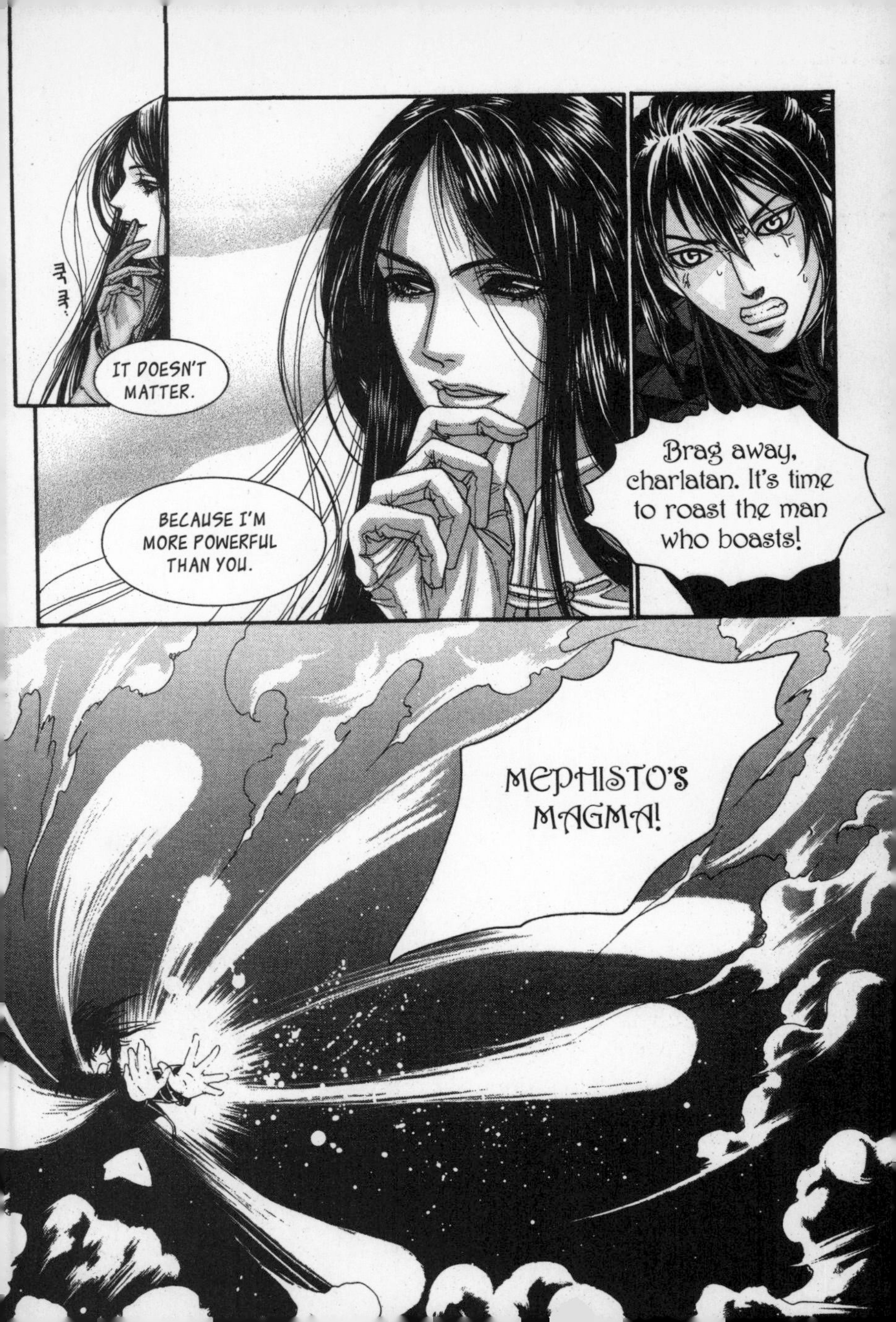
큭큭..
IT DOESN'T MATTER.
BECAUSE I'M MORE POWERFUL THAN YOU.
Brag away, charlatan. It's time to roast the man who boasts!
MEPHISTO'S MAGMA!

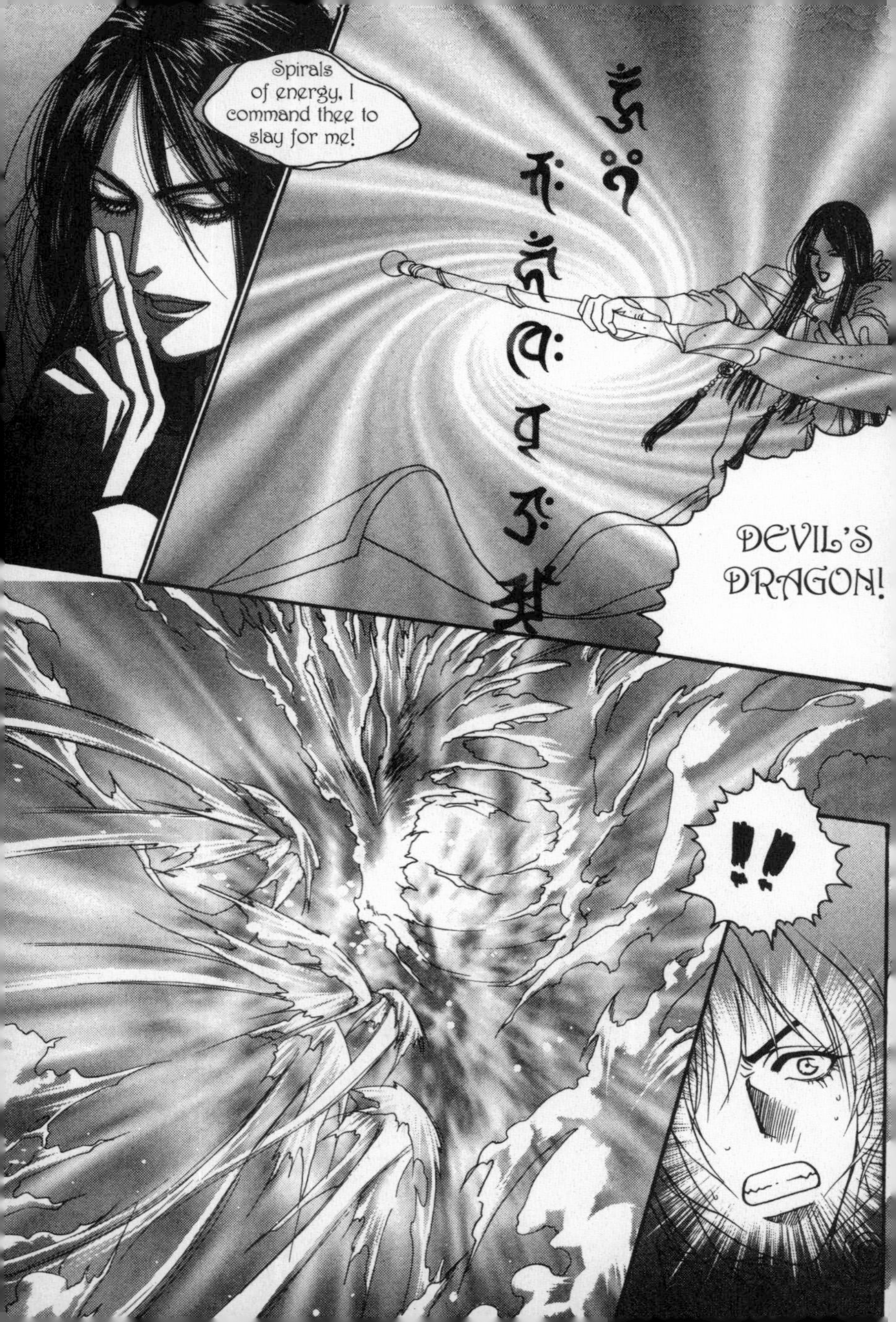
Spirals of energy, I command thee to slay for me!
DEVIL'S DRAGON!
!!

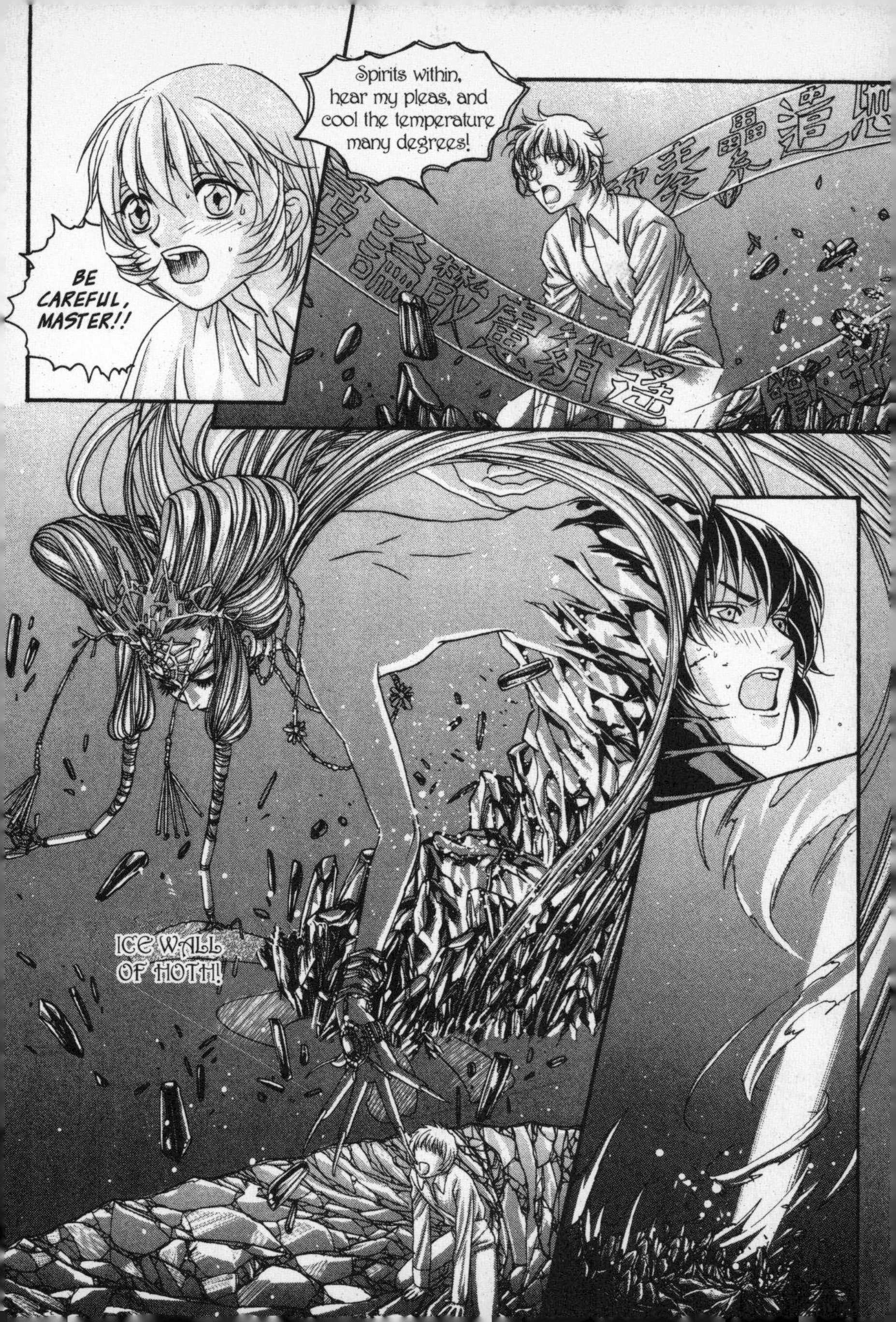
BE CAREFUL, MASTER!!
Spirits within, hear my pleas, and cool the temperature many degrees!
ICE WALL OF HOTH!

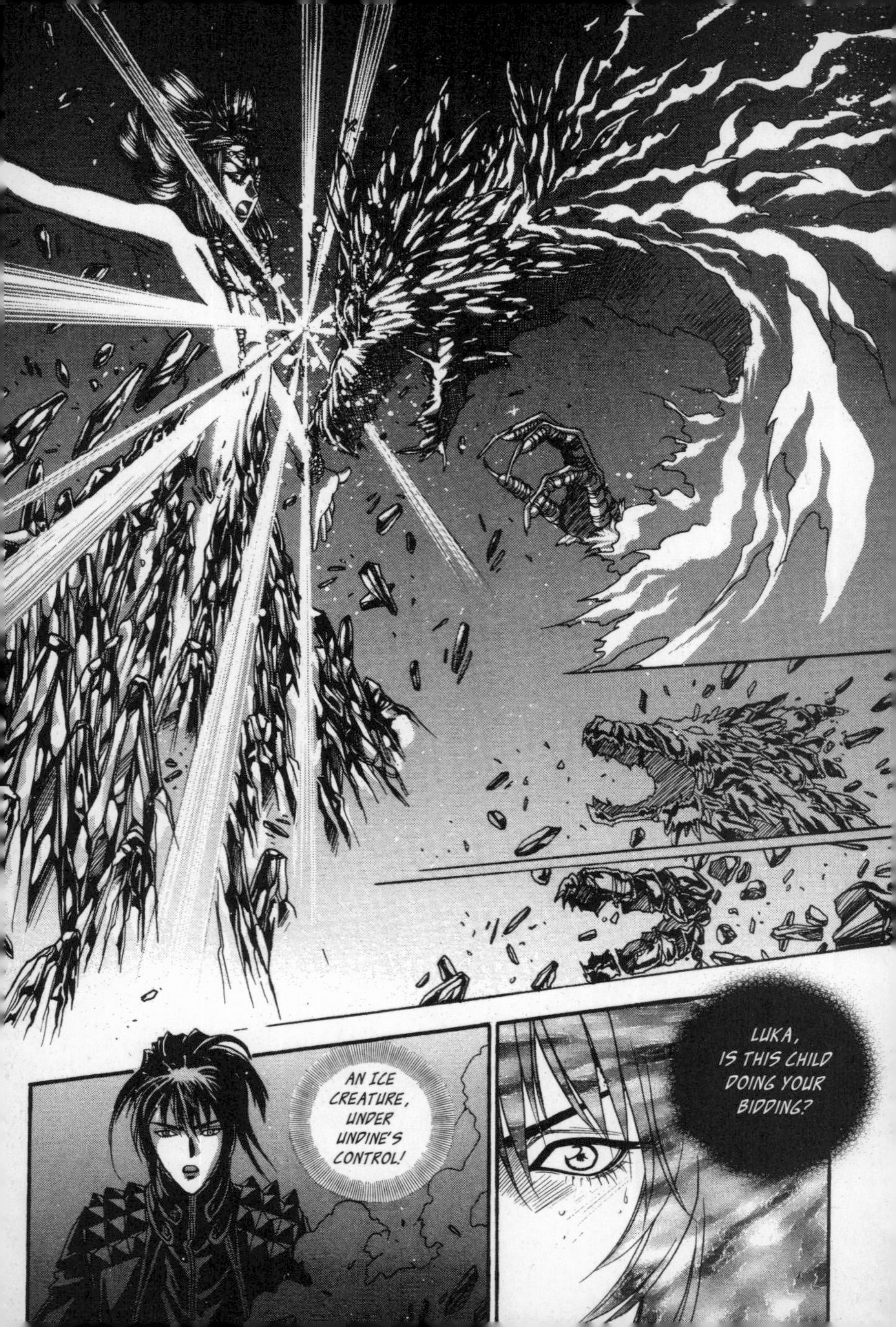
AN ICE CREATURE, UNDER UNDINE'S CONTROL!
LUKA, IS THIS CHILD DOING YOUR BIDDING?

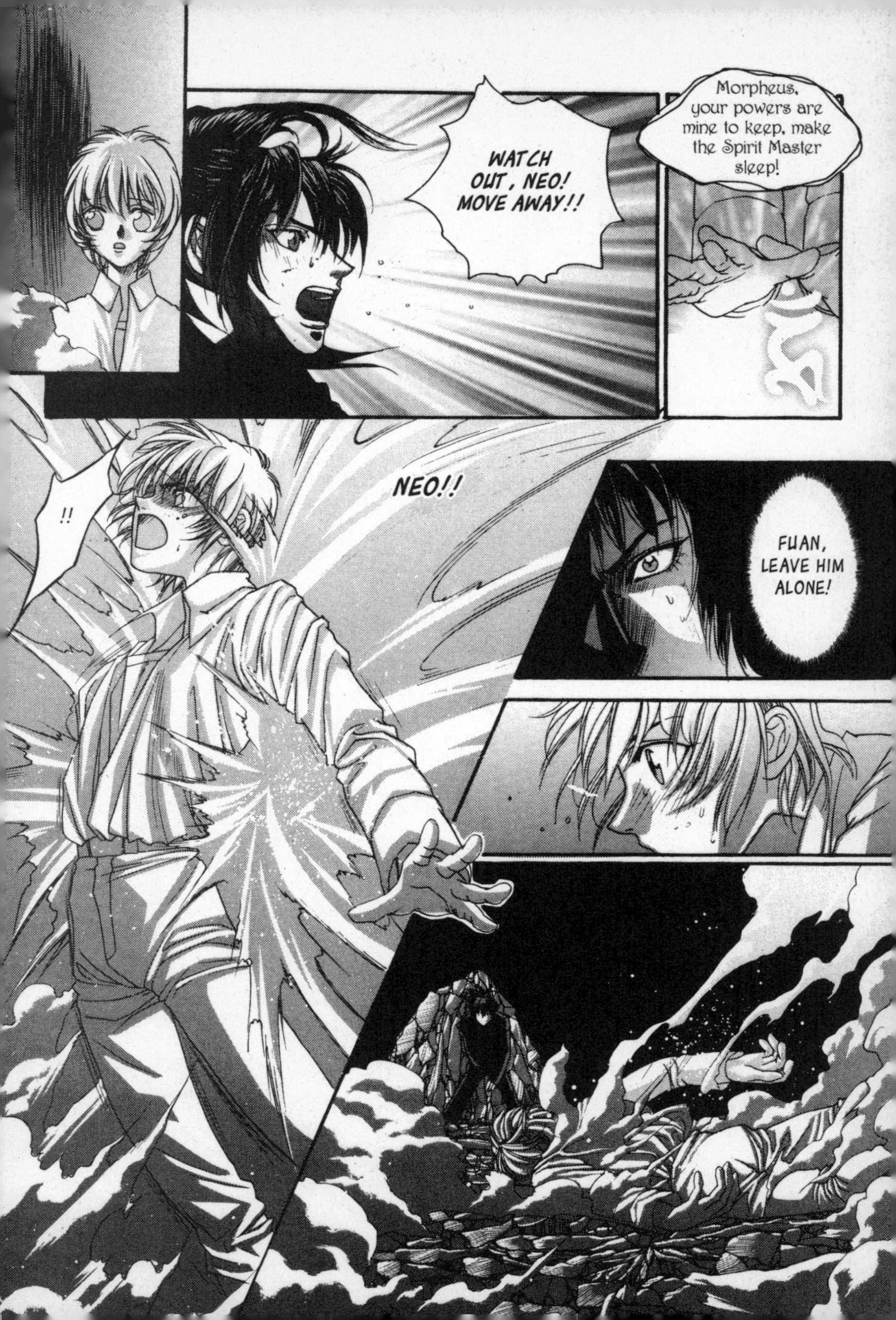
WATCH OUT, NEO! MOVE AWAY!!
Morpheus, your powers are mine to keep, make the Spirit Master sleep!
!!
NEO!!
FUAN, LEAVE HIM ALONE!

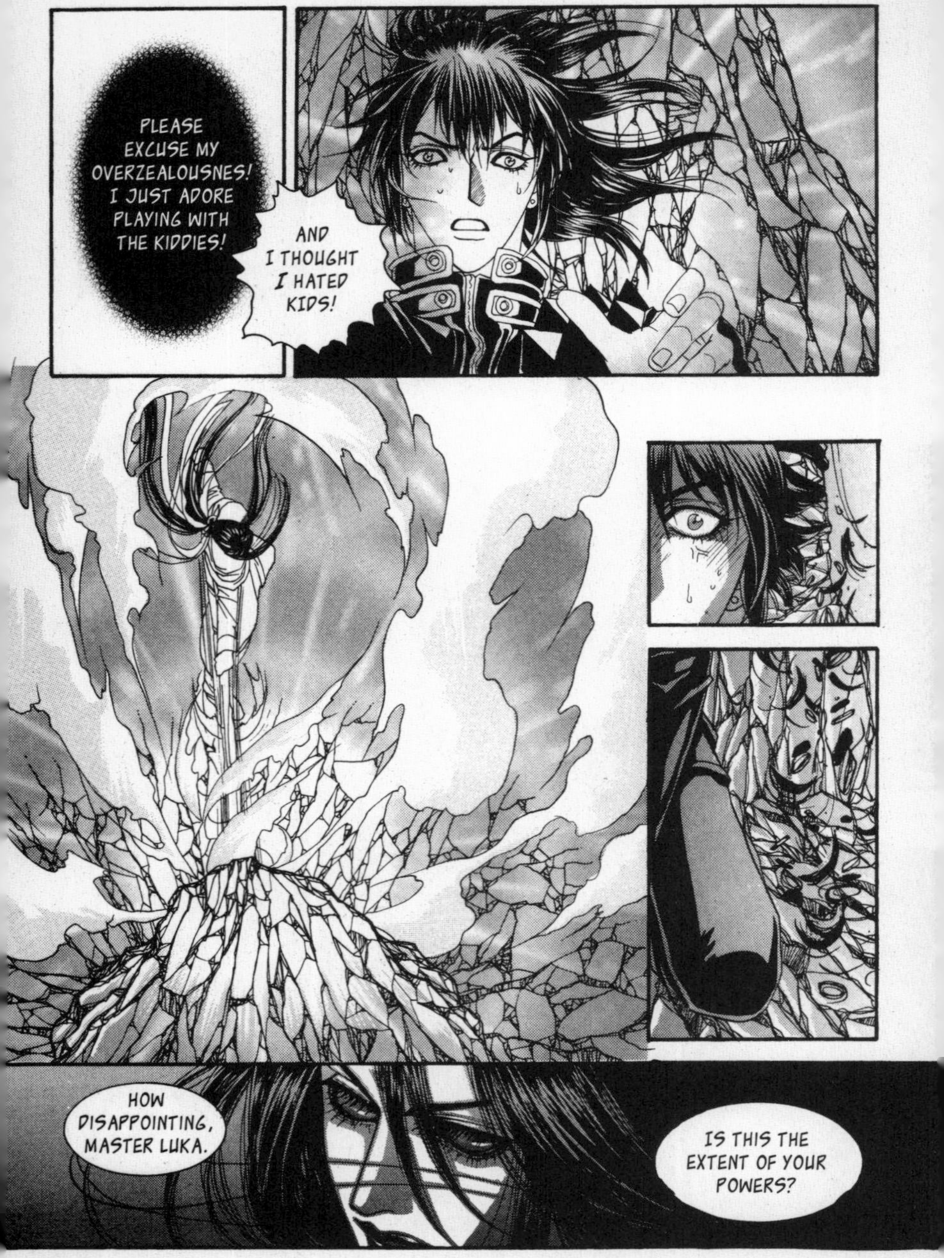
PLEASE EXCUSE MY OVERZEALOUSNES! I JUST ADORE PLAYING WITH THE KIDDIES!
AND I THOUGHT I HATED KIDS!
HOW DISAPPOINTING, MASTER LUKA.
IS THIS THE EXTENT OF YOUR POWERS?

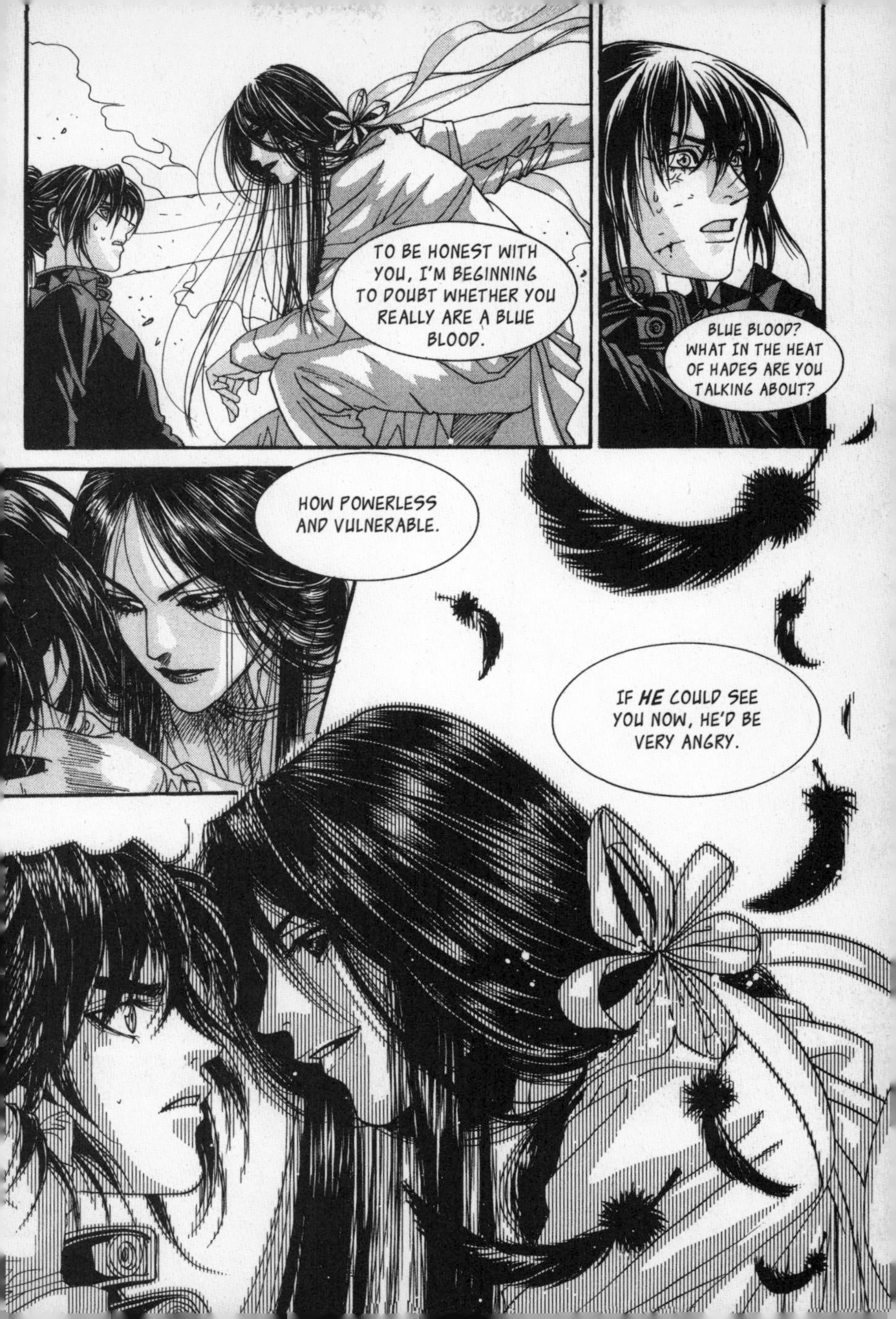
TO BE HONEST WITH YOU, I'M BEGINNING TO DOUBT WHETHER YOU REALLY ARE A BLUE BLOOD.
BLUE BLOOD? WHAT IN THE HEAT OF HADES ARE YOU TALKING ABOUT?
HOW POWERLESS AND VULNERABLE.
IF HE COULD SEE YOU NOW, HE'D BE VERY ANGRY.

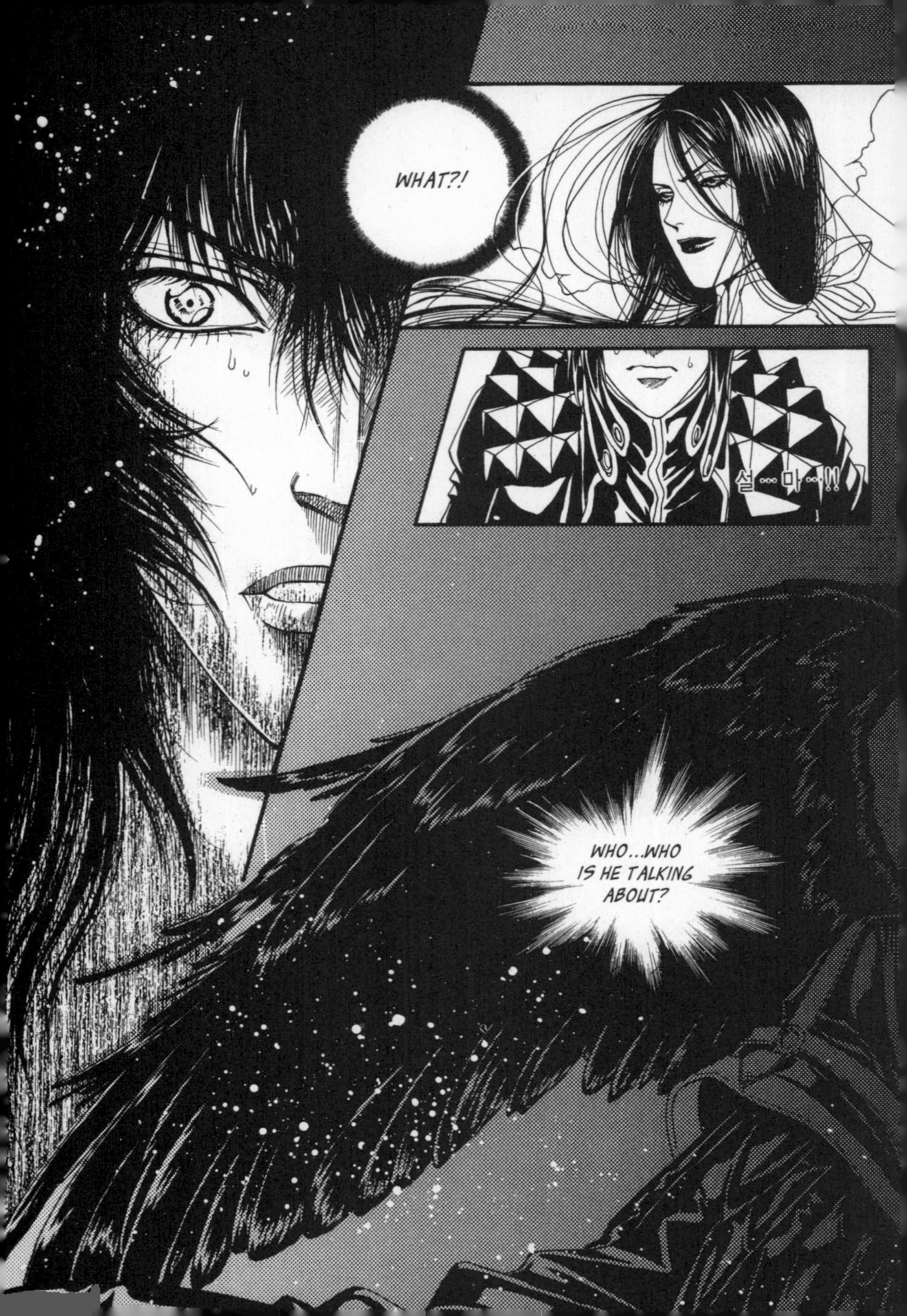
WHAT?!
설…마…!!
WHO...WHO IS HE TALKING ABOUT?

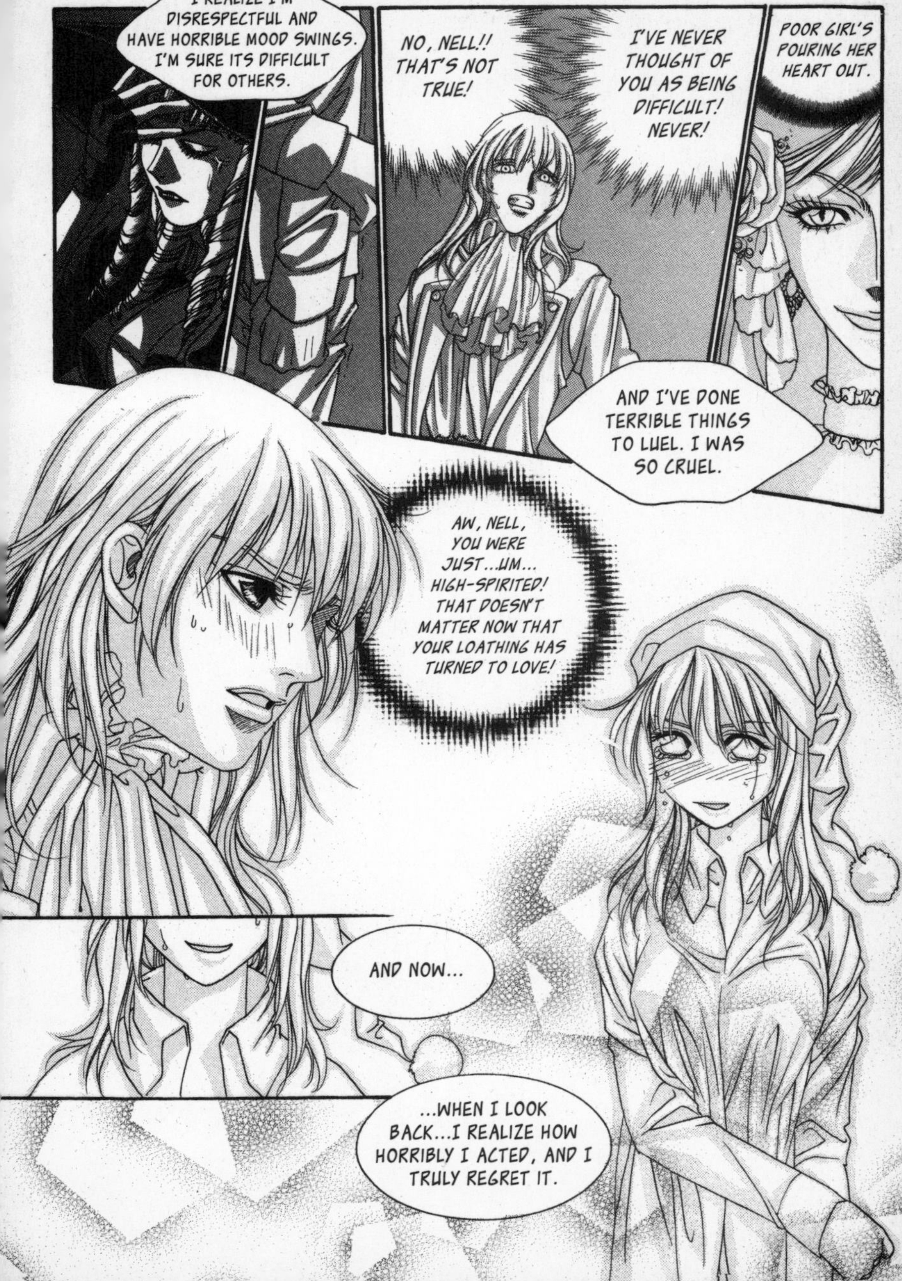

I REALIZE I'M DISRESPECTFUL AND HAVE HORRIBLE MOOD SWINGS. I'M SURE ITS DIFFICULT FOR OTHERS.
NO, NELL!! THAT'S NOT TRUE!
I'VE NEVER THOUGHT OF YOU AS BEING DIFFICULT! NEVER!
POOR GIRL'S POURING HER HEART OUT.
AND I'VE DONE TERRIBLE THINGS TO LUEL. I WAS SO CRUEL.
AW, NELL, YOU WERE JUST...UM... HIGH-SPIRITED! THAT DOESN'T MATTER NOW THAT YOUR LOATHING HAS TURNED TO LOVE!
AND NOW...
...WHEN I LOOK BACK...I REALIZE HOW HORRIBLY I ACTED, AND I TRULY REGRET IT.

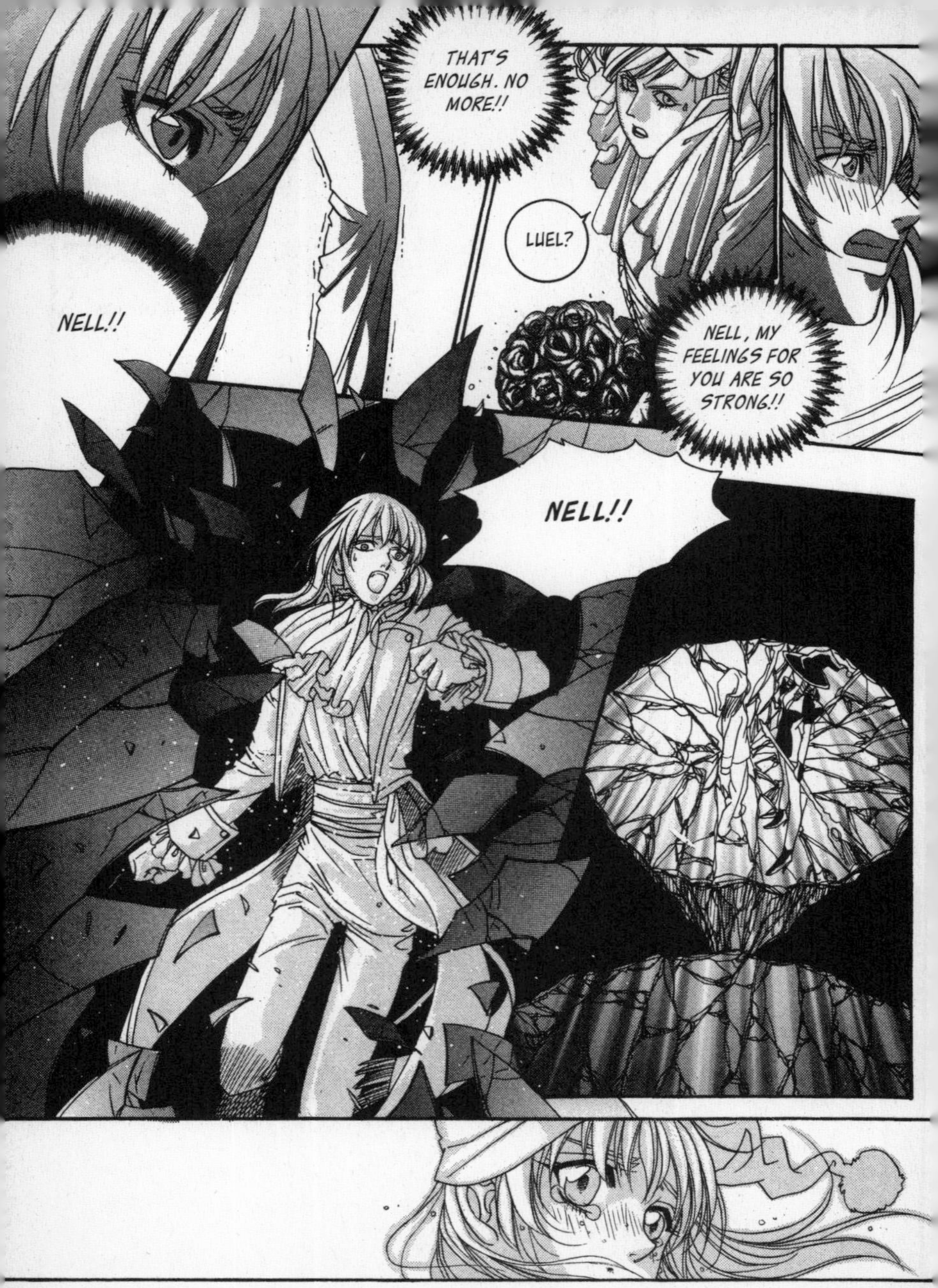
NELL!!
THAT'S ENOUGH. NO MORE!!
LUEL?
NELL, MY FEELINGS FOR YOU ARE SO STRONG!!
NELL!!

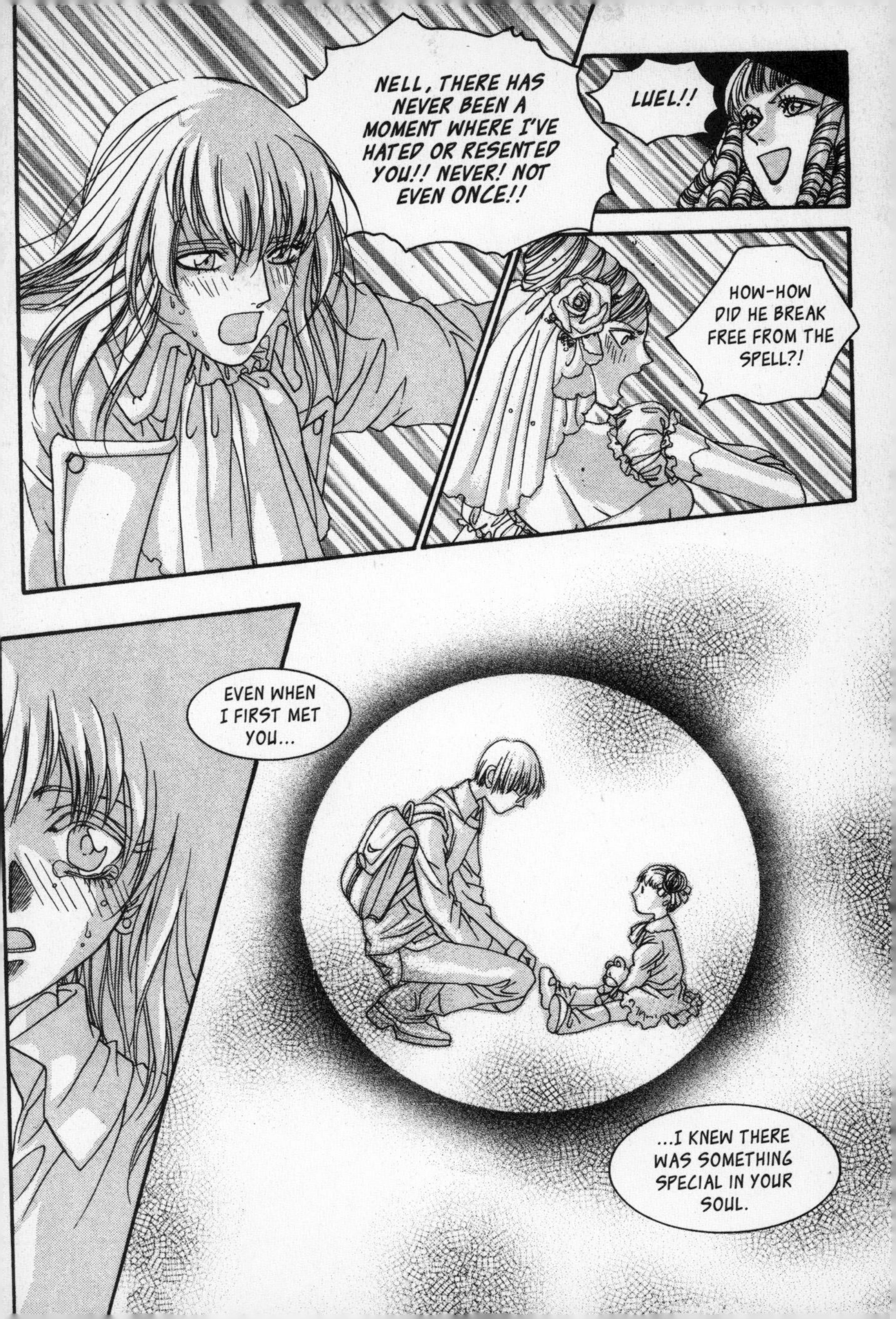
NELL, THERE HAS NEVER BEEN A MOMENT WHERE I'VE HATED OR RESENTED YOU!! NEVER! NOT EVEN ONCE!!
LUEL!!
HOW-HOW DID HE BREAK FREE FROM THE SPELL?!
EVEN WHEN I FIRST MET YOU...
...I KNEW THERE WAS SOMETHING SPECIAL IN YOUR SOUL.

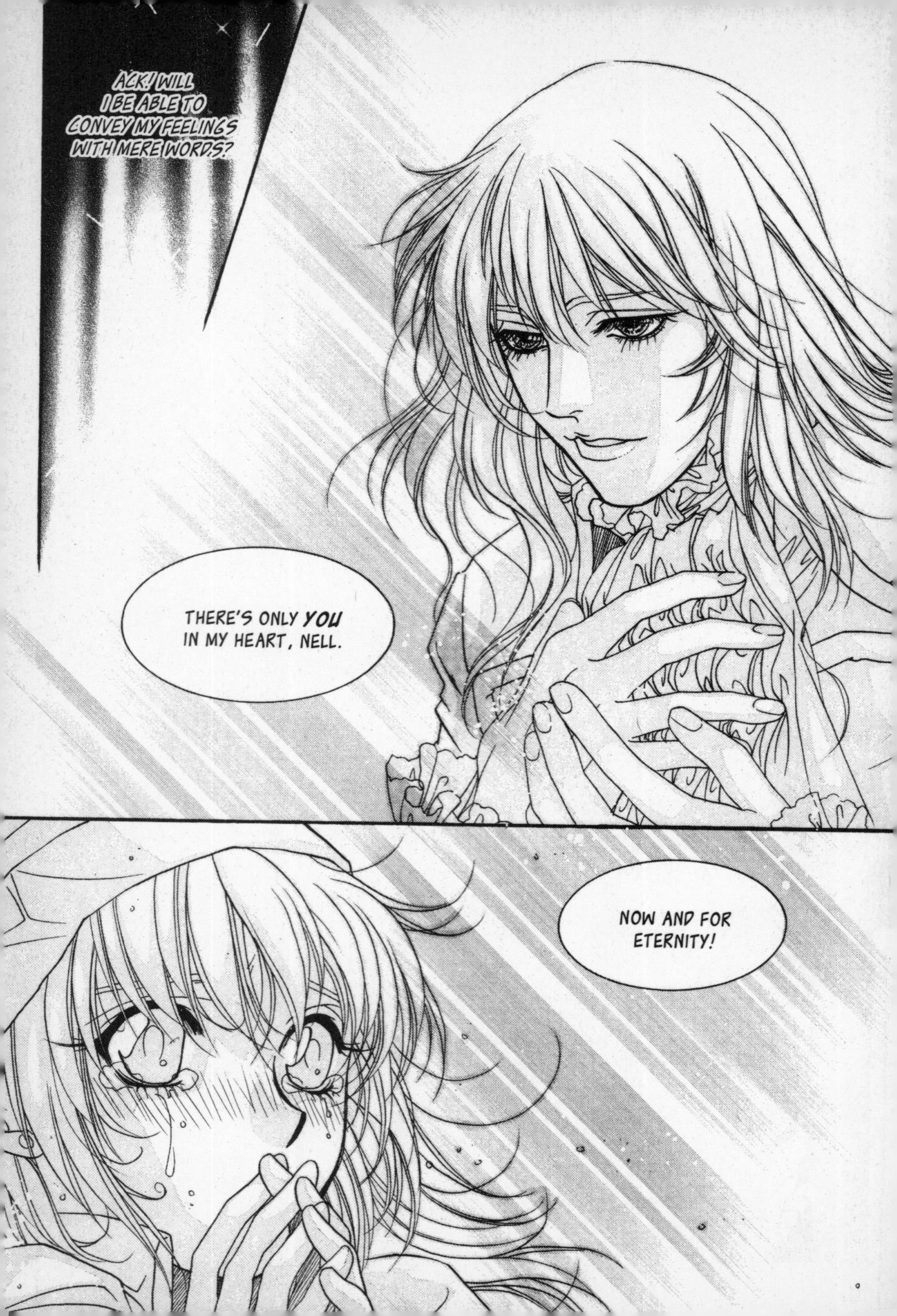
ACK! WILL I BE ABLE TO CONVEY MY FEELINGS WITH MERE WORDS?
THERE'S ONLY YOU IN MY HEART, NELL.
NOW AND FOR ETERNITY!

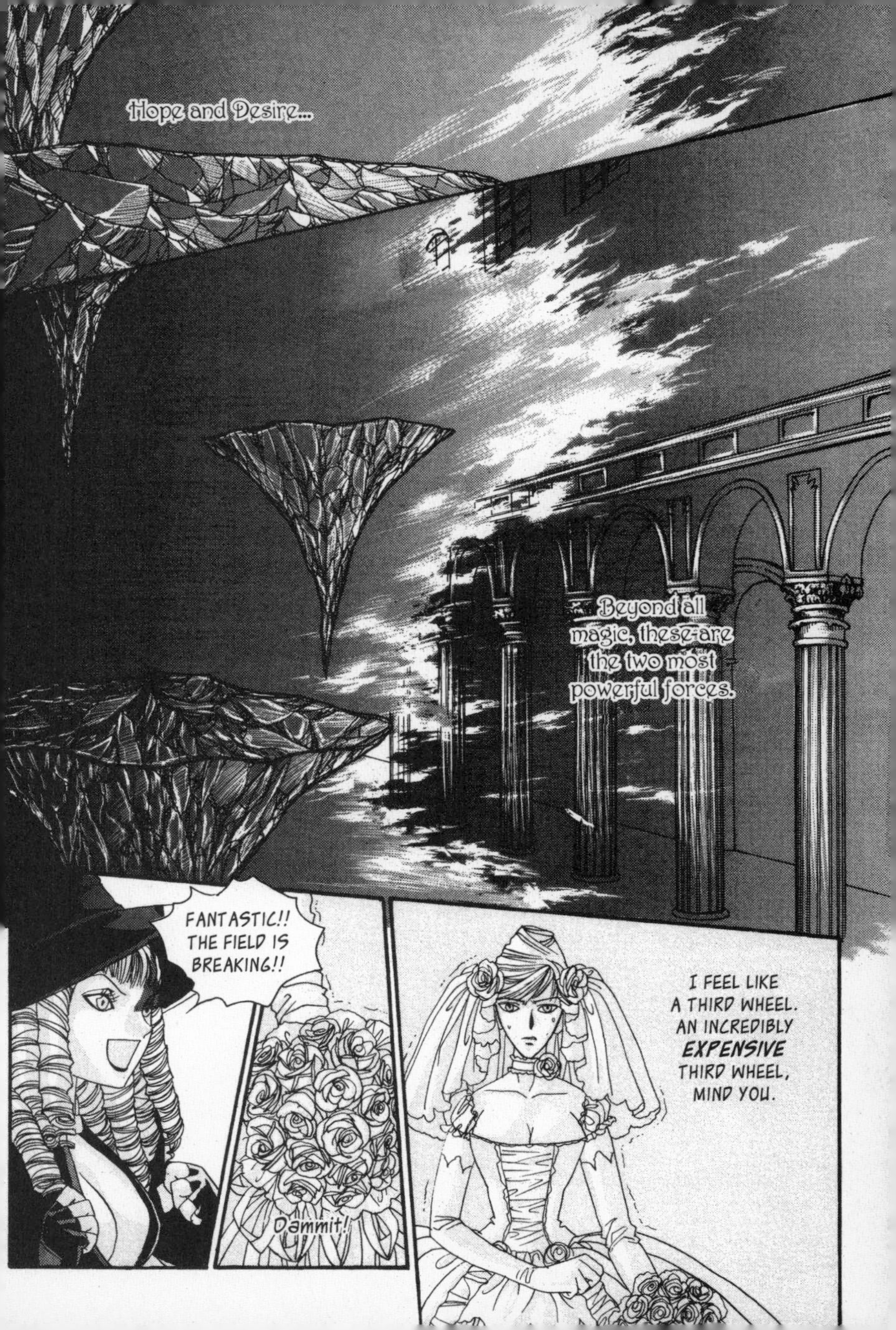
Hope and Desire...
Beyond all magic, these are the two most powerful forces.
FANTASTIC!! THE FIELD IS BREAKING!!
Dammit!
I FEEL LIKE A THIRD WHEEL. AN INCREDIBLY EXPENSIVE THIRD WHEEL, MIND YOU.

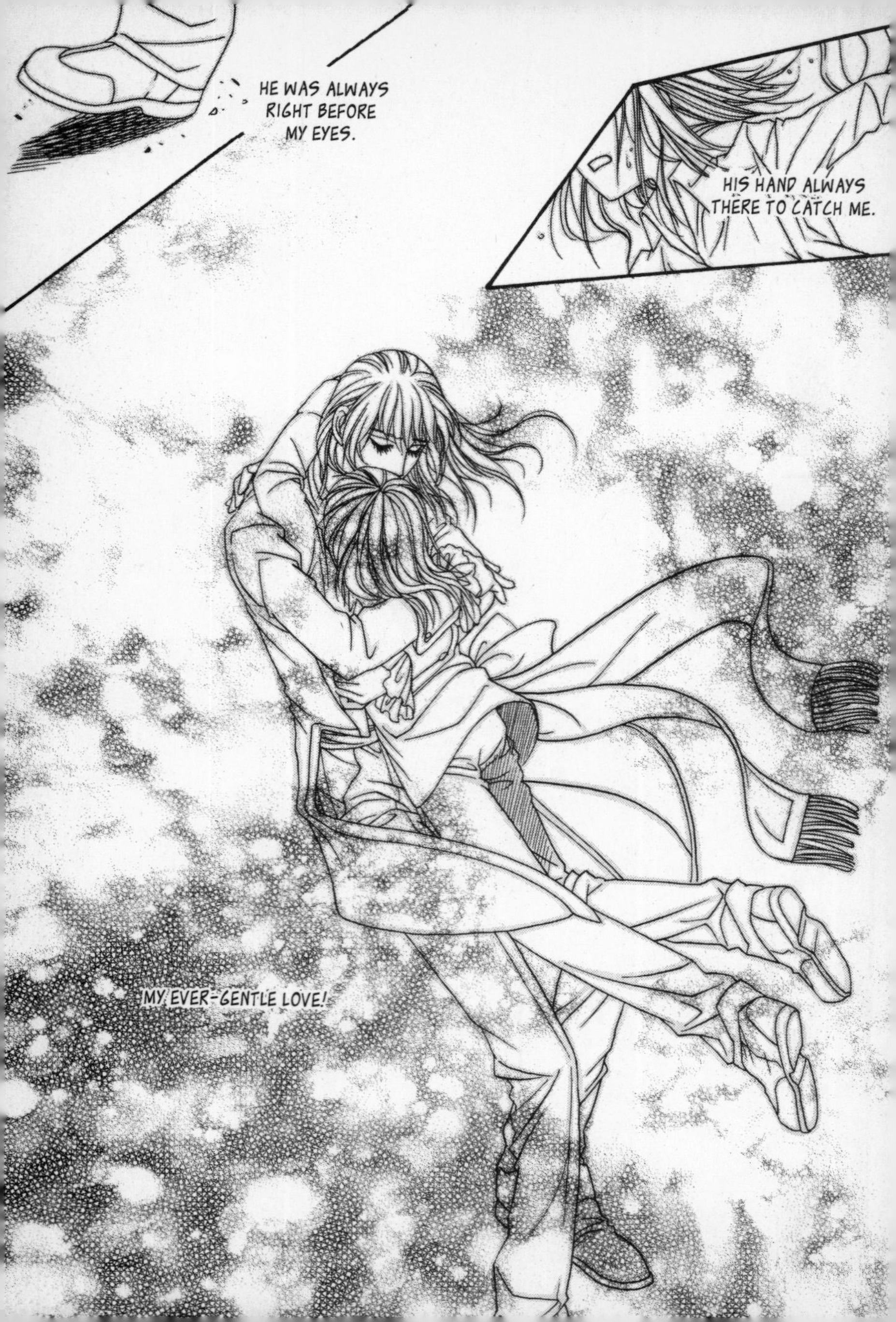
HE WAS ALWAYS RIGHT BEFORE MY EYES.
HIS HAND ALWAYS THERE TO CATCH ME.
MY EVER-GENTLE LOVE!

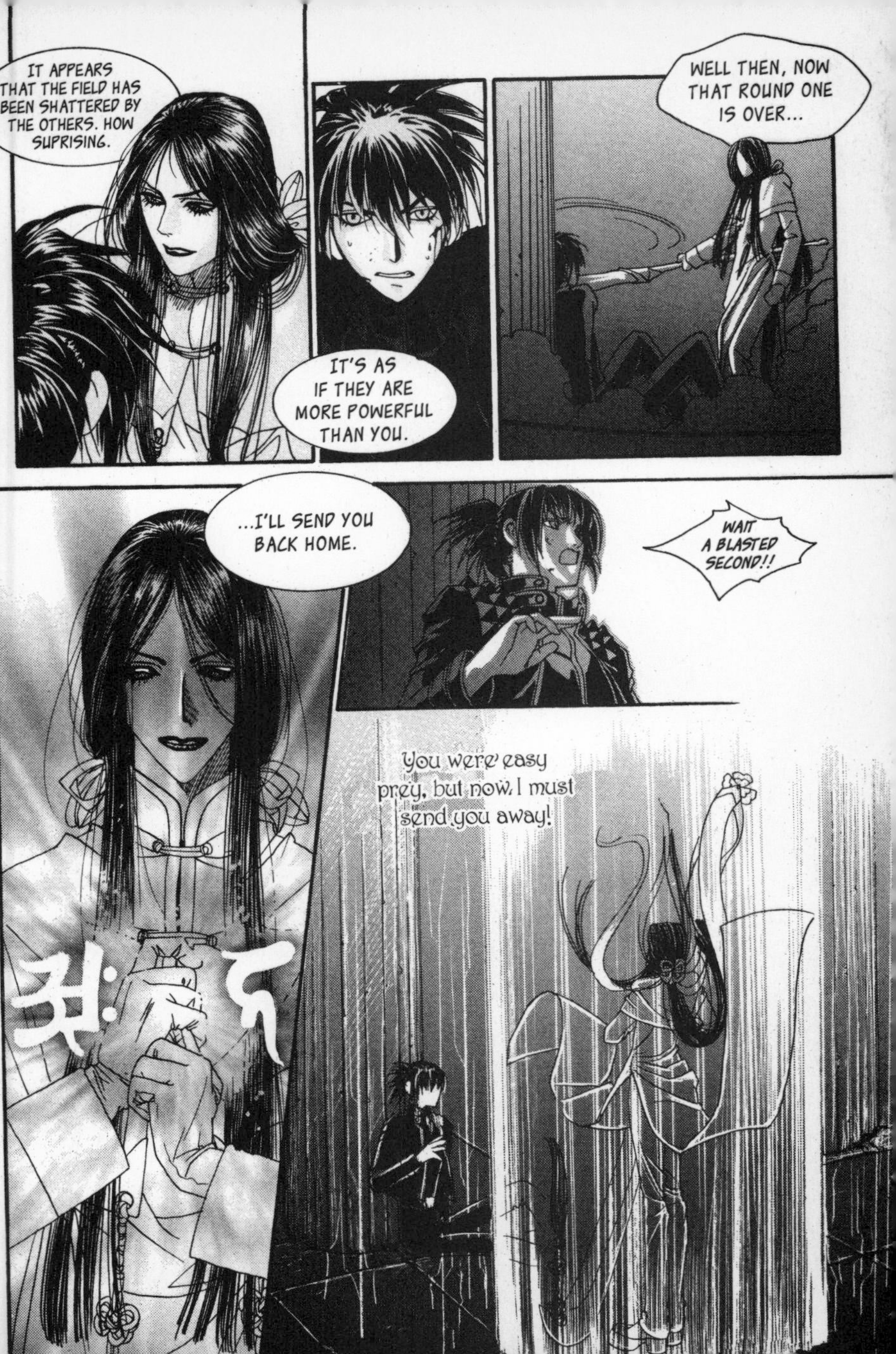
IT APPEARS THAT THE FIELD HAS BEEN SHATTERED BY THE OTHERS. HOW SUPRISING.
IT'S AS IF THEY ARE MORE POWERFUL THAN YOU.
WELL THEN, NOW THAT ROUND ONE IS OVER...
...I'LL SEND YOU BACK HOME.
WAIT A BLASTED SECOND!!
You were easy prey, but now, I must send you away!

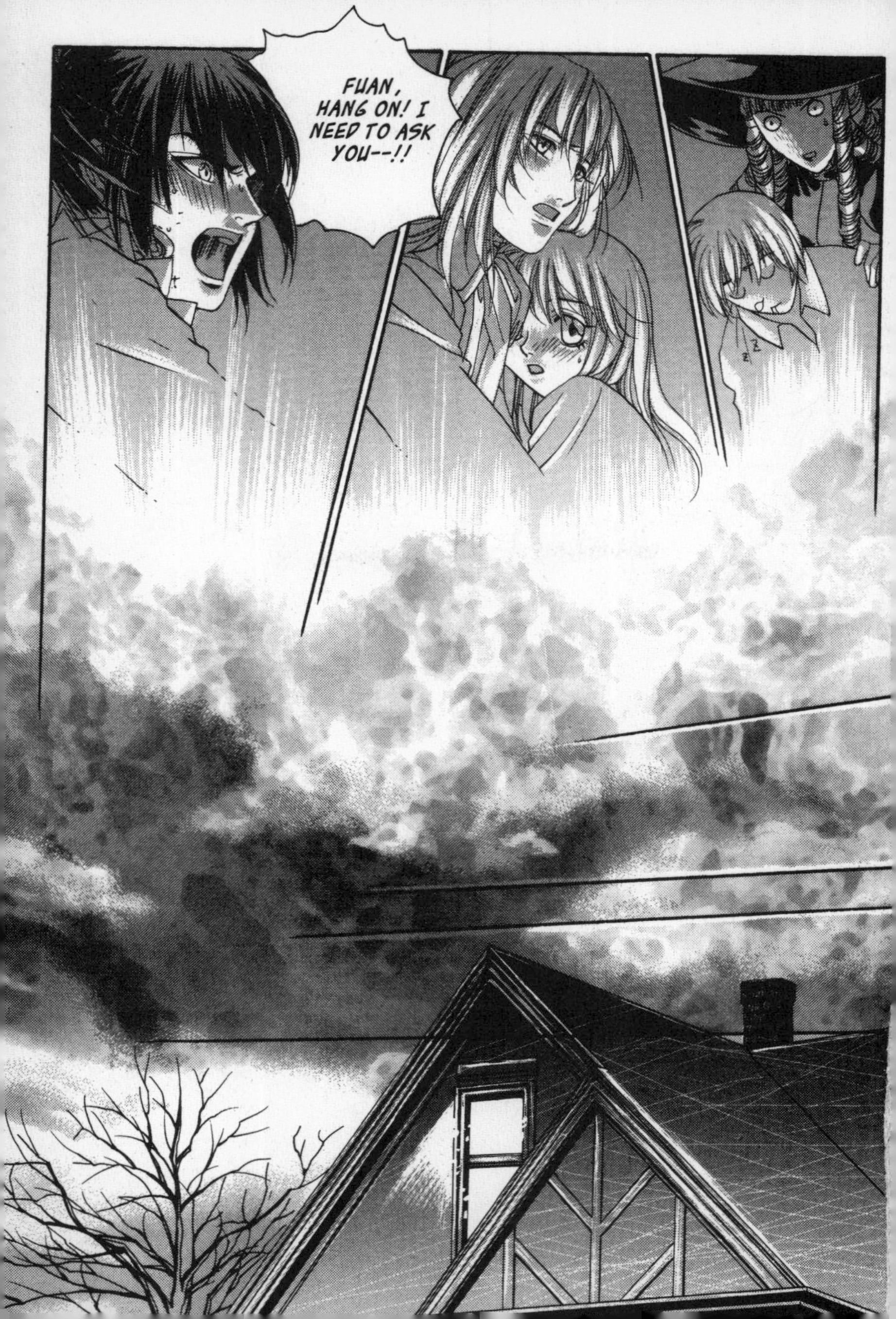
FUAN, HANG ON! I NEED TO ASK YOU--!!

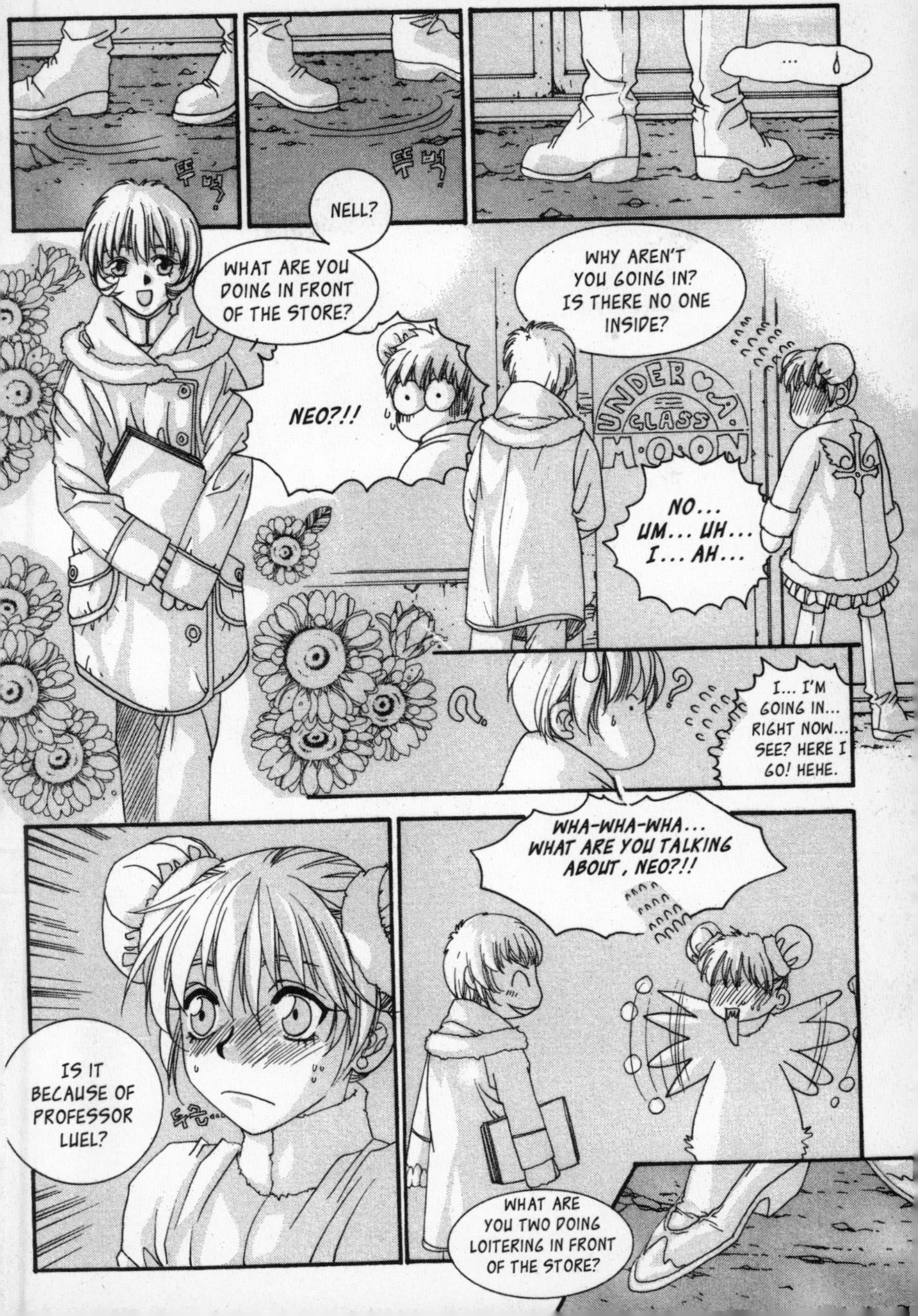

뚜벅
뚜벅
...
NELL?
WHAT ARE YOU DOING IN FRONT OF THE STORE?
NEO?!!
WHY AREN'T YOU GOING IN? IS THERE NO ONE INSIDE?
UNDER GLASS MOON
NO... UM... UH... I... AH...
I... I'M GOING IN... RIGHT NOW... SEE? HERE I GO! HEHE.
IS IT BECAUSE OF PROFESSOR LUEL?
WHA-WHA-WHA... WHAT ARE YOU TALKING ABOUT, NEO?!!
WHAT ARE YOU TWO DOING LOITERING IN FRONT OF THE STORE?

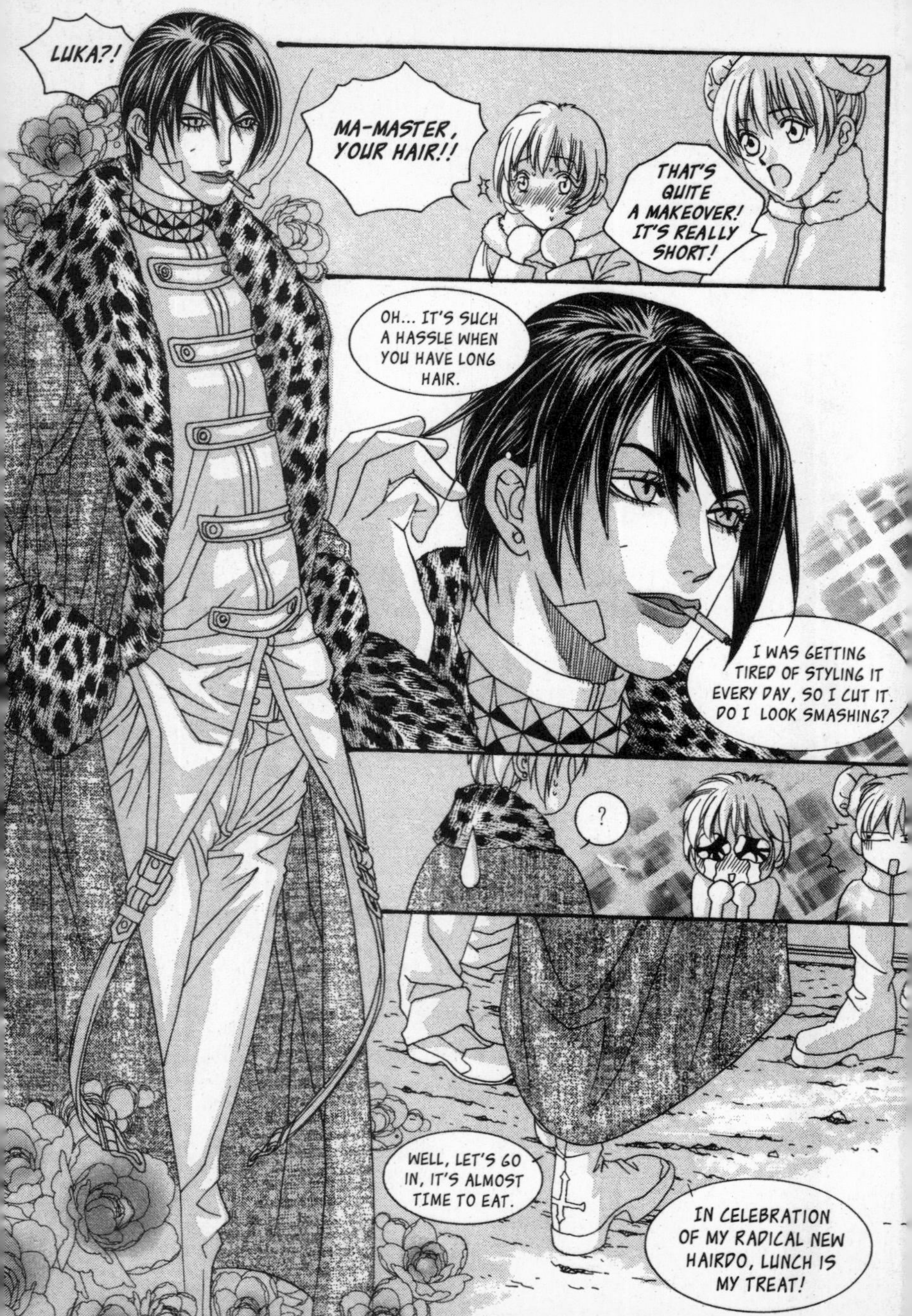
LUKA?!
MA-MASTER, YOUR HAIR!!
THAT'S QUITE A MAKEOVER! IT'S REALLY SHORT!
OH... IT'S SUCH A HASSLE WHEN YOU HAVE LONG HAIR.
I WAS GETTING TIRED OF STYLING IT EVERY DAY, SO I CUT IT. DO I LOOK SMASHING?
?
WELL, LET'S GO IN, IT'S ALMOST TIME TO EAT.
IN CELEBRATION OF MY RADICAL NEW HAIRDO, LUNCH IS MY TREAT!

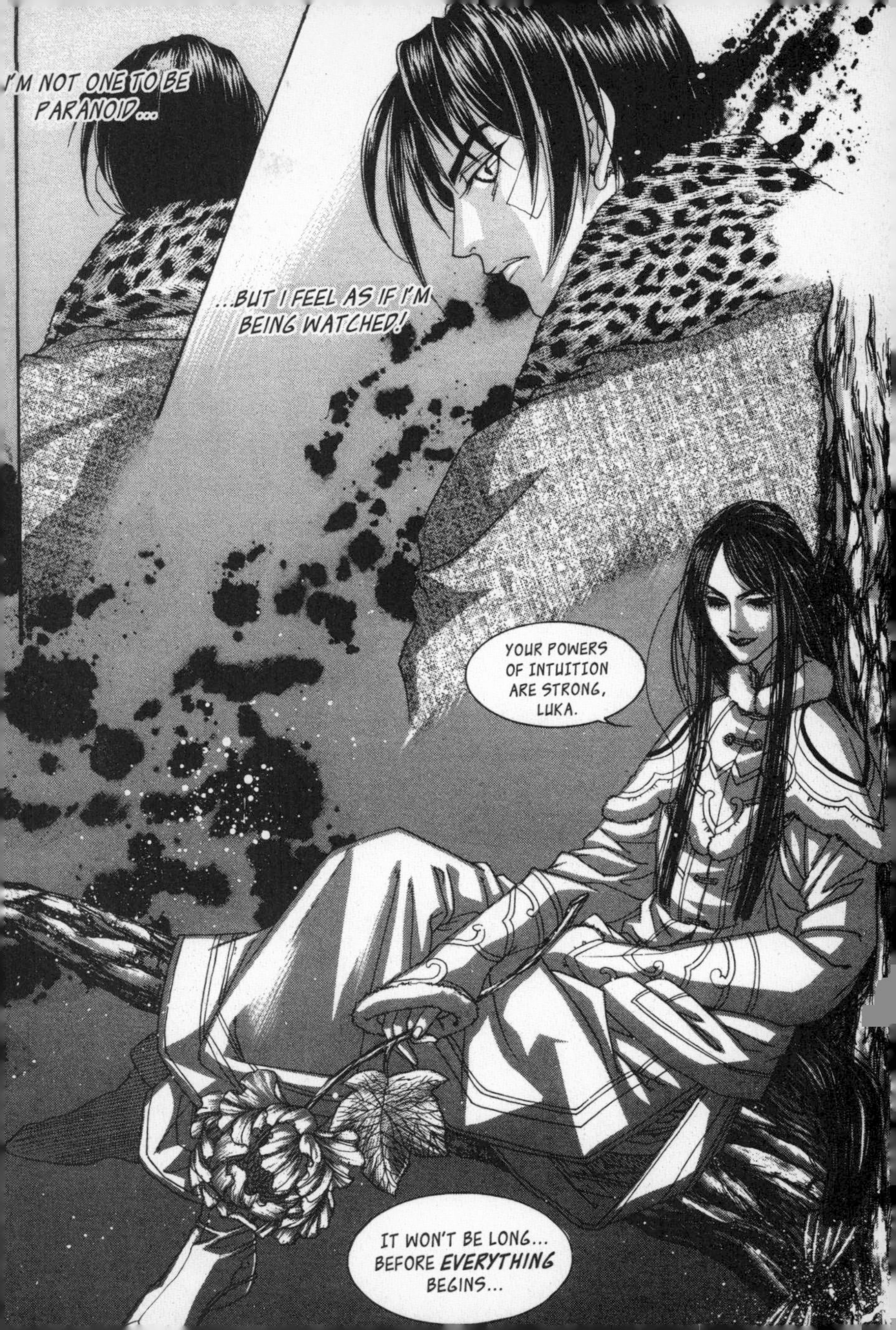
I'M NOT ONE TO BE PARANOID...
...BUT I FEEL AS IF I'M BEING WATCHED!
YOUR POWERS OF INTUITION ARE STRONG, LUKA.
IT WON'T BE LONG... BEFORE EVERYTHING BEGINS...

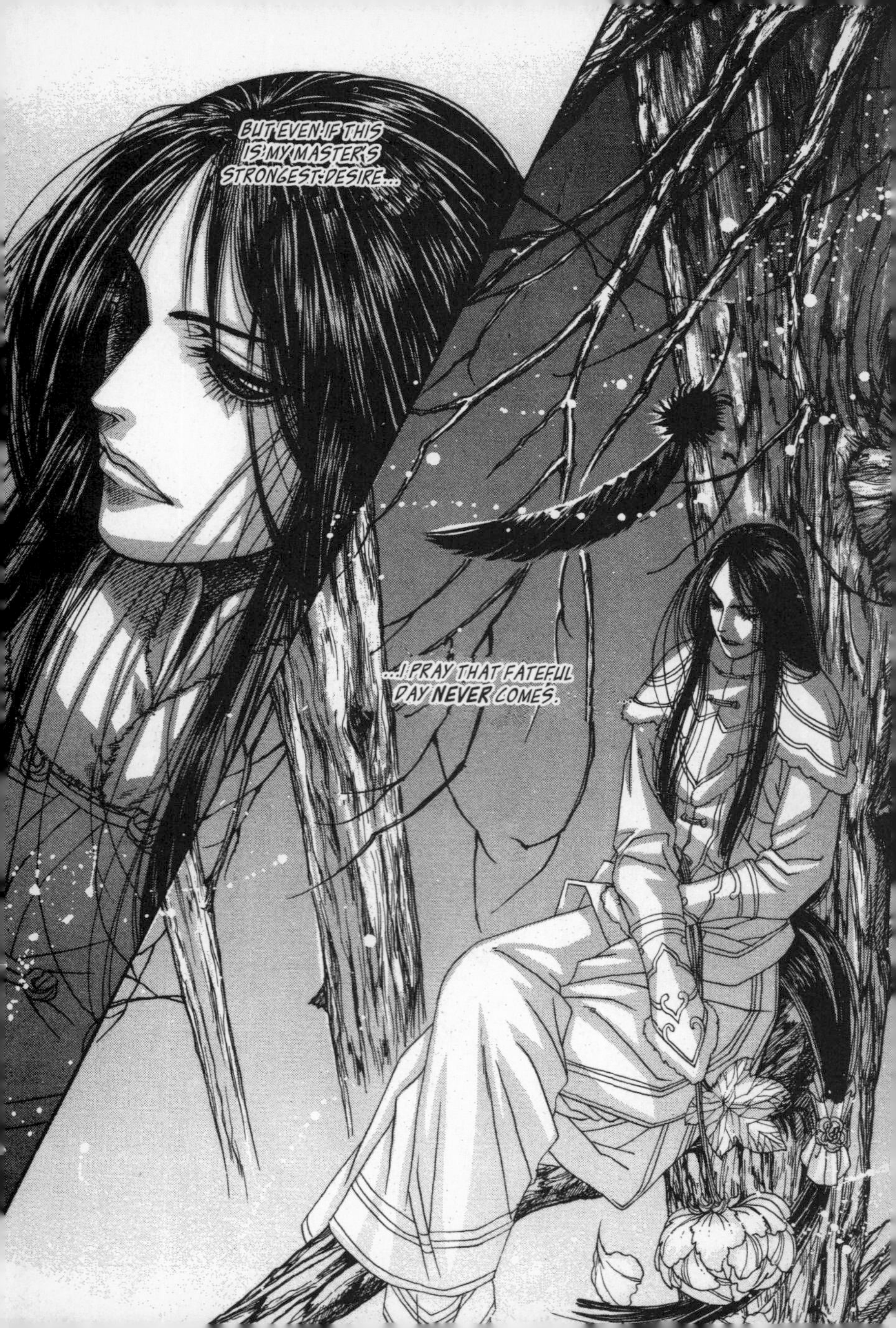
BUT EVEN IF THIS IS MY MASTER'S STRONGEST DESIRE...
...I PRAY THAT FATEFUL DAY **NEVER** COMES.

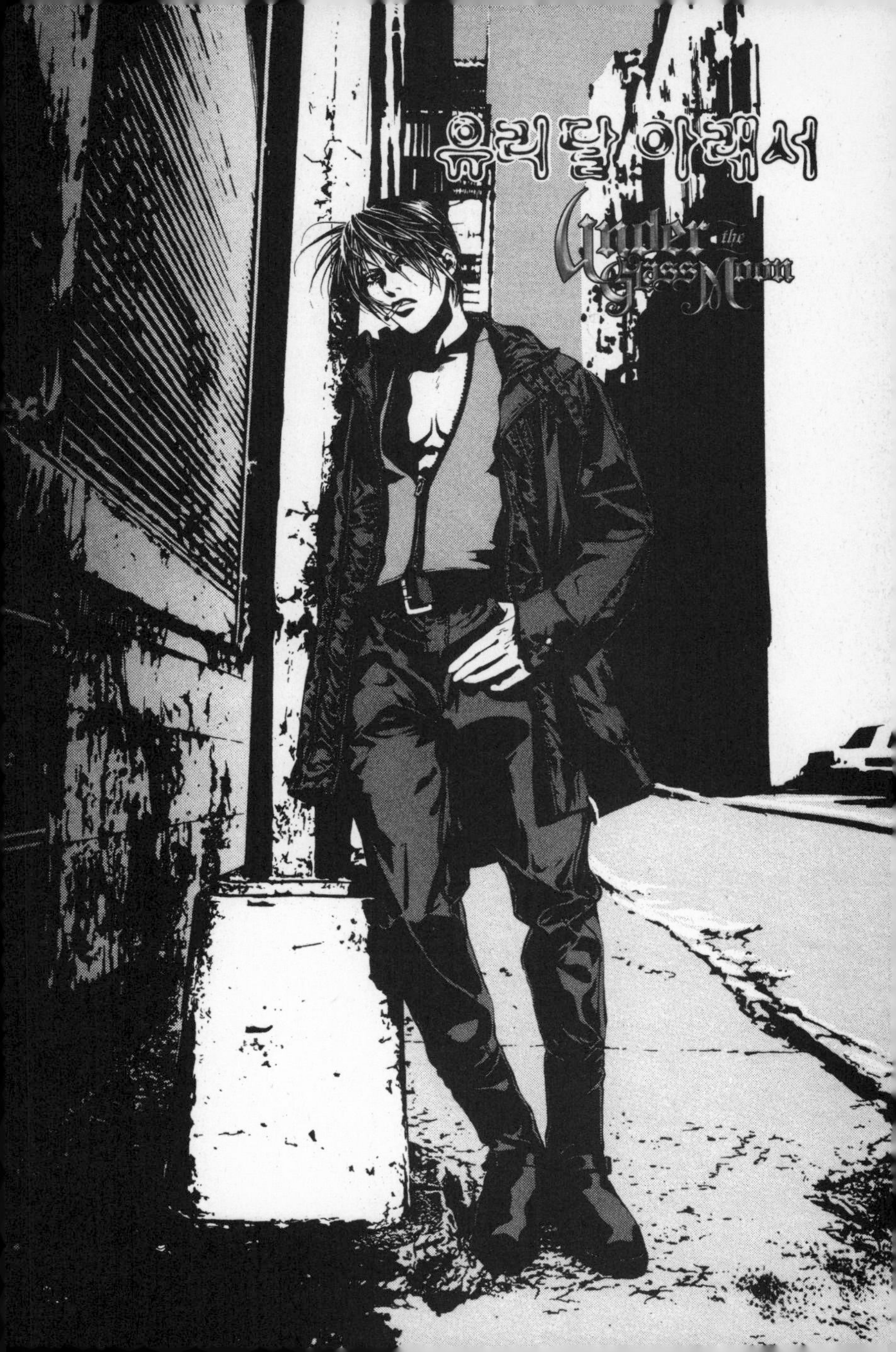
유리 달 아래서
Under the Glass Moon

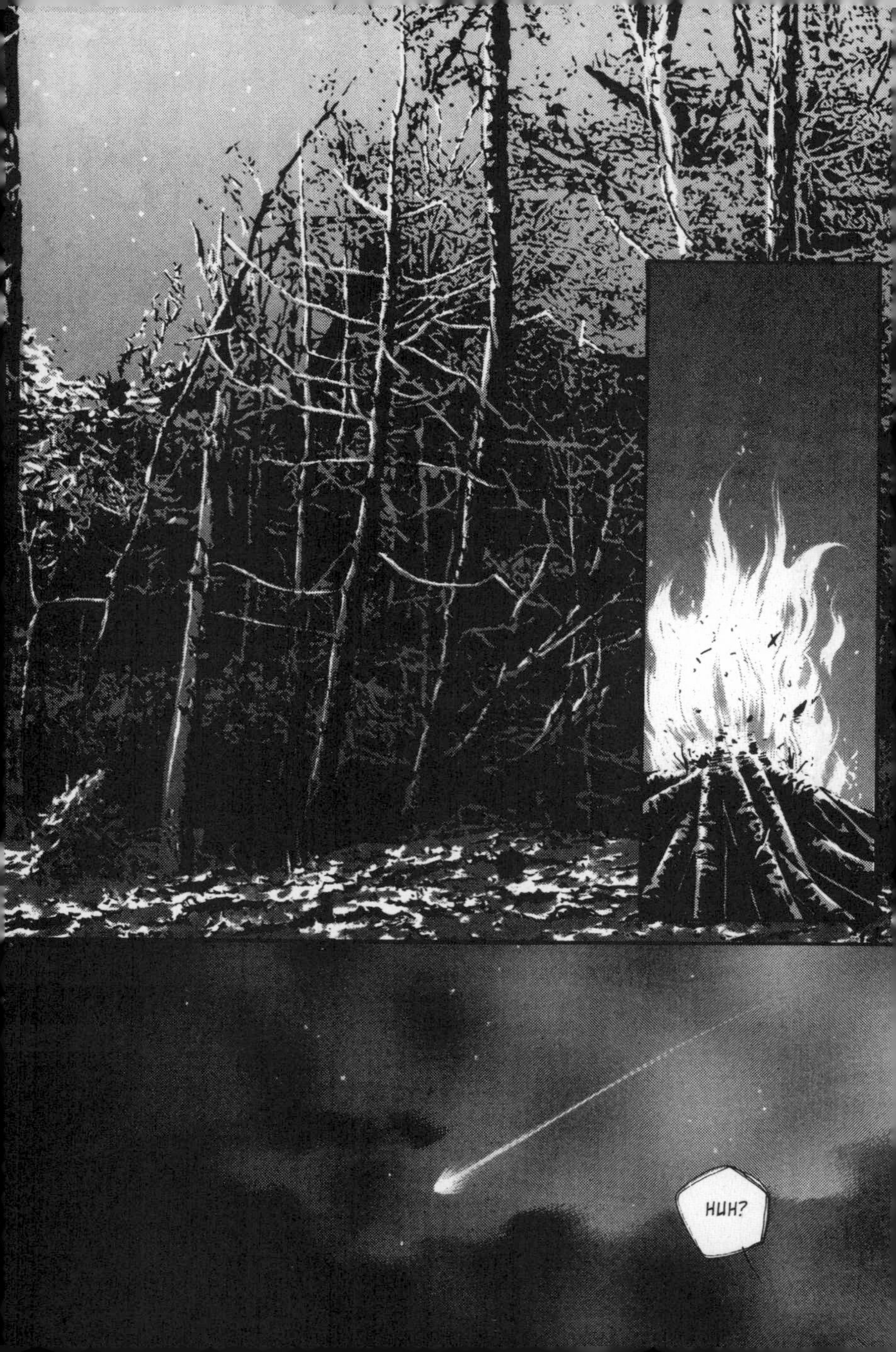
HUH?

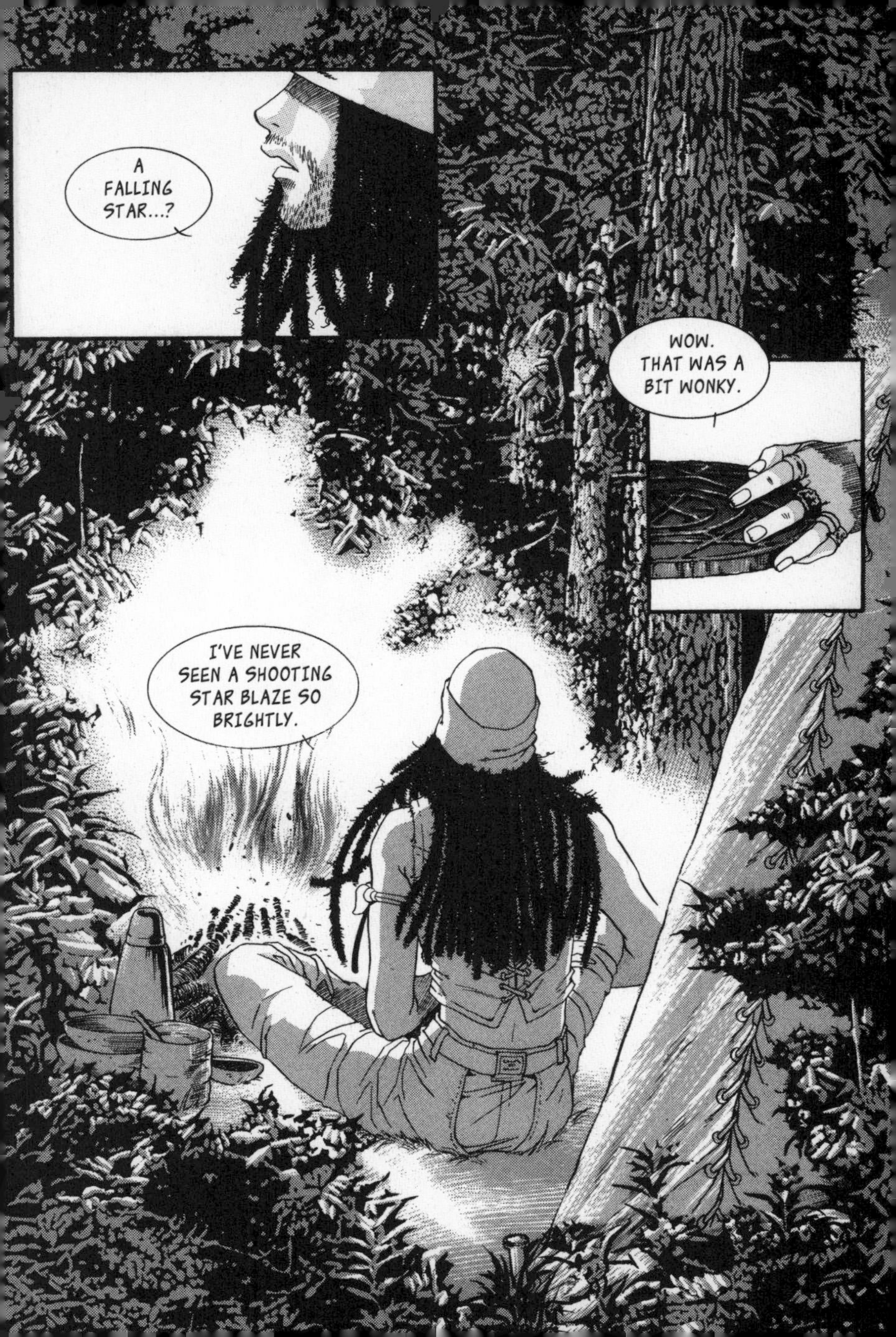
A FALLING STAR...?
WOW. THAT WAS A BIT WONKY.
I'VE NEVER SEEN A SHOOTING STAR BLAZE SO BRIGHTLY.

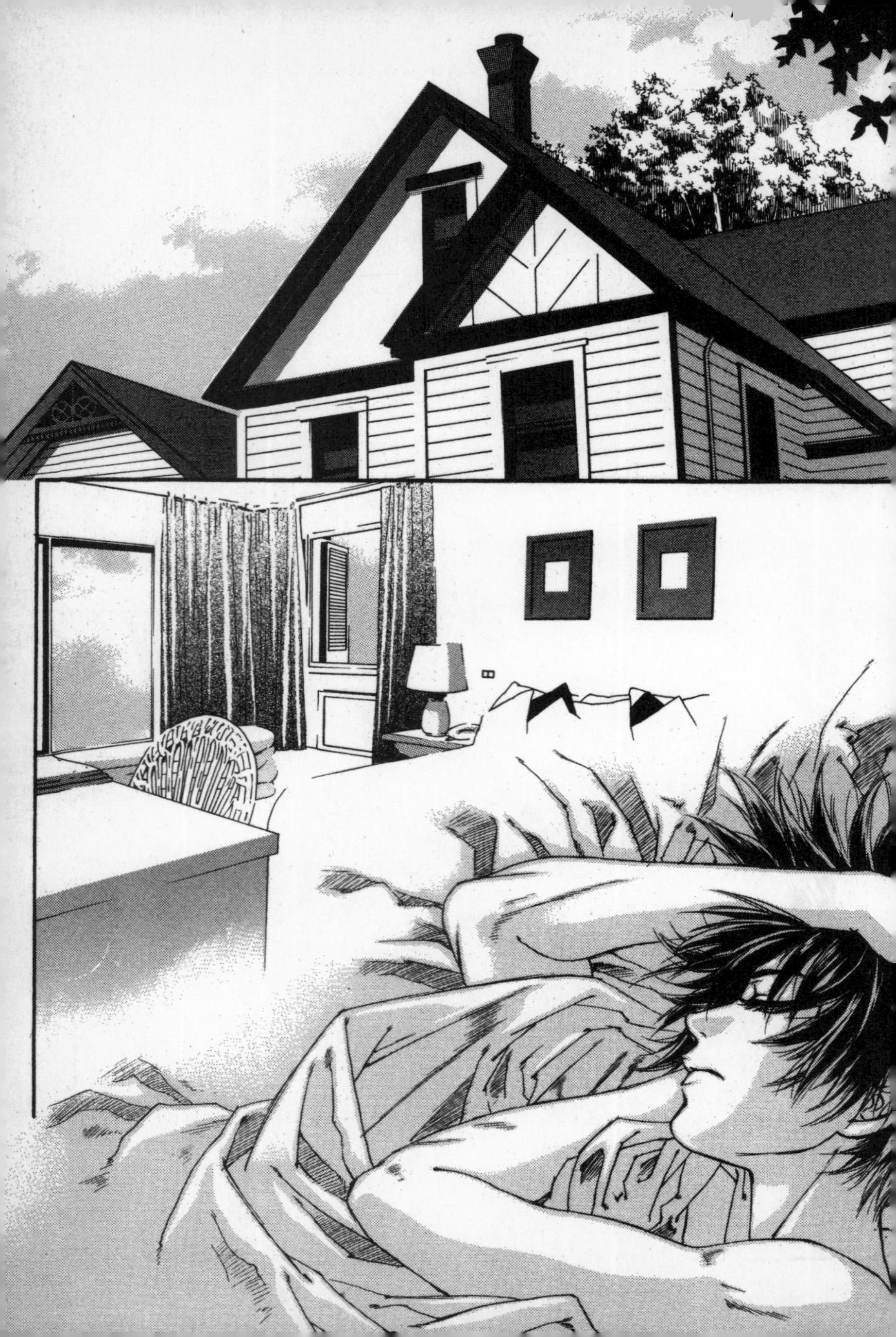

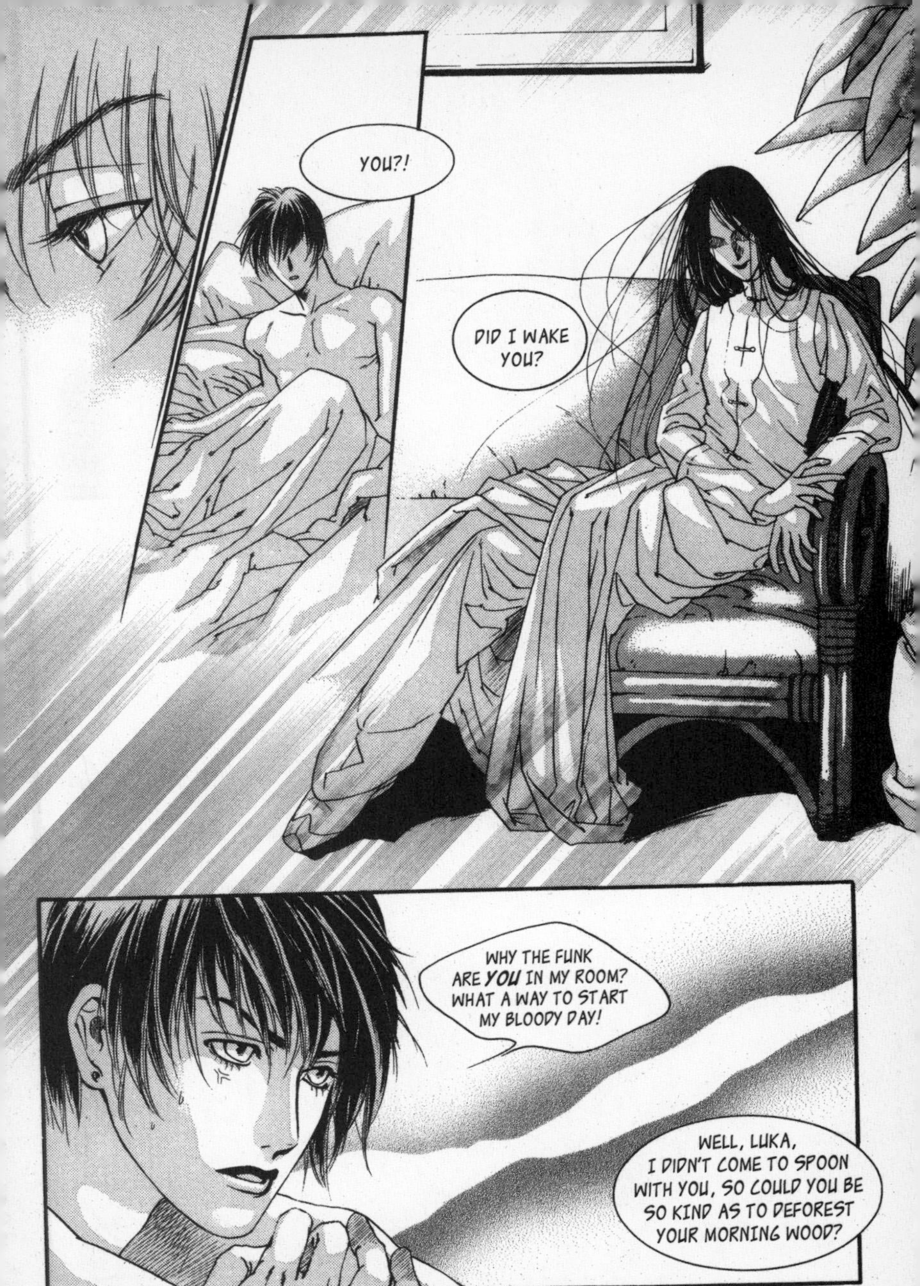
YOU?!
DID I WAKE YOU?
WHY THE FUNK ARE YOU IN MY ROOM? WHAT A WAY TO START MY BLOODY DAY!
WELL, LUKA, I DIDN'T COME TO SPOON WITH YOU, SO COULD YOU BE SO KIND AS TO DEFOREST YOUR MORNING WOOD?

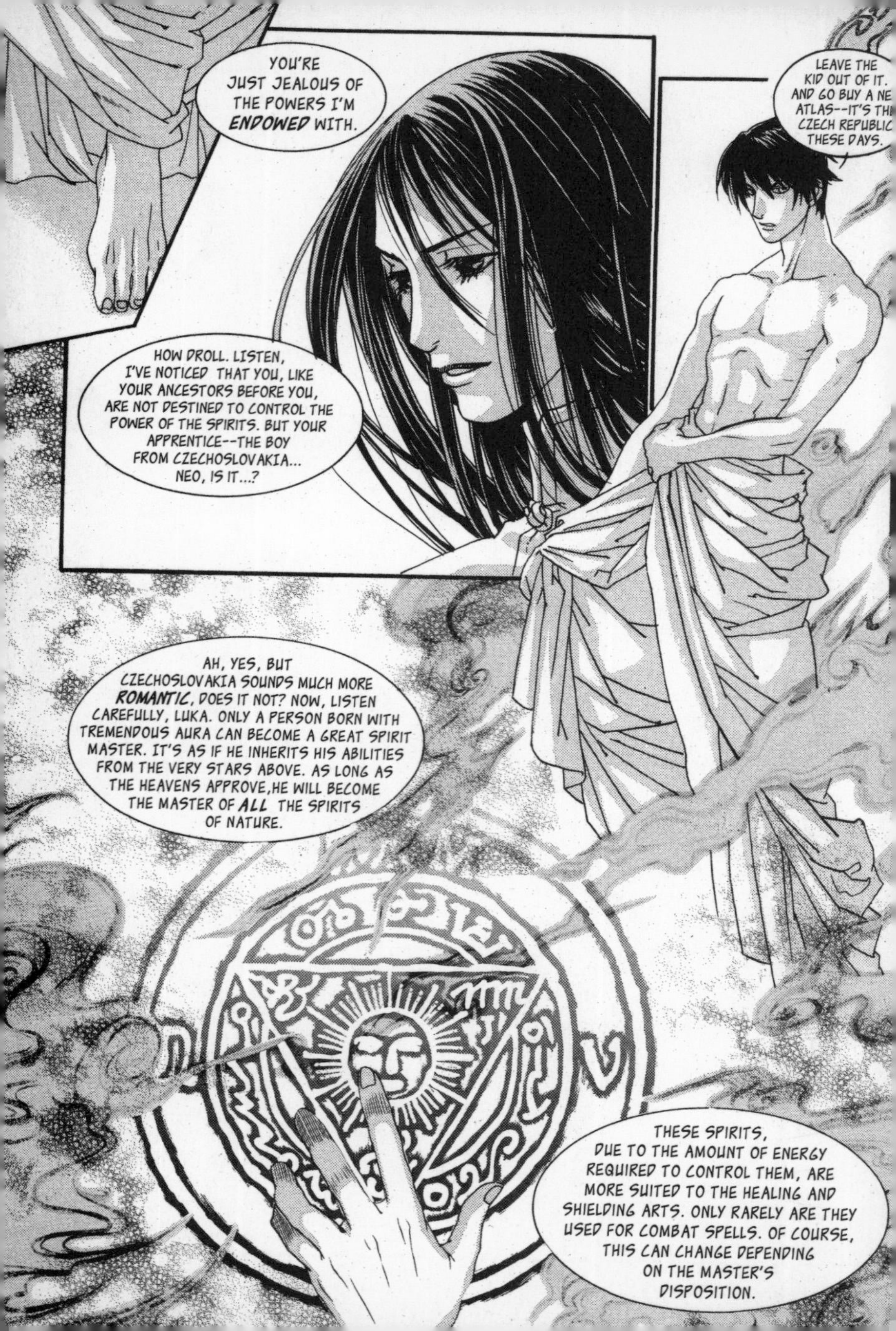
YOU'RE JUST JEALOUS OF THE POWERS I'M **ENDOWED** WITH.
LEAVE THE KID OUT OF IT. AND GO BUY A NE ATLAS--IT'S TH CZECH REPUBLIC THESE DAYS.
HOW DROLL. LISTEN, I'VE NOTICED THAT YOU, LIKE YOUR ANCESTORS BEFORE YOU, ARE NOT DESTINED TO CONTROL THE POWER OF THE SPIRITS. BUT YOUR APPRENTICE--THE BOY FROM CZECHOSLOVAKIA... NEO, IS IT...?
AH, YES, BUT CZECHOSLOVAKIA SOUNDS MUCH MORE **ROMANTIC**, DOES IT NOT? NOW, LISTEN CAREFULLY, LUKA. ONLY A PERSON BORN WITH TREMENDOUS AURA CAN BECOME A GREAT SPIRIT MASTER. IT'S AS IF HE INHERITS HIS ABILITIES FROM THE VERY STARS ABOVE. AS LONG AS THE HEAVENS APPROVE, HE WILL BECOME THE MASTER OF **ALL** THE SPIRITS OF NATURE.
THESE SPIRITS, DUE TO THE AMOUNT OF ENERGY REQUIRED TO CONTROL THEM, ARE MORE SUITED TO THE HEALING AND SHIELDING ARTS. ONLY RARELY ARE THEY USED FOR COMBAT SPELLS. OF COURSE, THIS CAN CHANGE DEPENDING ON THE MASTER'S DISPOSITION.

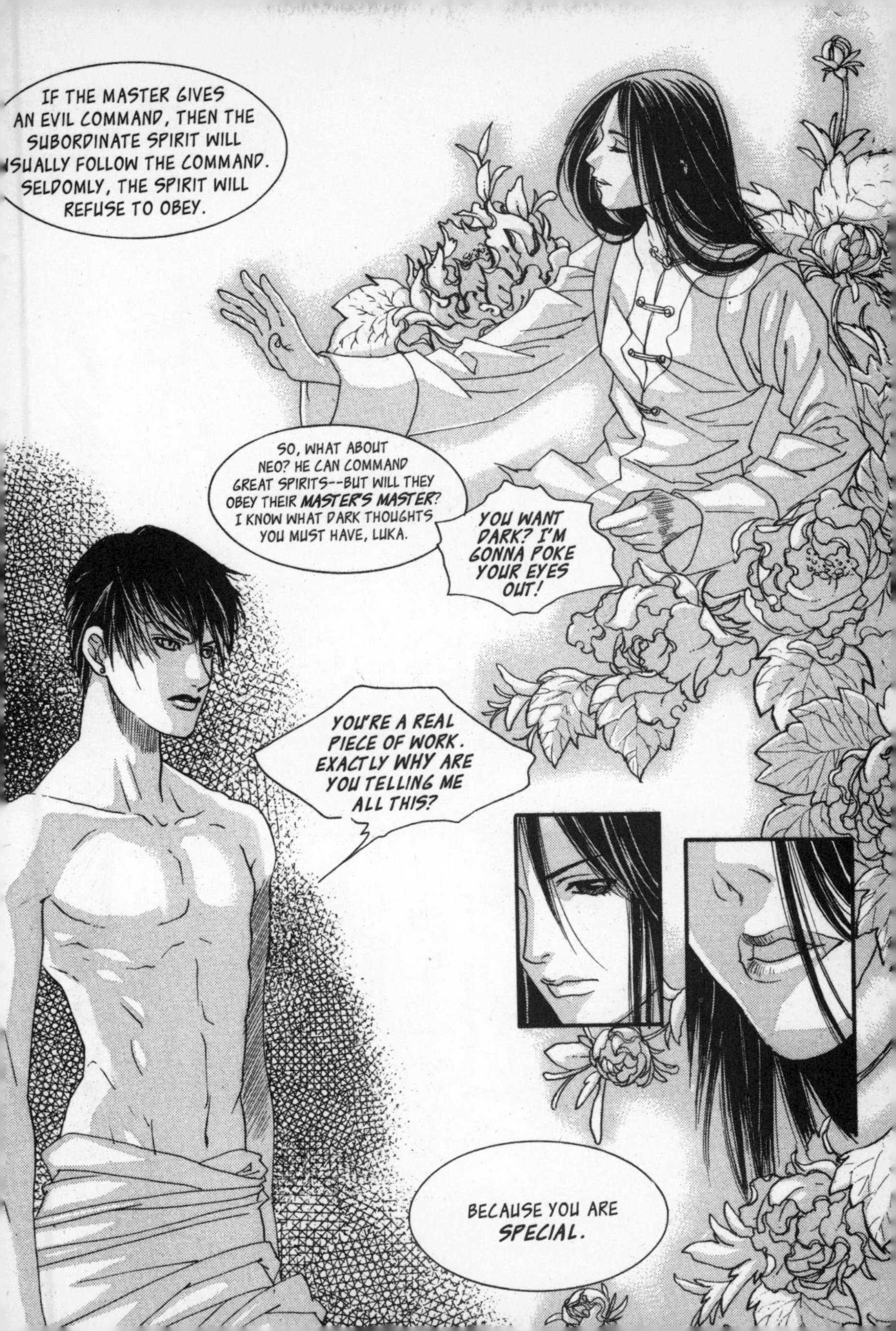
IF THE MASTER GIVES AN EVIL COMMAND, THEN THE SUBORDINATE SPIRIT WILL USUALLY FOLLOW THE COMMAND. SELDOMLY, THE SPIRIT WILL REFUSE TO OBEY.
SO, WHAT ABOUT NEO? HE CAN COMMAND GREAT SPIRITS--BUT WILL THEY OBEY THEIR MASTER'S MASTER? I KNOW WHAT DARK THOUGHTS YOU MUST HAVE, LUKA.
YOU WANT DARK? I'M GONNA POKE YOUR EYES OUT!
YOU'RE A REAL PIECE OF WORK. EXACTLY WHY ARE YOU TELLING ME ALL THIS?
BECAUSE YOU ARE SPECIAL.

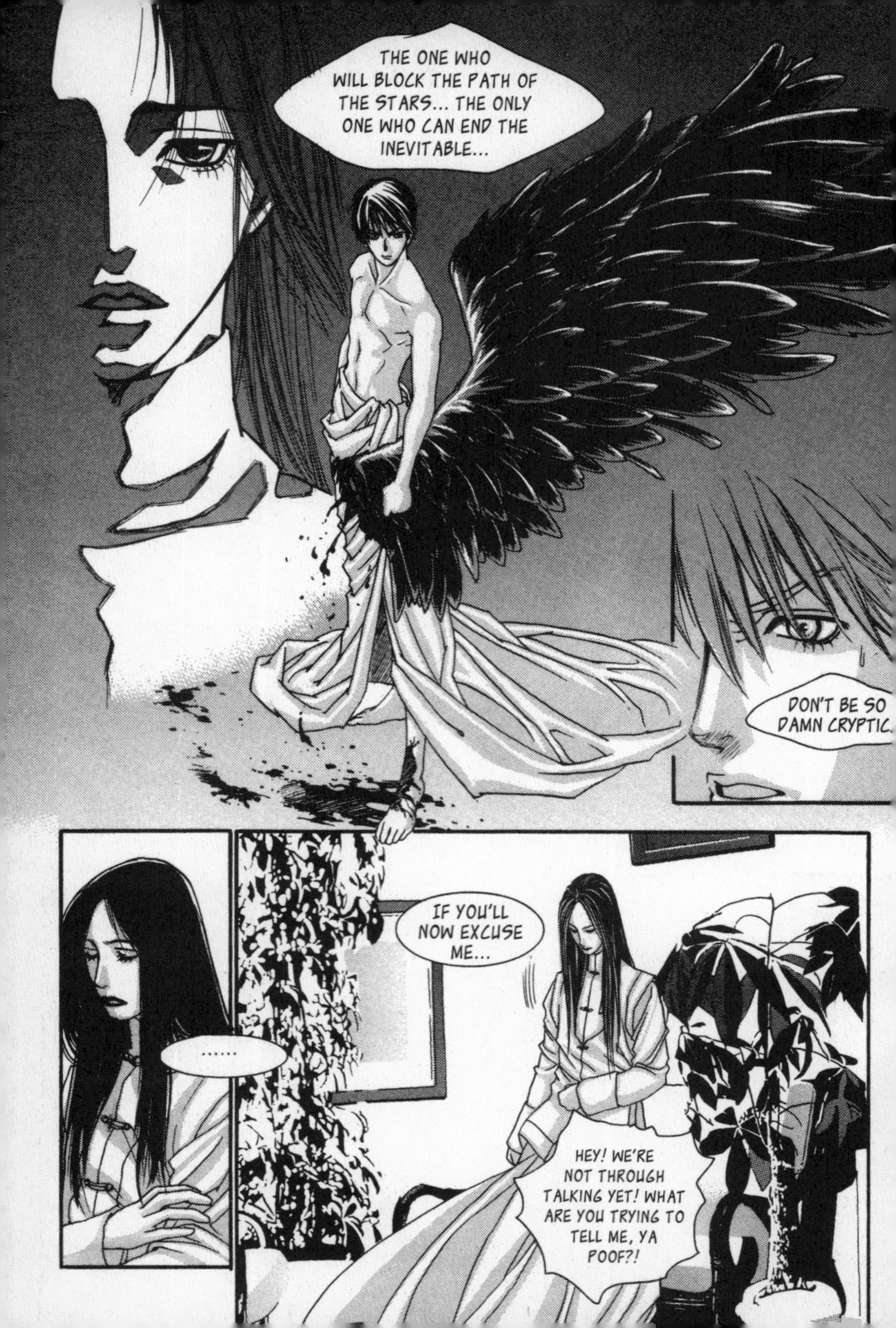
THE ONE WHO WILL BLOCK THE PATH OF THE STARS... THE ONLY ONE WHO CAN END THE INEVITABLE...
DON'T BE SO DAMN CRYPTIC.
......
IF YOU'LL NOW EXCUSE ME...
HEY! WE'RE NOT THROUGH TALKING YET! WHAT ARE YOU TRYING TO TELL ME, YA POOF?!

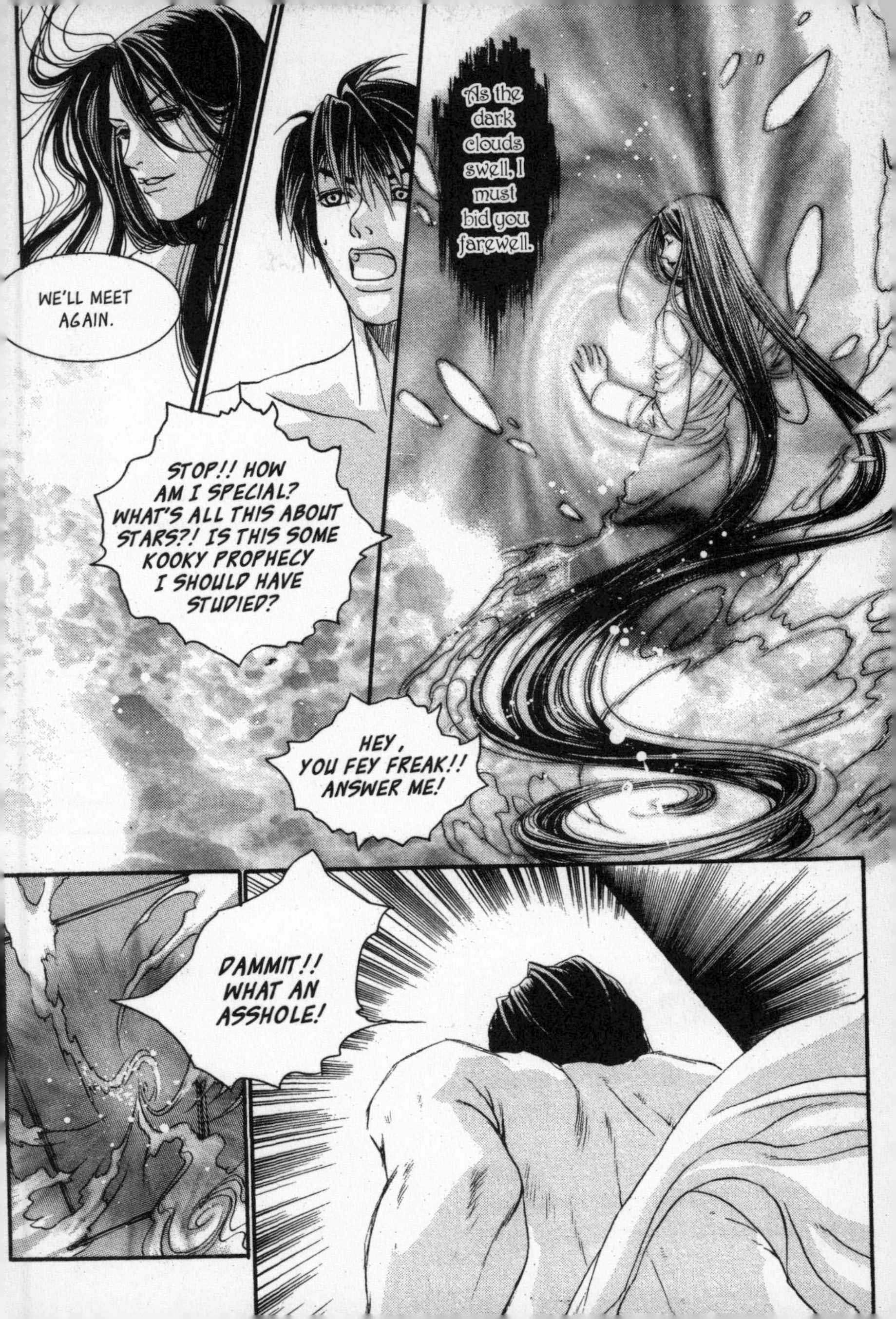
WE'LL MEET AGAIN.
STOP!! HOW AM I SPECIAL? WHAT'S ALL THIS ABOUT STARS?! IS THIS SOME KOOKY PROPHECY I SHOULD HAVE STUDIED?
As the dark clouds swell, I must bid you farewell.
HEY, YOU FEY FREAK!! ANSWER ME!
DAMMIT!! WHAT AN ASSHOLE!

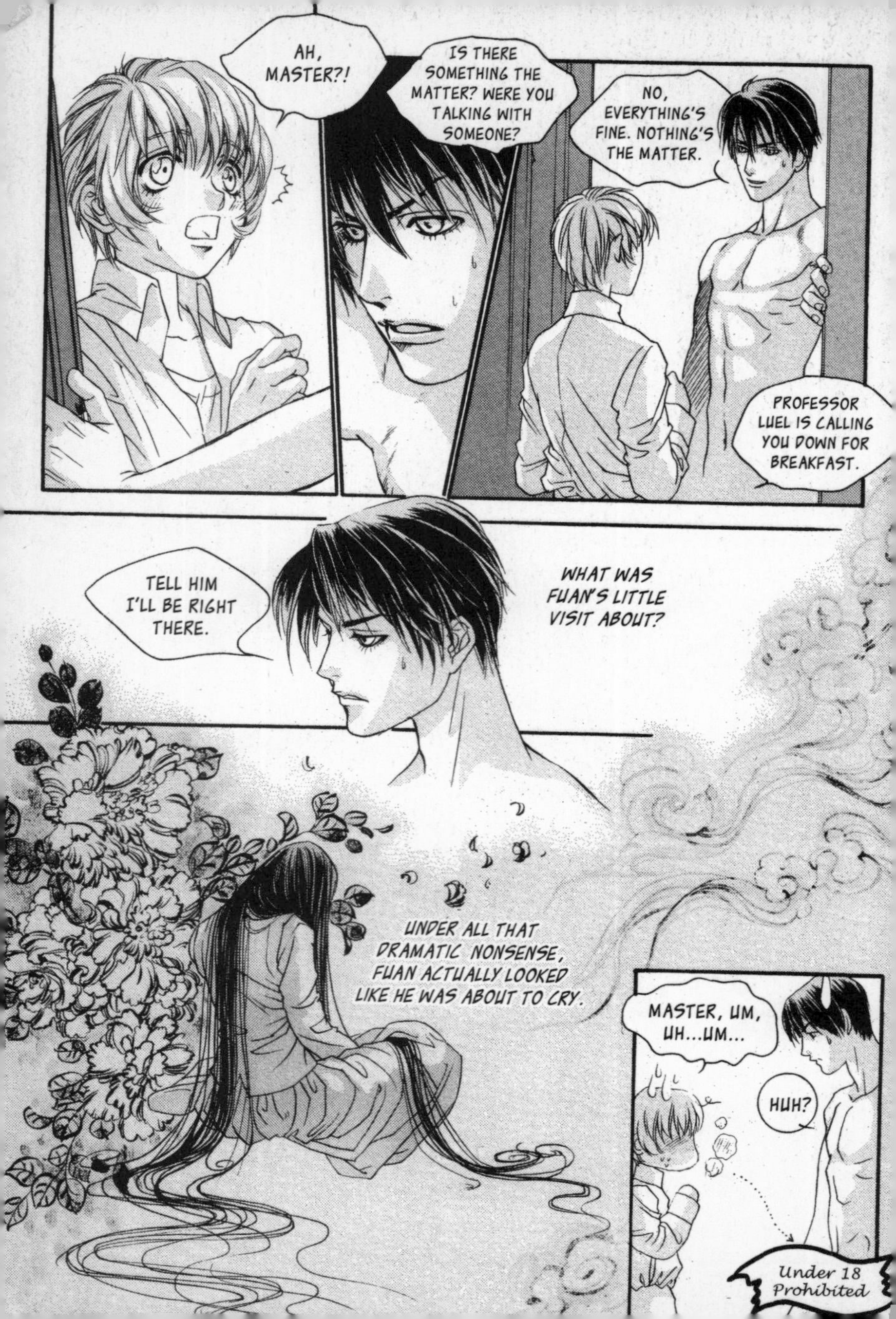
AH, MASTER?!
IS THERE SOMETHING THE MATTER? WERE YOU TALKING WITH SOMEONE?
NO, EVERYTHING'S FINE. NOTHING'S THE MATTER.
PROFESSOR LUEL IS CALLING YOU DOWN FOR BREAKFAST.
TELL HIM I'LL BE RIGHT THERE.
WHAT WAS FUAN'S LITTLE VISIT ABOUT?
UNDER ALL THAT DRAMATIC NONSENSE, FUAN ACTUALLY LOOKED LIKE HE WAS ABOUT TO CRY.
MASTER, UM, UH...UM...
HUH?
Under 18 Prohibited

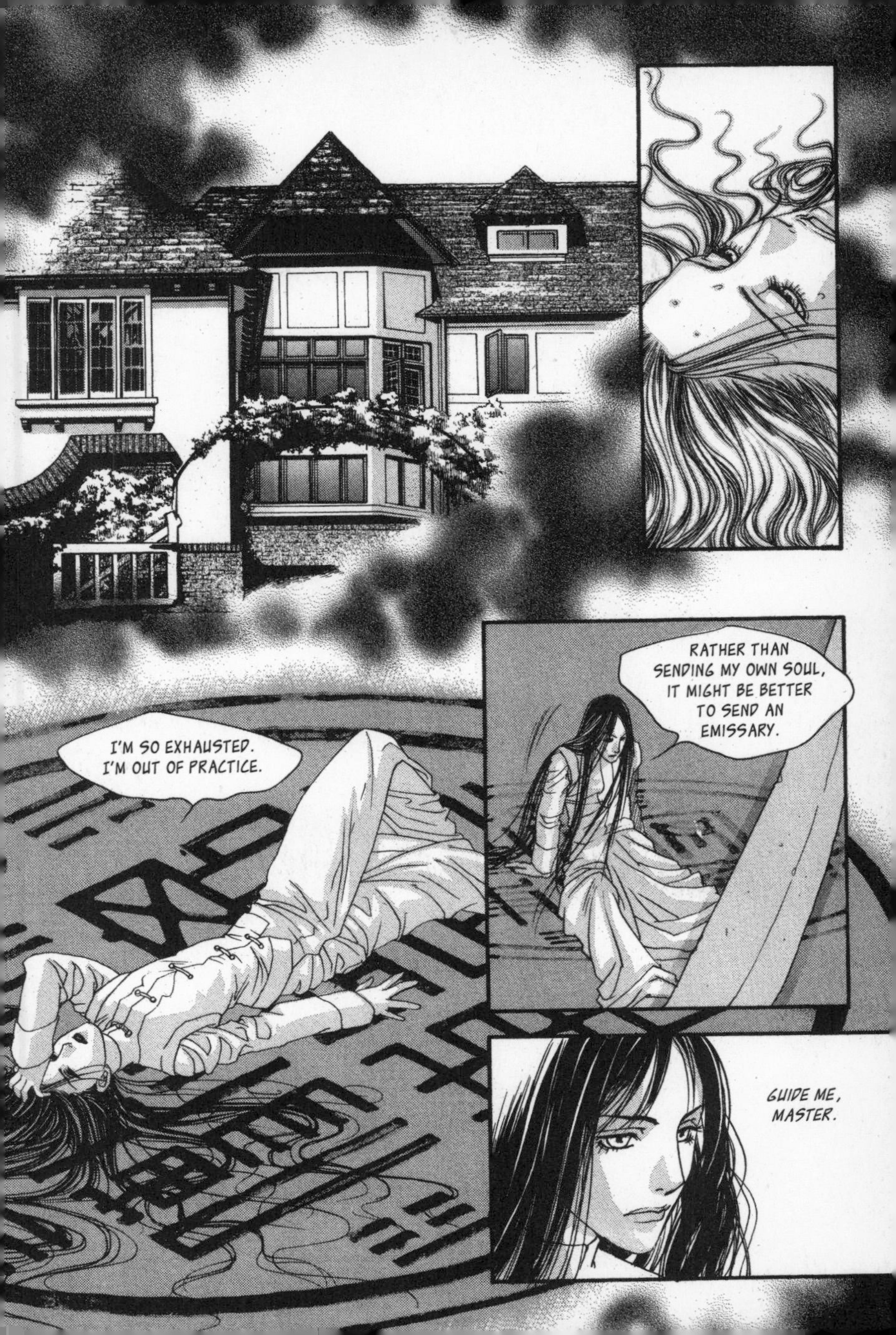
I'M SO EXHAUSTED. I'M OUT OF PRACTICE.
RATHER THAN SENDING MY OWN SOUL, IT MIGHT BE BETTER TO SEND AN EMISSARY.
GUIDE ME, MASTER.

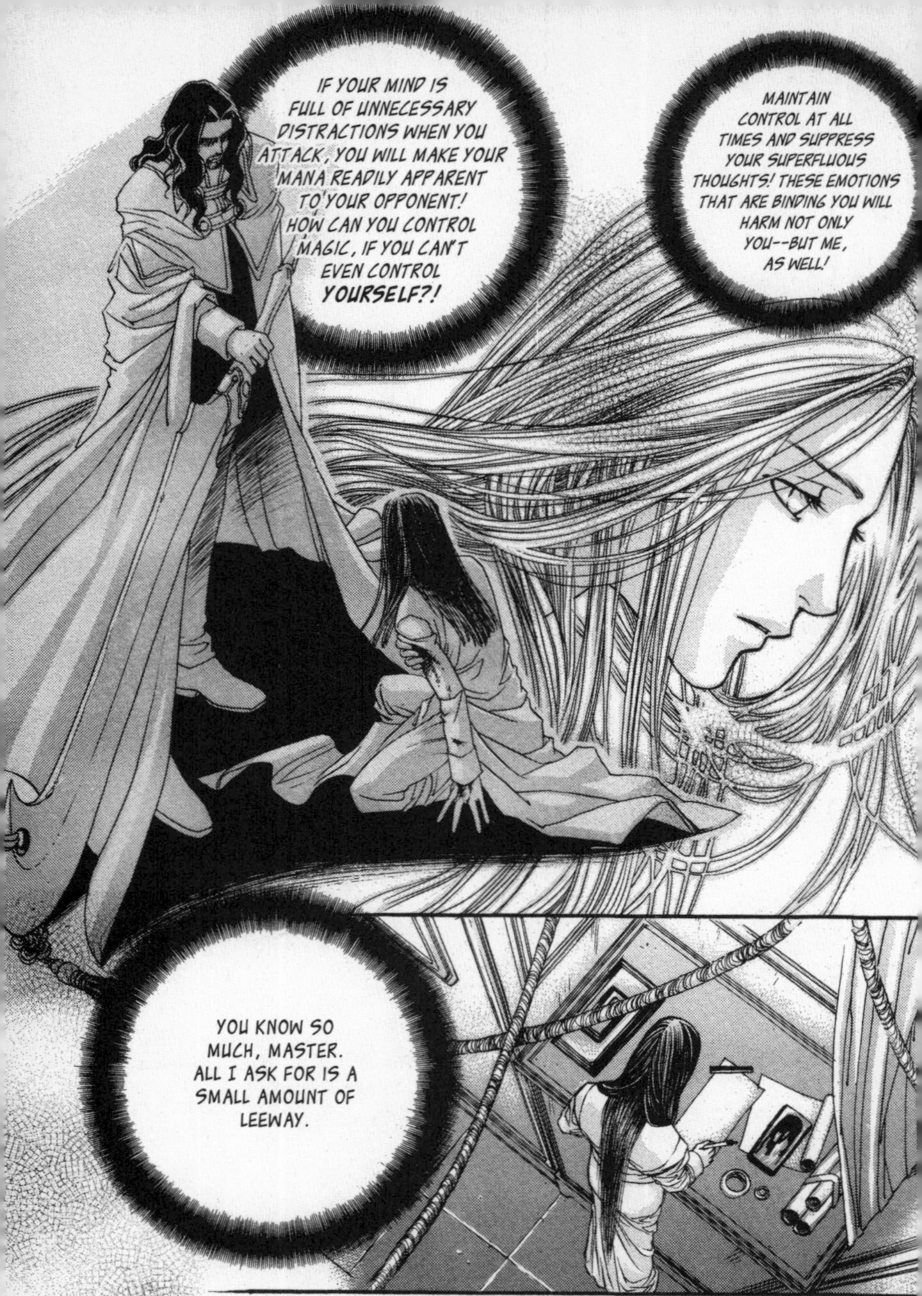
MAINTAIN CONTROL AT ALL TIMES AND SUPPRESS YOUR SUPERFLUOUS THOUGHTS! THESE EMOTIONS THAT ARE BINDING YOU WILL HARM NOT ONLY YOU--BUT ME, AS WELL!
IF YOUR MIND IS FULL OF UNNECESSARY DISTRACTIONS WHEN YOU ATTACK, YOU WILL MAKE YOUR MANA READILY APPARENT TO YOUR OPPONENT! HOW CAN YOU CONTROL MAGIC, IF YOU CAN'T EVEN CONTROL YOURSELF?!
YOU KNOW SO MUCH, MASTER. ALL I ASK FOR IS A SMALL AMOUNT OF LEEWAY.

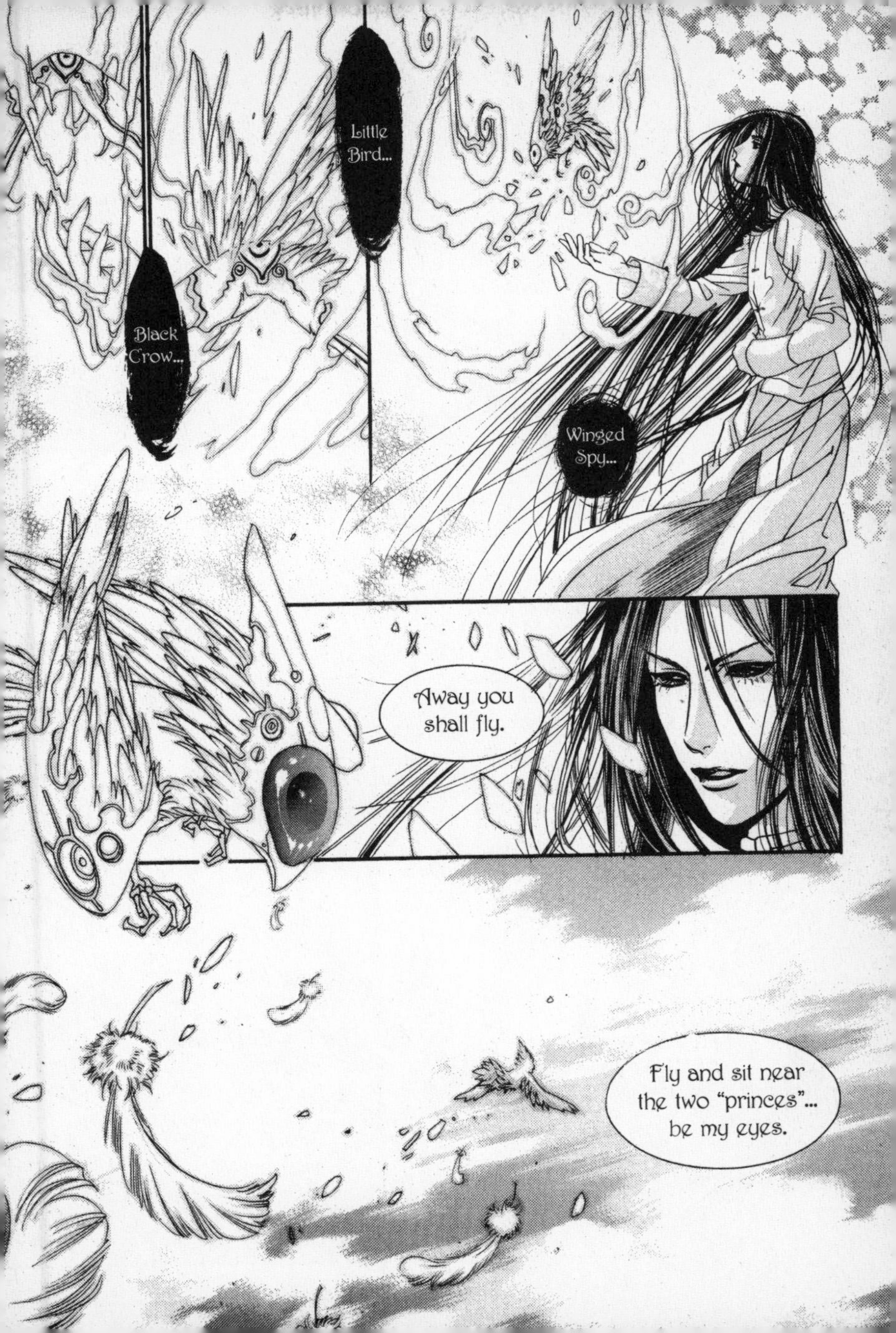
Black Crow...
Little Bird...
Winged Spy...
Away you shall fly.
Fly and sit near the two "princes"... be my eyes.

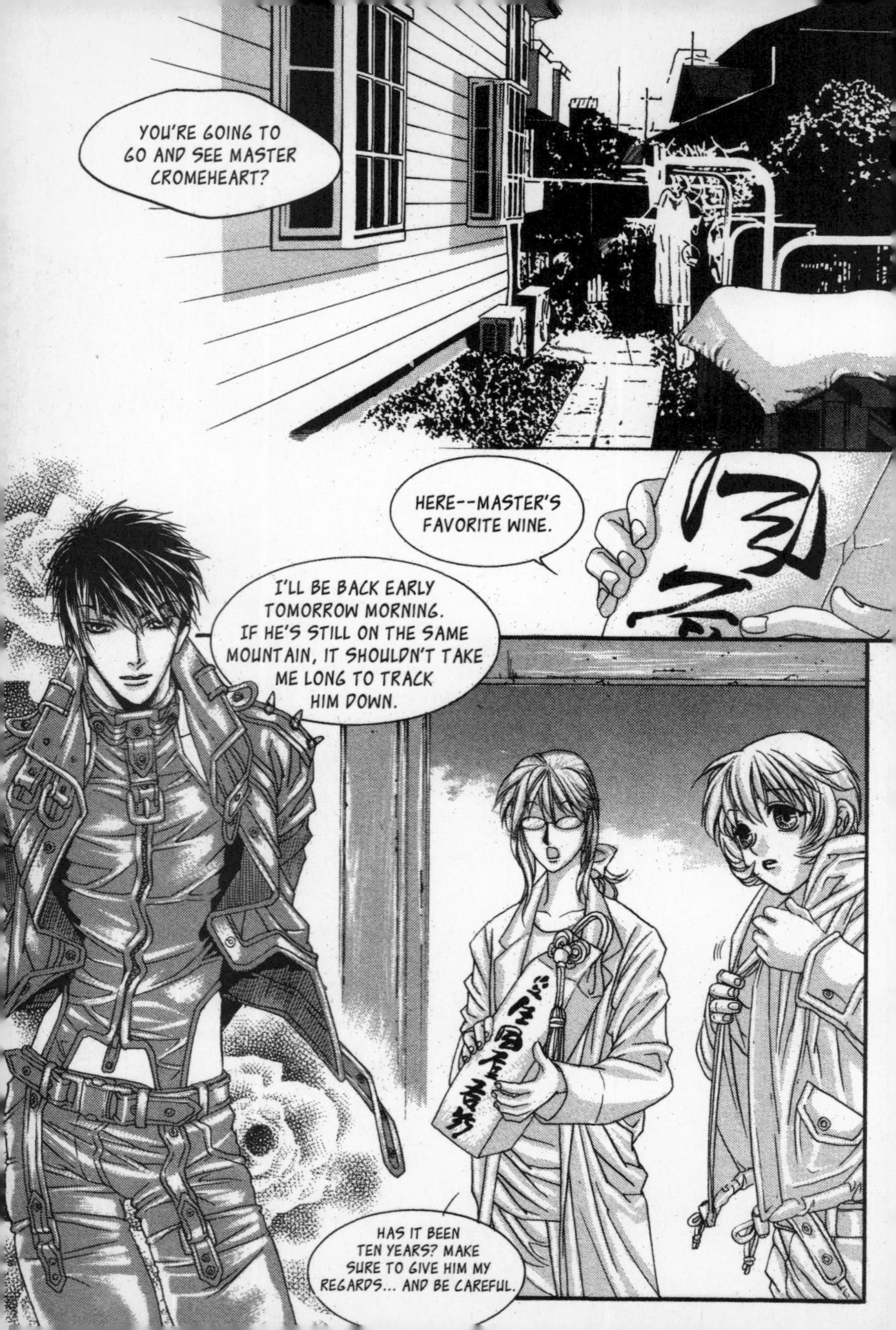
YOU'RE GOING TO GO AND SEE MASTER CROMEHEART?
I'LL BE BACK EARLY TOMORROW MORNING. IF HE'S STILL ON THE SAME MOUNTAIN, IT SHOULDN'T TAKE ME LONG TO TRACK HIM DOWN.
HERE--MASTER'S FAVORITE WINE.
HAS IT BEEN TEN YEARS? MAKE SURE TO GIVE HIM MY REGARDS... AND BE CAREFUL.

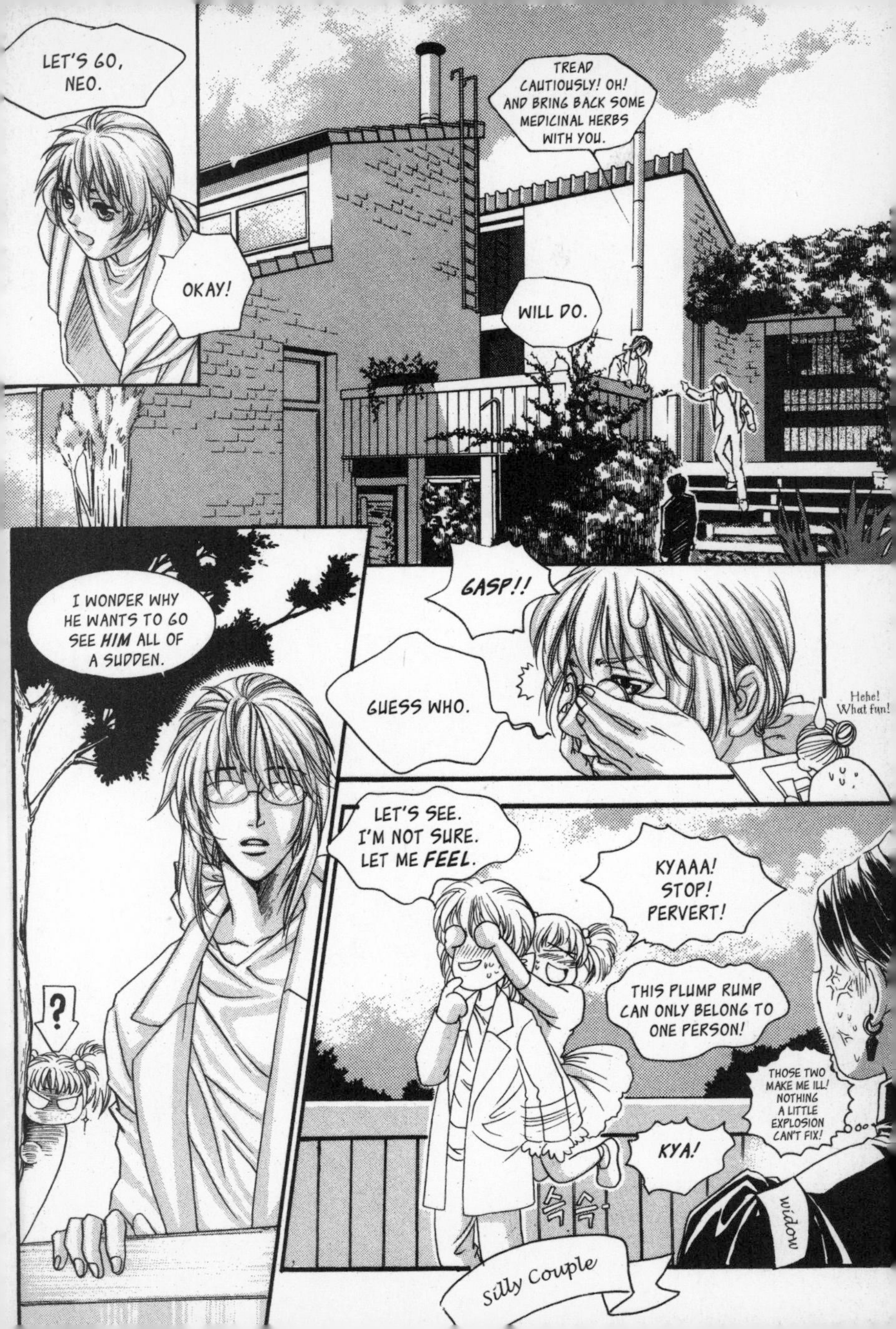
LET'S GO, NEO.
OKAY!
TREAD CAUTIOUSLY! OH! AND BRING BACK SOME MEDICINAL HERBS WITH YOU.
WILL DO.
I WONDER WHY HE WANTS TO GO SEE *HIM* ALL OF A SUDDEN.
?
GASP!!
GUESS WHO.
Hehe! What fun!
LET'S SEE. I'M NOT SURE. LET ME **FEEL**.
KYAAA! STOP! PERVERT!
THIS PLUMP RUMP CAN ONLY BELONG TO ONE PERSON!
THOSE TWO MAKE ME ILL! NOTHING A LITTLE EXPLOSION CAN'T FIX!
KYA!
슥슥
widow
Silly Couple

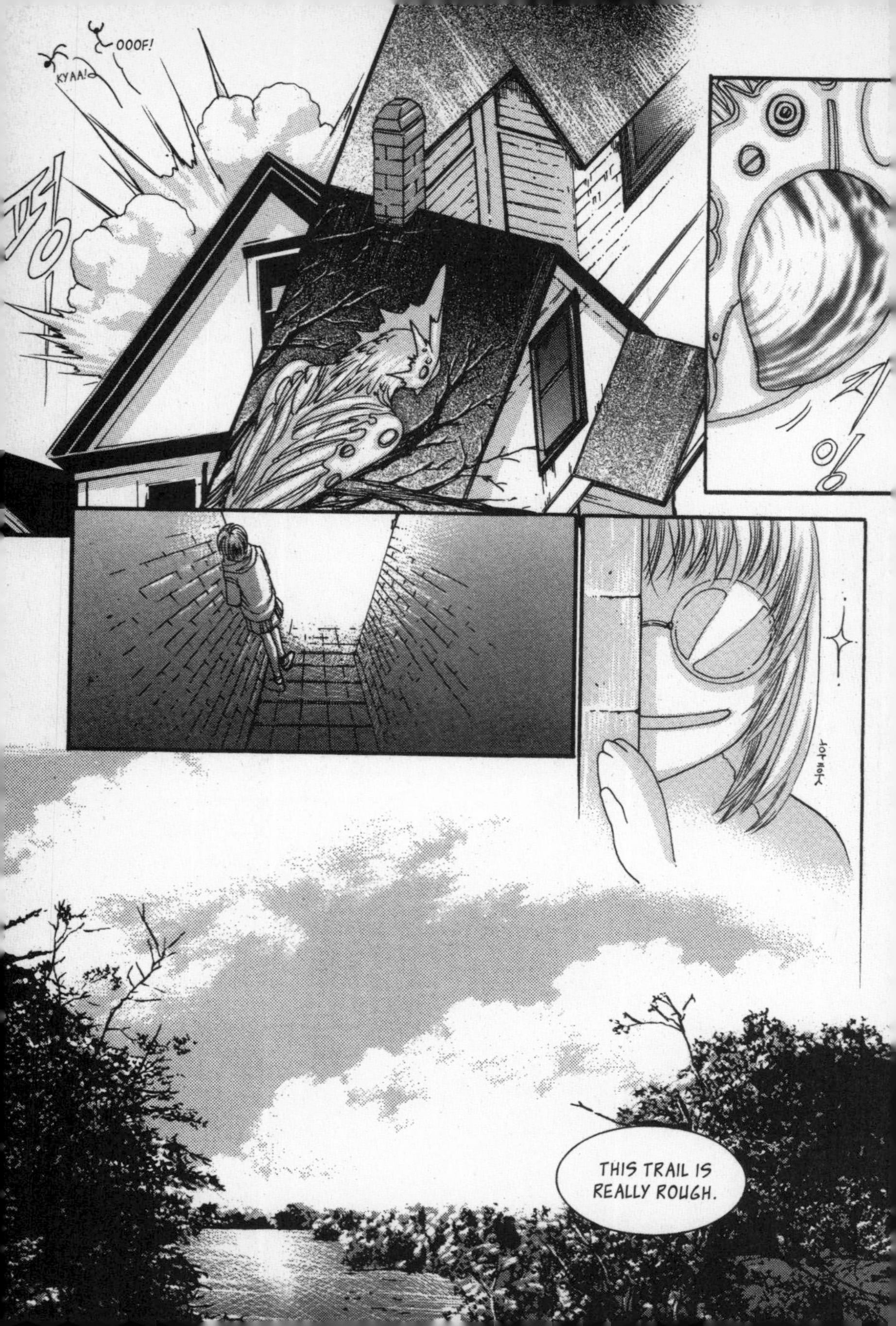
KYAA!
OOOF!
THIS TRAIL IS REALLY ROUGH.

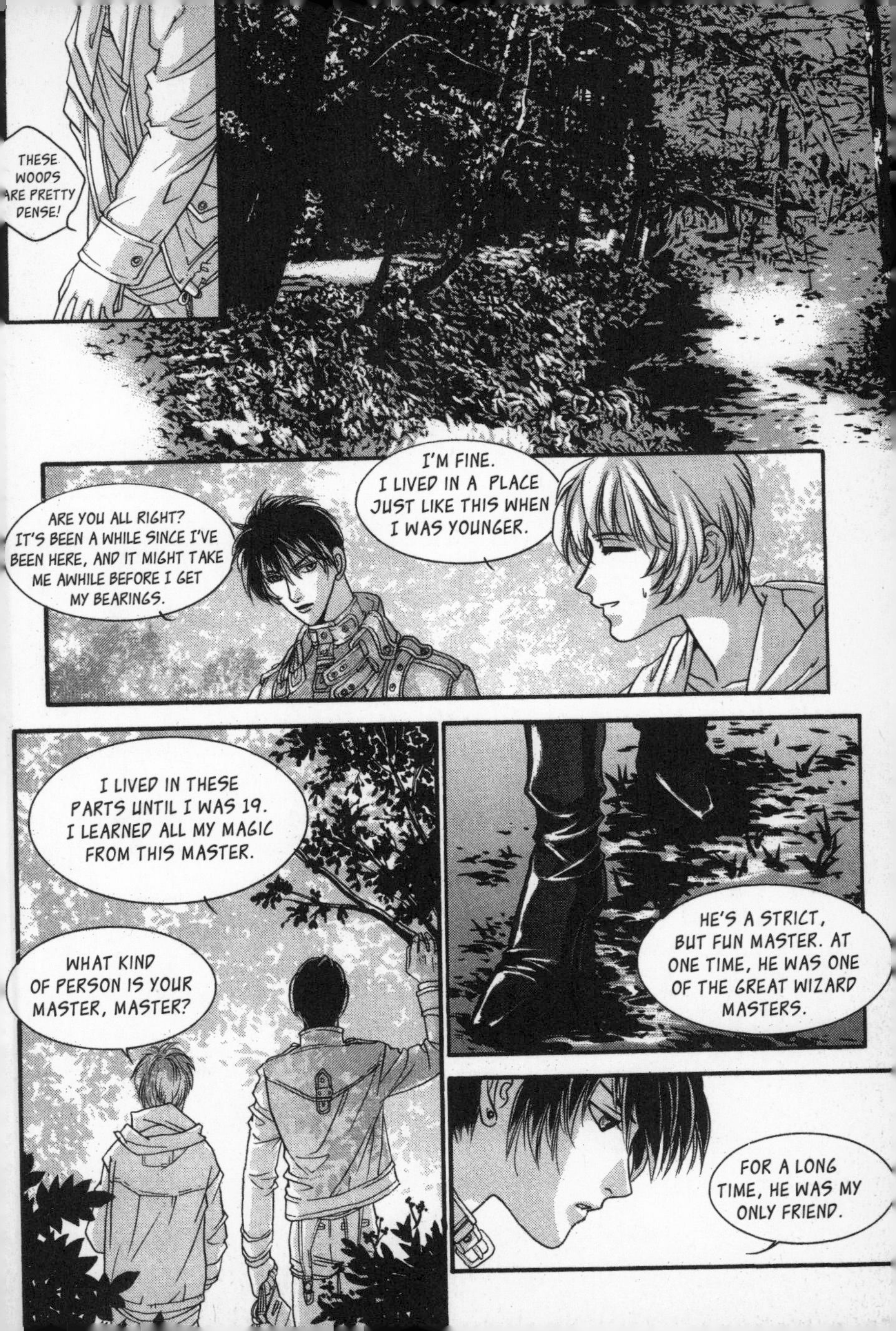
THESE WOODS ARE PRETTY DENSE!
ARE YOU ALL RIGHT? IT'S BEEN A WHILE SINCE I'VE BEEN HERE, AND IT MIGHT TAKE ME AWHILE BEFORE I GET MY BEARINGS.
I'M FINE. I LIVED IN A PLACE JUST LIKE THIS WHEN I WAS YOUNGER.
I LIVED IN THESE PARTS UNTIL I WAS 19. I LEARNED ALL MY MAGIC FROM THIS MASTER.
WHAT KIND OF PERSON IS YOUR MASTER, MASTER?
HE'S A STRICT, BUT FUN MASTER. AT ONE TIME, HE WAS ONE OF THE GREAT WIZARD MASTERS.
FOR A LONG TIME, HE WAS MY ONLY FRIEND.

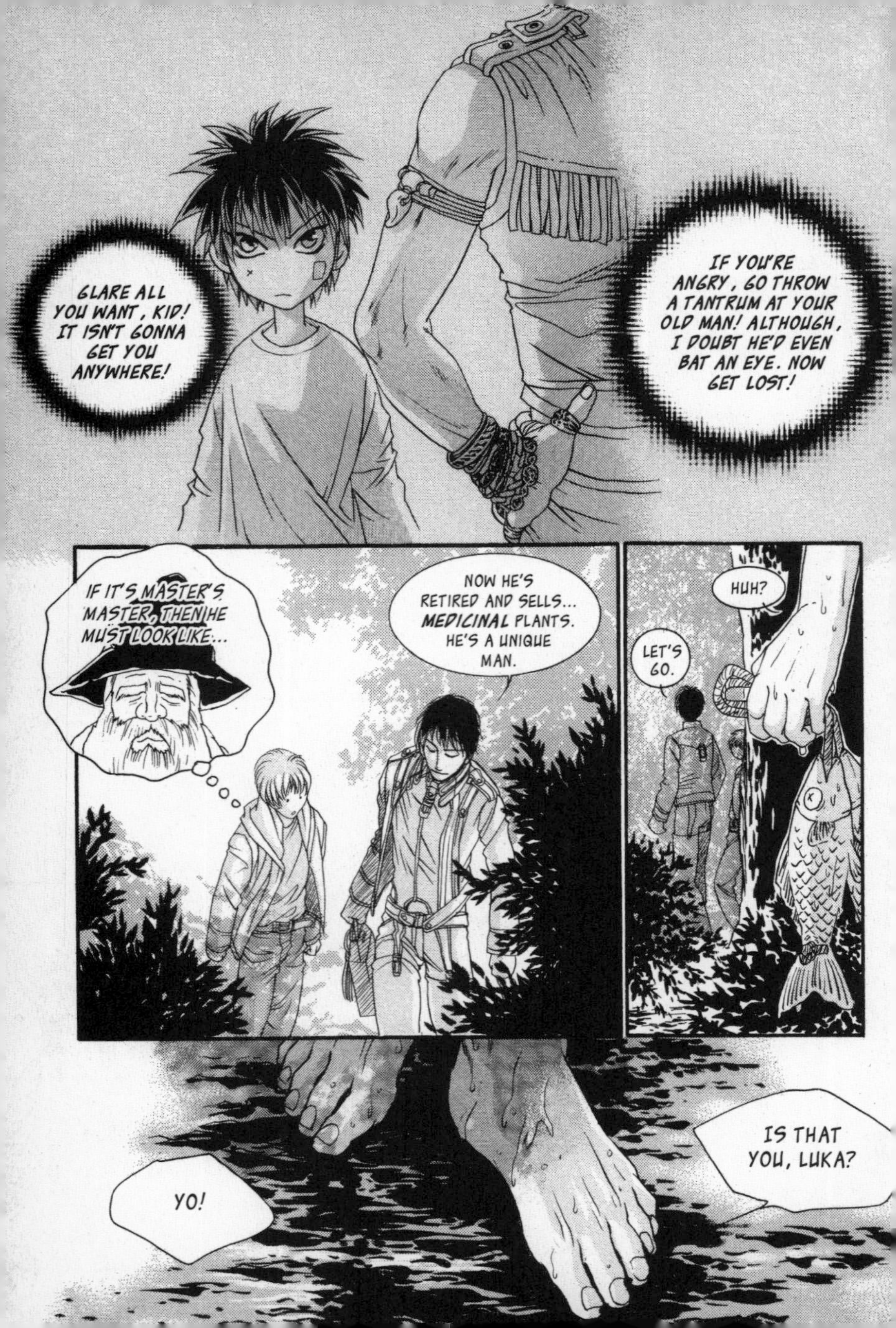
GLARE ALL YOU WANT, KID! IT ISN'T GONNA GET YOU ANYWHERE!
IF YOU'RE ANGRY, GO THROW A TANTRUM AT YOUR OLD MAN! ALTHOUGH, I DOUBT HE'D EVEN BAT AN EYE. NOW GET LOST!
IF IT'S MASTER'S MASTER, THEN HE MUST LOOK LIKE...
NOW HE'S RETIRED AND SELLS... MEDICINAL PLANTS. HE'S A UNIQUE MAN.
HUH?
LET'S GO.
YO!
IS THAT YOU, LUKA?

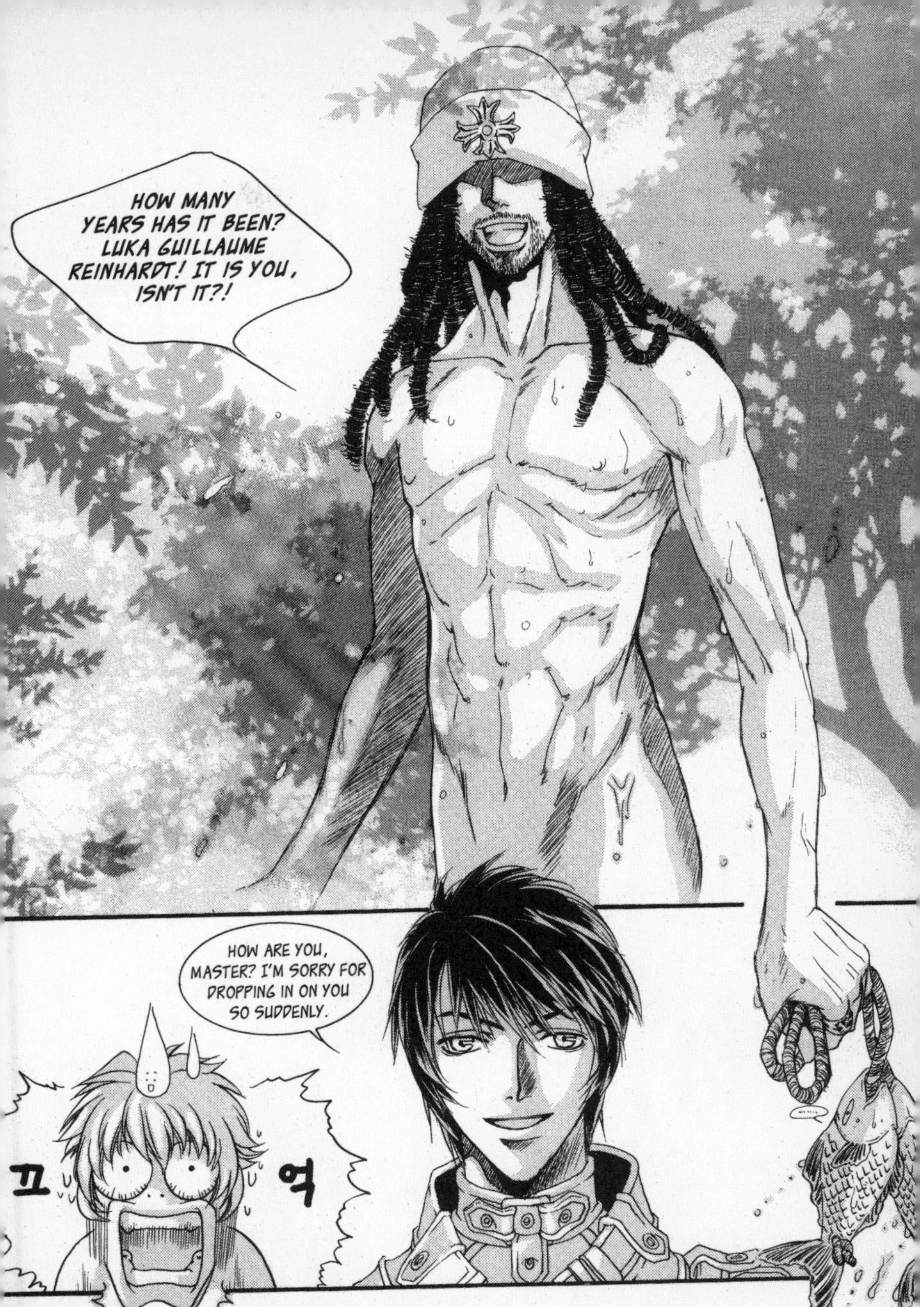
HOW MANY YEARS HAS IT BEEN? LUKA GUILLAUME REINHARDT! IT IS YOU, ISN'T IT?!
HOW ARE YOU, MASTER? I'M SORRY FOR DROPPING IN ON YOU SO SUDDENLY.
끄억

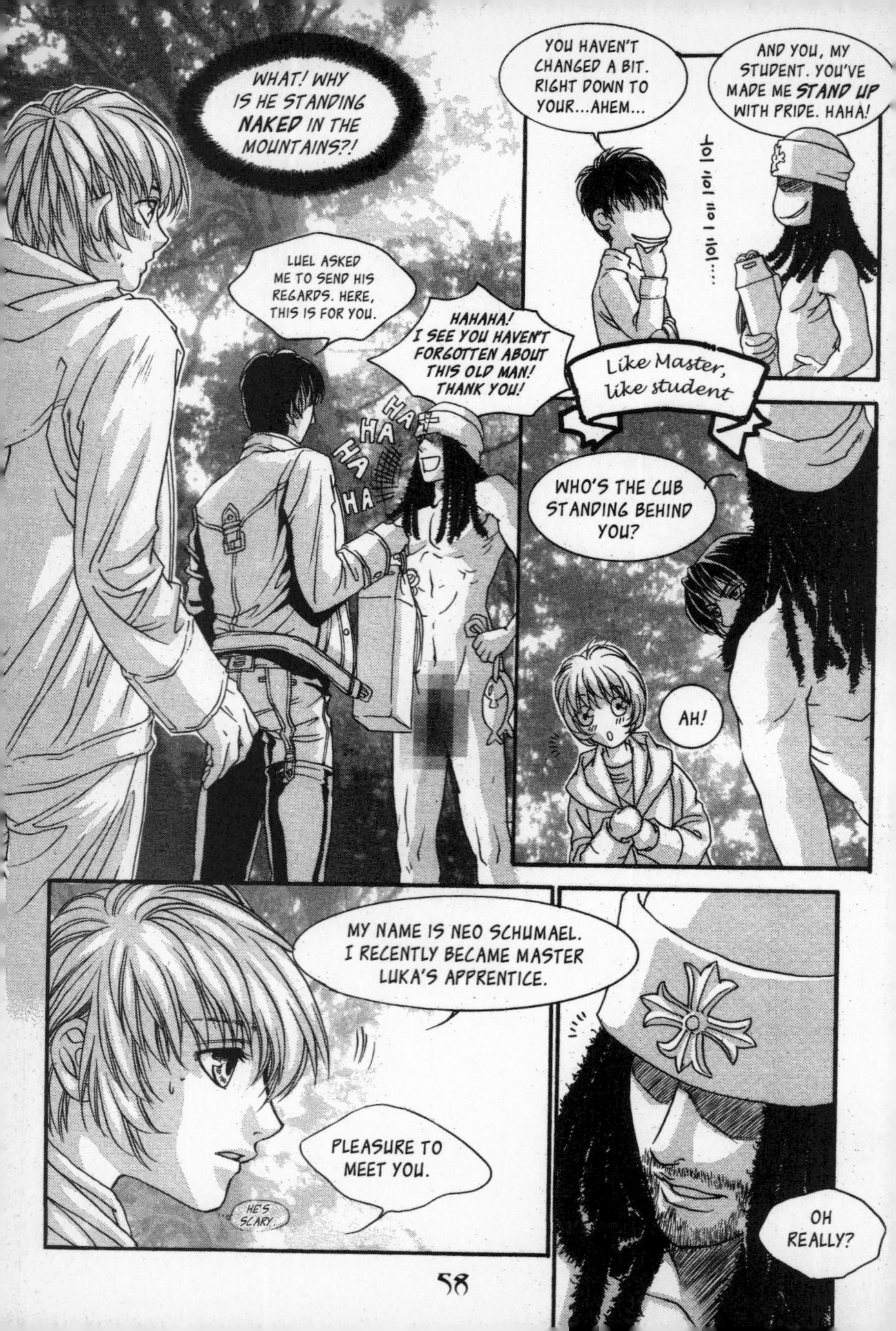
WHAT! WHY IS HE STANDING NAKED IN THE MOUNTAINS?!
LUEL ASKED ME TO SEND HIS REGARDS. HERE, THIS IS FOR YOU.
HAHAHA! I SEE YOU HAVEN'T FORGOTTEN ABOUT THIS OLD MAN! THANK YOU!
HA HA HA HA HA
YOU HAVEN'T CHANGED A BIT. RIGHT DOWN TO YOUR...AHEM...
AND YOU, MY STUDENT. YOU'VE MADE ME STAND UP WITH PRIDE. HAHA!
Like Master, like student
WHO'S THE CUB STANDING BEHIND YOU?
AH!
MY NAME IS NEO SCHUMAEL. I RECENTLY BECAME MASTER LUKA'S APPRENTICE.
PLEASURE TO MEET YOU.
HE'S SCARY
OH REALLY?

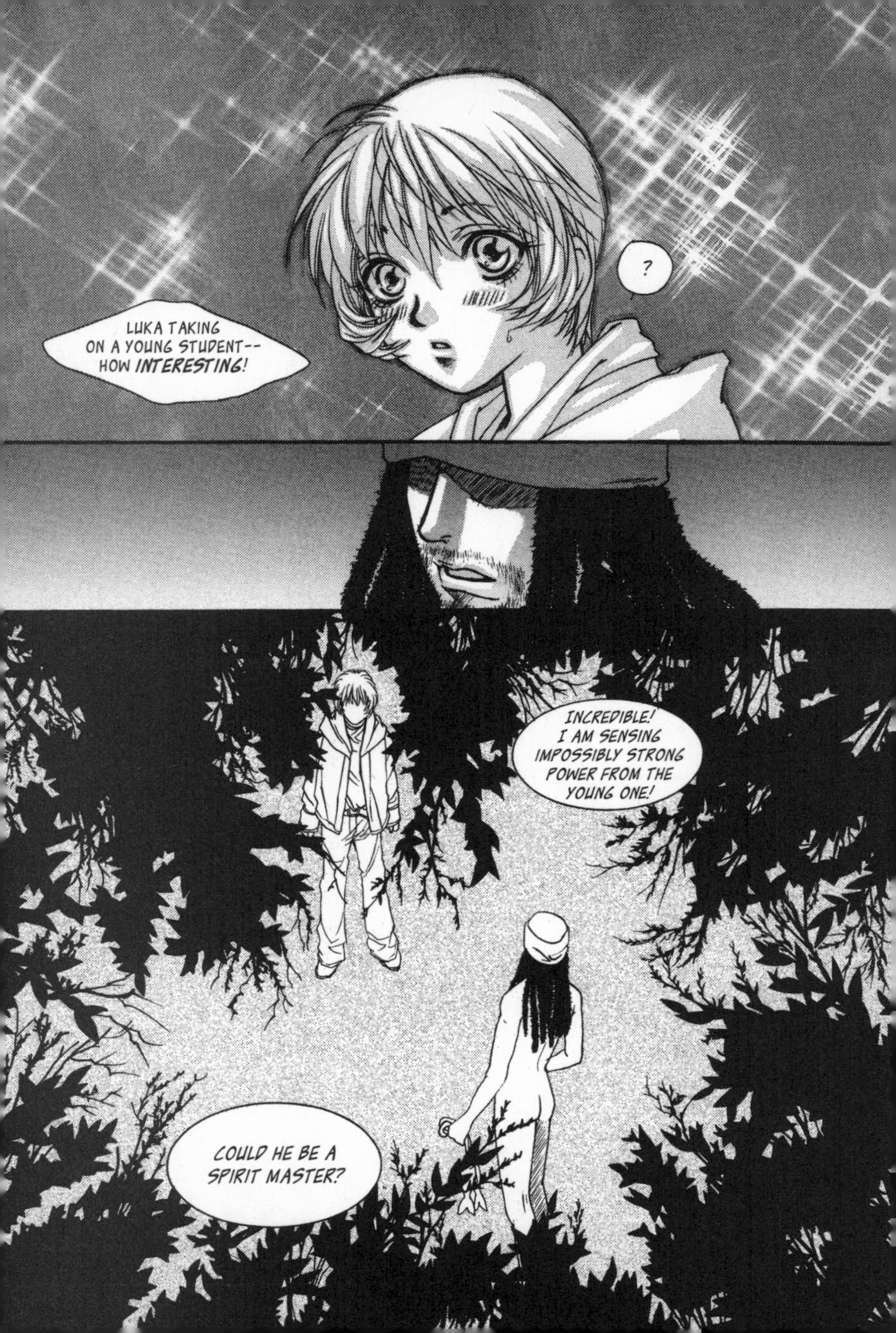
LUKA TAKING ON A YOUNG STUDENT--HOW INTERESTING!
?
INCREDIBLE! I AM SENSING IMPOSSIBLY STRONG POWER FROM THE YOUNG ONE!
COULD HE BE A SPIRIT MASTER?

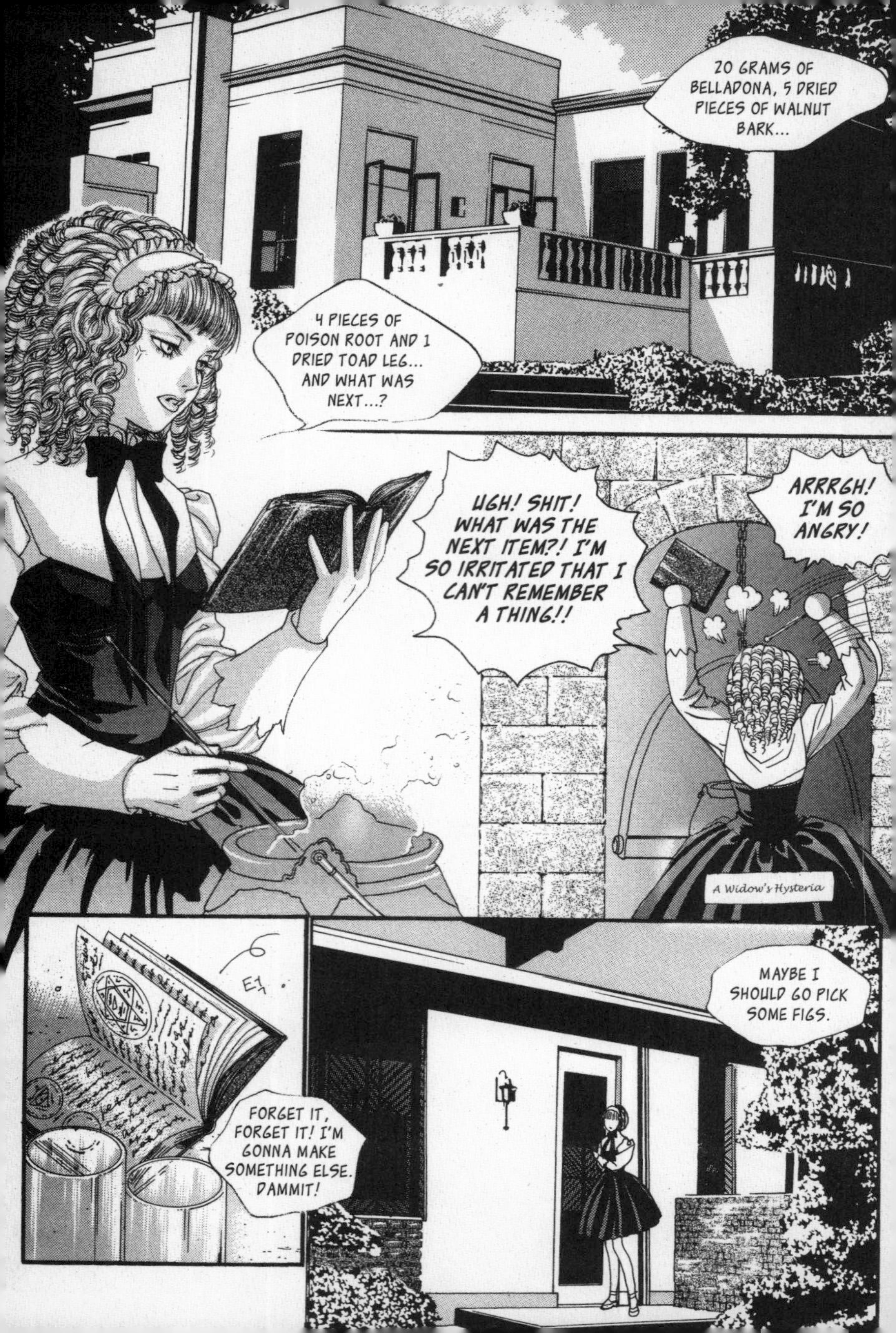
20 GRAMS OF BELLADONA, 5 DRIED PIECES OF WALNUT BARK...
4 PIECES OF POISON ROOT AND 1 DRIED TOAD LEG... AND WHAT WAS NEXT...?
UGH! SHIT! WHAT WAS THE NEXT ITEM?! I'M SO IRRITATED THAT I CAN'T REMEMBER A THING!!
ARRRGH! I'M SO ANGRY!
A Widow's Hysteria
FORGET IT, FORGET IT! I'M GONNA MAKE SOMETHING ELSE. DAMMIT!
MAYBE I SHOULD GO PICK SOME FIGS.

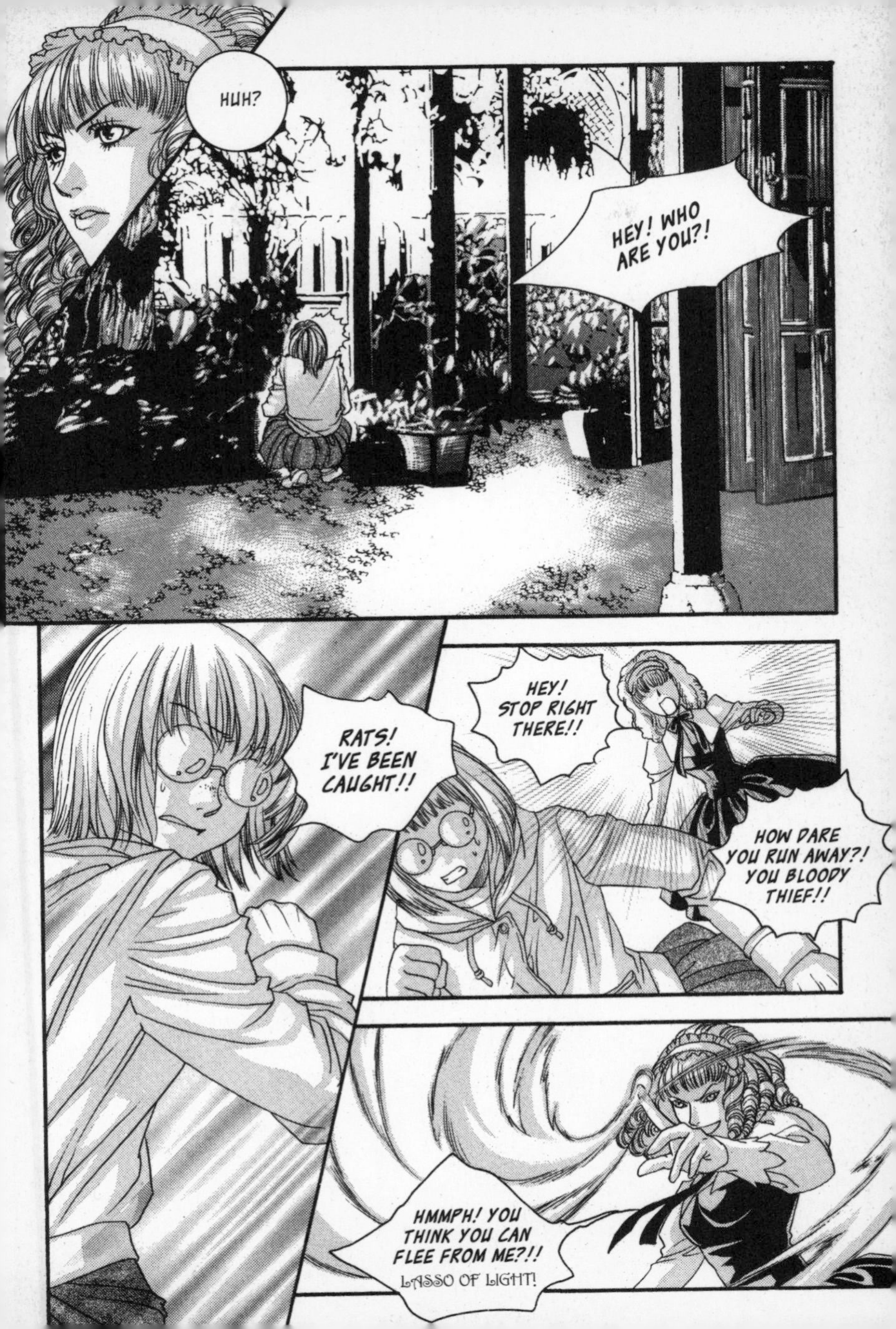
HUH?
HEY! WHO ARE YOU?!
RATS! I'VE BEEN CAUGHT!!
HEY! STOP RIGHT THERE!!
HOW DARE YOU RUN AWAY?! YOU BLOODY THIEF!!
HMMPH! YOU THINK YOU CAN FLEE FROM ME?!!
LASSO OF LIGHT!

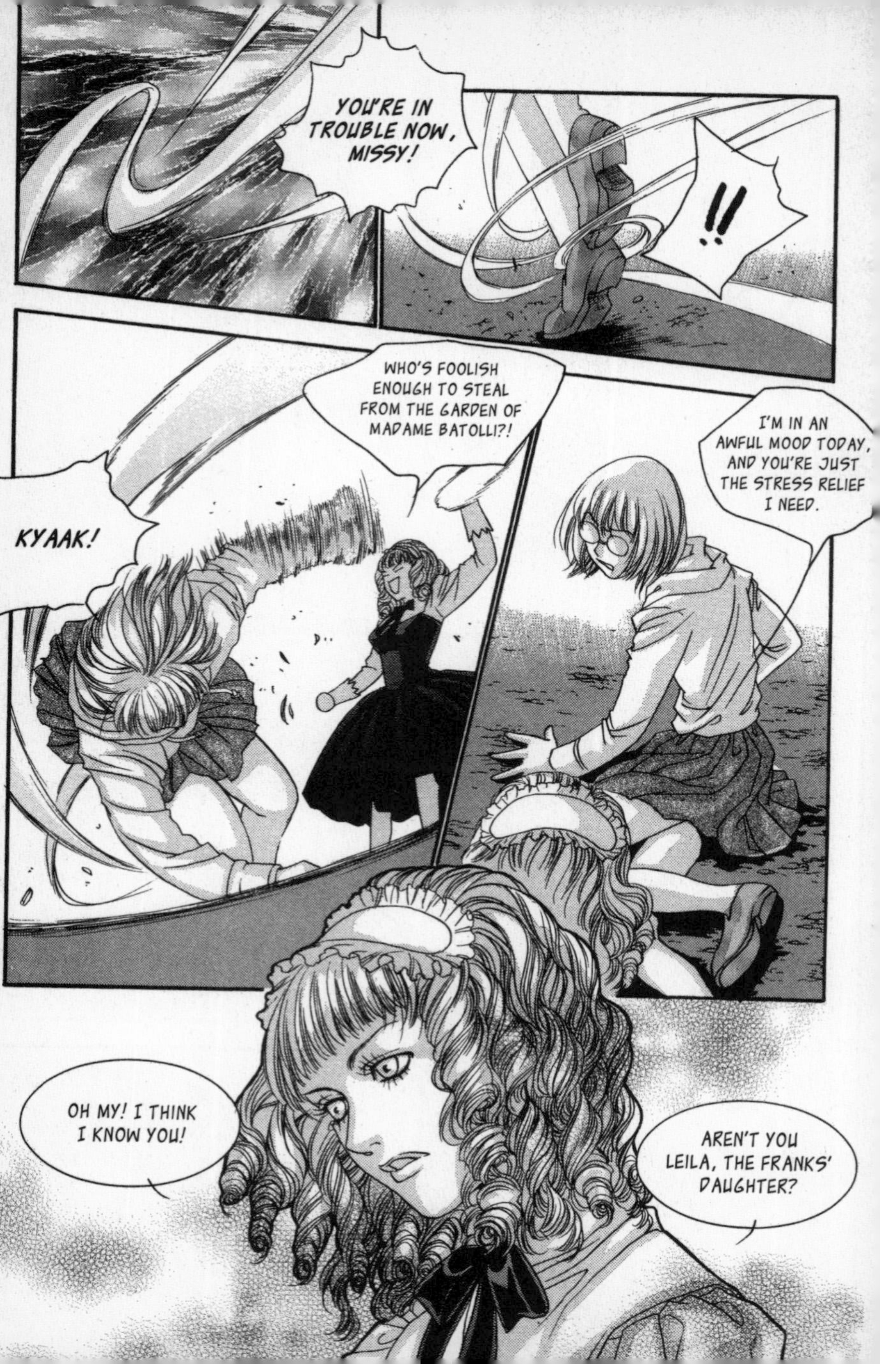
YOU'RE IN TROUBLE NOW, MISSY!
!!
WHO'S FOOLISH ENOUGH TO STEAL FROM THE GARDEN OF MADAME BATOLLI?!
KYAAK!
I'M IN AN AWFUL MOOD TODAY, AND YOU'RE JUST THE STRESS RELIEF I NEED.
OH MY! I THINK I KNOW YOU!
AREN'T YOU LEILA, THE FRANKS' DAUGHTER?

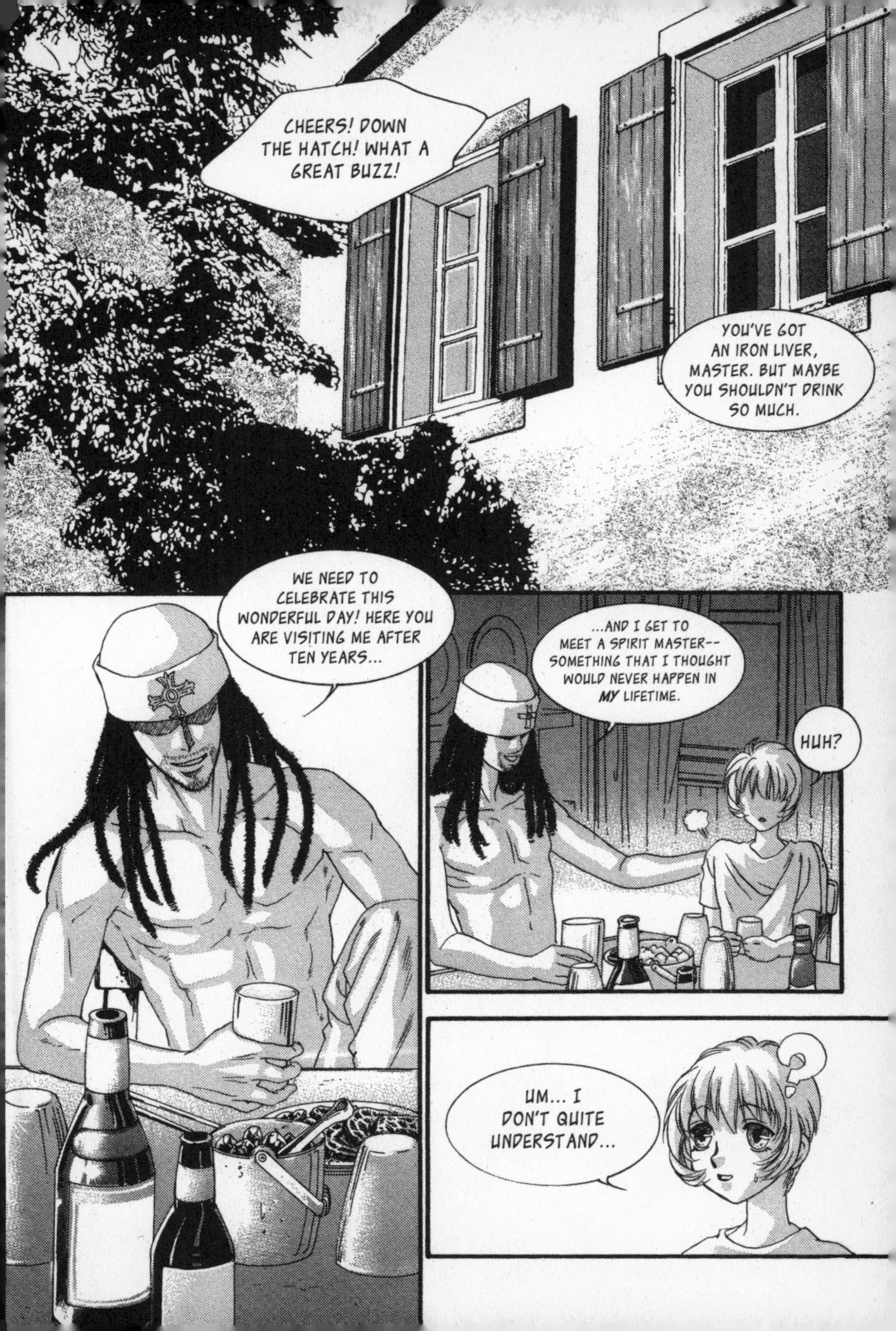
CHEERS! DOWN THE HATCH! WHAT A GREAT BUZZ!
YOU'VE GOT AN IRON LIVER, MASTER. BUT MAYBE YOU SHOULDN'T DRINK SO MUCH.
WE NEED TO CELEBRATE THIS WONDERFUL DAY! HERE YOU ARE VISITING ME AFTER TEN YEARS...
...AND I GET TO MEET A SPIRIT MASTER--SOMETHING THAT I THOUGHT WOULD NEVER HAPPEN IN MY LIFETIME.
HUH?
UM... I DON'T QUITE UNDERSTAND...

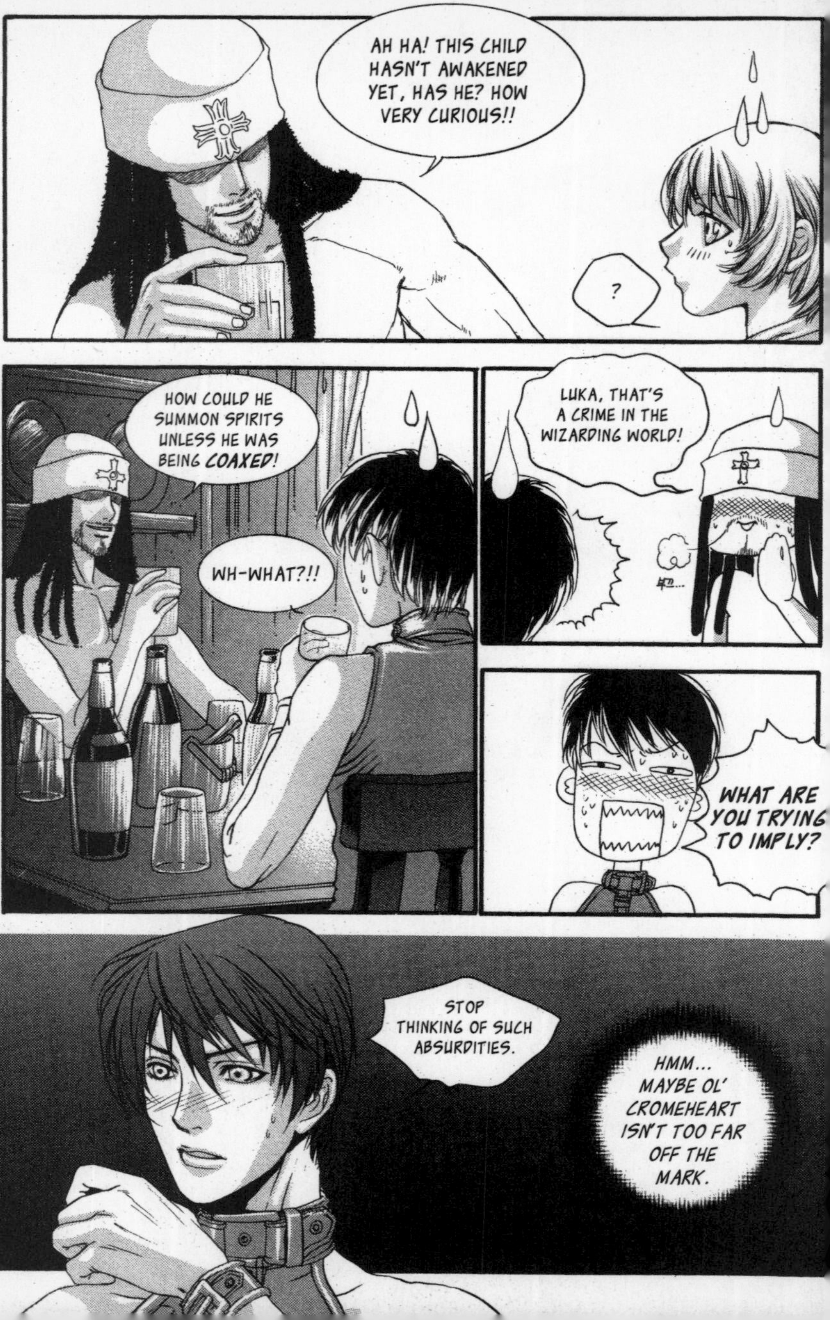
AH HA! THIS CHILD HASN'T AWAKENED YET, HAS HE? HOW VERY CURIOUS!!
?
HOW COULD HE SUMMON SPIRITS UNLESS HE WAS BEING COAXED!
WH-WHAT?!!
LUKA, THAT'S A CRIME IN THE WIZARDING WORLD!
WHAT ARE YOU TRYING TO IMPLY?
STOP THINKING OF SUCH ABSURDITIES.
HMM... MAYBE OL' CROMEHEART ISN'T TOO FAR OFF THE MARK.

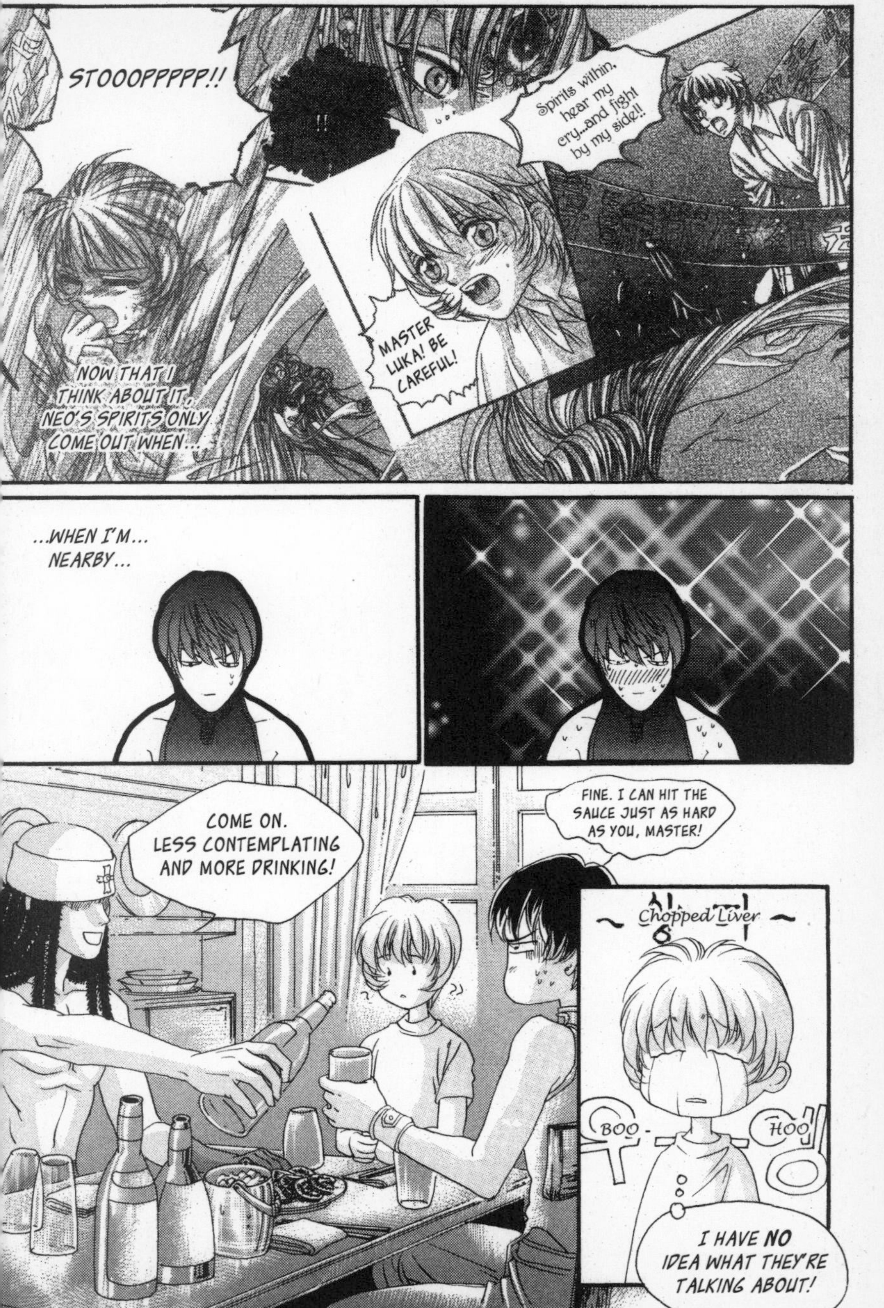
STOOOPPPPP!!
!!
Spirits within, hear my cry...and fight by my side!!
MASTER LUKA! BE CAREFUL!
NOW THAT I THINK ABOUT IT, NEO'S SPIRITS ONLY COME OUT WHEN...
...WHEN I'M... NEARBY...
COME ON. LESS CONTEMPLATING AND MORE DRINKING!
FINE. I CAN HIT THE SAUCE JUST AS HARD AS YOU, MASTER!
~ Chopped Liver ~
BOO-
HOO
I HAVE **NO** IDEA WHAT THEY'RE TALKING ABOUT!

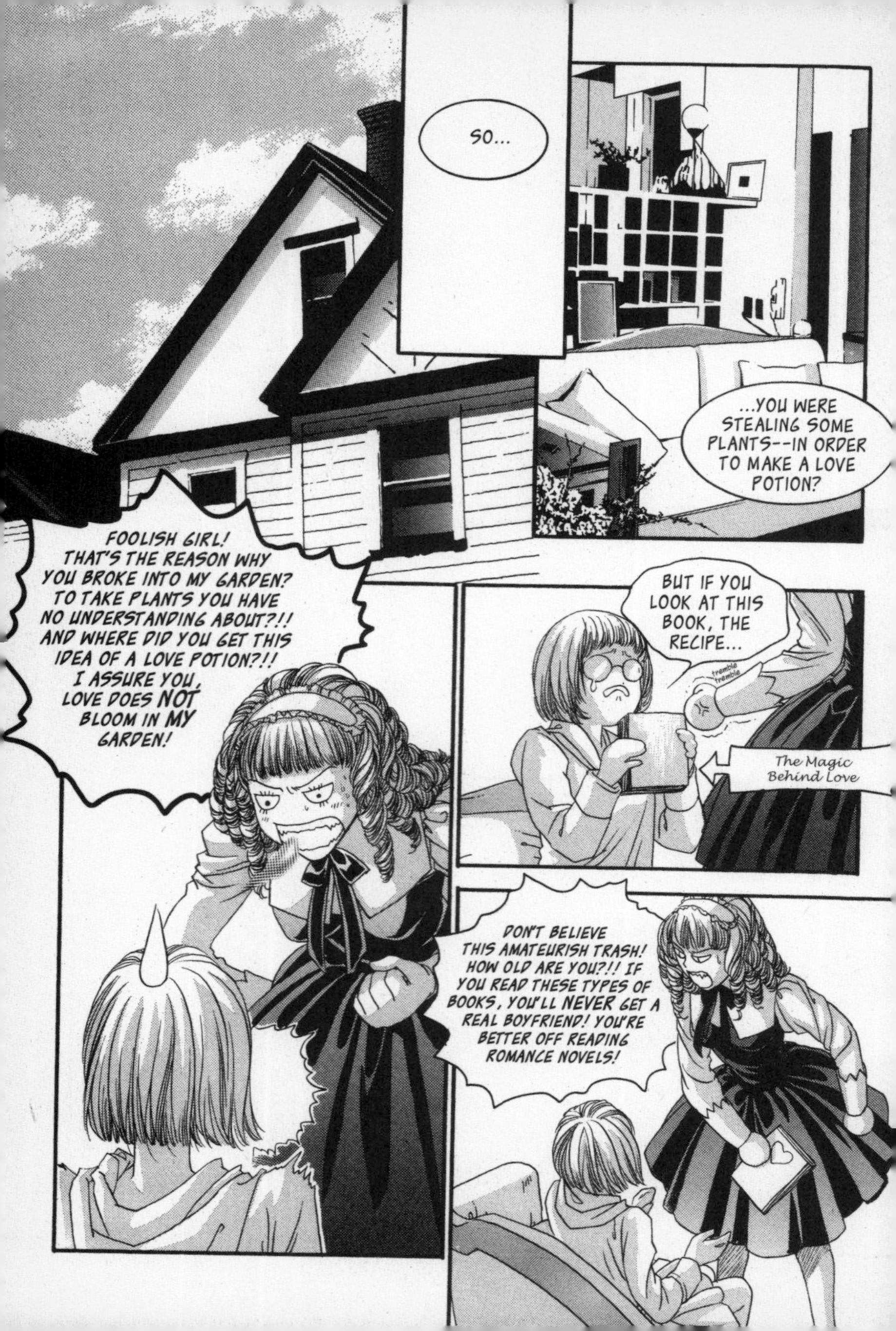
SO...
...YOU WERE STEALING SOME PLANTS--IN ORDER TO MAKE A LOVE POTION?
FOOLISH GIRL! THAT'S THE REASON WHY YOU BROKE INTO MY GARDEN? TO TAKE PLANTS YOU HAVE NO UNDERSTANDING ABOUT?!! AND WHERE DID YOU GET THIS IDEA OF A LOVE POTION?!! I ASSURE YOU, LOVE DOES NOT BLOOM IN MY GARDEN!
BUT IF YOU LOOK AT THIS BOOK, THE RECIPE...
tremble tremble
The Magic Behind Love
DON'T BELIEVE THIS AMATEURISH TRASH! HOW OLD ARE YOU?!! IF YOU READ THESE TYPES OF BOOKS, YOU'LL NEVER GET A REAL BOYFRIEND! YOU'RE BETTER OFF READING ROMANCE NOVELS!

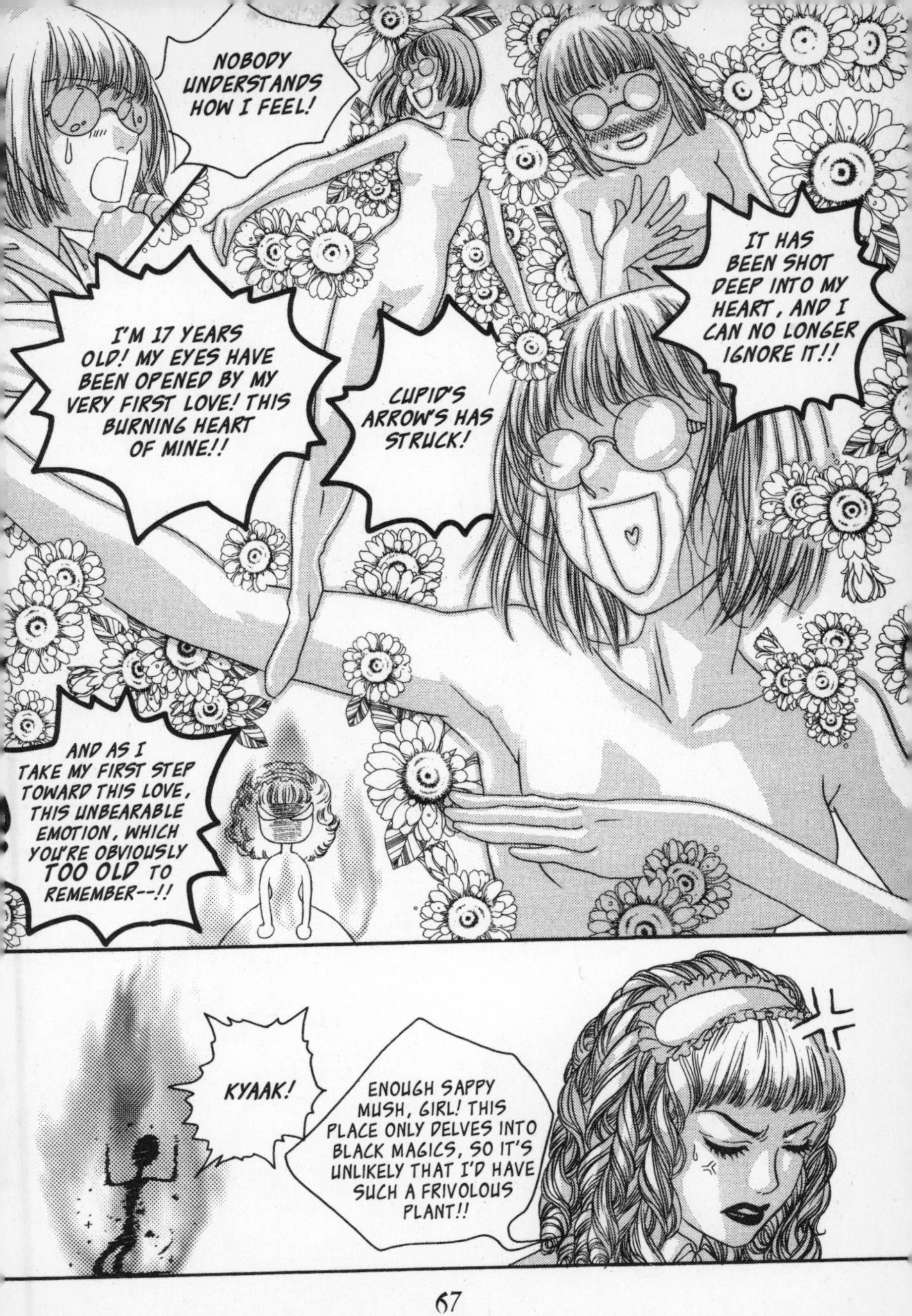
NOBODY UNDERSTANDS HOW I FEEL!
I'M 17 YEARS OLD! MY EYES HAVE BEEN OPENED BY MY VERY FIRST LOVE! THIS BURNING HEART OF MINE!!
CUPID'S ARROW'S HAS STRUCK!
IT HAS BEEN SHOT DEEP INTO MY HEART, AND I CAN NO LONGER IGNORE IT!!
AND AS I TAKE MY FIRST STEP TOWARD THIS LOVE, THIS UNBEARABLE EMOTION, WHICH YOU'RE OBVIOUSLY TOO OLD TO REMEMBER--!!
KYAAK!
ENOUGH SAPPY MUSH, GIRL! THIS PLACE ONLY DELVES INTO BLACK MAGICS, SO IT'S UNLIKELY THAT I'D HAVE SUCH A FRIVOLOUS PLANT!!

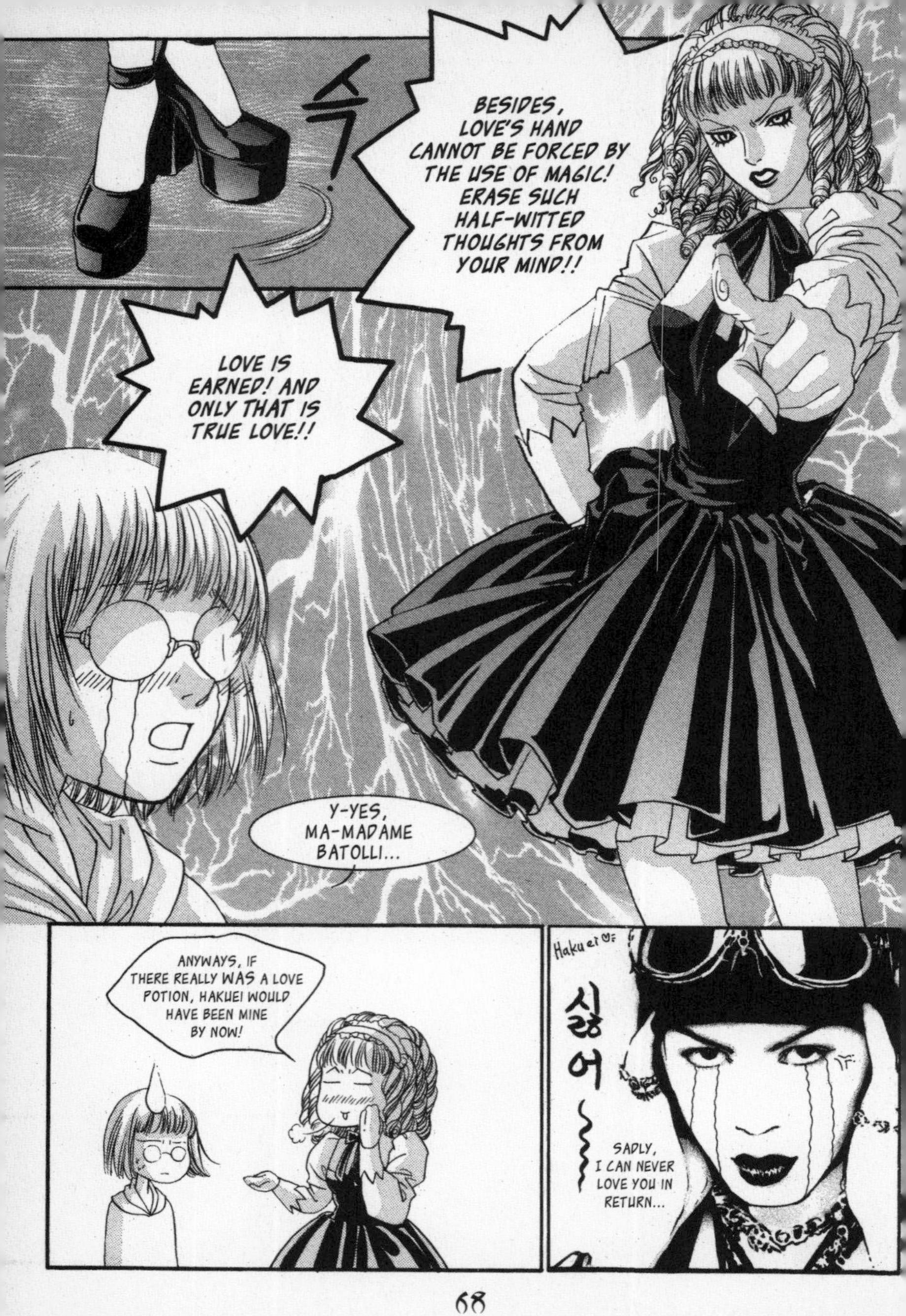
BESIDES, LOVE'S HAND CANNOT BE FORCED BY THE USE OF MAGIC! ERASE SUCH HALF-WITTED THOUGHTS FROM YOUR MIND!!
LOVE IS EARNED! AND ONLY THAT IS TRUE LOVE!!
Y-YES, MA-MADAME BATOLLI...
ANYWAYS, IF THERE REALLY WAS A LOVE POTION, HAKUEI WOULD HAVE BEEN MINE BY NOW!
Hakuei
싫어~
SADLY, I CAN NEVER LOVE YOU IN RETURN...

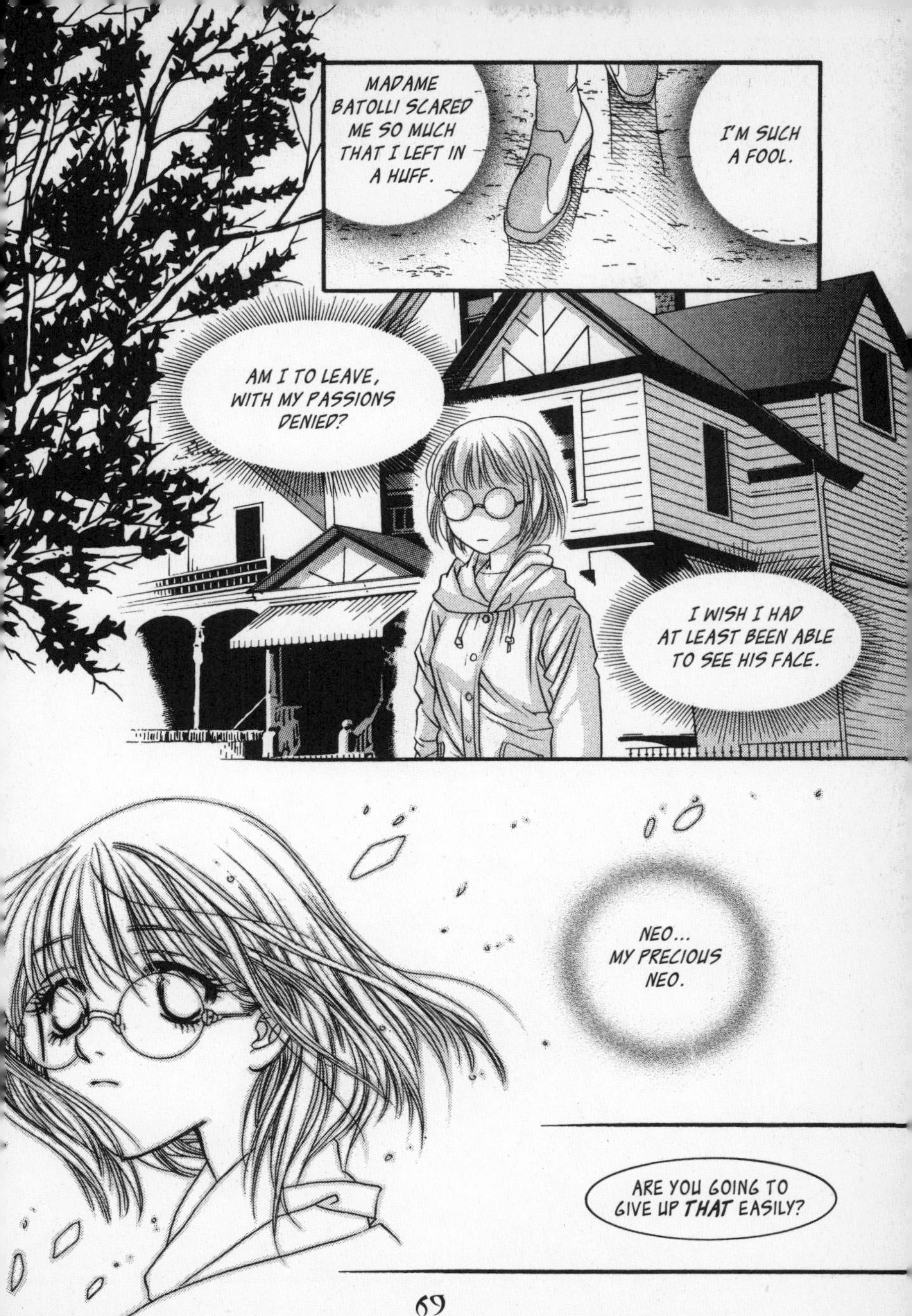
MADAME BATOLLI SCARED ME SO MUCH THAT I LEFT IN A HUFF.
I'M SUCH A FOOL.
AM I TO LEAVE, WITH MY PASSIONS DENIED?
I WISH I HAD AT LEAST BEEN ABLE TO SEE HIS FACE.
NEO... MY PRECIOUS NEO.
ARE YOU GOING TO GIVE UP **THAT** EASILY?

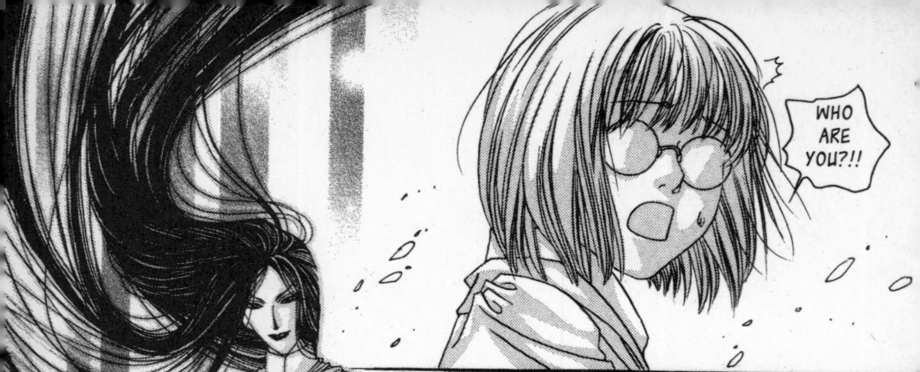
WHO ARE YOU?!!

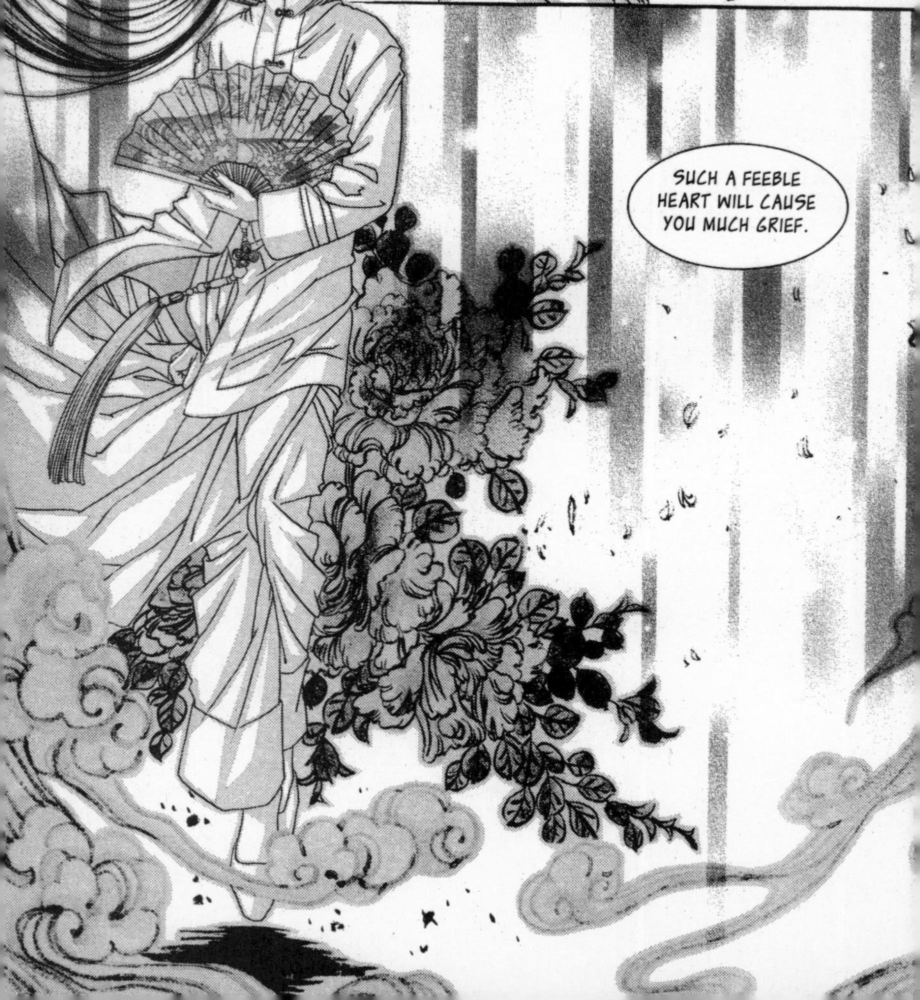
SUCH A FEEBLE HEART WILL CAUSE YOU MUCH GRIEF.

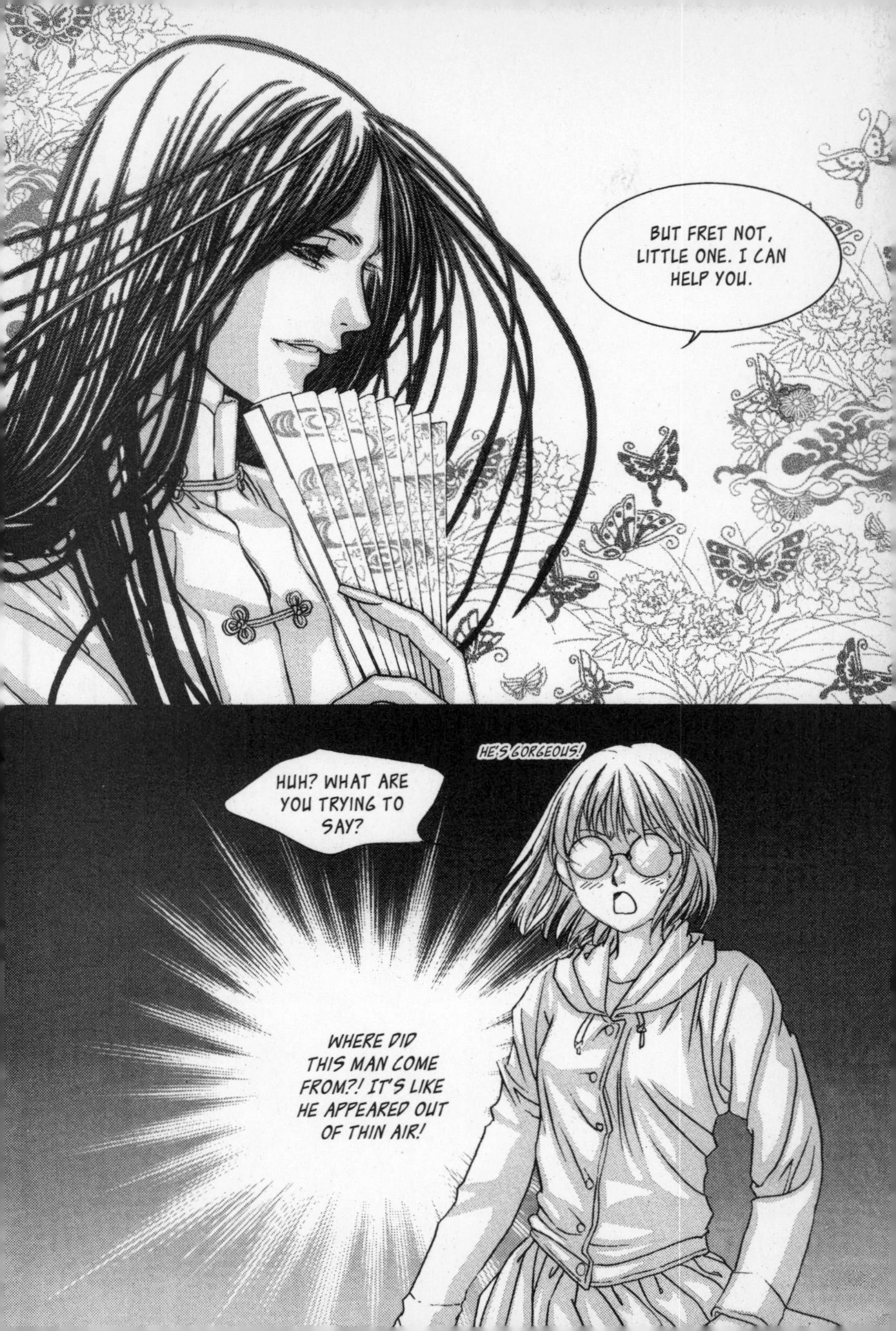
BUT FRET NOT, LITTLE ONE. I CAN HELP YOU.
HE'S GORGEOUS!
HUH? WHAT ARE YOU TRYING TO SAY?
WHERE DID THIS MAN COME FROM?! IT'S LIKE HE APPEARED OUT OF THIN AIR!

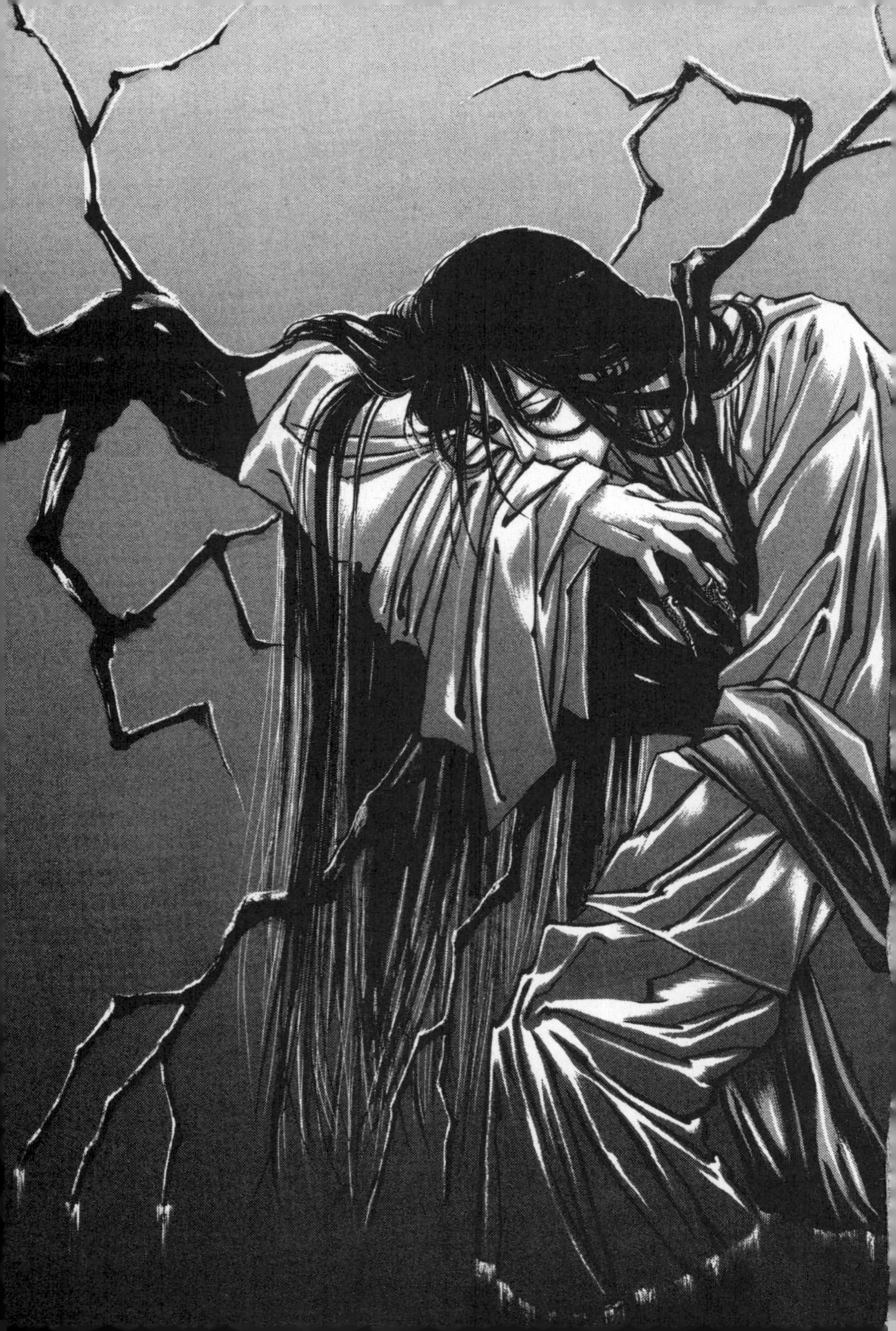

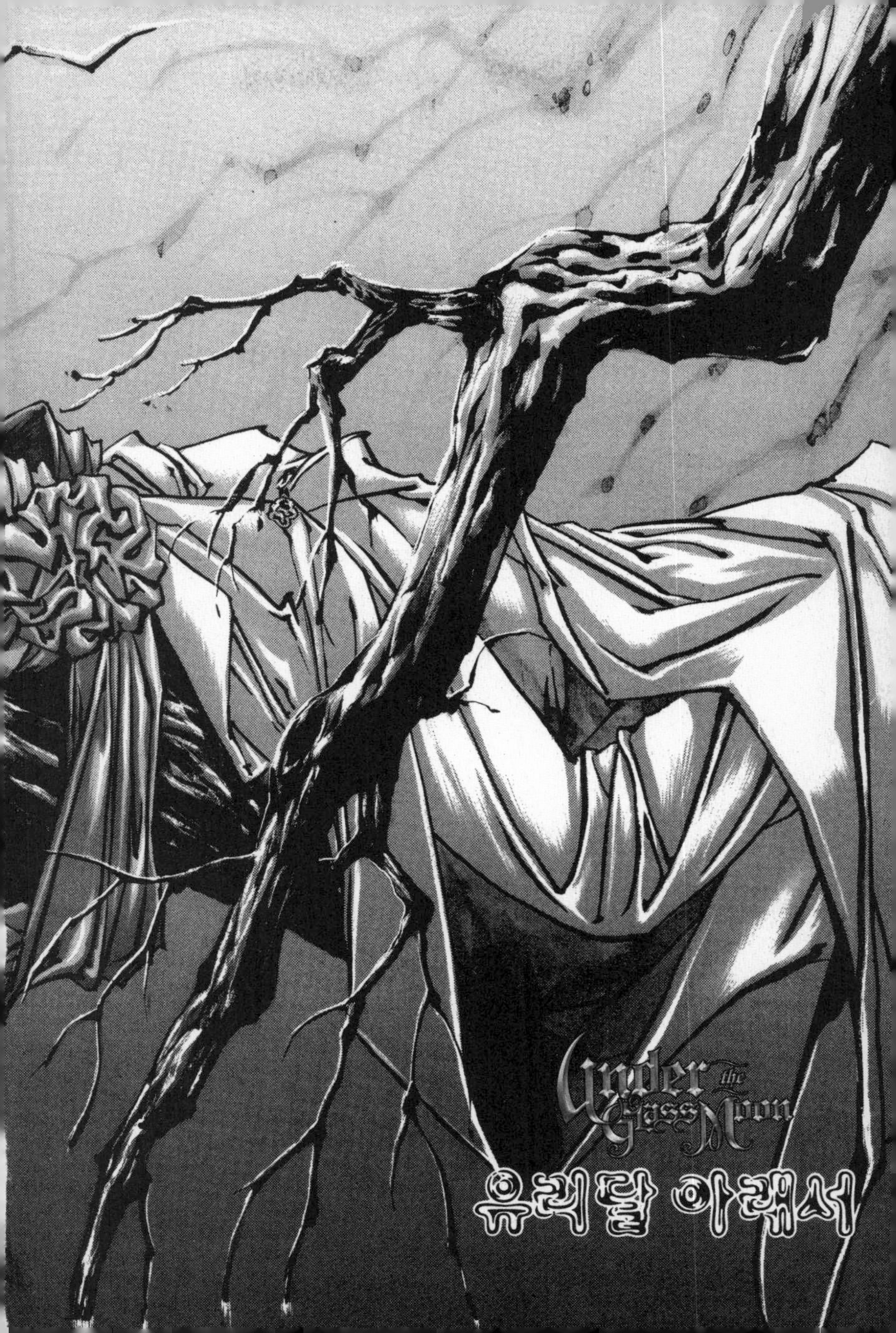
Under the Glass Moon
유리달 아래서

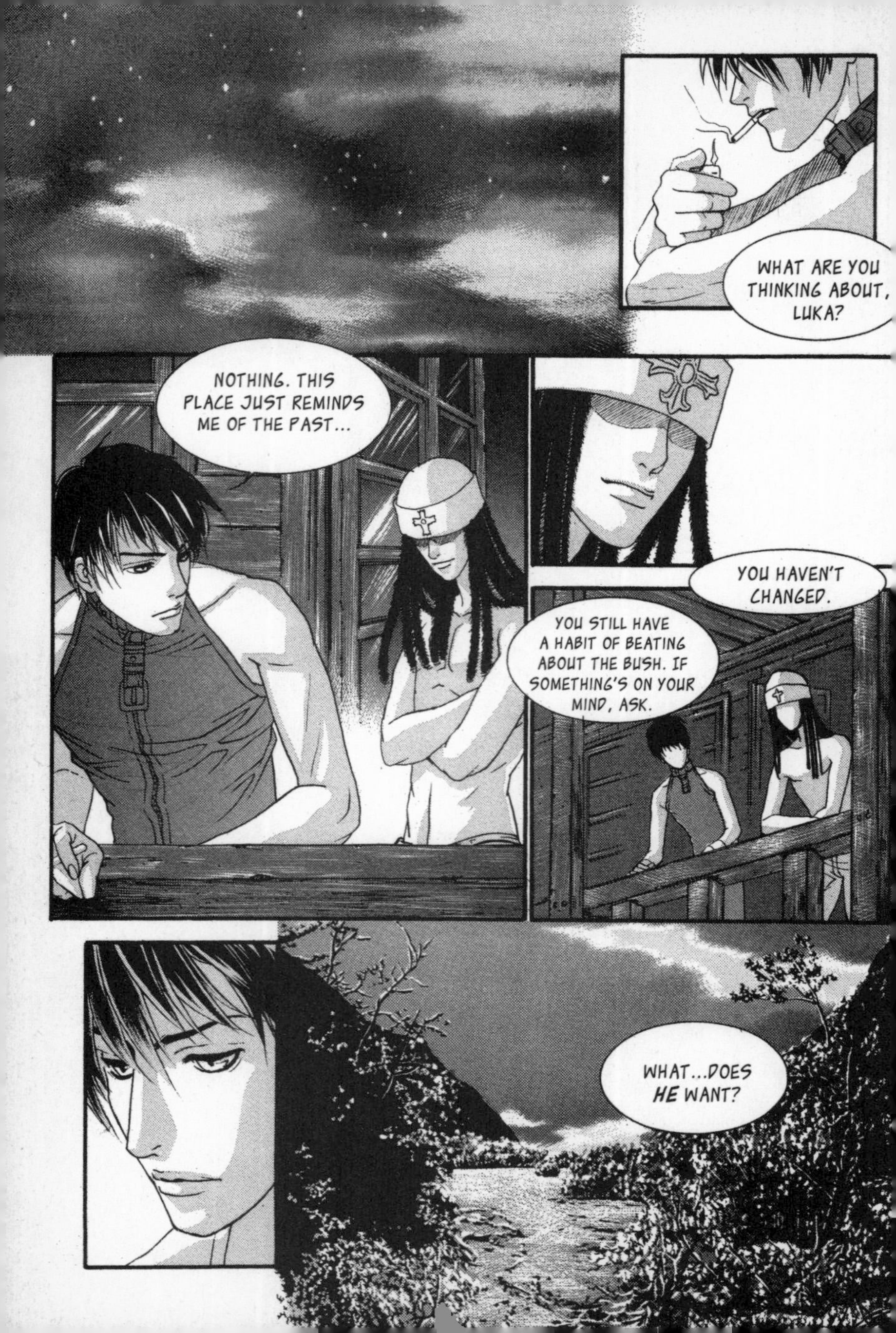
WHAT ARE YOU THINKING ABOUT, LUKA?
NOTHING. THIS PLACE JUST REMINDS ME OF THE PAST...
YOU HAVEN'T CHANGED.
YOU STILL HAVE A HABIT OF BEATING ABOUT THE BUSH. IF SOMETHING'S ON YOUR MIND, ASK.
WHAT...DOES *HE* WANT?

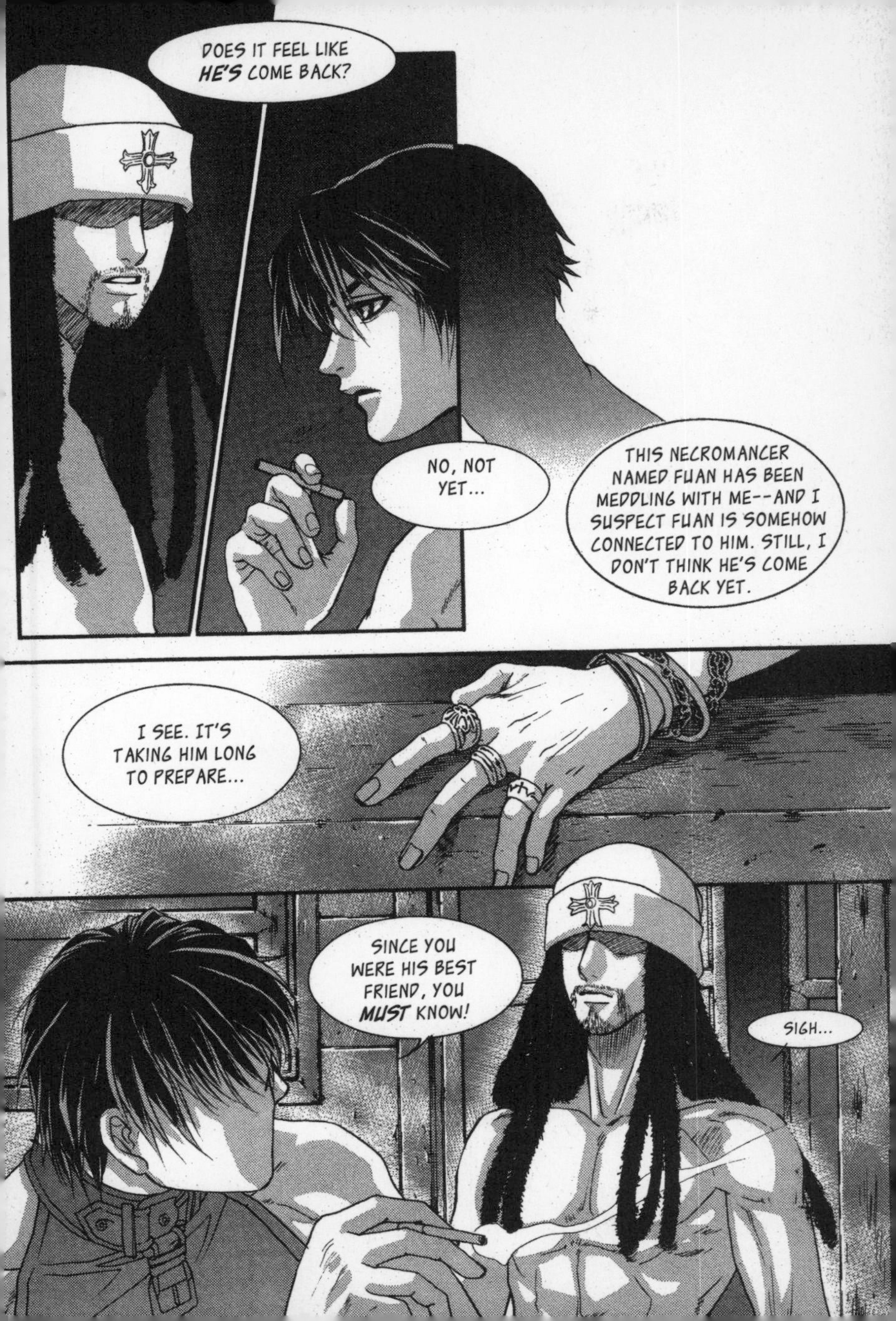
DOES IT FEEL LIKE HE'S COME BACK?
NO, NOT YET...
THIS NECROMANCER NAMED FUAN HAS BEEN MEDDLING WITH ME--AND I SUSPECT FUAN IS SOMEHOW CONNECTED TO HIM. STILL, I DON'T THINK HE'S COME BACK YET.
I SEE. IT'S TAKING HIM LONG TO PREPARE...
SINCE YOU WERE HIS BEST FRIEND, YOU MUST KNOW!
SIGH...

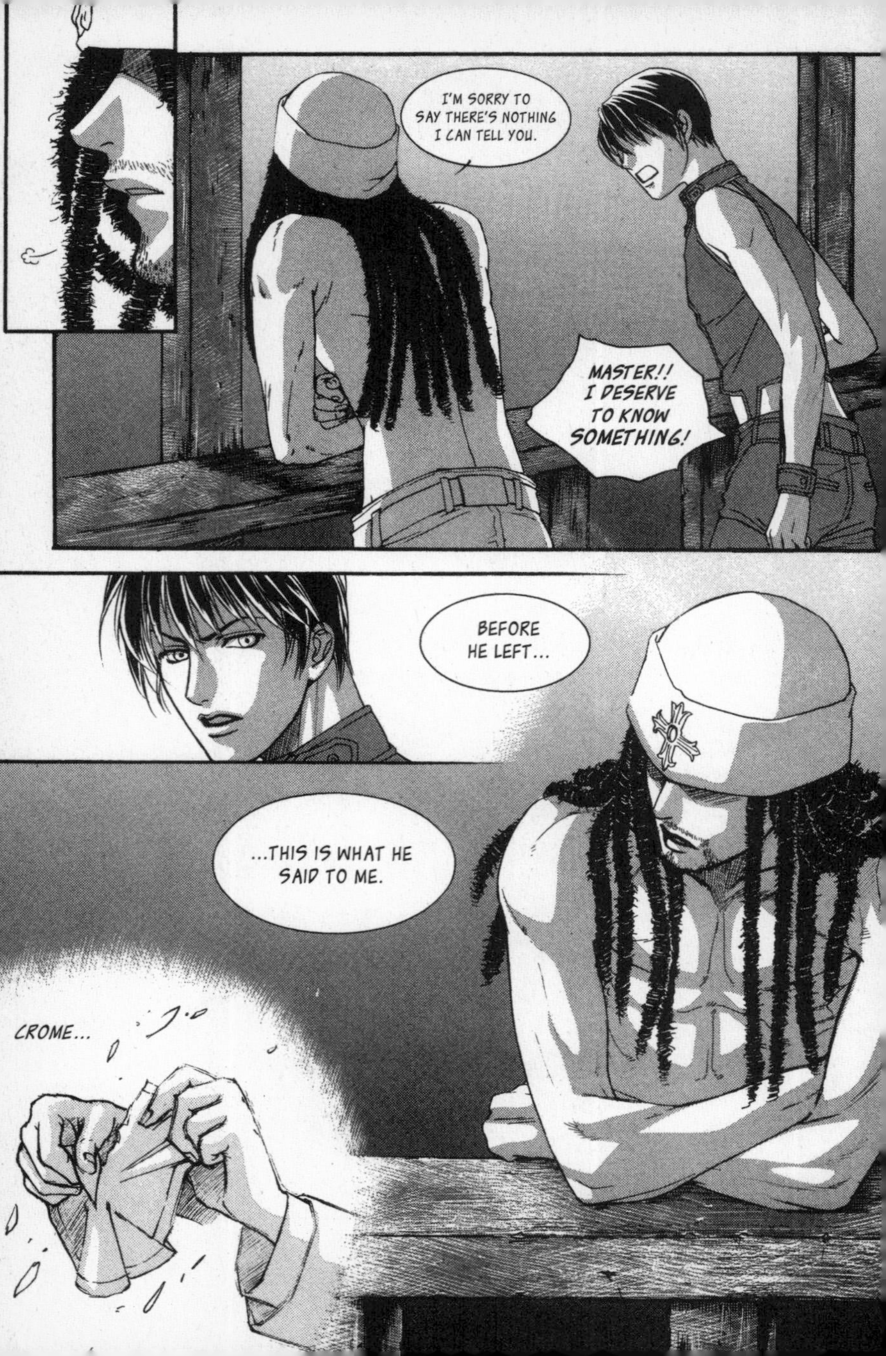
I'M SORRY TO SAY THERE'S NOTHING I CAN TELL YOU.
MASTER!! I DESERVE TO KNOW SOMETHING!
BEFORE HE LEFT...
...THIS IS WHAT HE SAID TO ME.
CROME...

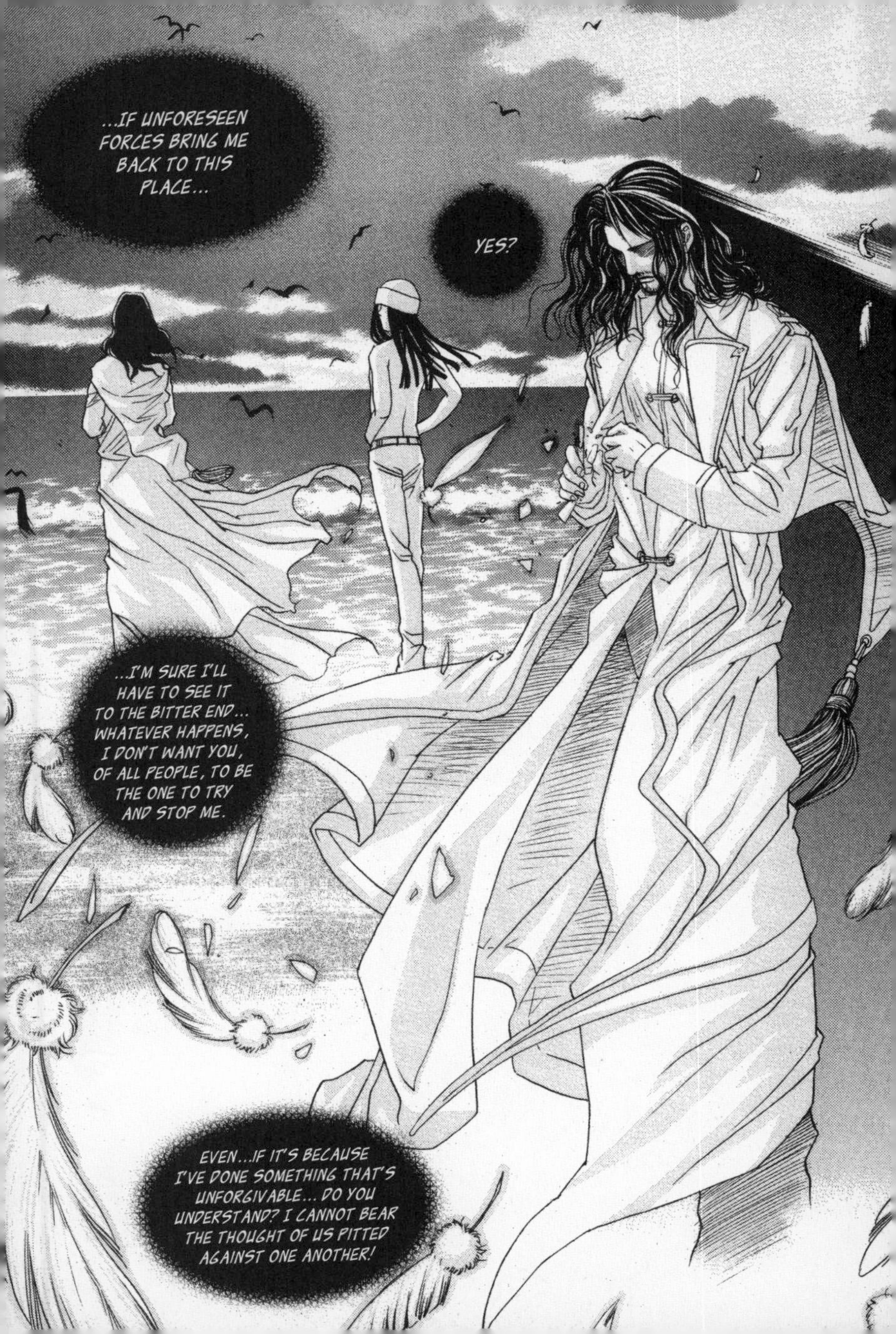
...IF UNFORESEEN FORCES BRING ME BACK TO THIS PLACE...
YES?
...I'M SURE I'LL HAVE TO SEE IT TO THE BITTER END... WHATEVER HAPPENS, I DON'T WANT YOU, OF ALL PEOPLE, TO BE THE ONE TO TRY AND STOP ME.
EVEN...IF IT'S BECAUSE I'VE DONE SOMETHING THAT'S UNFORGIVABLE... DO YOU UNDERSTAND? I CANNOT BEAR THE THOUGHT OF US PITTED AGAINST ONE ANOTHER!

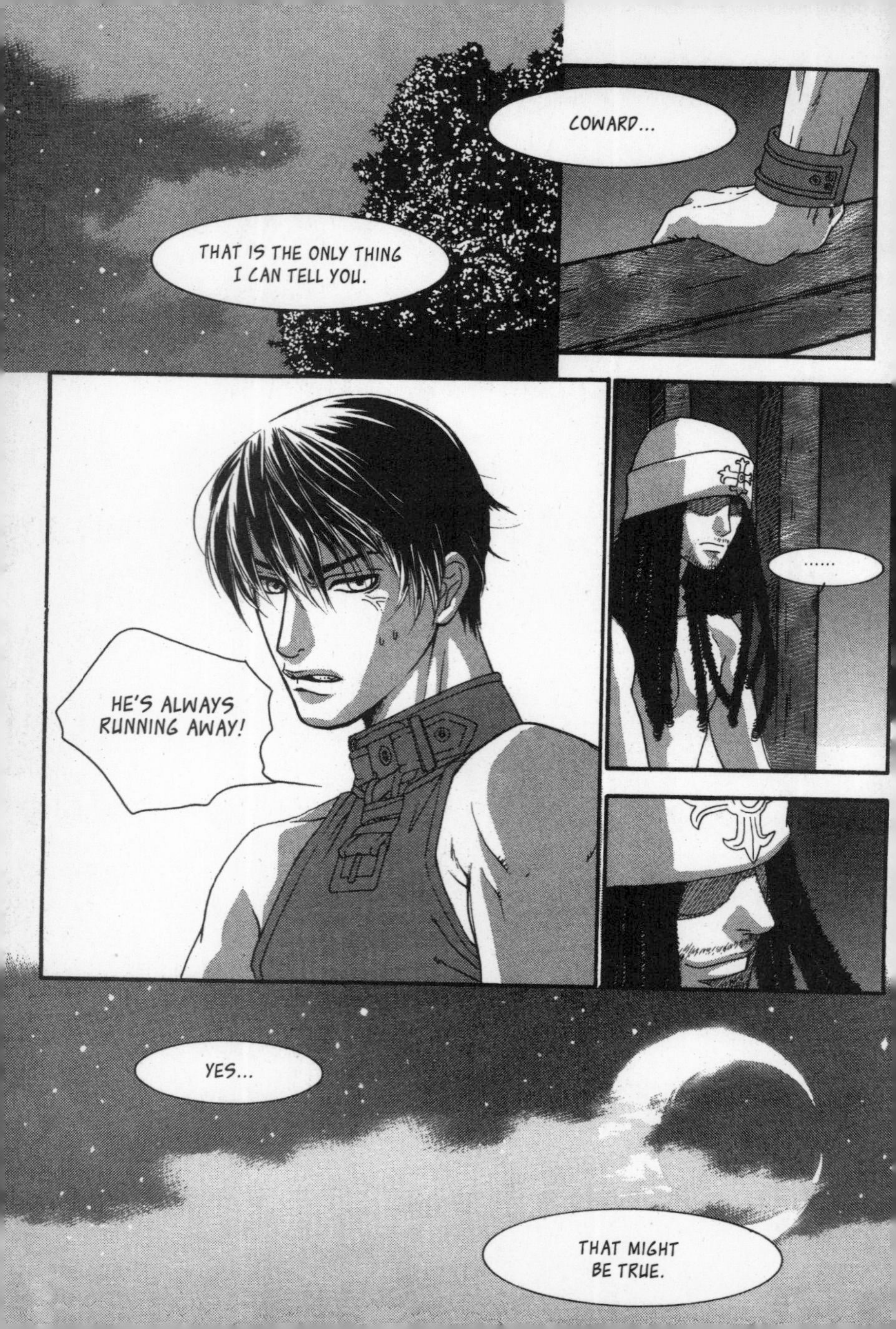
THAT IS THE ONLY THING I CAN TELL YOU.
COWARD...
HE'S ALWAYS RUNNING AWAY!
......
YES...
THAT MIGHT BE TRUE.

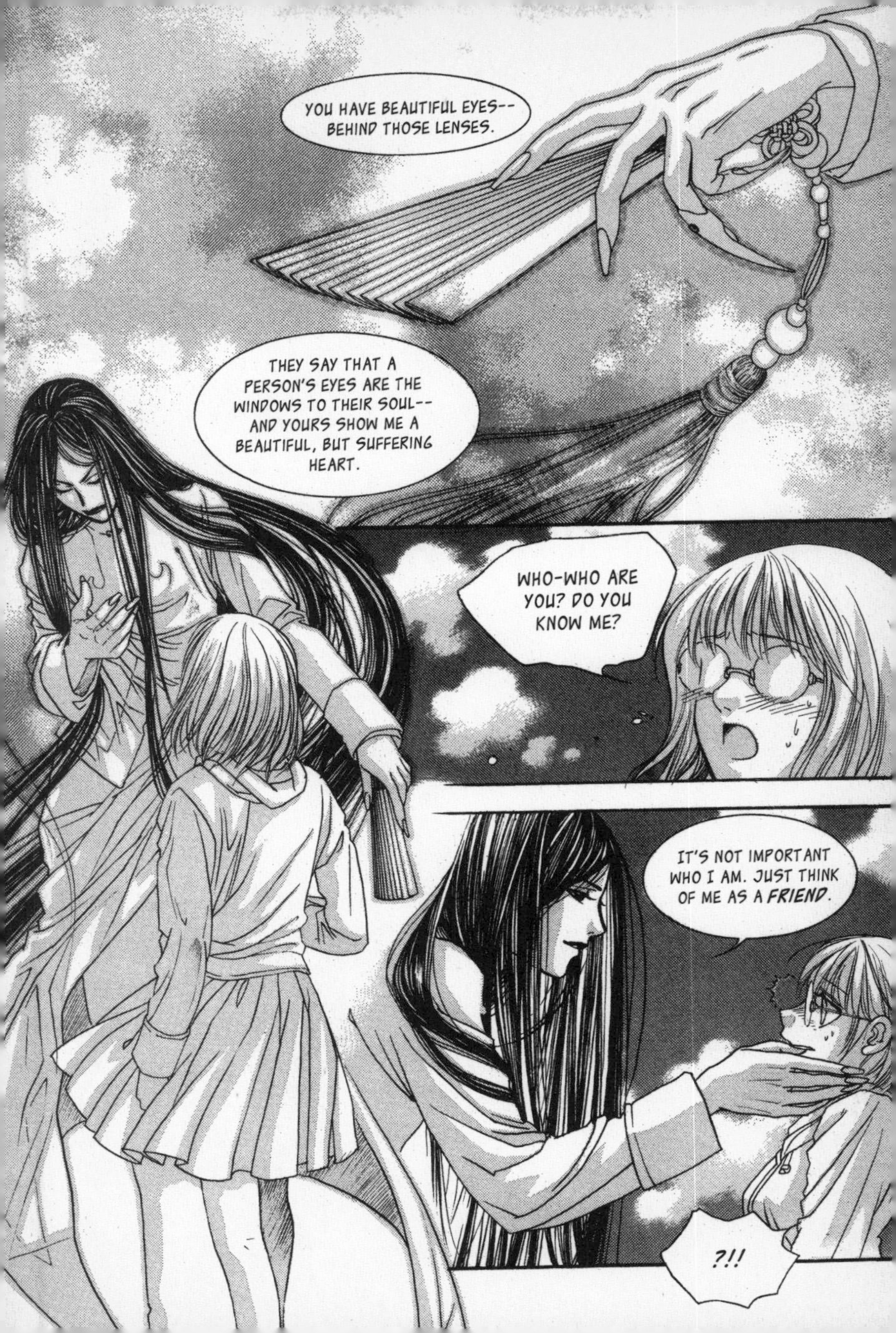
YOU HAVE BEAUTIFUL EYES-- BEHIND THOSE LENSES.
THEY SAY THAT A PERSON'S EYES ARE THE WINDOWS TO THEIR SOUL-- AND YOURS SHOW ME A BEAUTIFUL, BUT SUFFERING HEART.
WHO-WHO ARE YOU? DO YOU KNOW ME?
IT'S NOT IMPORTANT WHO I AM. JUST THINK OF ME AS A *FRIEND*.
?!!

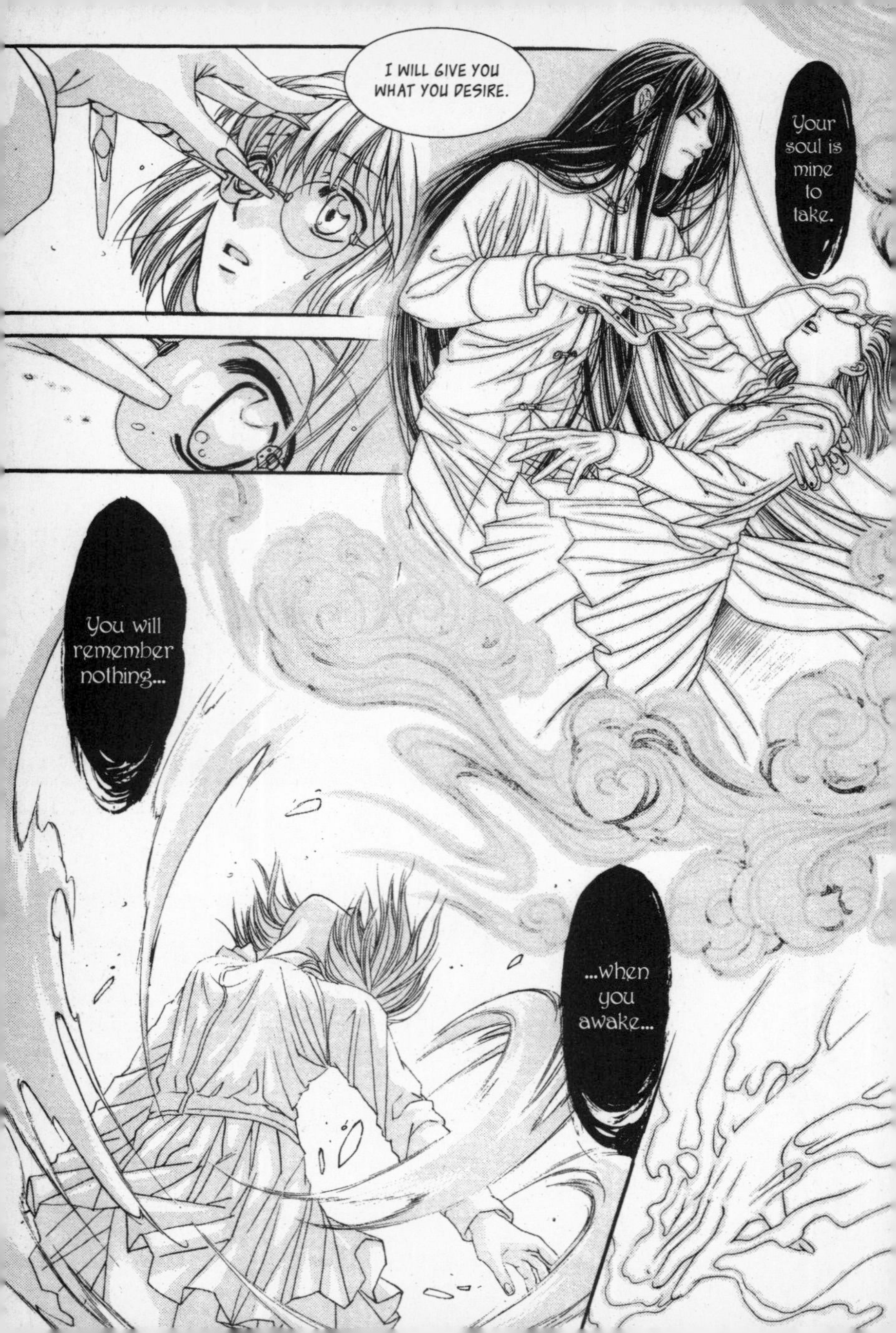
I WILL GIVE YOU WHAT YOU DESIRE.
Your soul is mine to take.
You will remember nothing...
...when you awake...

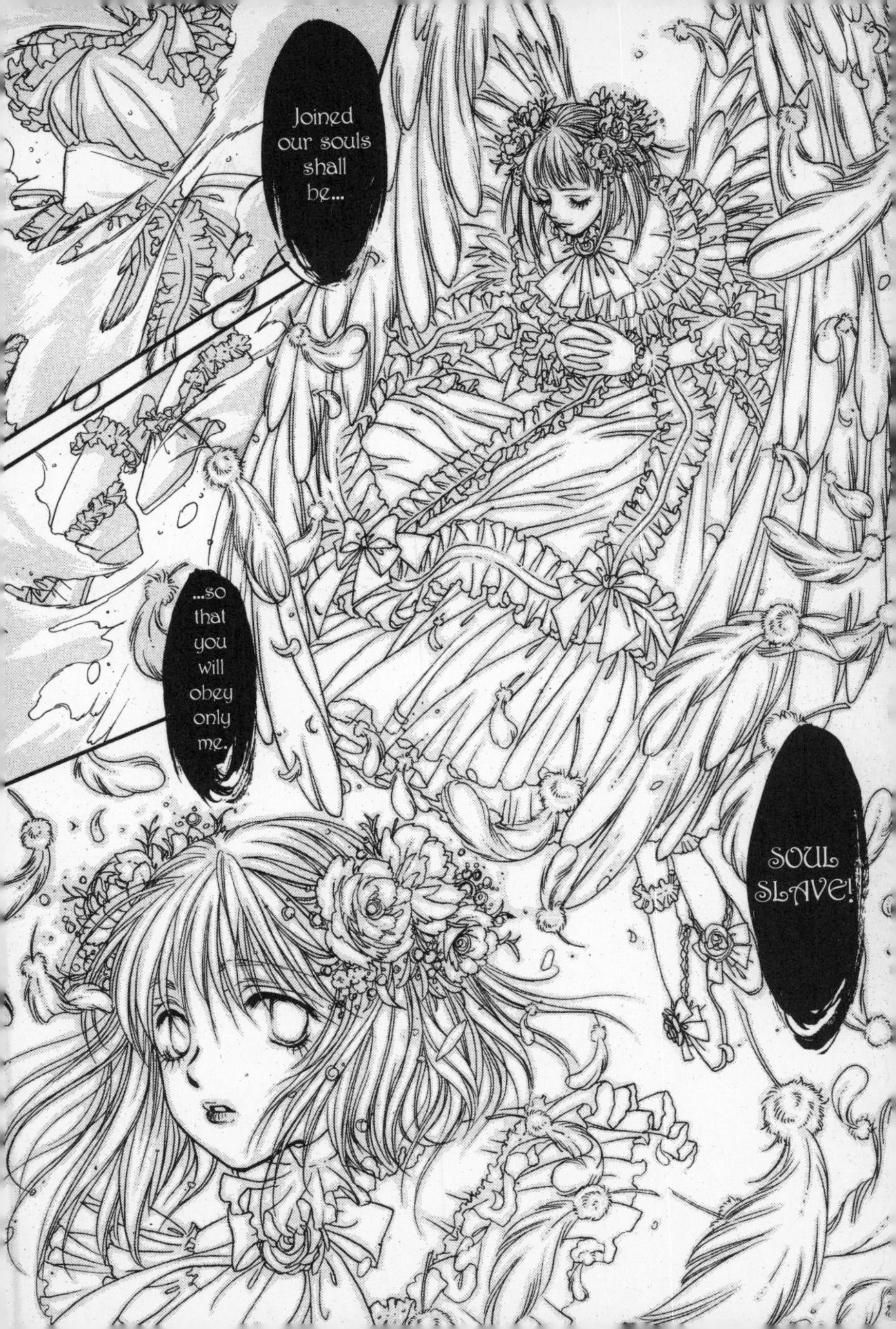
Joined our souls shall be...
...so that you will obey only me.
SOUL SLAVE!

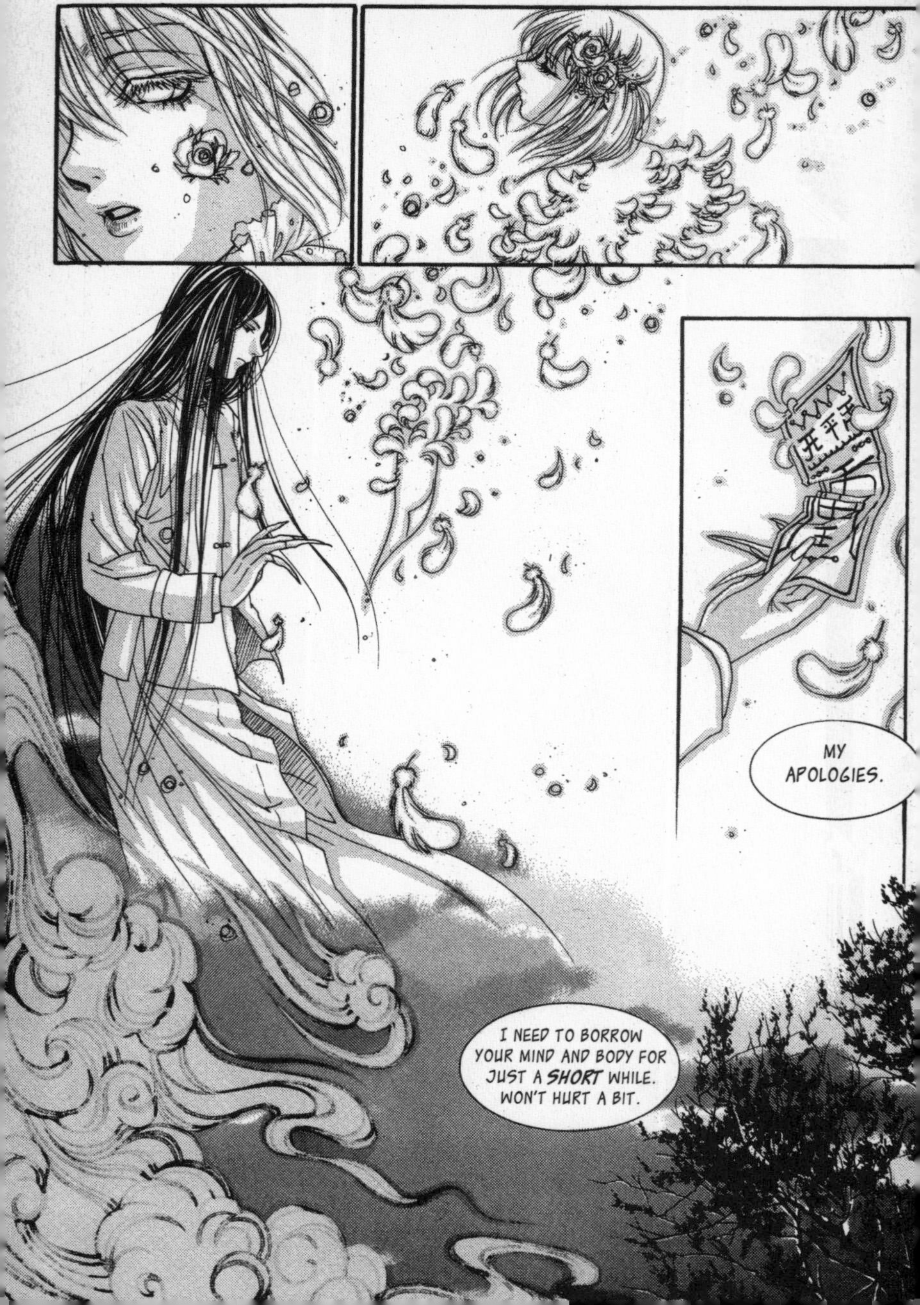
MY APOLOGIES.
I NEED TO BORROW YOUR MIND AND BODY FOR JUST A SHORT WHILE. WON'T HURT A BIT.

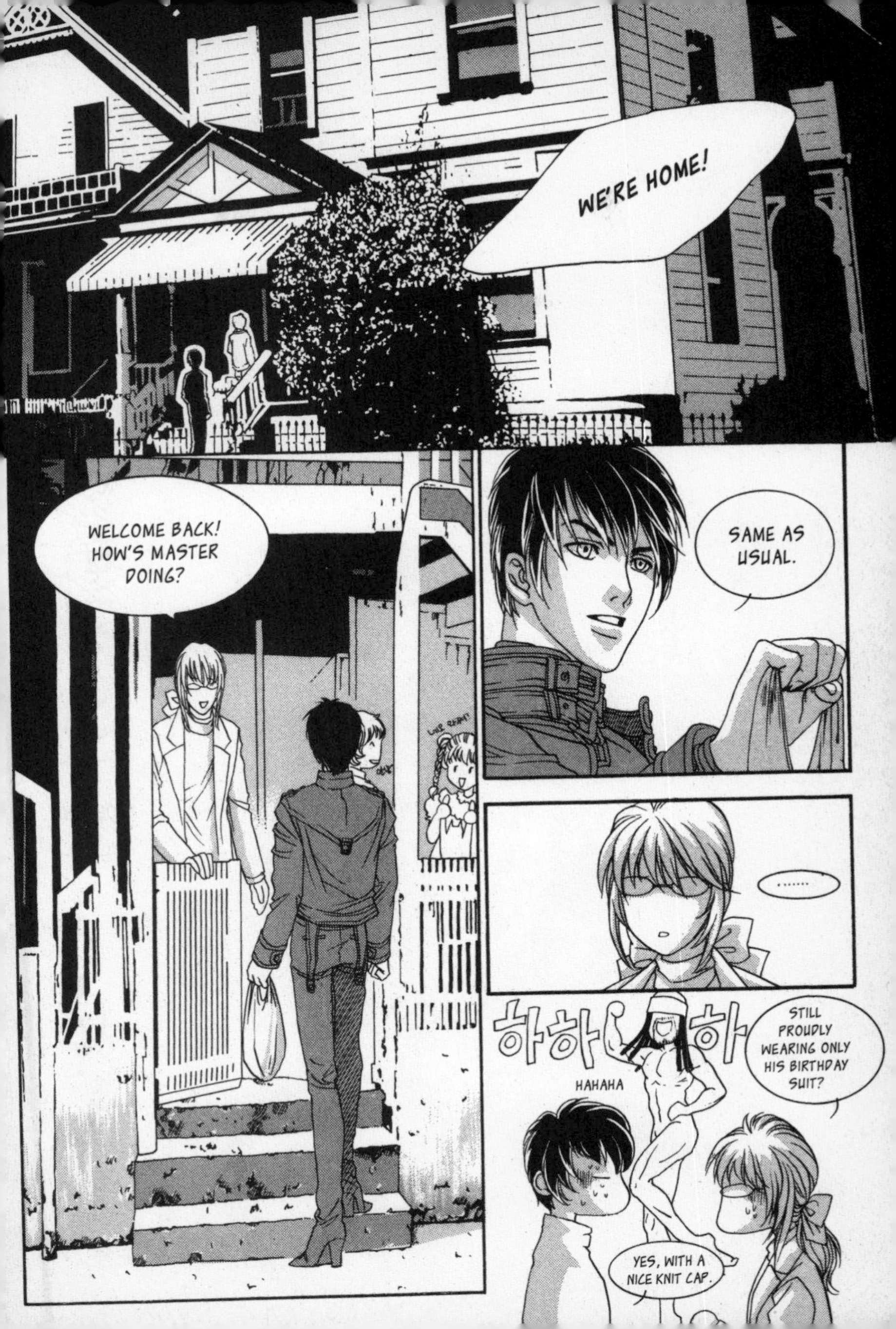
WE'RE HOME!
WELCOME BACK! HOW'S MASTER DOING?
SAME AS USUAL.
......
하하하
STILL PROUDLY WEARING ONLY HIS BIRTHDAY SUIT?
HAHAHA
YES, WITH A NICE KNIT CAP.

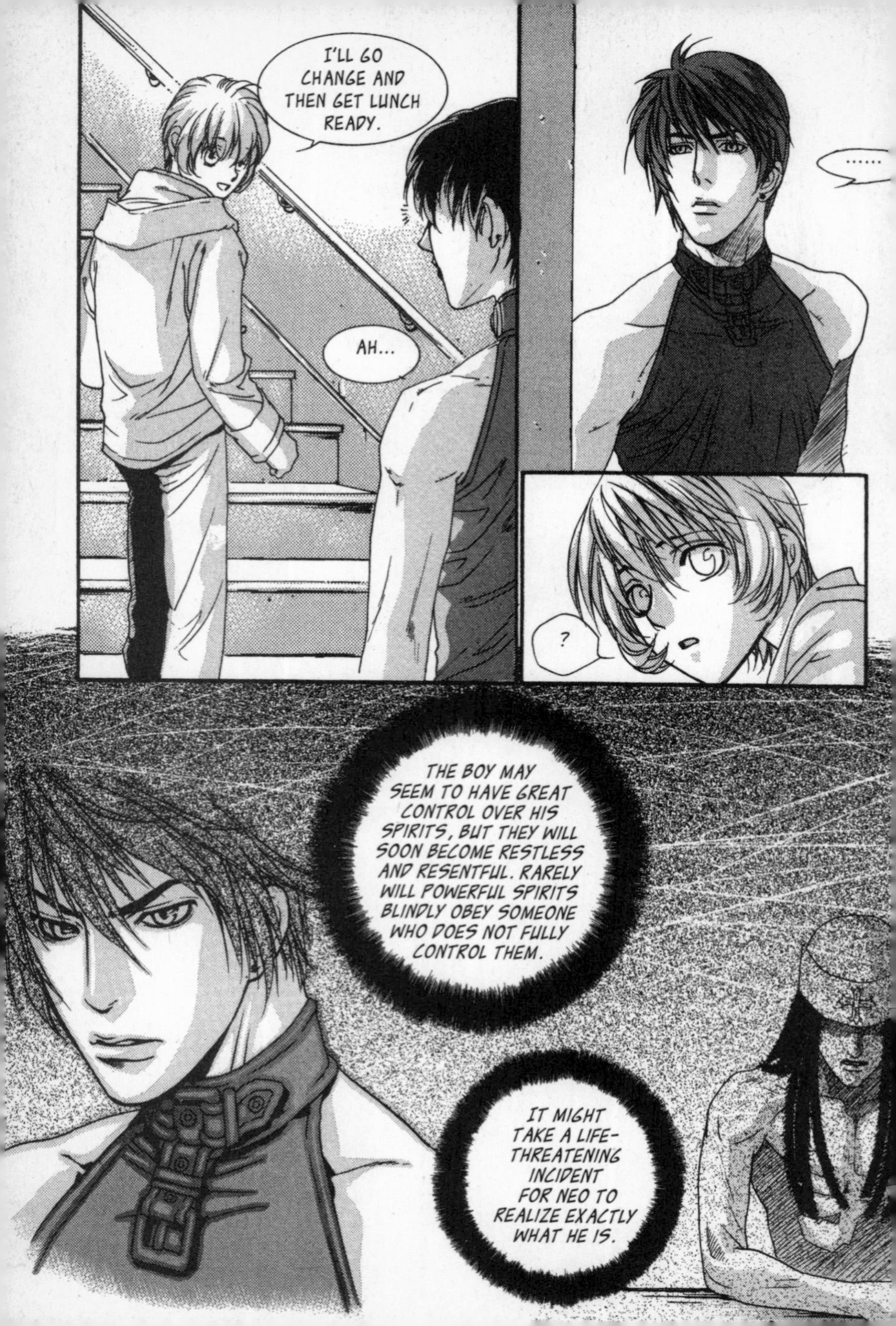
I'LL GO CHANGE AND THEN GET LUNCH READY.
AH...
......
?
THE BOY MAY SEEM TO HAVE GREAT CONTROL OVER HIS SPIRITS, BUT THEY WILL SOON BECOME RESTLESS AND RESENTFUL. RARELY WILL POWERFUL SPIRITS BLINDLY OBEY SOMEONE WHO DOES NOT FULLY CONTROL THEM.
IT MIGHT TAKE A LIFE-THREATENING INCIDENT FOR NEO TO REALIZE EXACTLY WHAT HE IS.

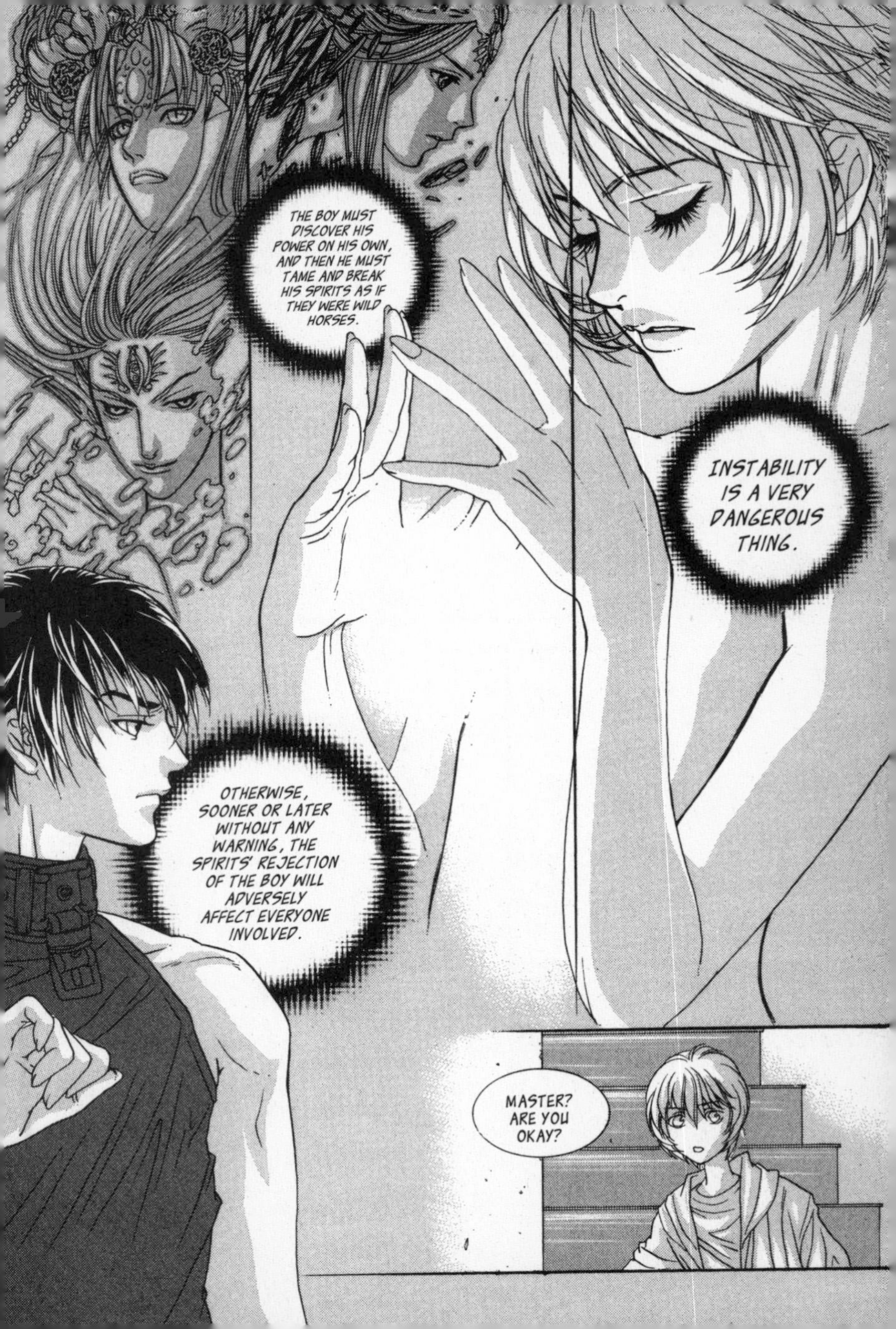
THE BOY MUST DISCOVER HIS POWER ON HIS OWN, AND THEN HE MUST TAME AND BREAK HIS SPIRITS AS IF THEY WERE WILD HORSES.
INSTABILITY IS A VERY DANGEROUS THING.
OTHERWISE, SOONER OR LATER WITHOUT ANY WARNING, THE SPIRITS' REJECTION OF THE BOY WILL ADVERSELY AFFECT EVERYONE INVOLVED.
MASTER? ARE YOU OKAY?

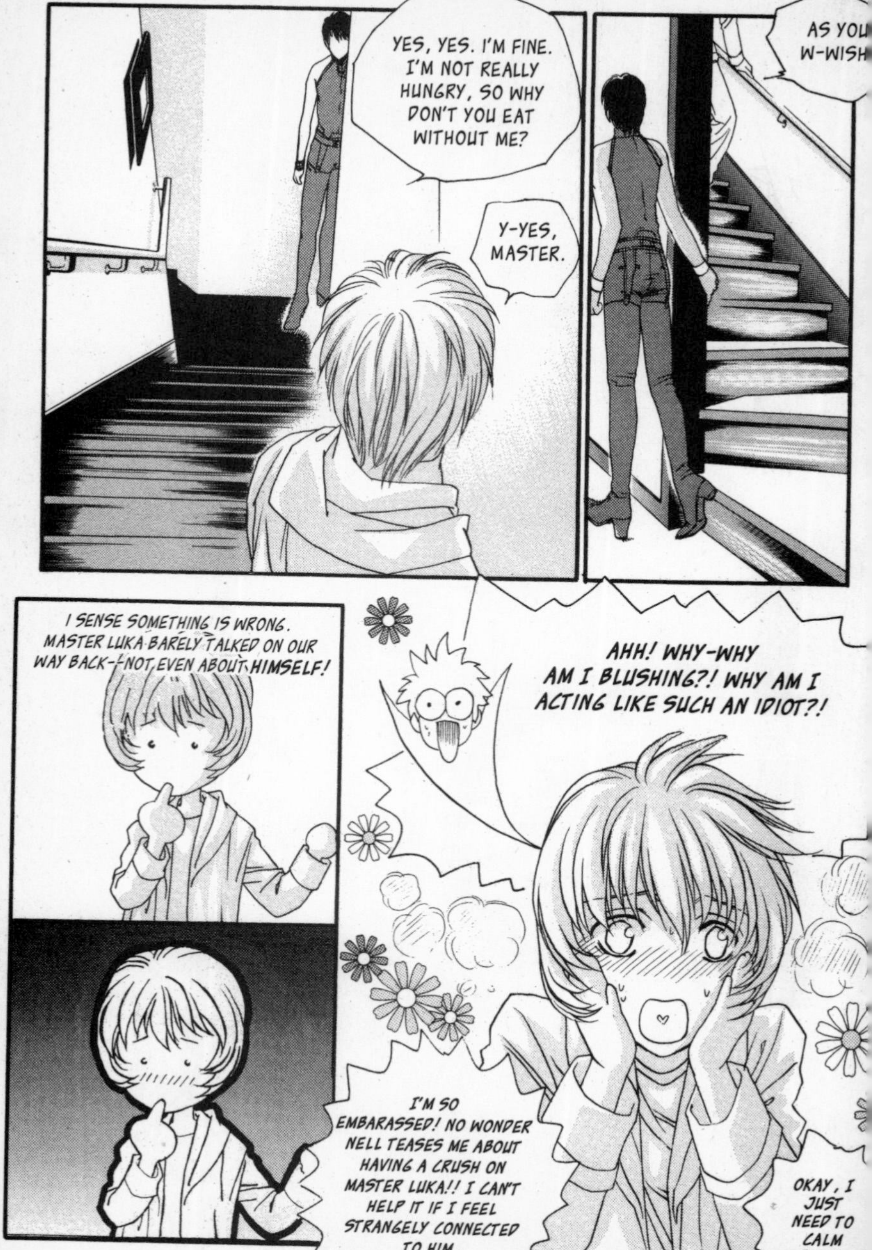
YES, YES. I'M FINE. I'M NOT REALLY HUNGRY, SO WHY DON'T YOU EAT WITHOUT ME?
Y-YES, MASTER.
AS YOU W-WISH
I SENSE SOMETHING IS WRONG. MASTER LUKA BARELY TALKED ON OUR WAY BACK--NOT EVEN ABOUT HIMSELF!
AHH! WHY-WHY AM I BLUSHING?! WHY AM I ACTING LIKE SUCH AN IDIOT?!
I'M SO EMBARASSED! NO WONDER NELL TEASES ME ABOUT HAVING A CRUSH ON MASTER LUKA!! I CAN'T HELP IT IF I FEEL STRANGELY CONNECTED TO HIM.
OKAY, I JUST NEED TO CALM DOWN.

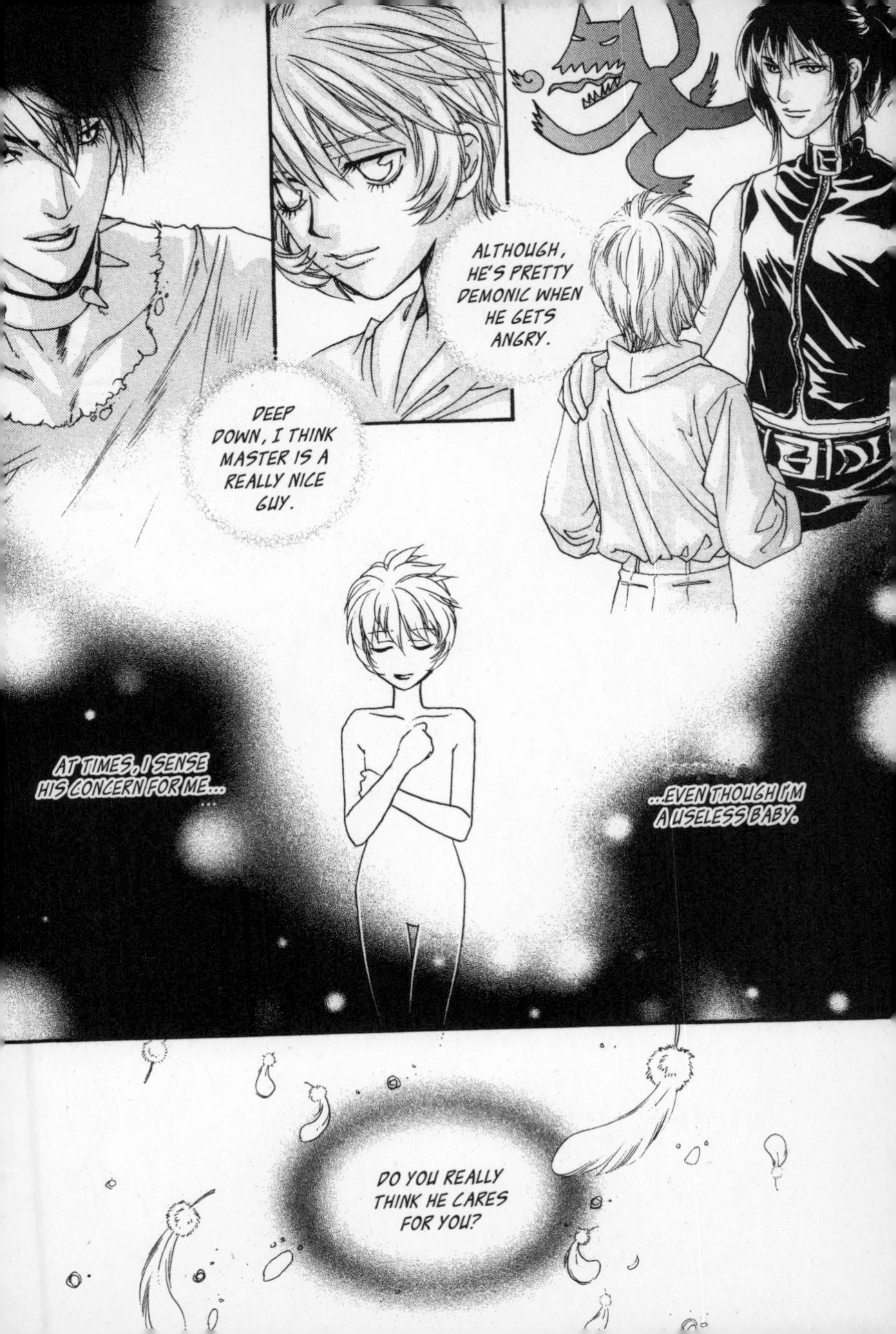
DEEP DOWN, I THINK MASTER IS A REALLY NICE GUY.
ALTHOUGH, HE'S PRETTY DEMONIC WHEN HE GETS ANGRY.
AT TIMES, I SENSE HIS CONCERN FOR ME...
...EVEN THOUGH I'M A USELESS BABY.
DO YOU REALLY THINK HE CARES FOR YOU?

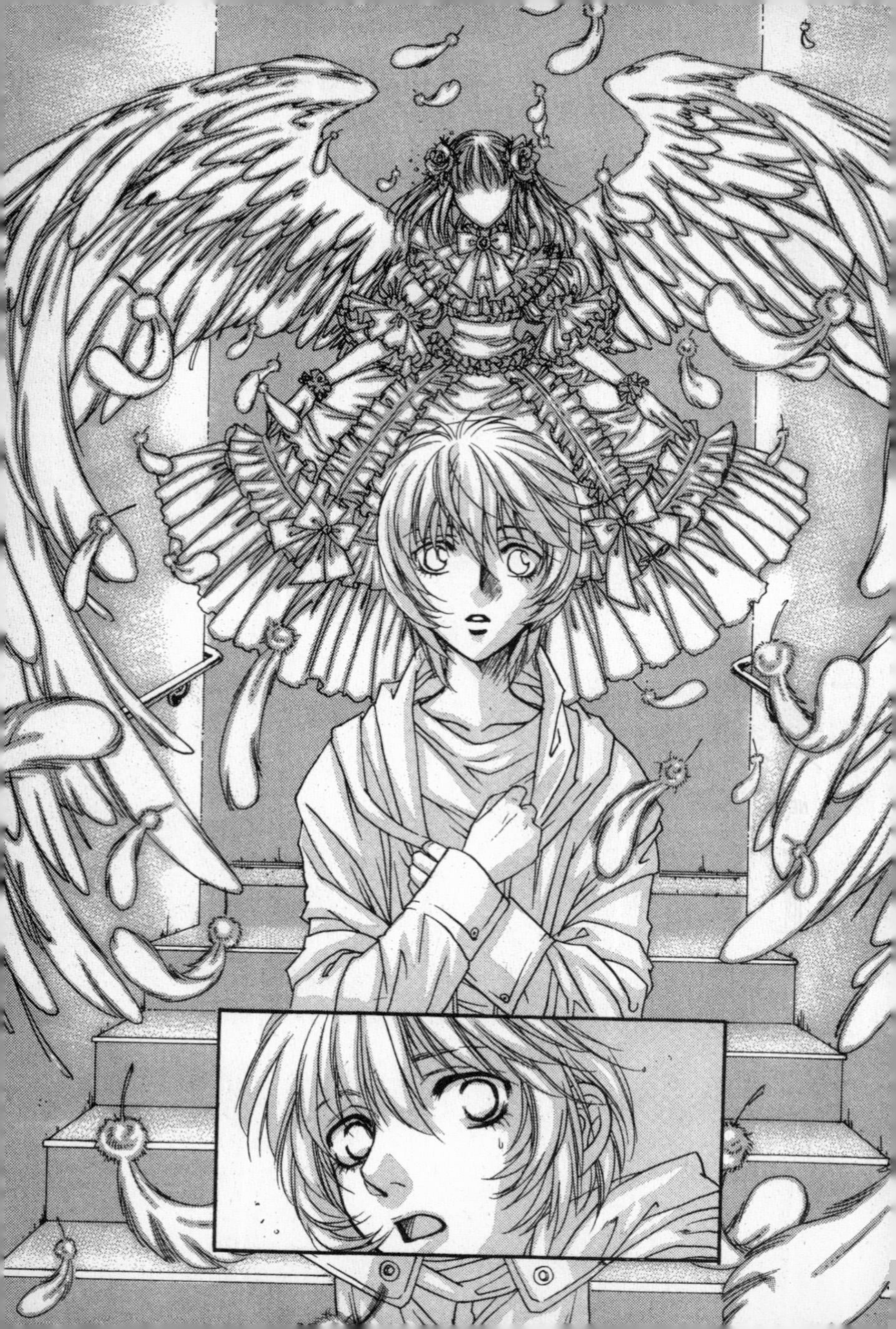

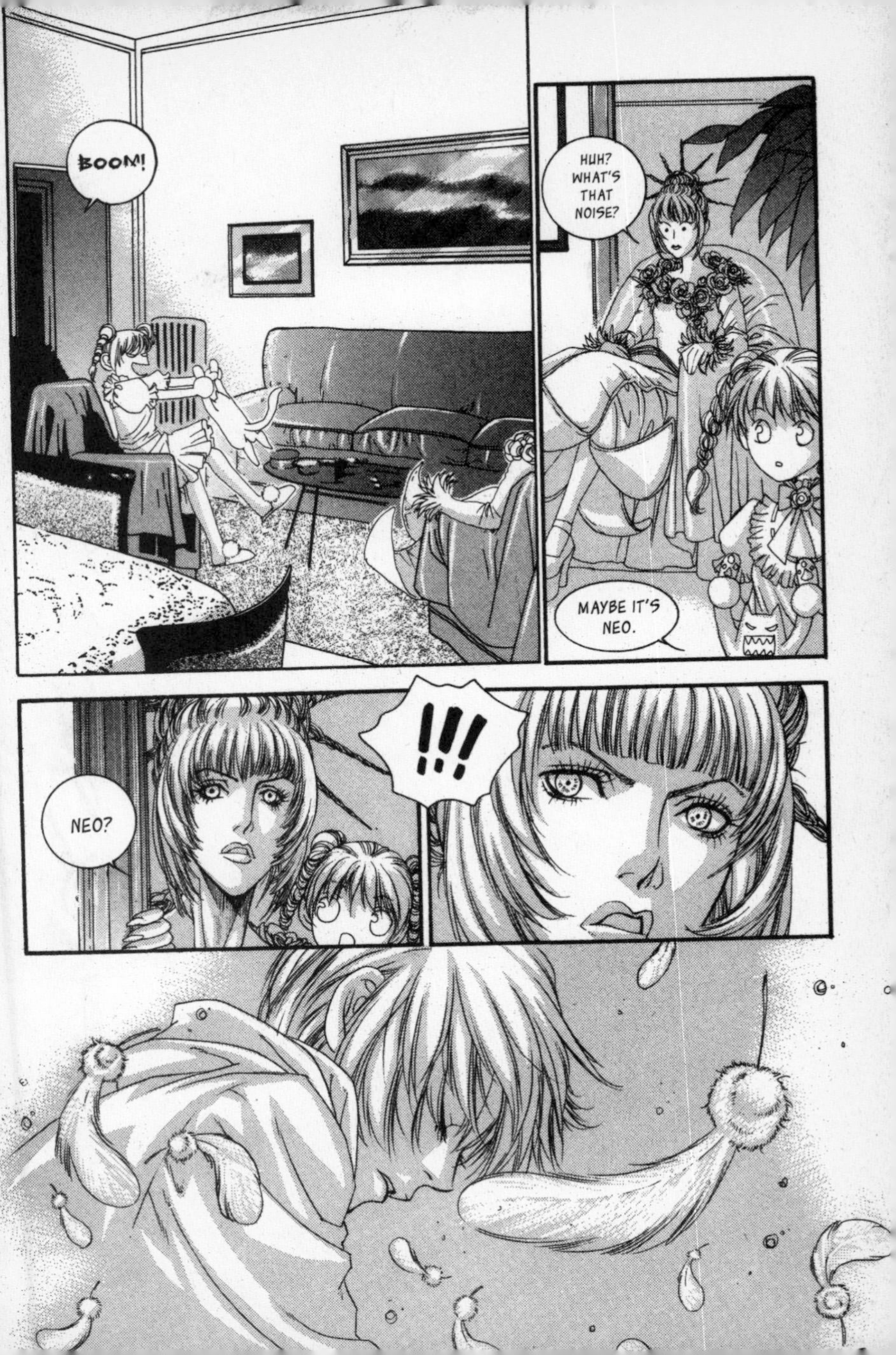
BOOM!
HUH? WHAT'S THAT NOISE?
MAYBE IT'S NEO.
NEO?
!!!

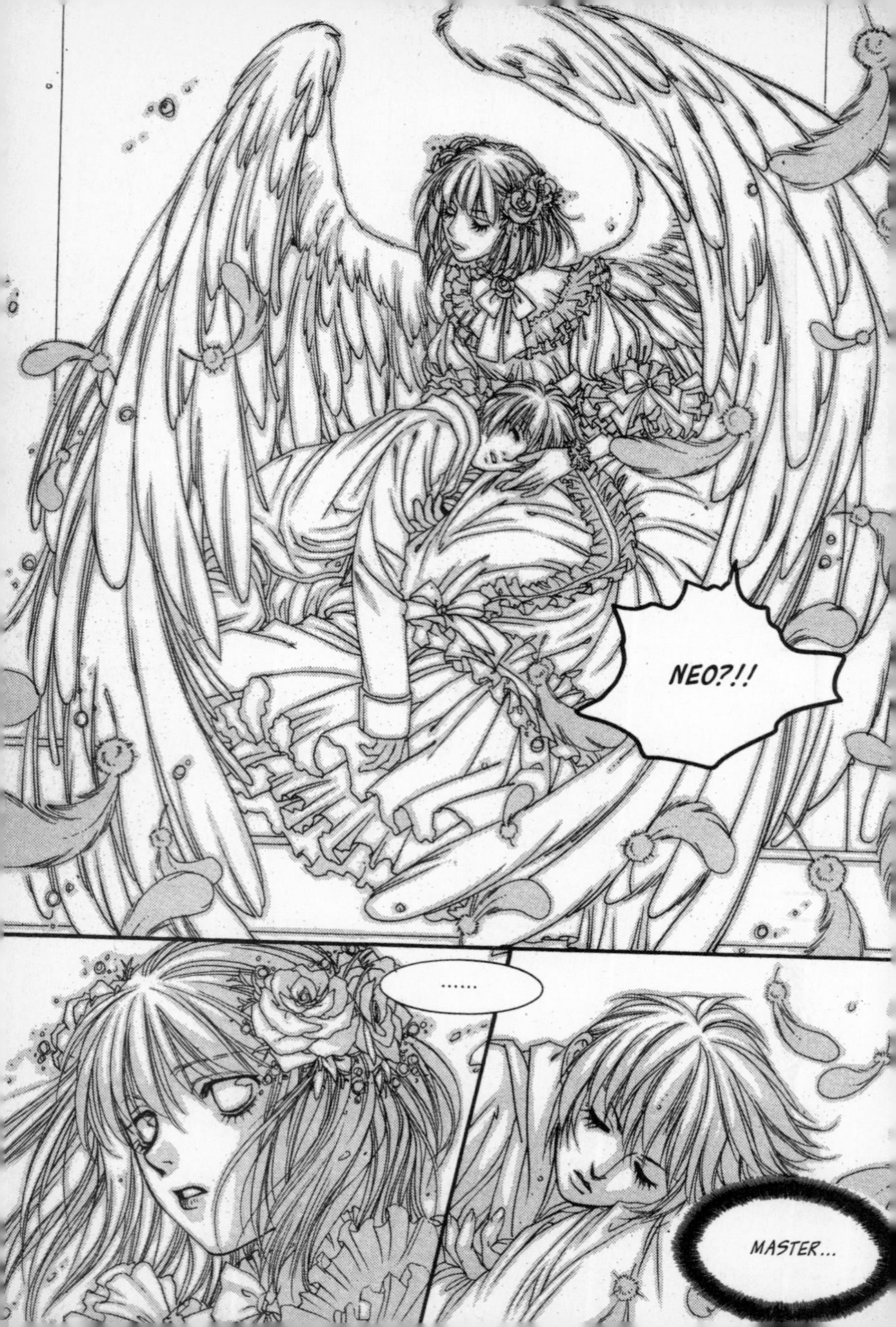
NEO?!!
......
MASTER...

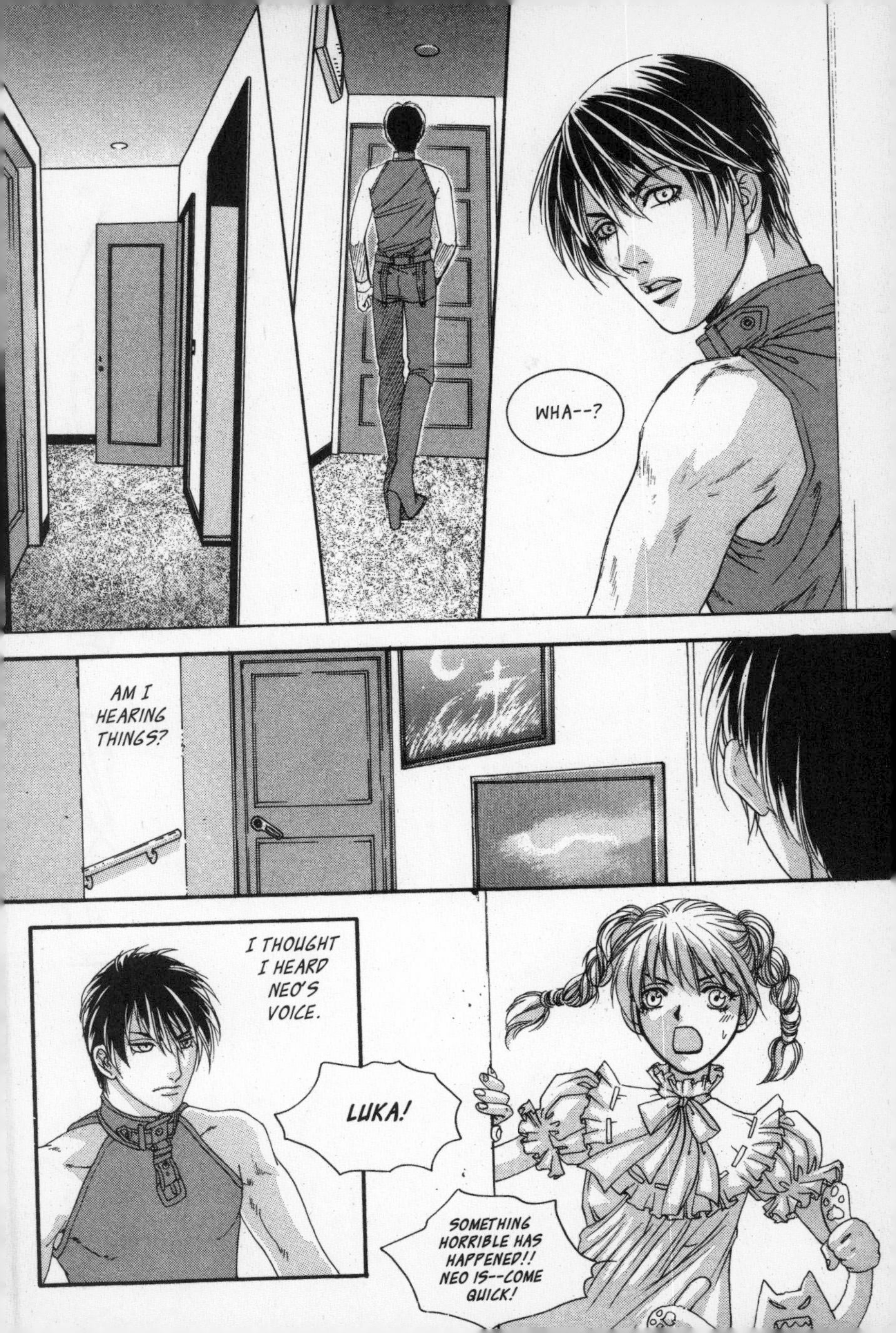
WHA--?
AM I HEARING THINGS?
I THOUGHT I HEARD NEO'S VOICE.
LUKA!
SOMETHING HORRIBLE HAS HAPPENED!! NEO IS--COME QUICK!

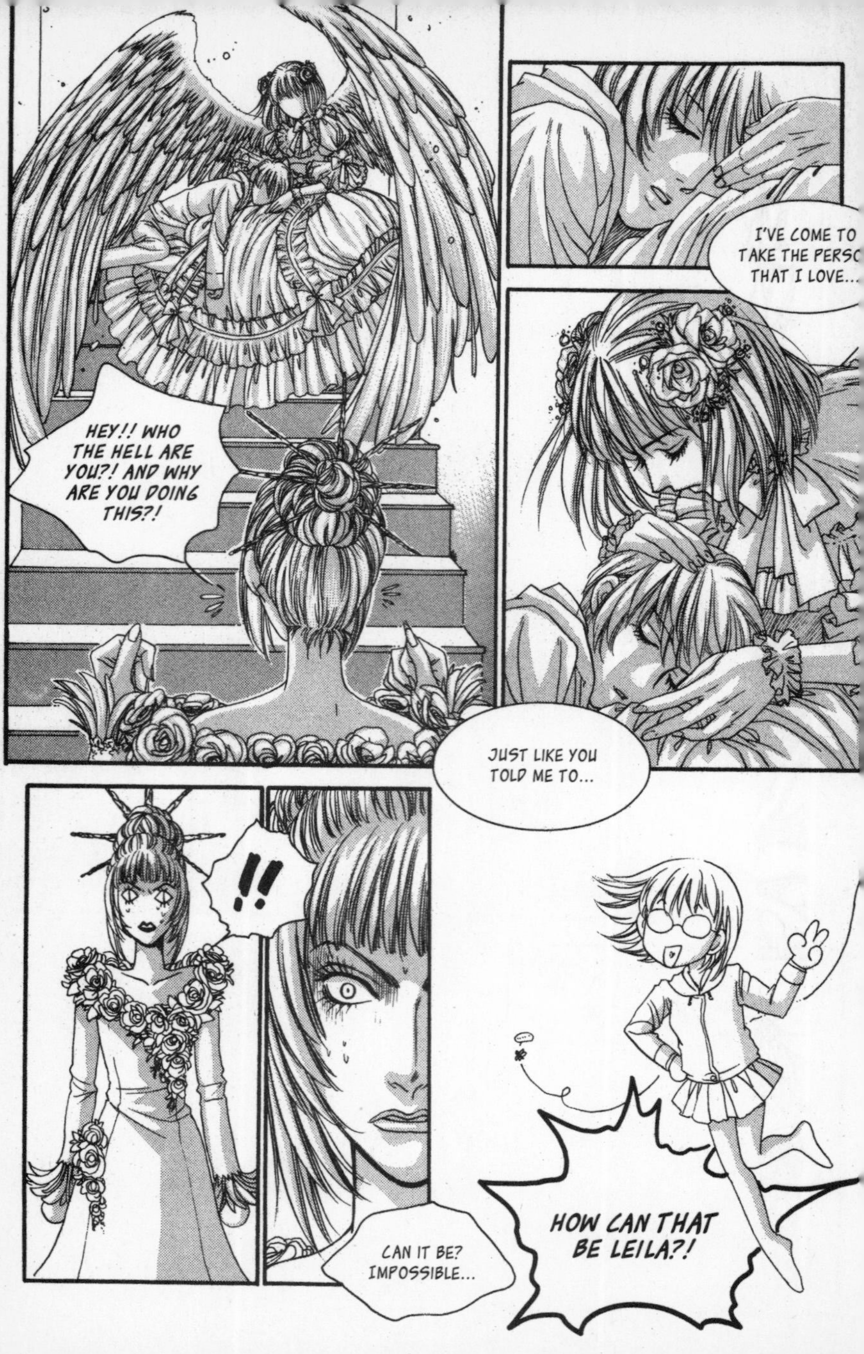
HEY!! WHO THE HELL ARE YOU?! AND WHY ARE YOU DOING THIS?!
I'VE COME TO TAKE THE PERSO THAT I LOVE...
JUST LIKE YOU TOLD ME TO...
!!
CAN IT BE? IMPOSSIBLE...
HOW CAN THAT BE LEILA?!

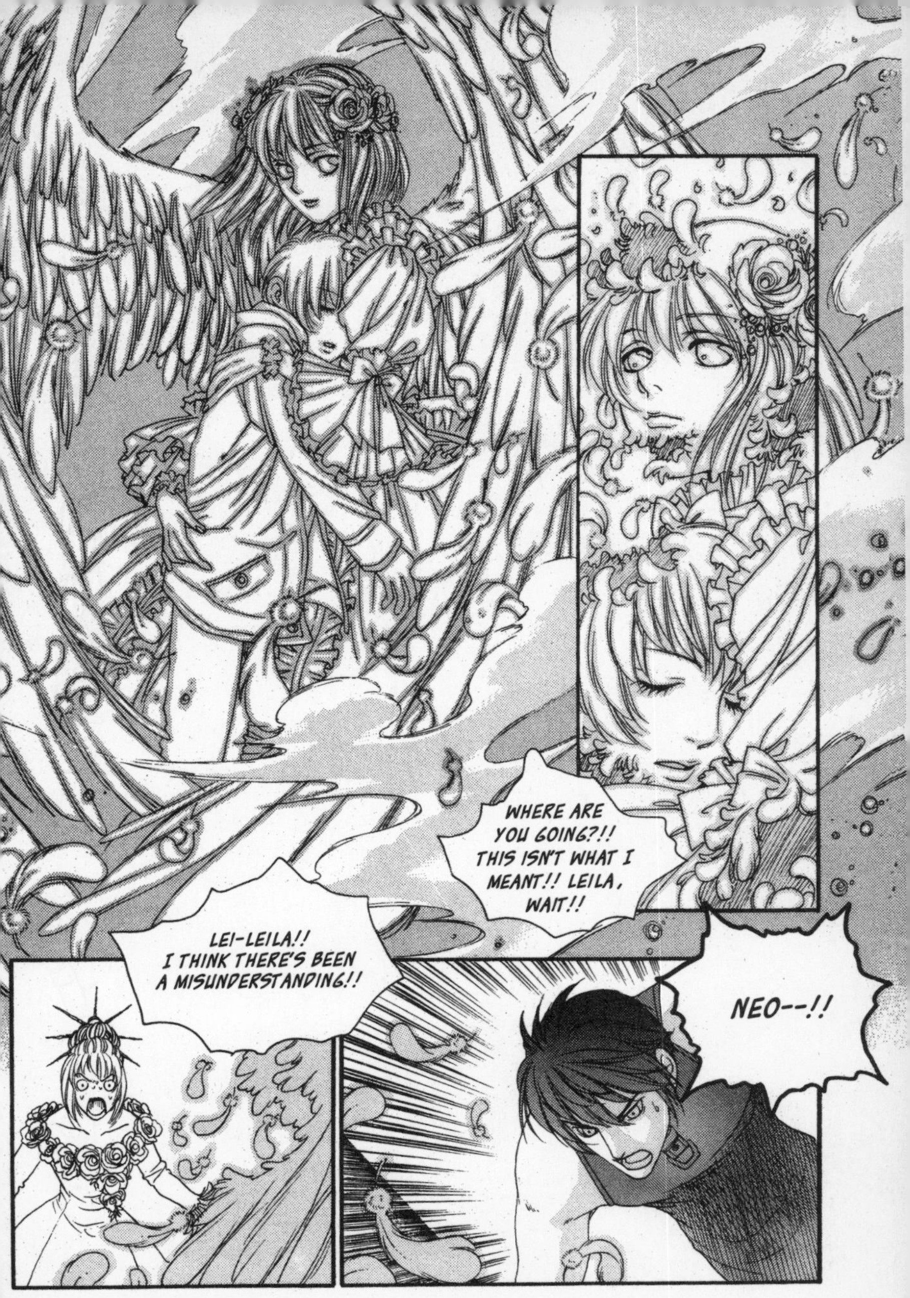
WHERE ARE YOU GOING?!! THIS ISN'T WHAT I MEANT!! LEILA, WAIT!!
LEI-LEILA!! I THINK THERE'S BEEN A MISUNDERSTANDING!!
NEO--!!

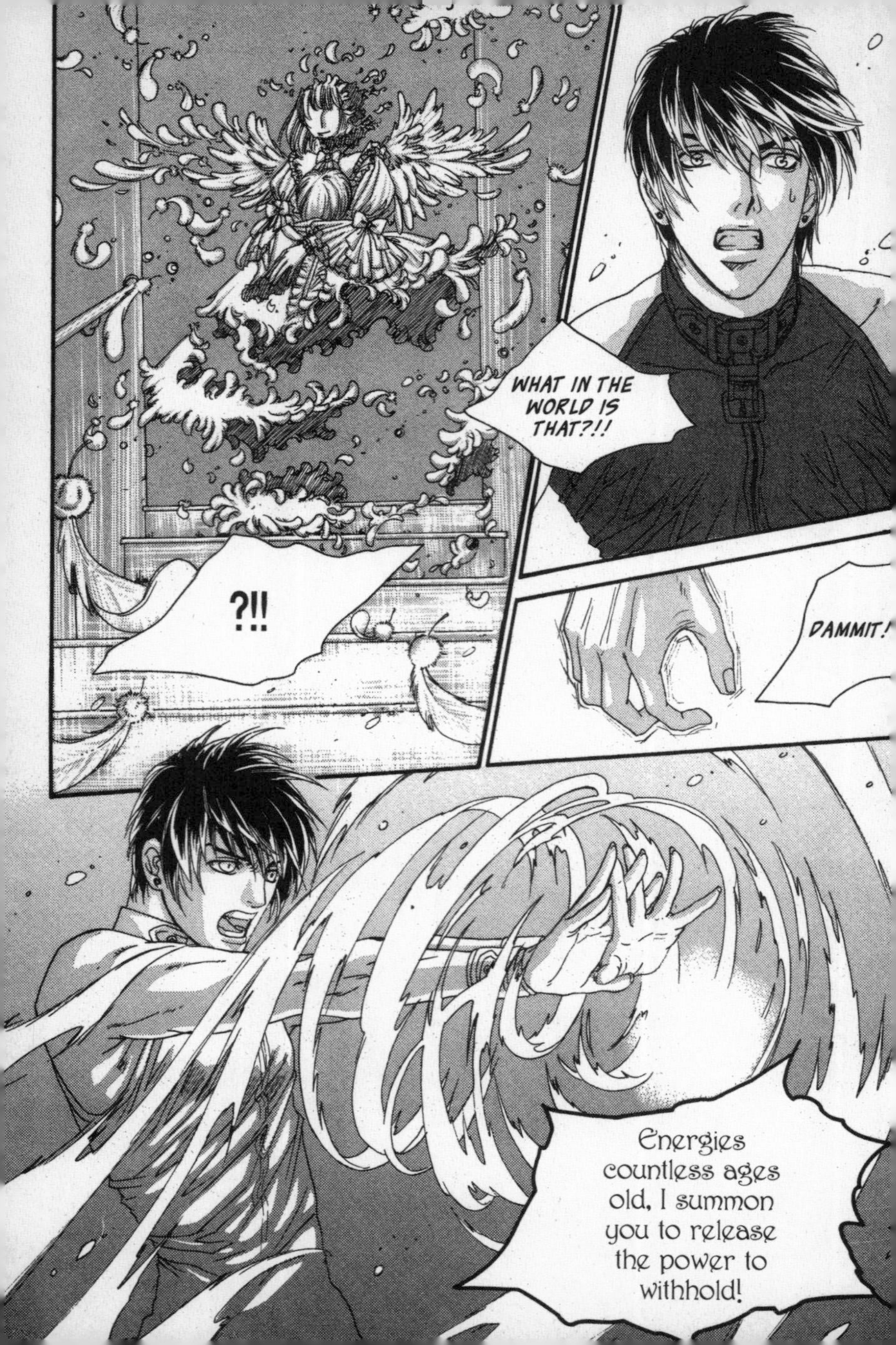
WHAT IN THE WORLD IS THAT?!!
?!!
DAMMIT!
Energies countless ages old, I summon you to release the power to withhold!

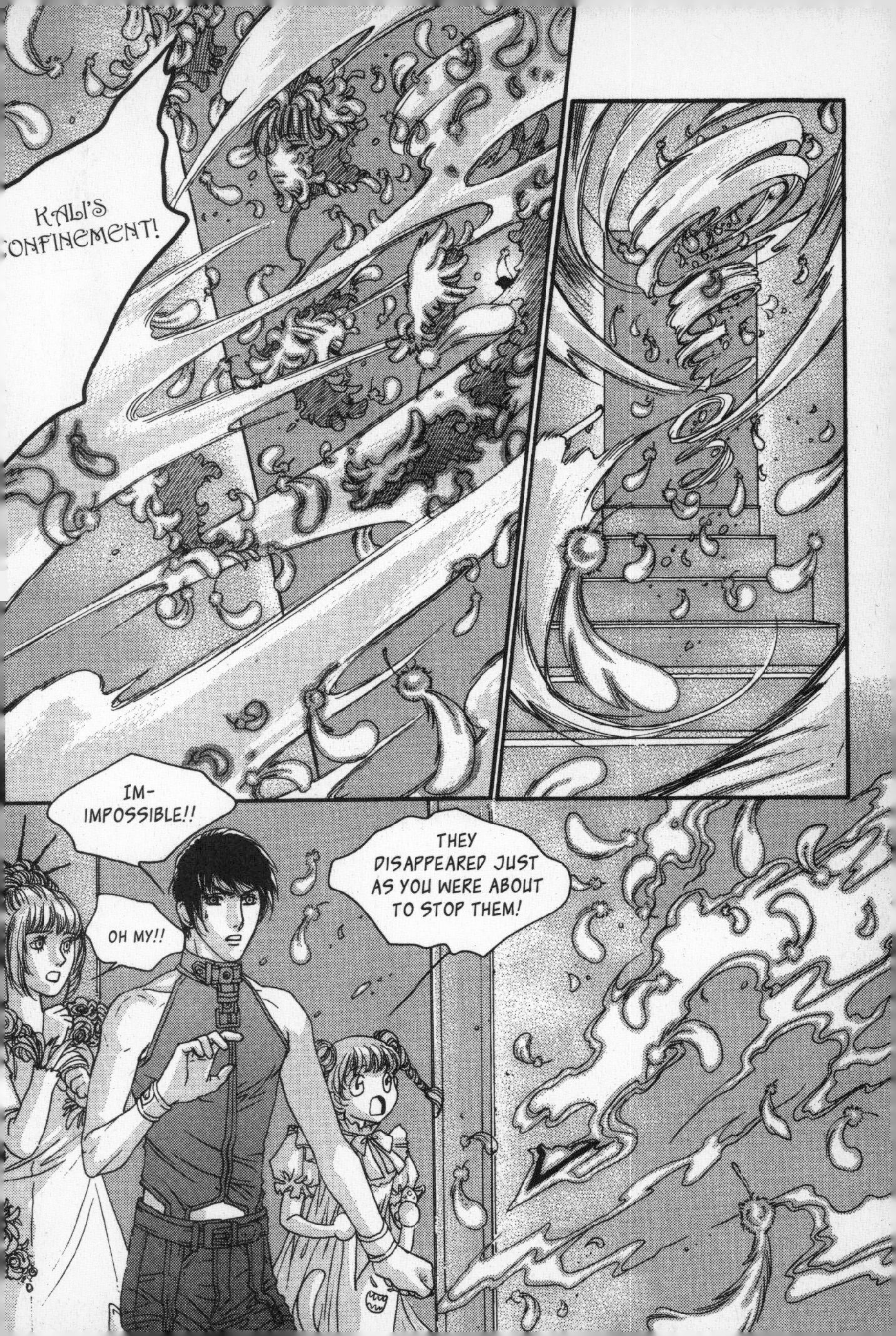
KALI'S CONFINEMENT!
IM- IMPOSSIBLE!!
THEY DISAPPEARED JUST AS YOU WERE ABOUT TO STOP THEM!
OH MY!!

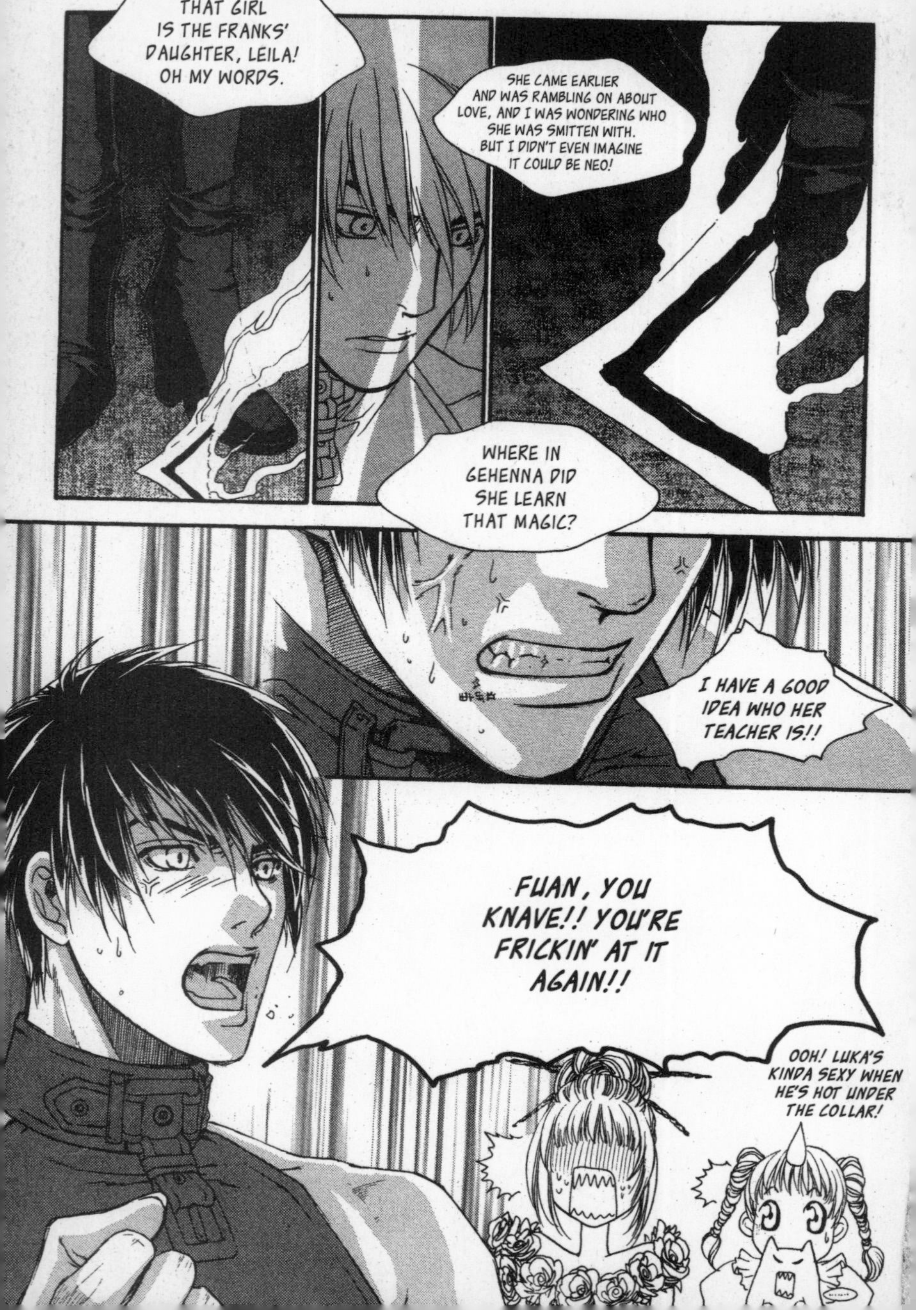
THAT GIRL IS THE FRANKS' DAUGHTER, LEILA! OH MY WORDS.
SHE CAME EARLIER AND WAS RAMBLING ON ABOUT LOVE, AND I WAS WONDERING WHO SHE WAS SMITTEN WITH. BUT I DIDN'T EVEN IMAGINE IT COULD BE NEO!
WHERE IN GEHENNA DID SHE LEARN THAT MAGIC?
I HAVE A GOOD IDEA WHO HER TEACHER IS!!
FUAN, YOU KNAVE!! YOU'RE FRICKIN' AT IT AGAIN!!
OOH! LUKA'S KINDA SEXY WHEN HE'S HOT UNDER THE COLLAR!

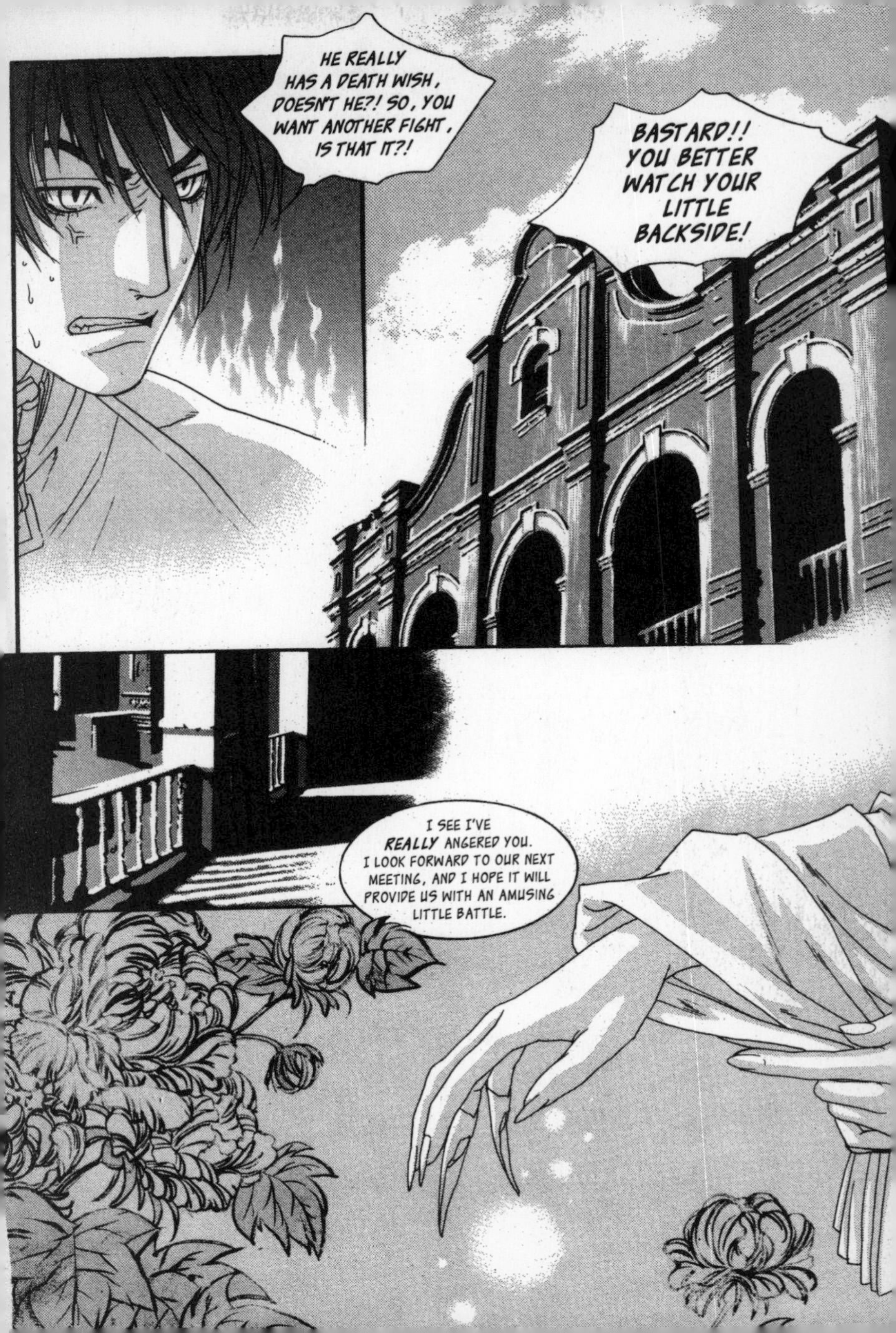
HE REALLY HAS A DEATH WISH, DOESN'T HE?! SO, YOU WANT ANOTHER FIGHT, IS THAT IT?!
BASTARD!! YOU BETTER WATCH YOUR LITTLE BACKSIDE!
I SEE I'VE REALLY ANGERED YOU. I LOOK FORWARD TO OUR NEXT MEETING, AND I HOPE IT WILL PROVIDE US WITH AN AMUSING LITTLE BATTLE.

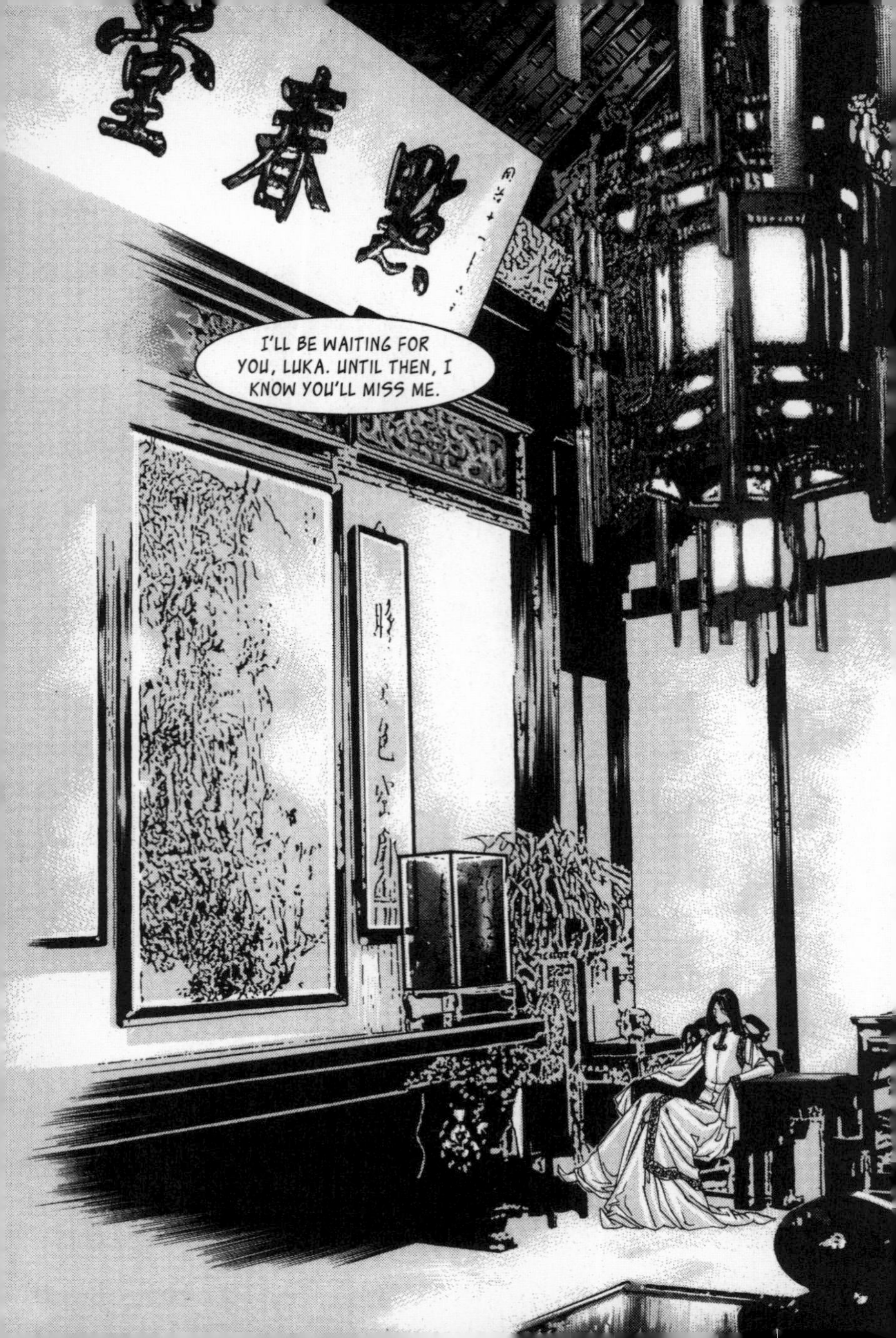
I'LL BE WAITING FOR YOU, LUKA. UNTIL THEN, I KNOW YOU'LL MISS ME.

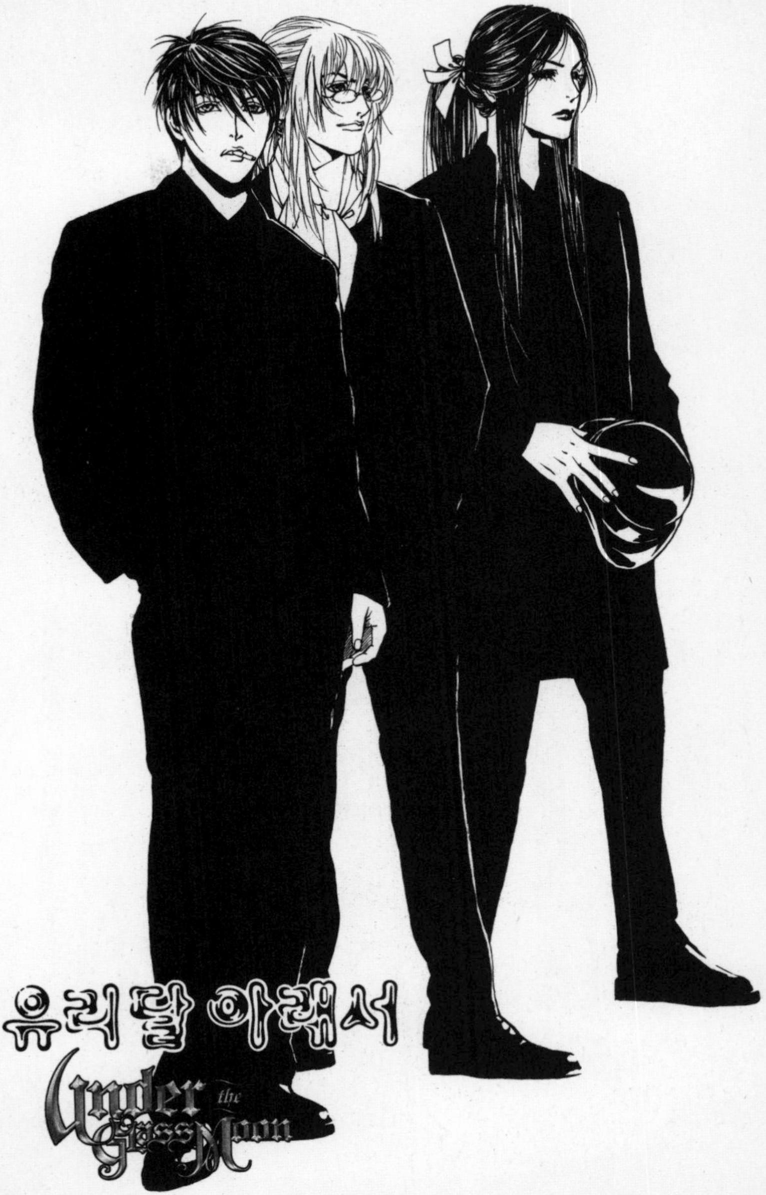
유리달 아래서
Under the Glass Moon

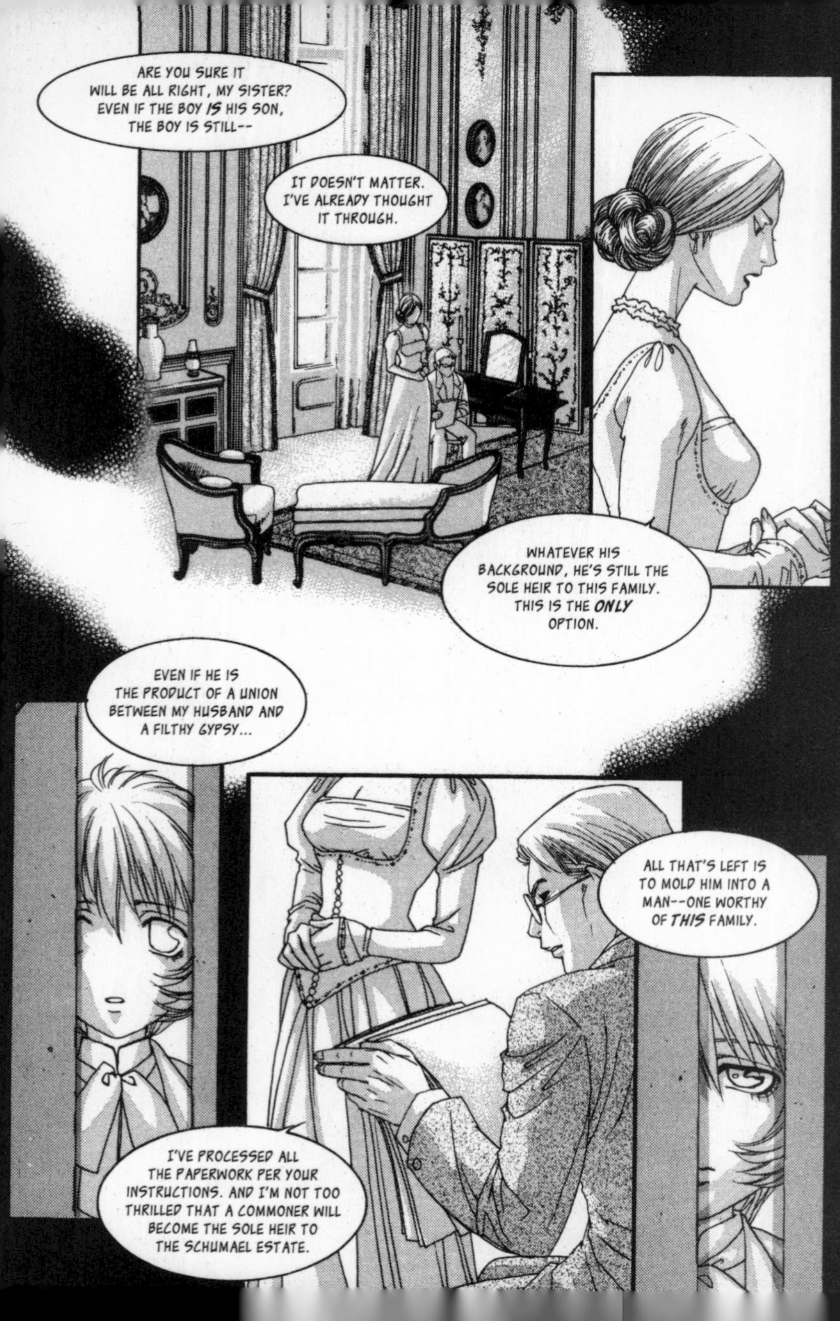
ARE YOU SURE IT WILL BE ALL RIGHT, MY SISTER? EVEN IF THE BOY *IS* HIS SON, THE BOY IS STILL--
IT DOESN'T MATTER. I'VE ALREADY THOUGHT IT THROUGH.
WHATEVER HIS BACKGROUND, HE'S STILL THE SOLE HEIR TO THIS FAMILY. THIS IS THE *ONLY* OPTION.
EVEN IF HE IS THE PRODUCT OF A UNION BETWEEN MY HUSBAND AND A FILTHY GYPSY...
I'VE PROCESSED ALL THE PAPERWORK PER YOUR INSTRUCTIONS. AND I'M NOT TOO THRILLED THAT A COMMONER WILL BECOME THE SOLE HEIR TO THE SCHUMAEL ESTATE.
ALL THAT'S LEFT IS TO MOLD HIM INTO A MAN--ONE WORTHY OF *THIS* FAMILY.

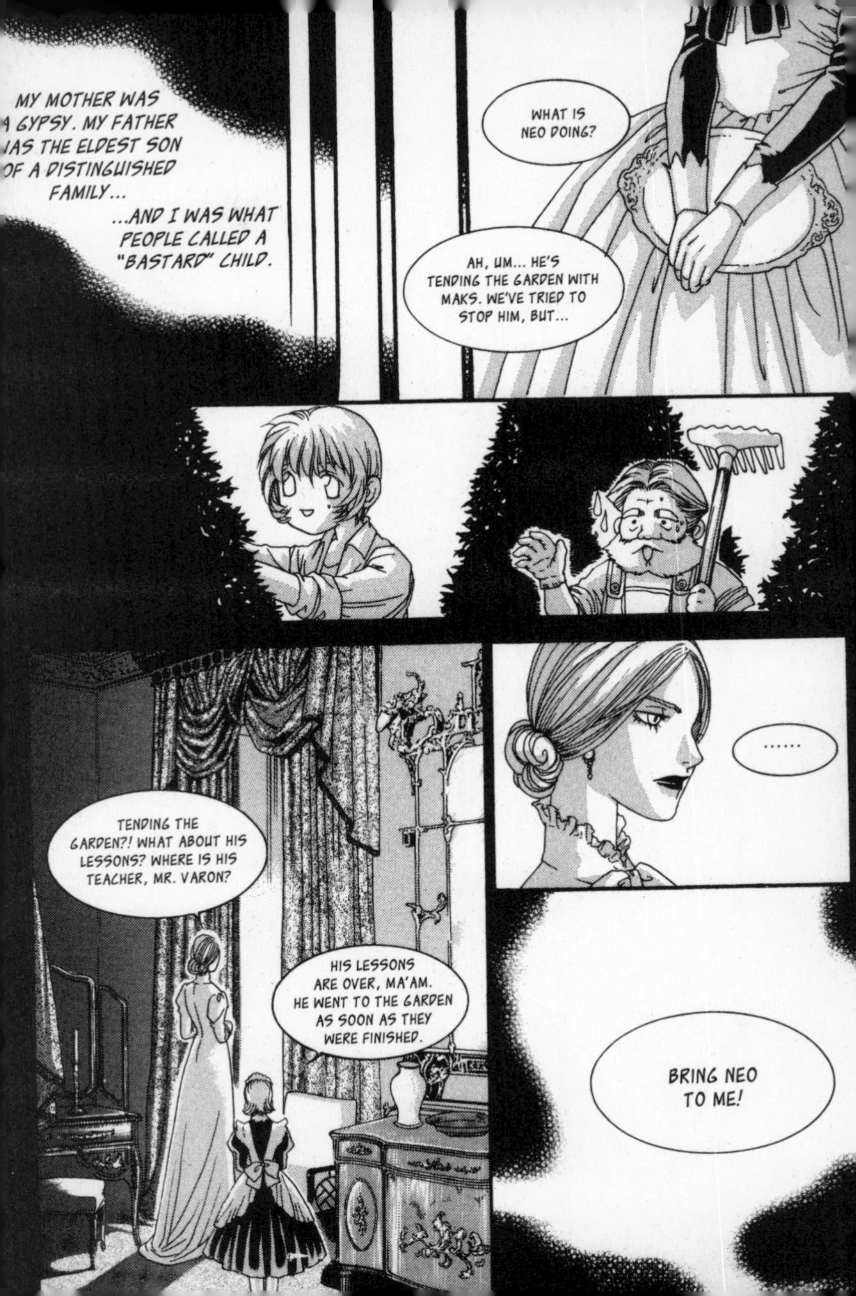
MY MOTHER WAS A GYPSY. MY FATHER WAS THE ELDEST SON OF A DISTINGUISHED FAMILY...
...AND I WAS WHAT PEOPLE CALLED A "BASTARD" CHILD.
WHAT IS NEO DOING?
AH, UM... HE'S TENDING THE GARDEN WITH MAKS. WE'VE TRIED TO STOP HIM, BUT...
TENDING THE GARDEN?! WHAT ABOUT HIS LESSONS? WHERE IS HIS TEACHER, MR. VARON?
HIS LESSONS ARE OVER, MA'AM. HE WENT TO THE GARDEN AS SOON AS THEY WERE FINISHED.
......
BRING NEO TO ME!

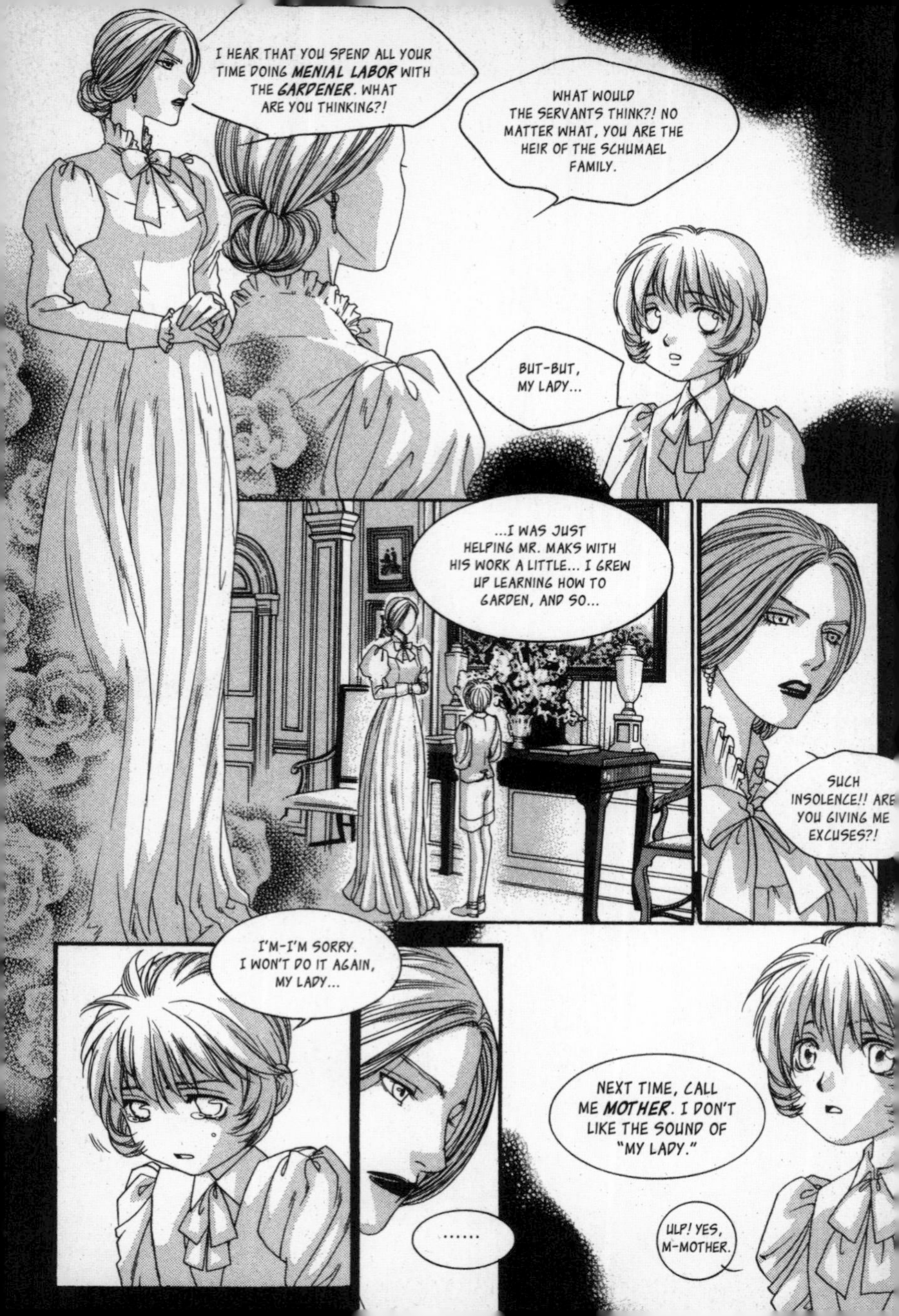
I HEAR THAT YOU SPEND ALL YOUR TIME DOING MENIAL LABOR WITH THE GARDENER. WHAT ARE YOU THINKING?!
WHAT WOULD THE SERVANTS THINK?! NO MATTER WHAT, YOU ARE THE HEIR OF THE SCHUMAEL FAMILY.
BUT-BUT, MY LADY...
...I WAS JUST HELPING MR. MAKS WITH HIS WORK A LITTLE... I GREW UP LEARNING HOW TO GARDEN, AND SO...
SUCH INSOLENCE!! ARE YOU GIVING ME EXCUSES?!
I'M-I'M SORRY. I WON'T DO IT AGAIN, MY LADY...
......
NEXT TIME, CALL ME MOTHER. I DON'T LIKE THE SOUND OF "MY LADY."
ULP! YES, M-MOTHER.

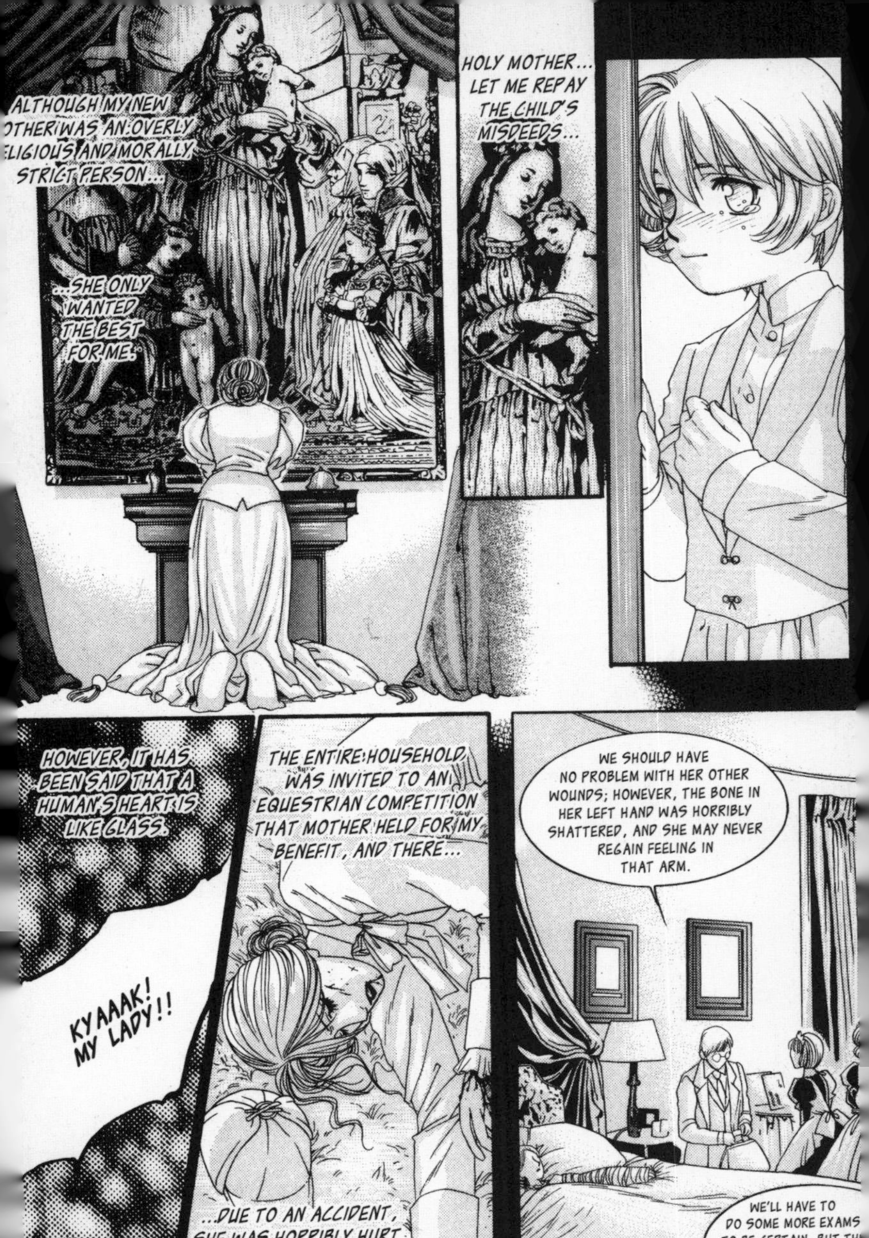
ALTHOUGH MY NEW MOTHER WAS AN OVERLY RELIGIOUS AND MORALLY STRICT PERSON...
...SHE ONLY WANTED THE BEST FOR ME.
HOLY MOTHER... LET ME REPAY THE CHILD'S MISDEEDS...
HOWEVER, IT HAS BEEN SAID THAT A HUMAN'S HEART IS LIKE GLASS.
KYAAAK! MY LADY!!
THE ENTIRE HOUSEHOLD WAS INVITED TO AN EQUESTRIAN COMPETITION THAT MOTHER HELD FOR MY BENEFIT, AND THERE...
...DUE TO AN ACCIDENT, SHE WAS HORRIBLY HURT.
WE SHOULD HAVE NO PROBLEM WITH HER OTHER WOUNDS; HOWEVER, THE BONE IN HER LEFT HAND WAS HORRIBLY SHATTERED, AND SHE MAY NEVER REGAIN FEELING IN THAT ARM.
WE'LL HAVE TO DO SOME MORE EXAMS TO BE CERTAIN, BUT THE PATIENT SHOULD BE MAD AWARE OF SUCH A POSSIBILITY.

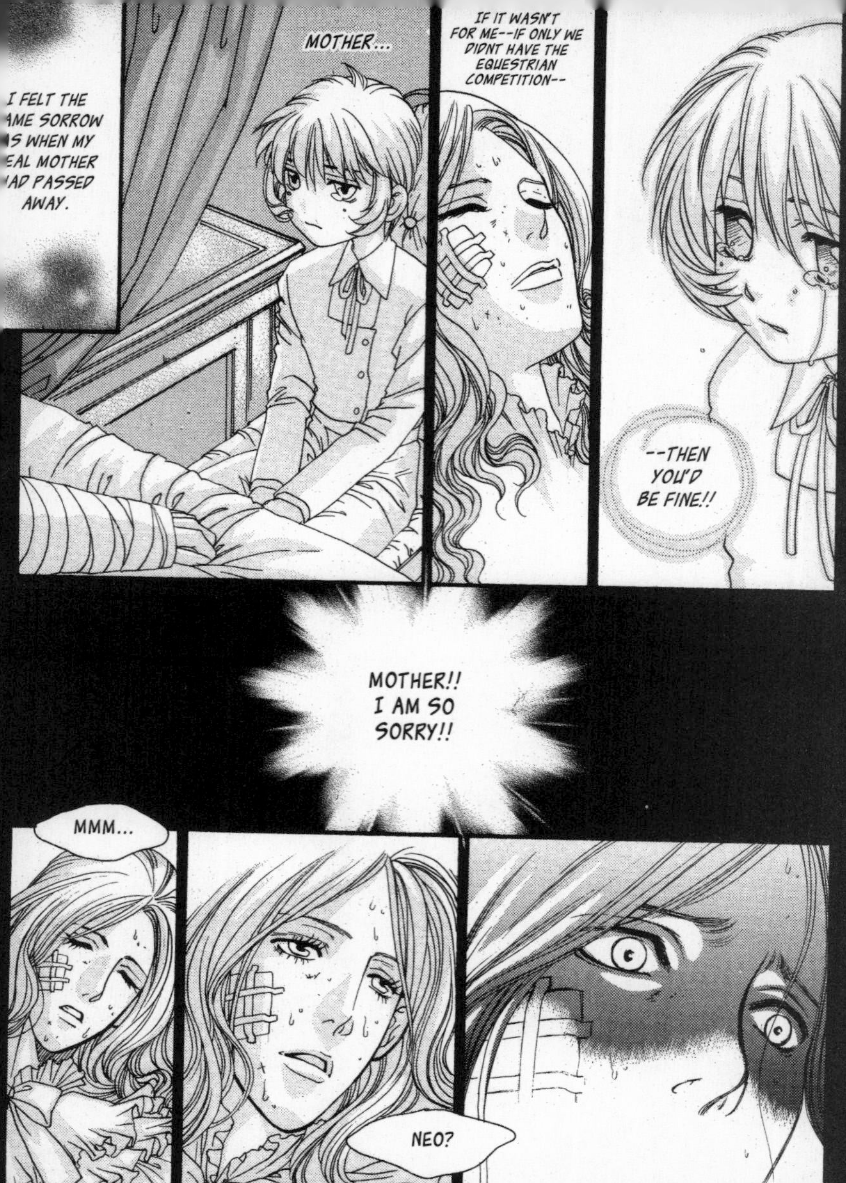
I FELT THE AME SORROW S WHEN MY EAL MOTHER AD PASSED AWAY.
MOTHER...
IF IT WASN'T FOR ME--IF ONLY WE DIDNT HAVE THE EQUESTRIAN COMPETITION--
--THEN YOU'D BE FINE!!
MOTHER!! I AM SO SORRY!!
MMM...
NEO?

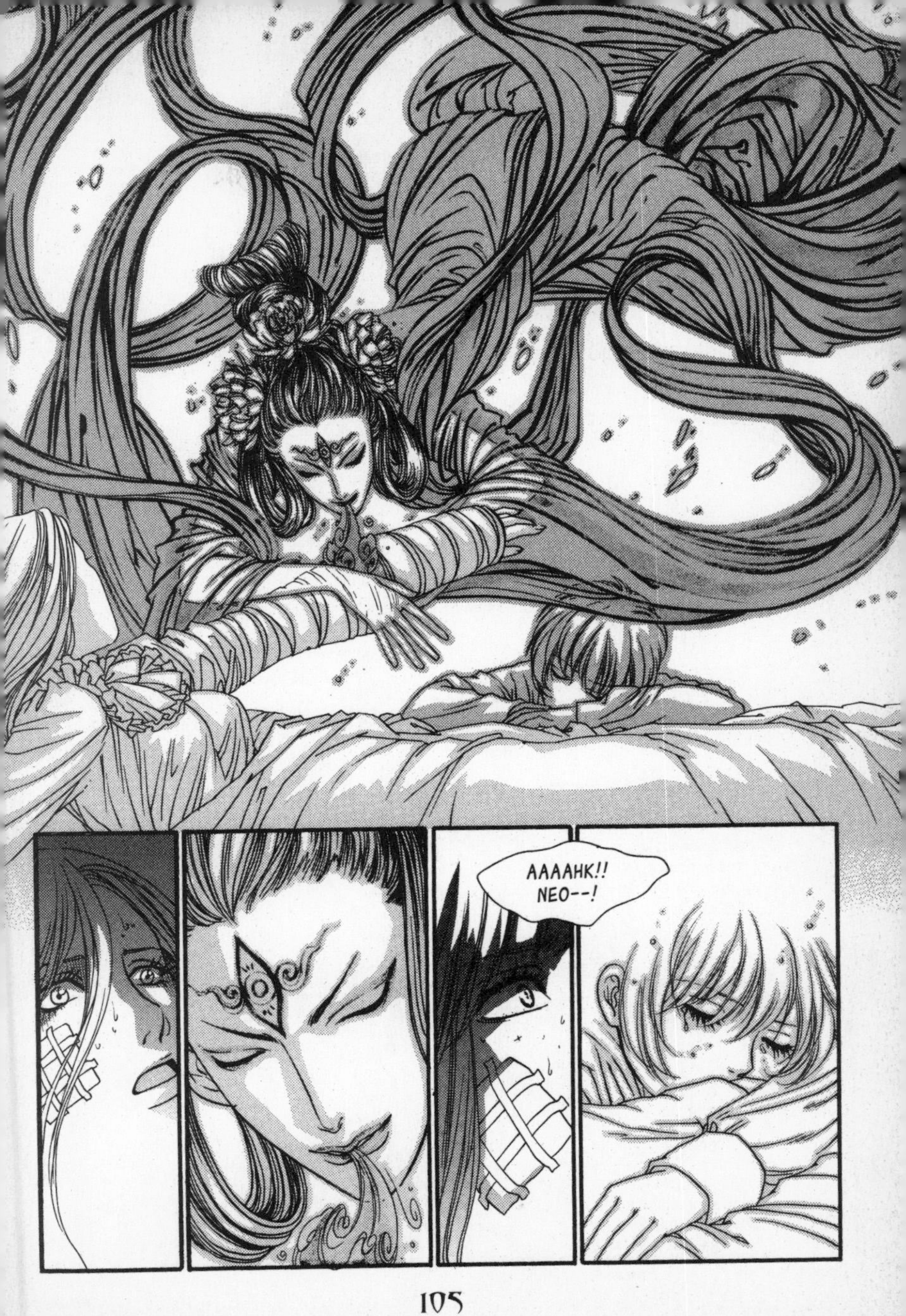
AAAAHK!! NEO--!

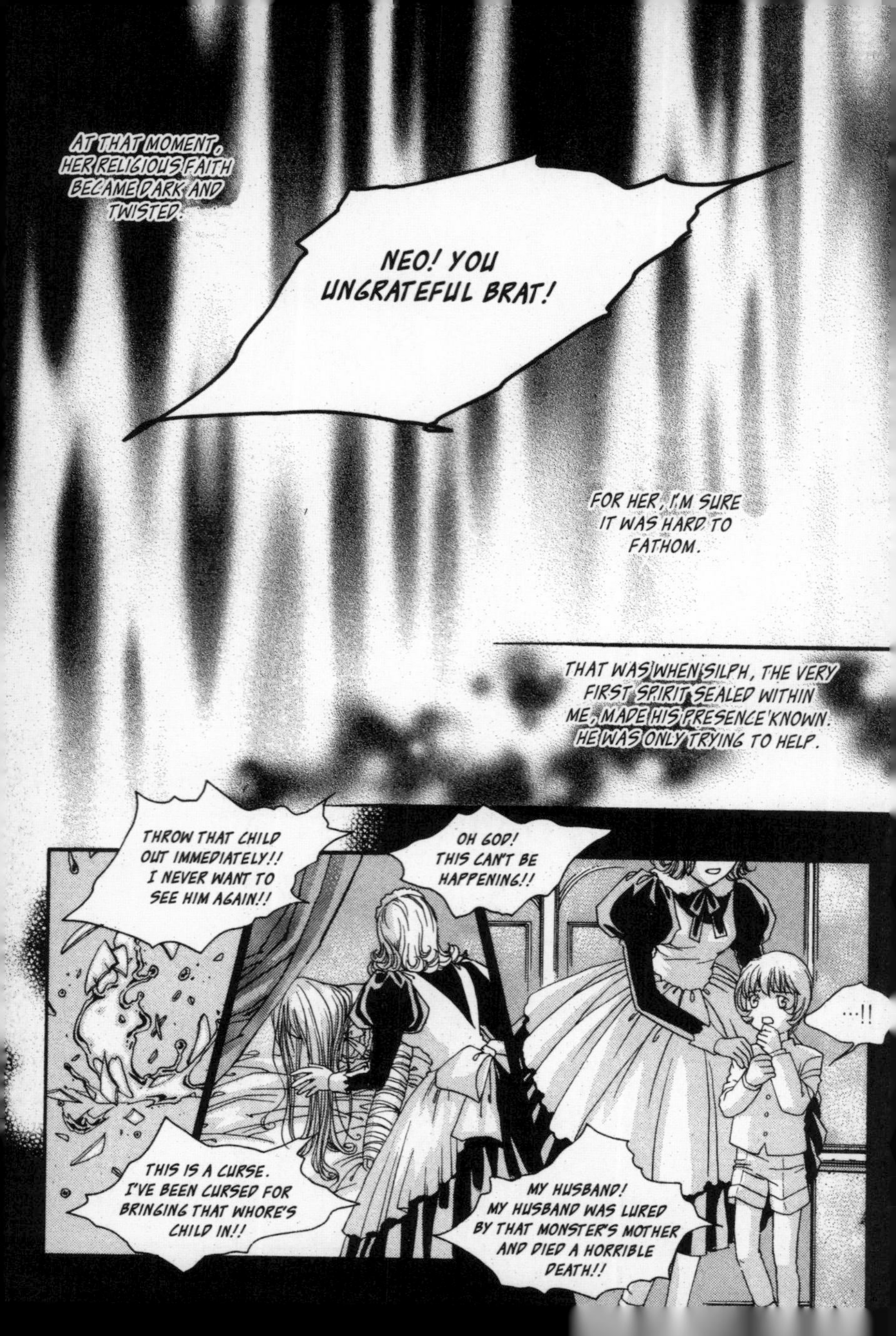
AT THAT MOMENT, HER RELIGIOUS FAITH BECAME DARK AND TWISTED.
NEO! YOU UNGRATEFUL BRAT!
FOR HER, I'M SURE IT WAS HARD TO FATHOM.
THAT WAS WHEN SILPH, THE VERY FIRST SPIRIT SEALED WITHIN ME, MADE HIS PRESENCE KNOWN. HE WAS ONLY TRYING TO HELP.
THROW THAT CHILD OUT IMMEDIATELY!! I NEVER WANT TO SEE HIM AGAIN!!
OH GOD! THIS CAN'T BE HAPPENING!!
...!!
THIS IS A CURSE. I'VE BEEN CURSED FOR BRINGING THAT WHORE'S CHILD IN!!
MY HUSBAND! MY HUSBAND WAS LURED BY THAT MONSTER'S MOTHER AND DIED A HORRIBLE DEATH!!

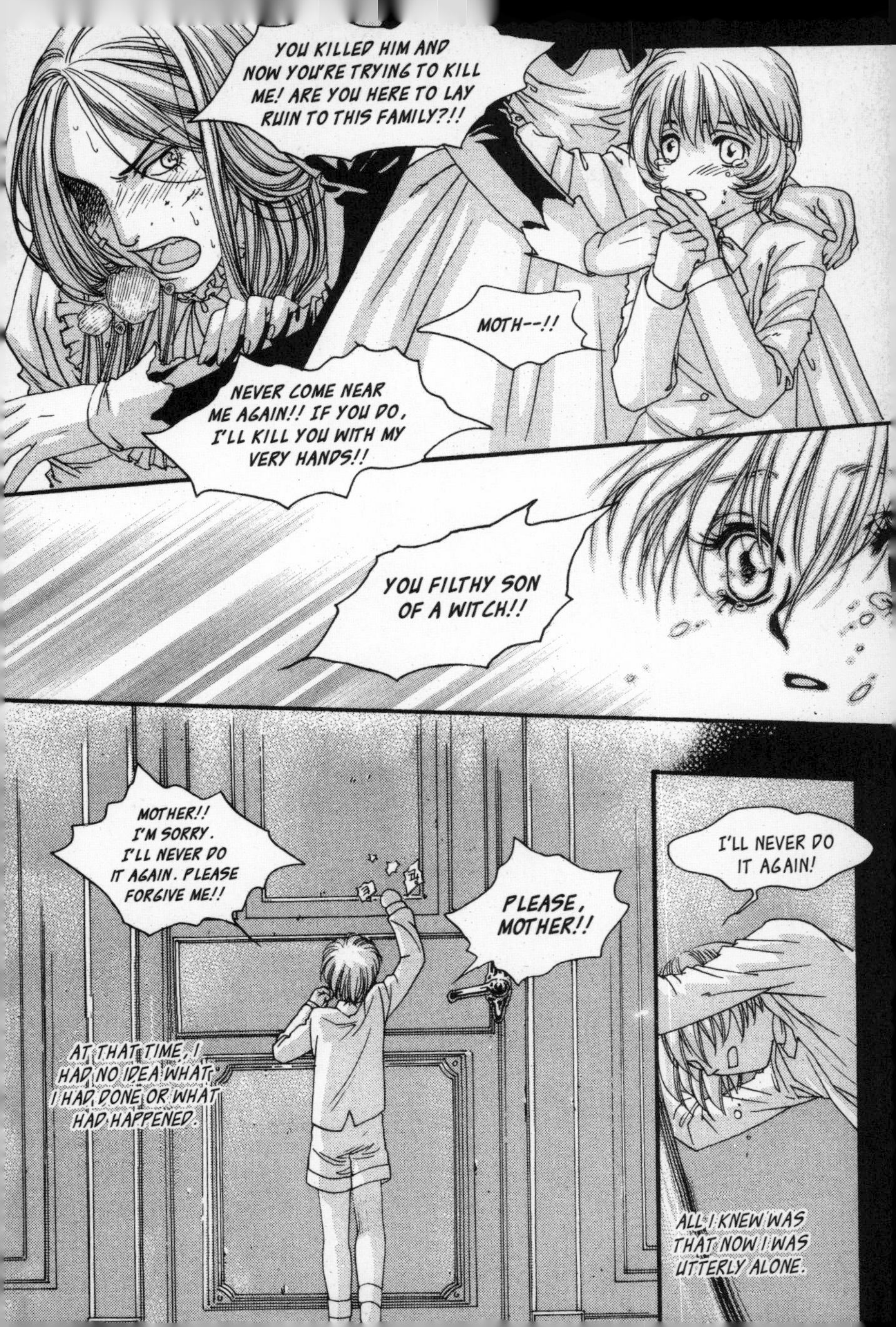
YOU KILLED HIM AND NOW YOU'RE TRYING TO KILL ME! ARE YOU HERE TO LAY RUIN TO THIS FAMILY?!!
MOTH--!!
NEVER COME NEAR ME AGAIN!! IF YOU DO, I'LL KILL YOU WITH MY VERY HANDS!!
YOU FILTHY SON OF A WITCH!!
MOTHER!! I'M SORRY. I'LL NEVER DO IT AGAIN. PLEASE FORGIVE ME!!
PLEASE, MOTHER!!
AT THAT TIME, I HAD NO IDEA WHAT I HAD DONE OR WHAT HAD HAPPENED.
I'LL NEVER DO IT AGAIN!
ALL I KNEW WAS THAT NOW I WAS UTTERLY ALONE.

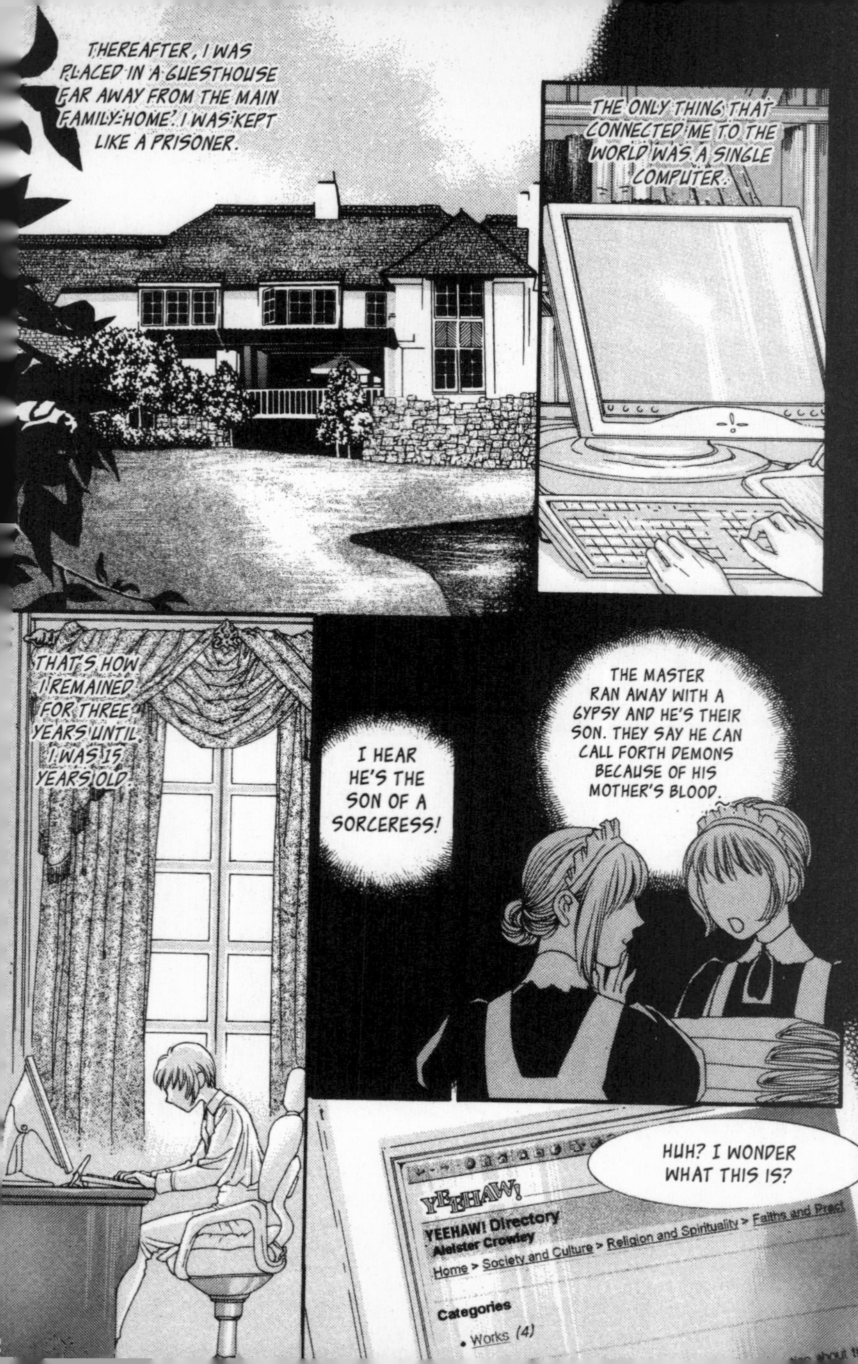
THEREAFTER, I WAS PLACED IN A GUESTHOUSE FAR AWAY FROM THE MAIN FAMILY HOME. I WAS KEPT LIKE A PRISONER.
THE ONLY THING THAT CONNECTED ME TO THE WORLD WAS A SINGLE COMPUTER.
THAT'S HOW I REMAINED FOR THREE YEARS UNTIL I WAS 15 YEARS OLD.
I HEAR HE'S THE SON OF A SORCERESS!
THE MASTER RAN AWAY WITH A GYPSY AND HE'S THEIR SON. THEY SAY HE CAN CALL FORTH DEMONS BECAUSE OF HIS MOTHER'S BLOOD.
HUH? I WONDER WHAT THIS IS?
YEEHAW!
YEEHAW! Directory
Aleister Crowley
Home > Society and Culture > Religion and Spirituality > Faiths and Pract
Categories
• Works (4)

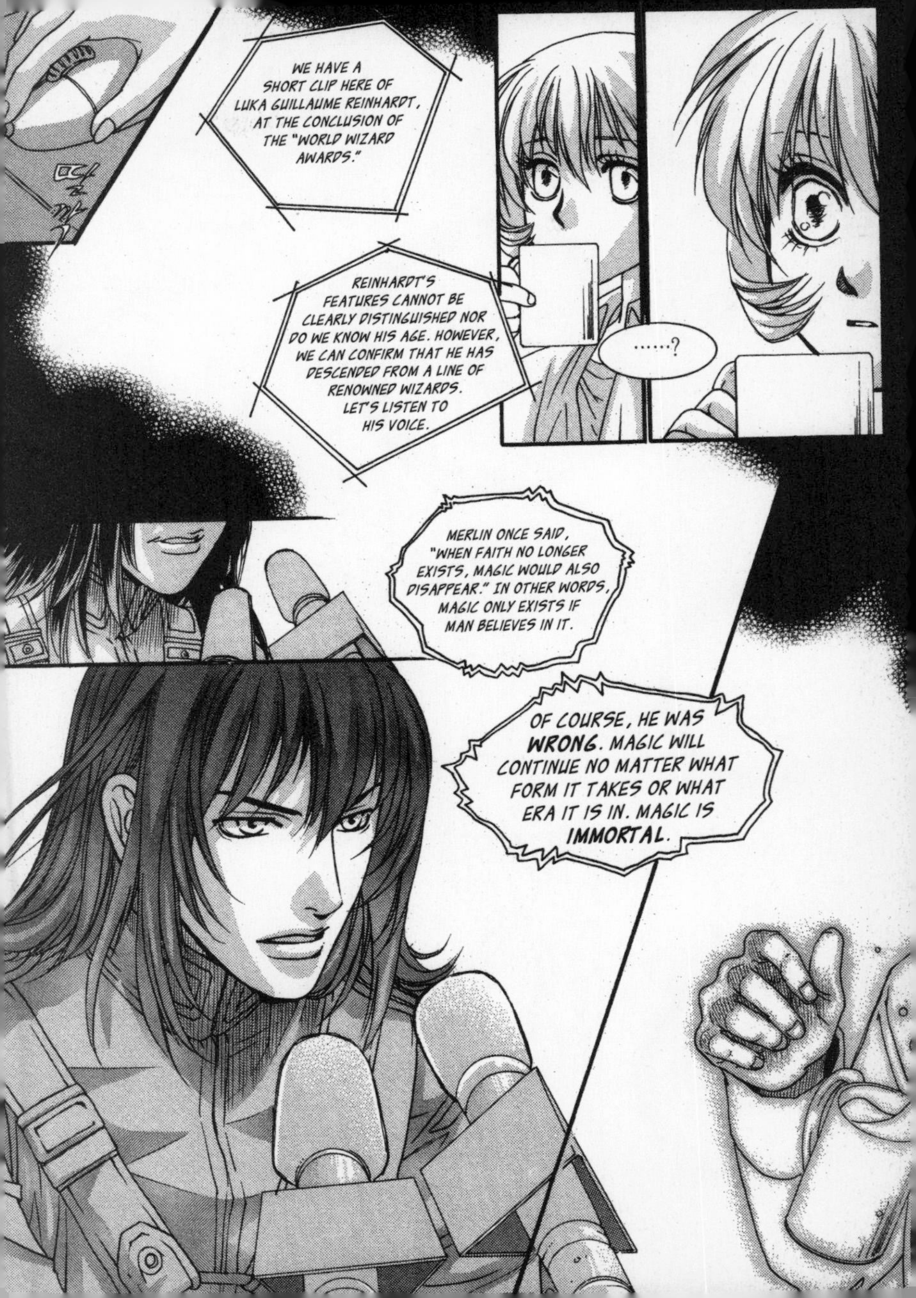
WE HAVE A SHORT CLIP HERE OF LUKA GUILLAUME REINHARDT, AT THE CONCLUSION OF THE "WORLD WIZARD AWARDS."
REINHARDT'S FEATURES CANNOT BE CLEARLY DISTINGUISHED NOR DO WE KNOW HIS AGE. HOWEVER, WE CAN CONFIRM THAT HE HAS DESCENDED FROM A LINE OF RENOWNED WIZARDS. LET'S LISTEN TO HIS VOICE.
......?
MERLIN ONCE SAID, "WHEN FAITH NO LONGER EXISTS, MAGIC WOULD ALSO DISAPPEAR." IN OTHER WORDS, MAGIC ONLY EXISTS IF MAN BELIEVES IN IT.
OF COURSE, HE WAS **WRONG**. MAGIC WILL CONTINUE NO MATTER WHAT FORM IT TAKES OR WHAT ERA IT IS IN. MAGIC IS **IMMORTAL**.

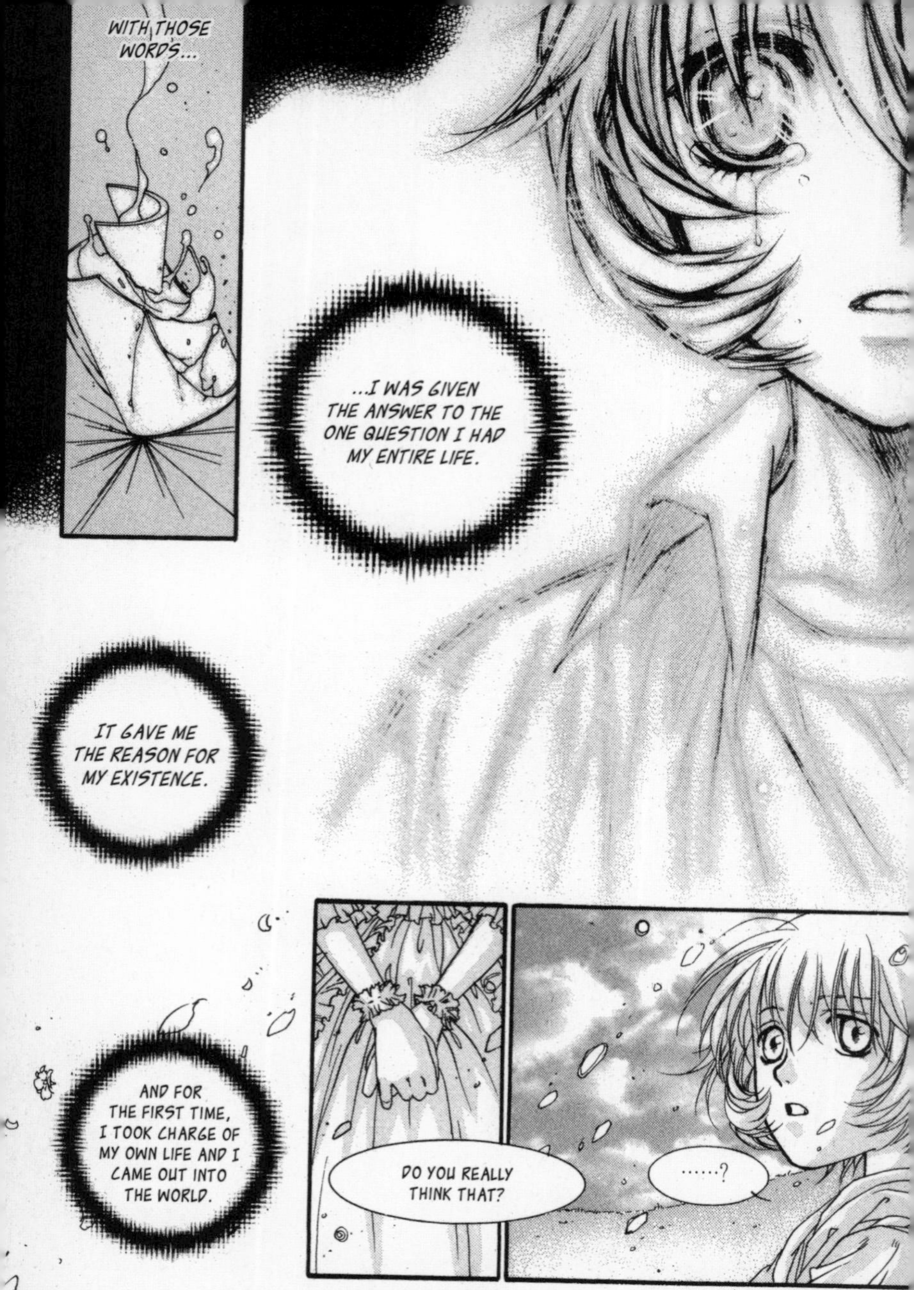
WITH THOSE WORDS...
...I WAS GIVEN THE ANSWER TO THE ONE QUESTION I HAD MY ENTIRE LIFE.
IT GAVE ME THE REASON FOR MY EXISTENCE.
AND FOR THE FIRST TIME, I TOOK CHARGE OF MY OWN LIFE AND I CAME OUT INTO THE WORLD.
DO YOU REALLY THINK THAT?
......?

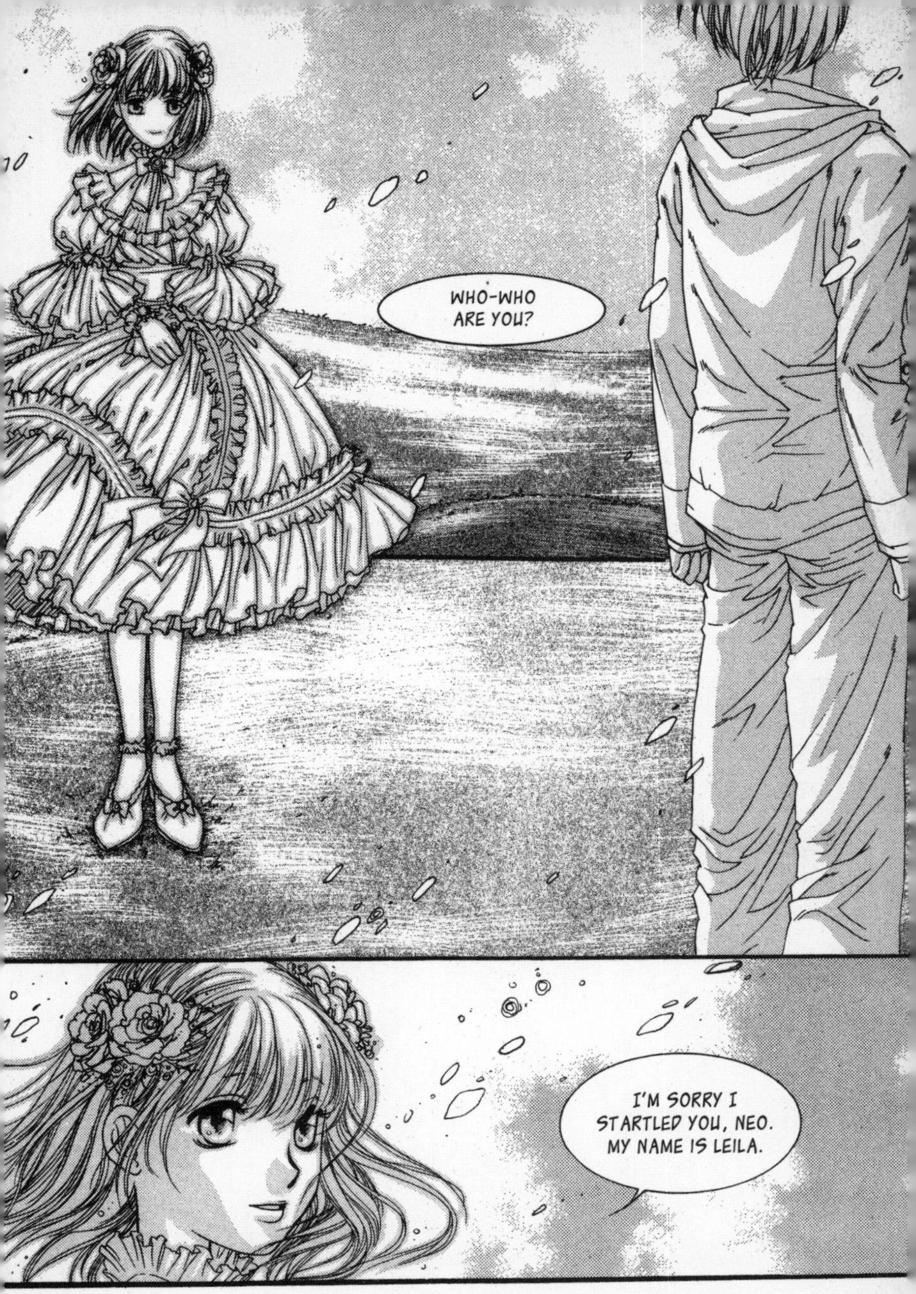
WHO-WHO ARE YOU?
I'M SORRY I STARTLED YOU, NEO. MY NAME IS LEILA.

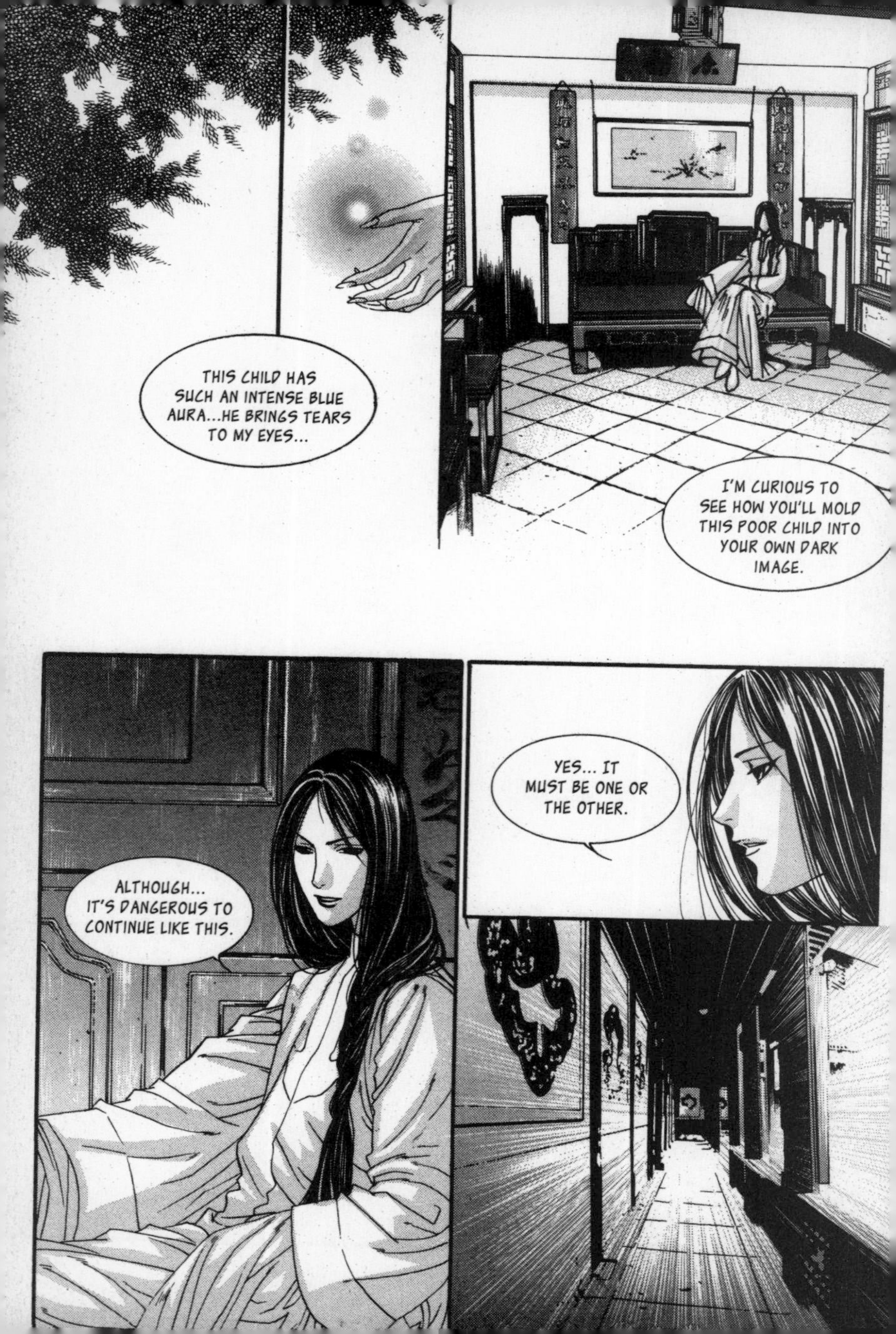
THIS CHILD HAS SUCH AN INTENSE BLUE AURA...HE BRINGS TEARS TO MY EYES...
I'M CURIOUS TO SEE HOW YOU'LL MOLD THIS POOR CHILD INTO YOUR OWN DARK IMAGE.
ALTHOUGH... IT'S DANGEROUS TO CONTINUE LIKE THIS.
YES... IT MUST BE ONE OR THE OTHER.

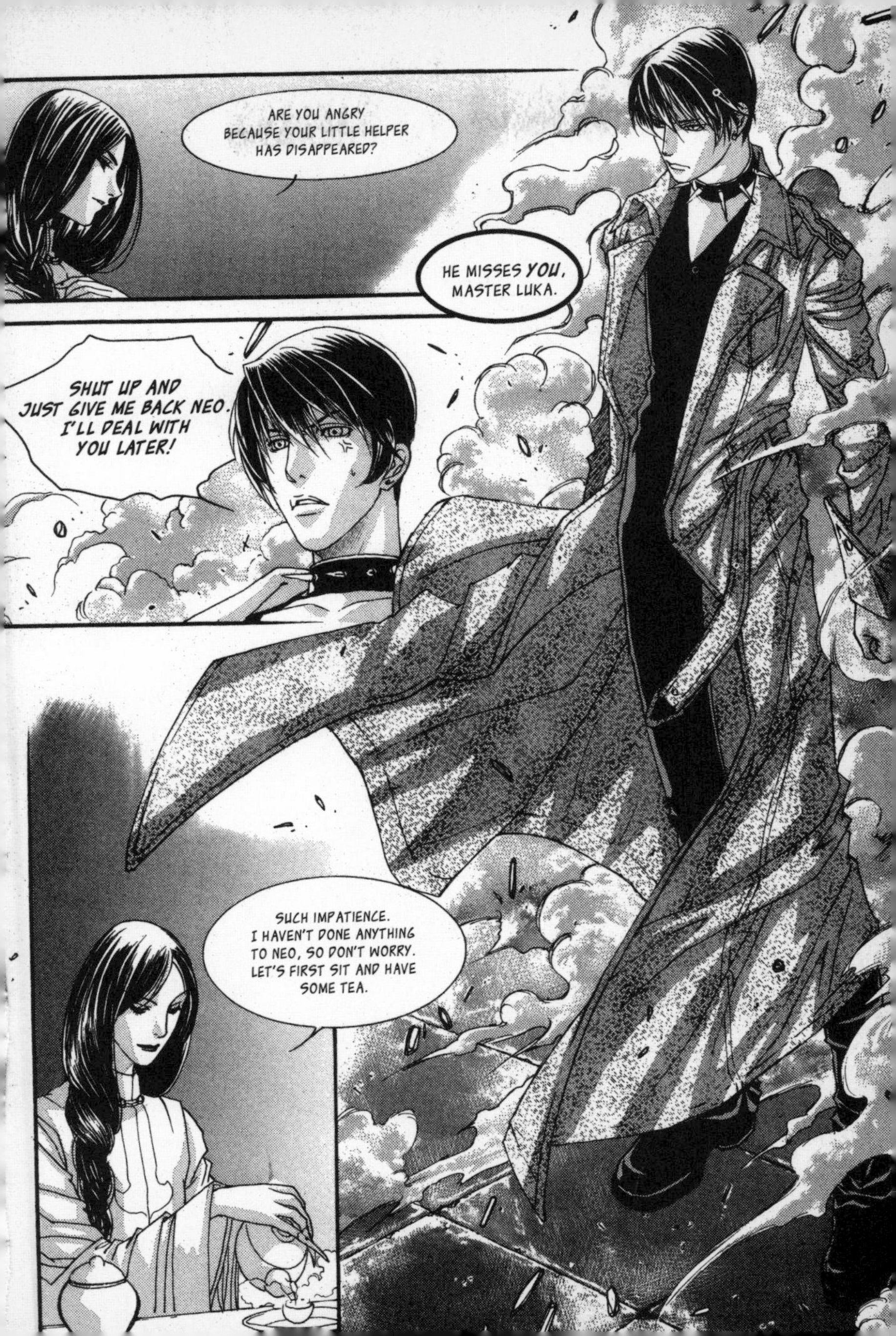
ARE YOU ANGRY BECAUSE YOUR LITTLE HELPER HAS DISAPPEARED?
HE MISSES YOU, MASTER LUKA.
SHUT UP AND JUST GIVE ME BACK NEO. I'LL DEAL WITH YOU LATER!
SUCH IMPATIENCE. I HAVEN'T DONE ANYTHING TO NEO, SO DON'T WORRY. LET'S FIRST SIT AND HAVE SOME TEA.

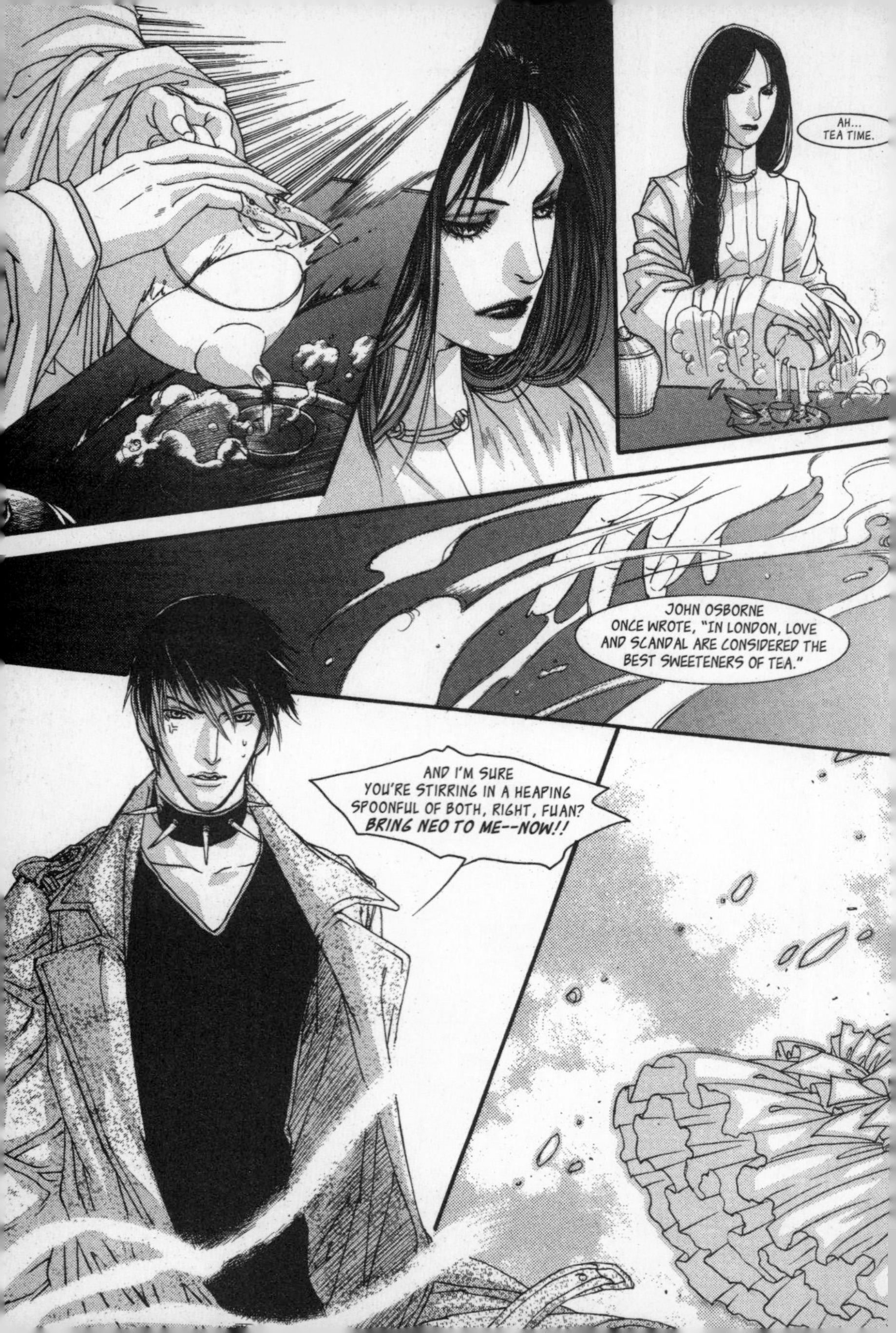
AH... TEA TIME.
JOHN OSBORNE ONCE WROTE, "IN LONDON, LOVE AND SCANDAL ARE CONSIDERED THE BEST SWEETENERS OF TEA."
AND I'M SURE YOU'RE STIRRING IN A HEAPING SPOONFUL OF BOTH, RIGHT, FUAN? ***BRING NEO TO ME--NOW!!***

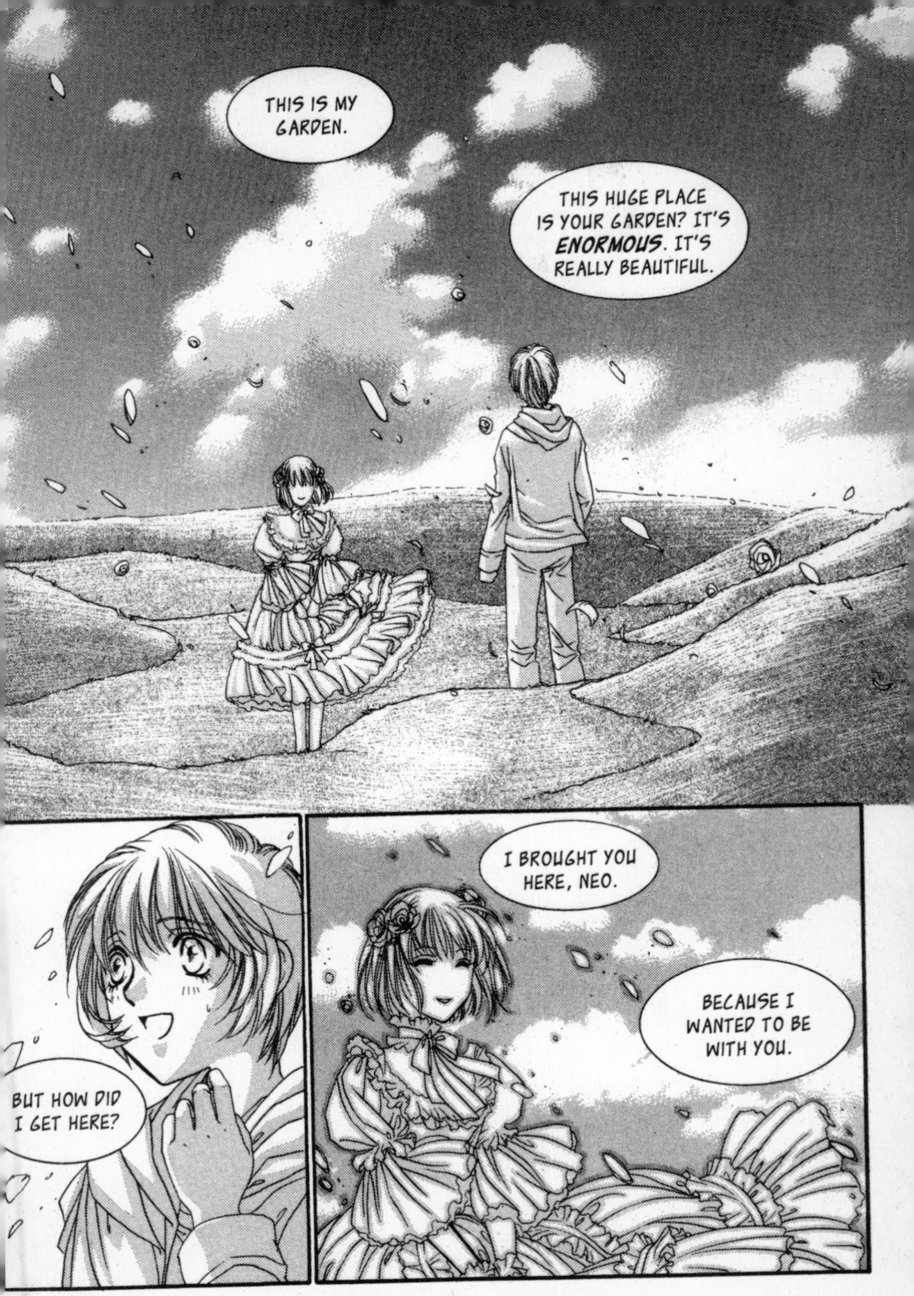
THIS IS MY GARDEN.
THIS HUGE PLACE IS YOUR GARDEN? IT'S **ENORMOUS**. IT'S REALLY BEAUTIFUL.
BUT HOW DID I GET HERE?
I BROUGHT YOU HERE, NEO.
BECAUSE I WANTED TO BE WITH YOU.

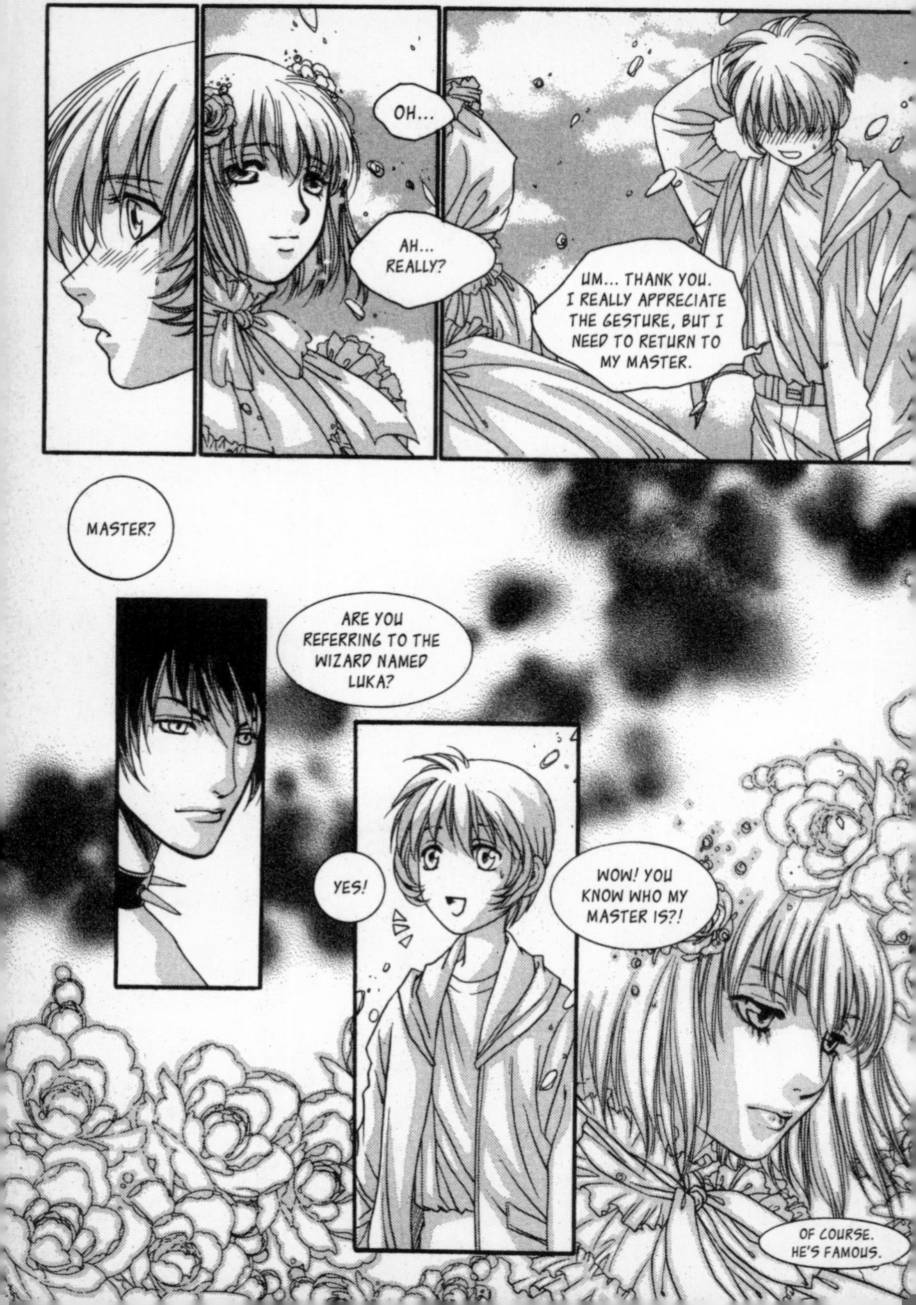
OH...
AH... REALLY?
UM... THANK YOU. I REALLY APPRECIATE THE GESTURE, BUT I NEED TO RETURN TO MY MASTER.
MASTER?
ARE YOU REFERRING TO THE WIZARD NAMED LUKA?
YES!
WOW! YOU KNOW WHO MY MASTER IS?!
OF COURSE. HE'S FAMOUS.

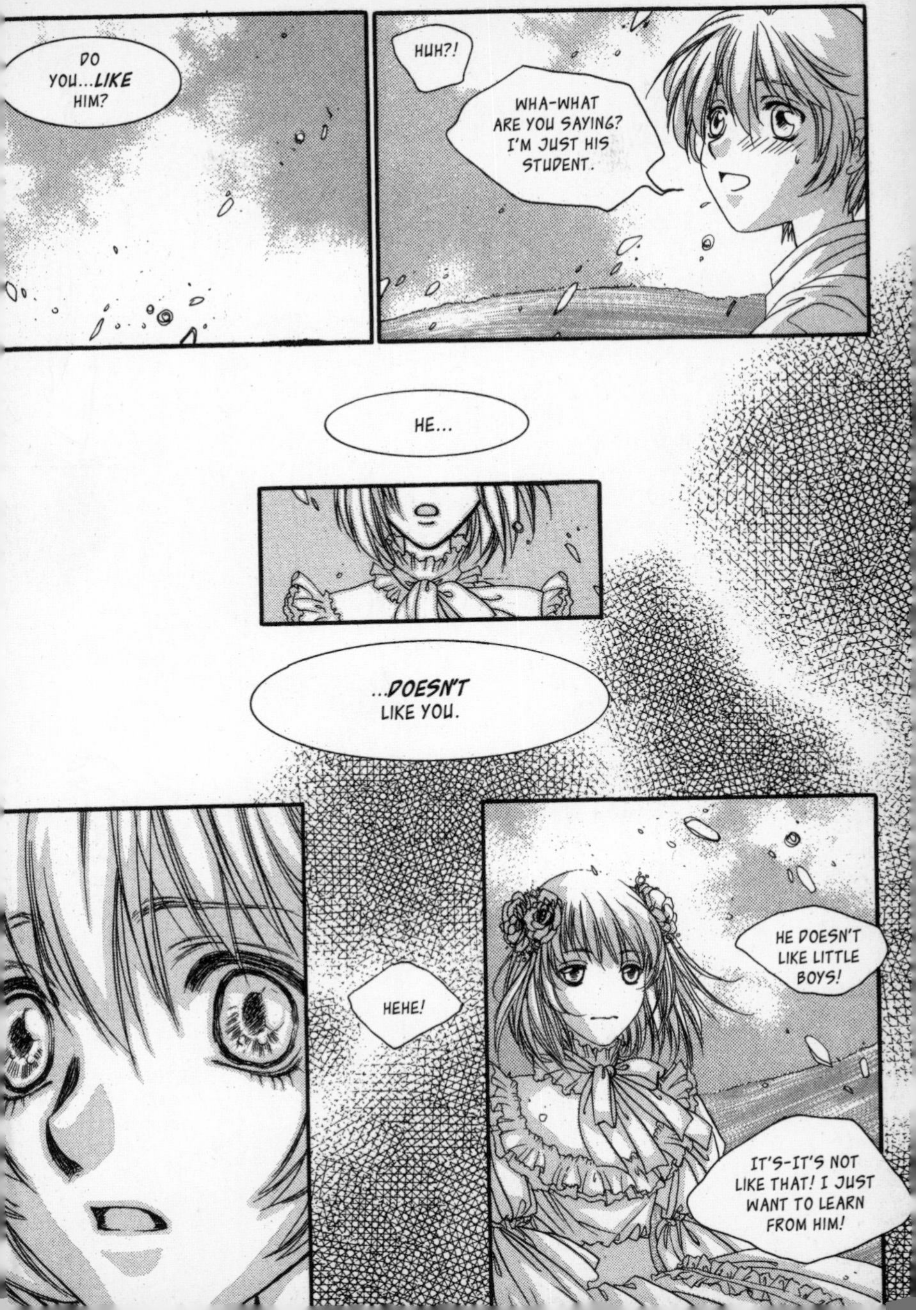
DO YOU...LIKE HIM?
HUH?!
WHA-WHAT ARE YOU SAYING? I'M JUST HIS STUDENT.
HE...
...DOESN'T LIKE YOU.
HEHE!
HE DOESN'T LIKE LITTLE BOYS!
IT'S-IT'S NOT LIKE THAT! I JUST WANT TO LEARN FROM HIM!

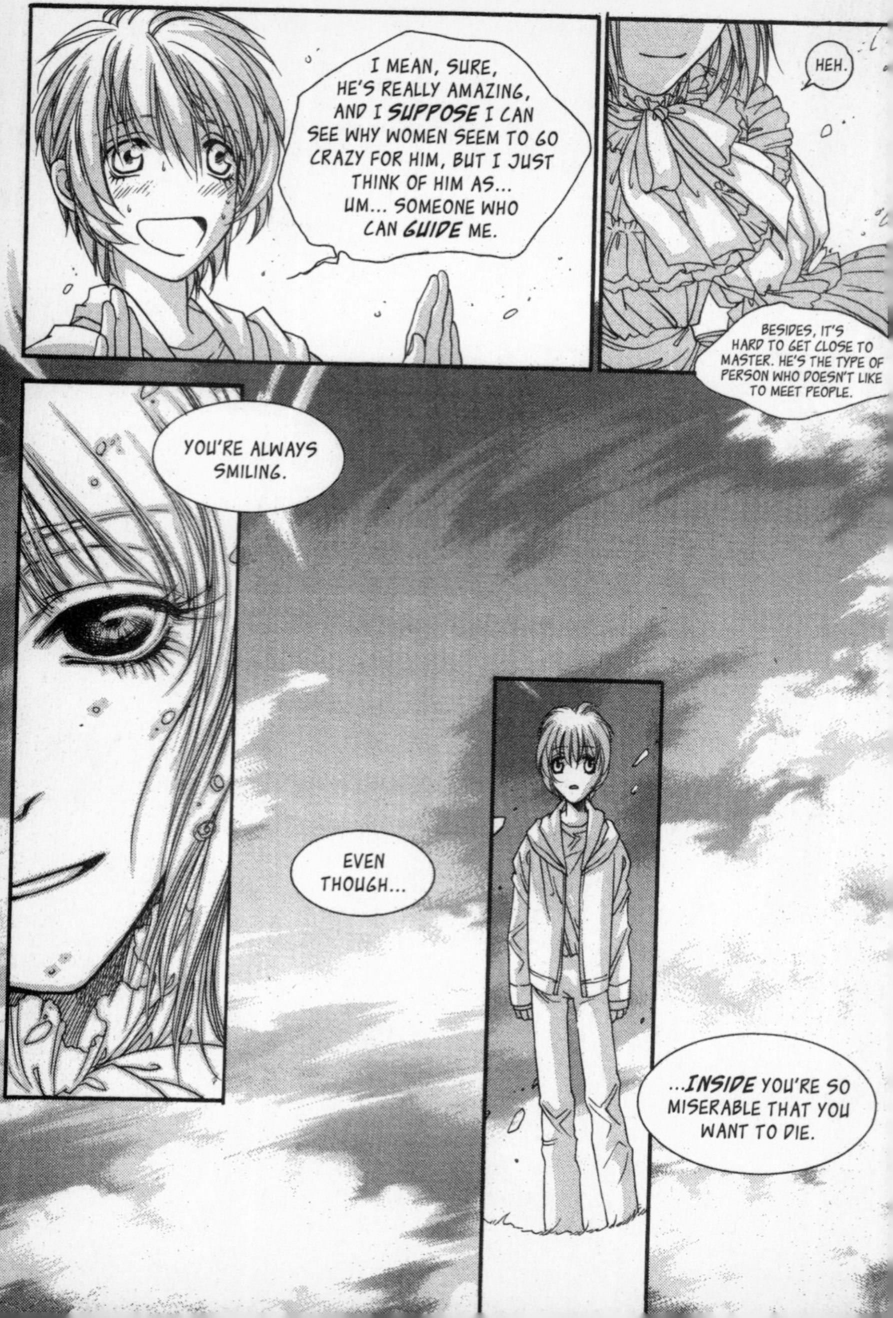
I MEAN, SURE, HE'S REALLY AMAZING, AND I SUPPOSE I CAN SEE WHY WOMEN SEEM TO GO CRAZY FOR HIM, BUT I JUST THINK OF HIM AS... UM... SOMEONE WHO CAN GUIDE ME.
HEH.
BESIDES, IT'S HARD TO GET CLOSE TO MASTER. HE'S THE TYPE OF PERSON WHO DOESN'T LIKE TO MEET PEOPLE.
YOU'RE ALWAYS SMILING.
EVEN THOUGH...
...INSIDE YOU'RE SO MISERABLE THAT YOU WANT TO DIE.

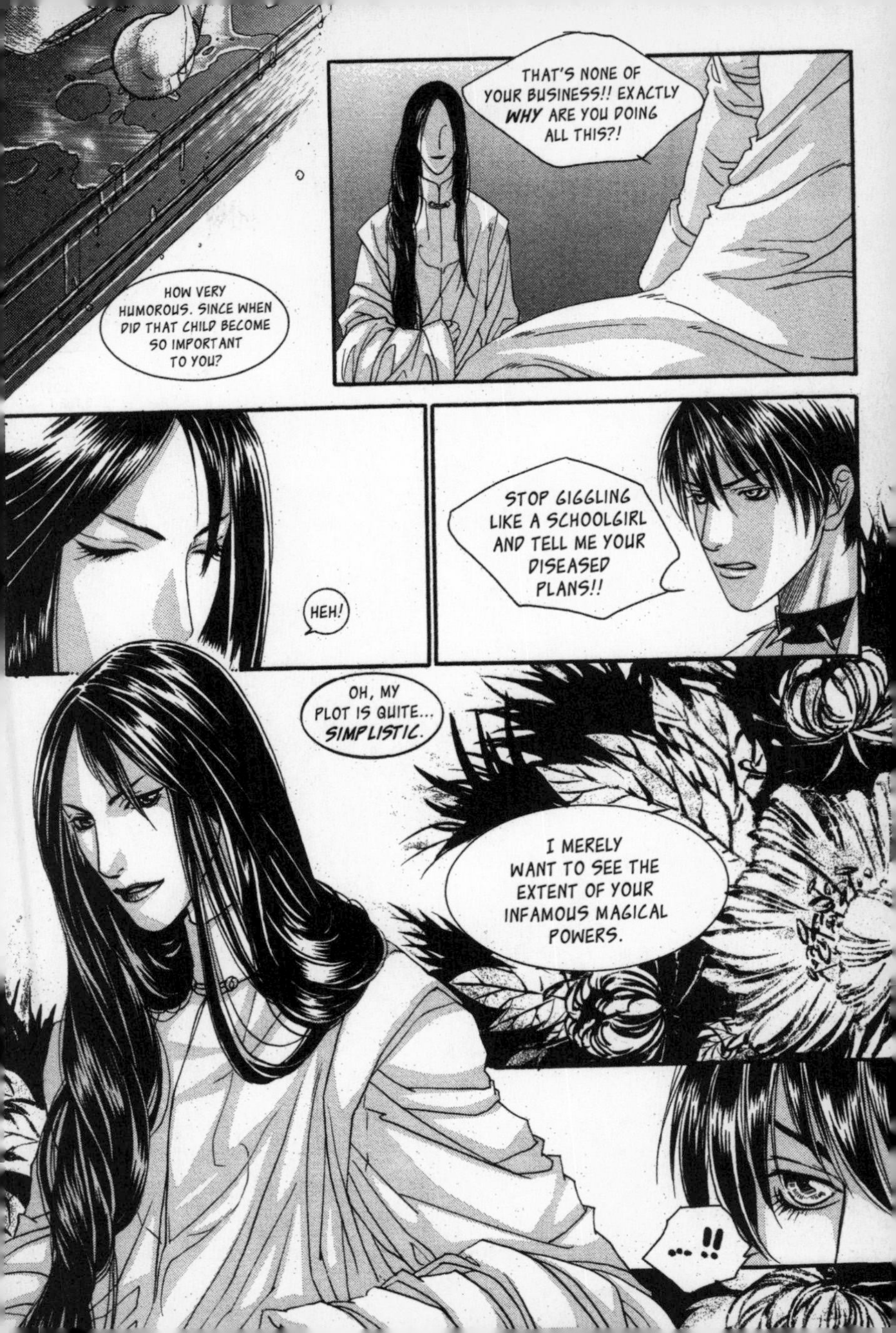
HOW VERY HUMOROUS. SINCE WHEN DID THAT CHILD BECOME SO IMPORTANT TO YOU?
THAT'S NONE OF YOUR BUSINESS!! EXACTLY WHY ARE YOU DOING ALL THIS?!
HEH!
STOP GIGGLING LIKE A SCHOOLGIRL AND TELL ME YOUR DISEASED PLANS!!
OH, MY PLOT IS QUITE... SIMPLISTIC.
I MERELY WANT TO SEE THE EXTENT OF YOUR INFAMOUS MAGICAL POWERS.
...!!

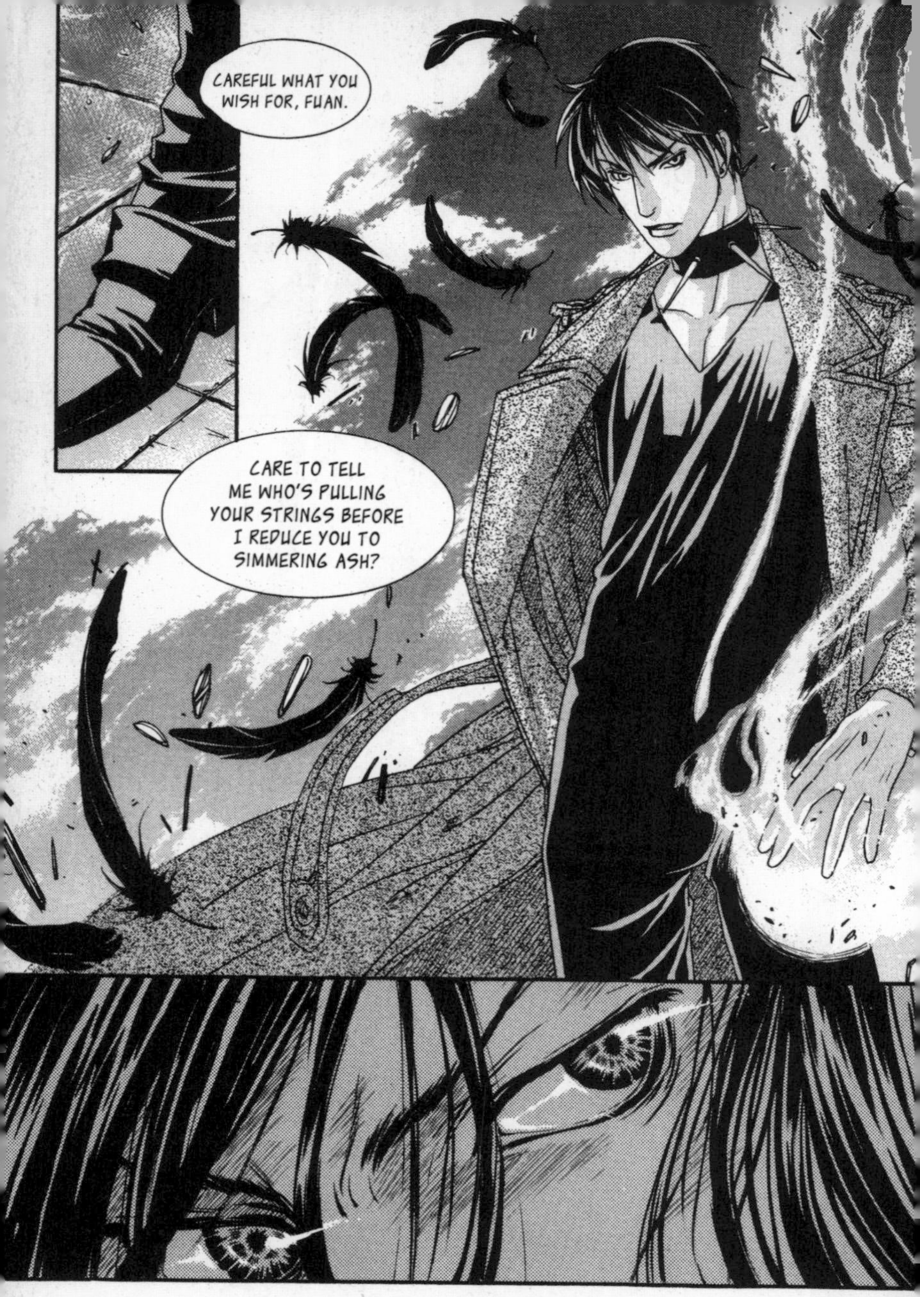
CAREFUL WHAT YOU WISH FOR, FUAN.
CARE TO TELL ME WHO'S PULLING YOUR STRINGS BEFORE I REDUCE YOU TO SIMMERING ASH?

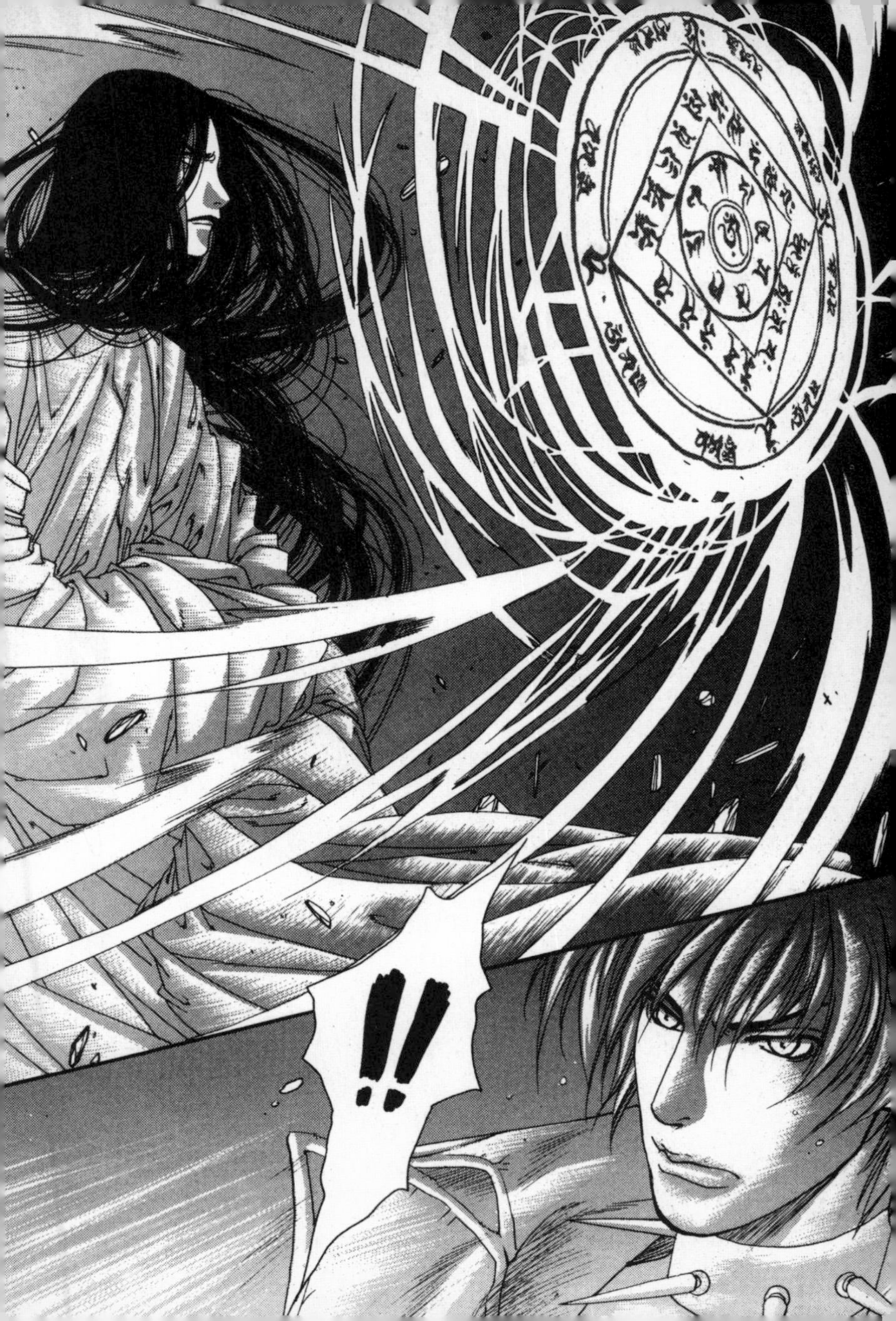
!!

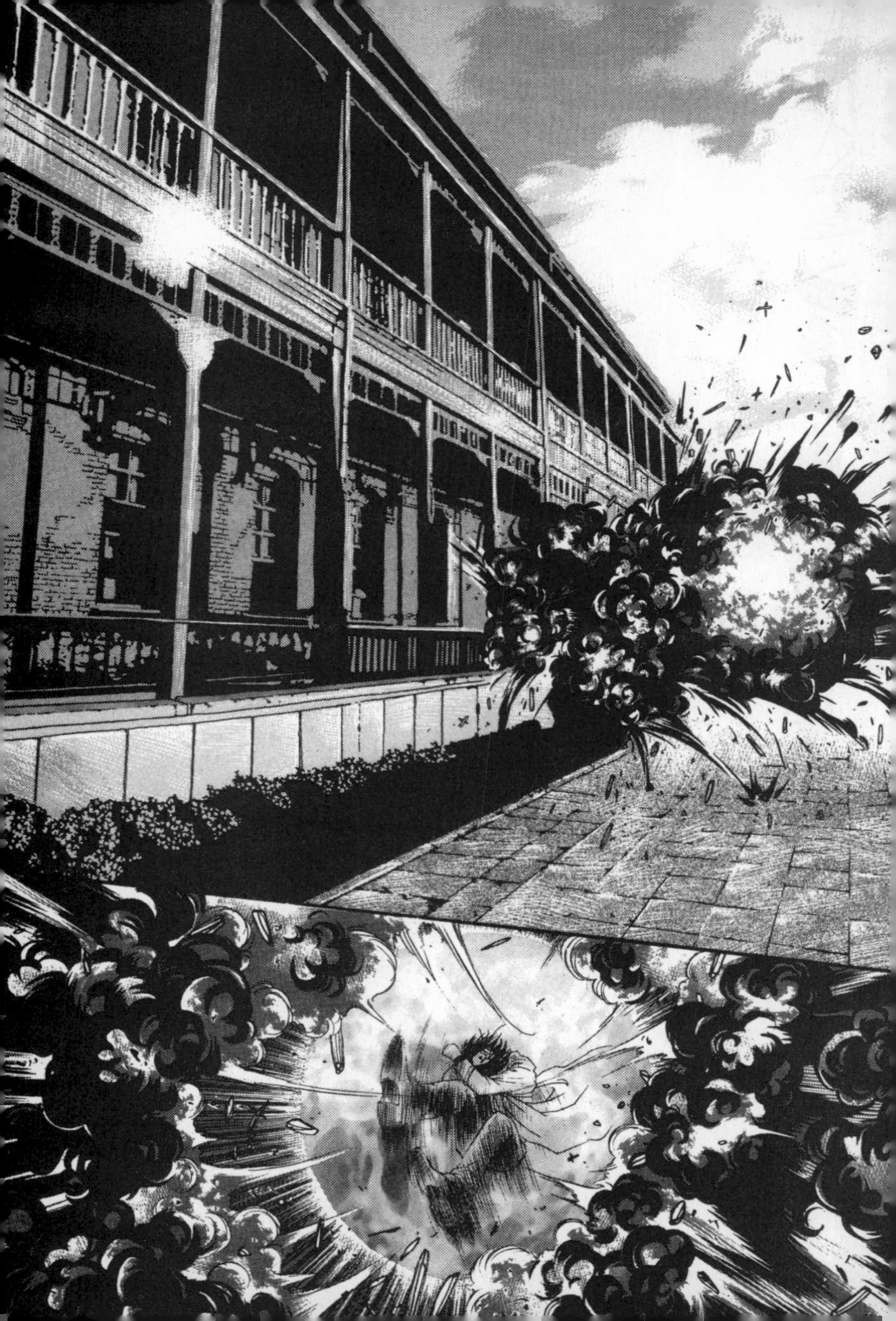

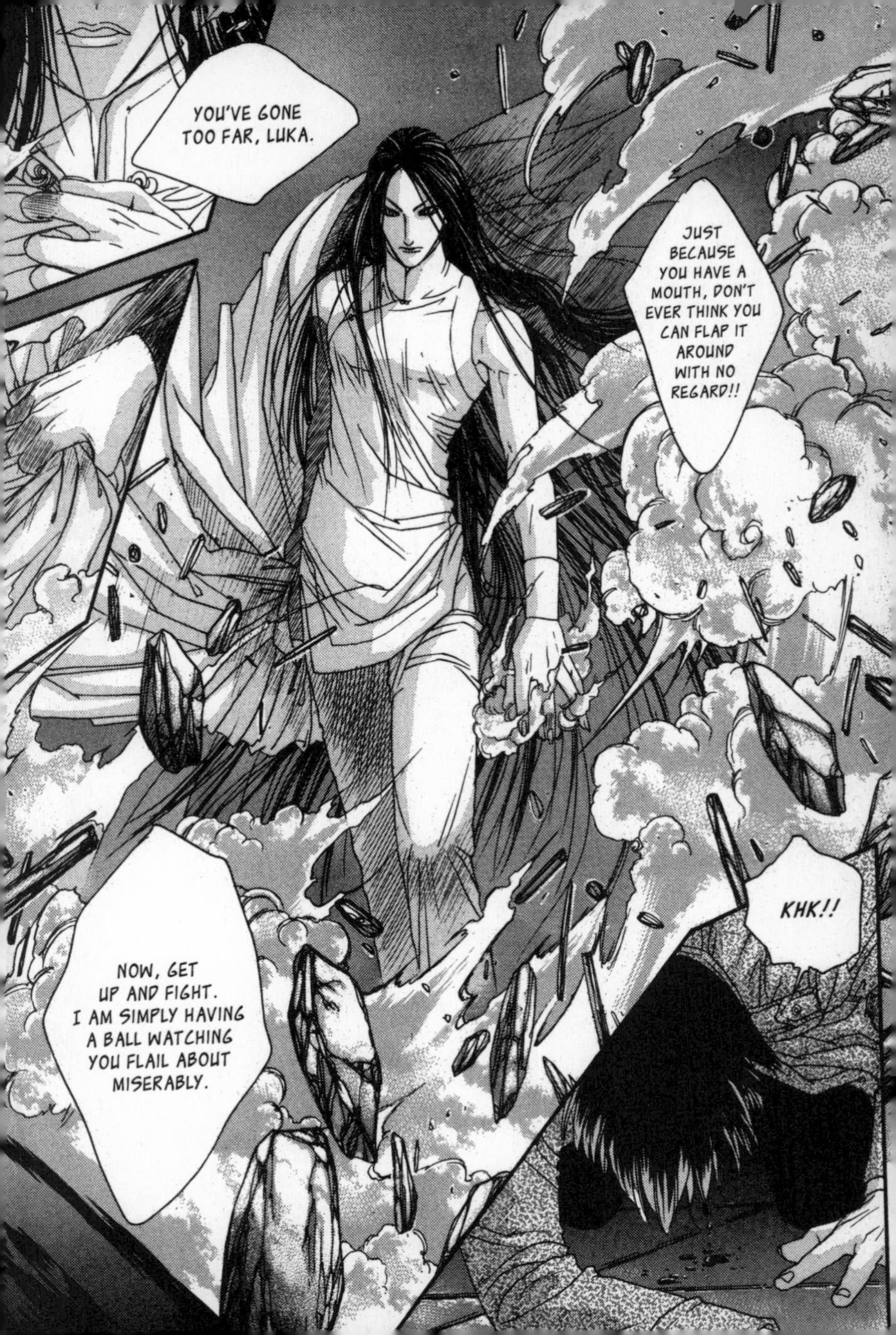
YOU'VE GONE TOO FAR, LUKA.
JUST BECAUSE YOU HAVE A MOUTH, DON'T EVER THINK YOU CAN FLAP IT AROUND WITH NO REGARD!!
NOW, GET UP AND FIGHT. I AM SIMPLY HAVING A BALL WATCHING YOU FLAIL ABOUT MISERABLY.
KHK!!

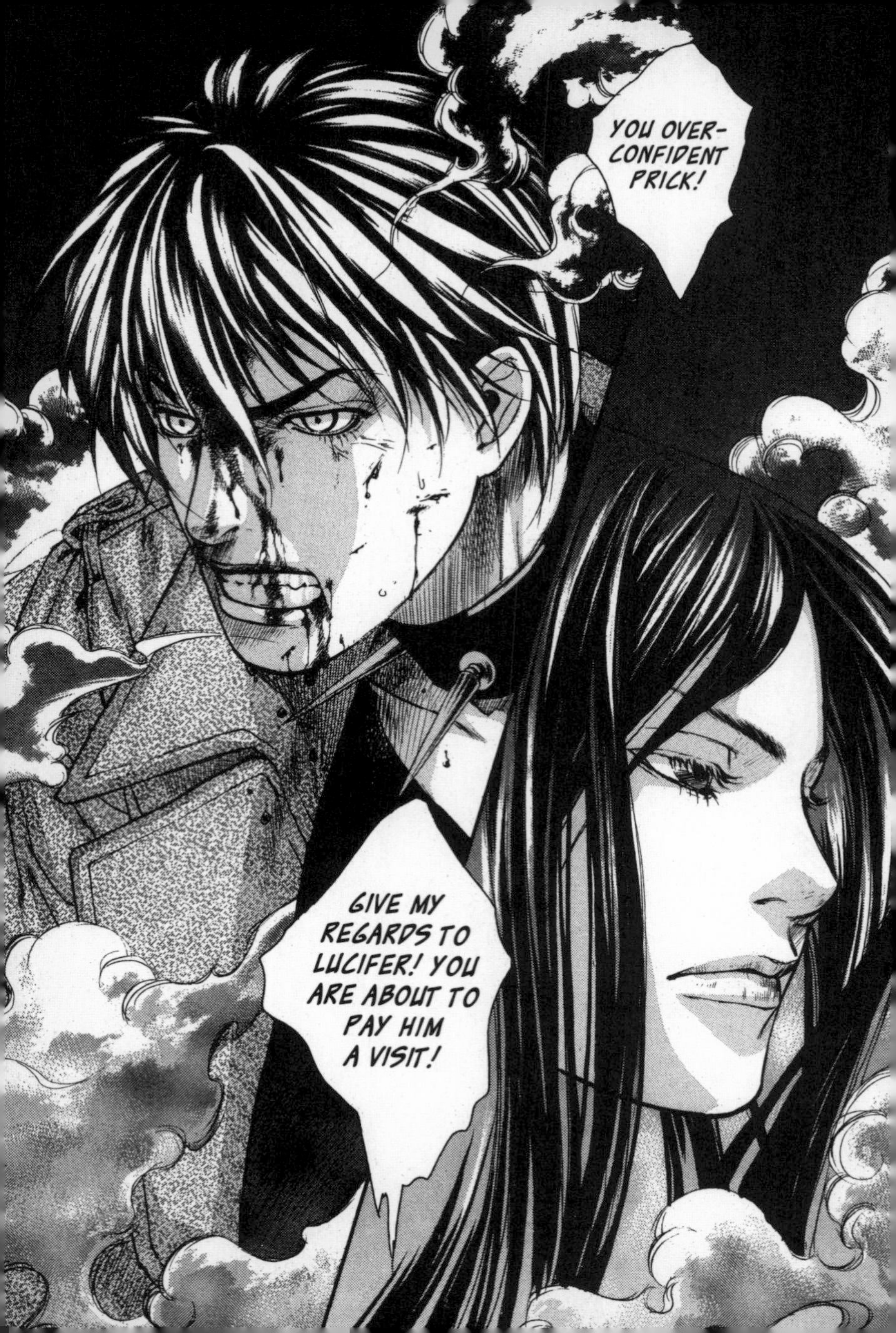
YOU OVER-CONFIDENT PRICK!
GIVE MY REGARDS TO LUCIFER! YOU ARE ABOUT TO PAY HIM A VISIT!

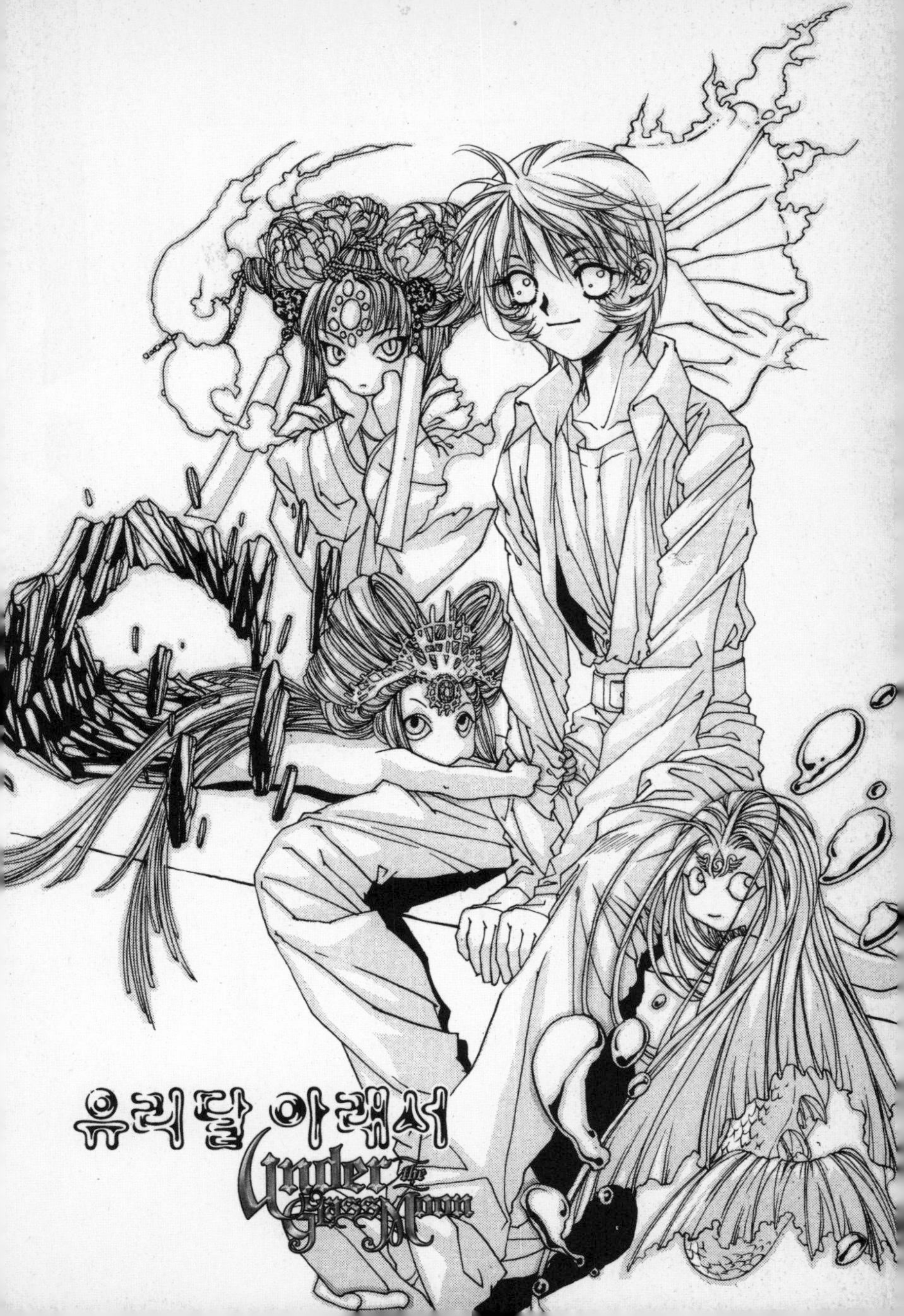
유리달 아래서
Under the Glass Moon

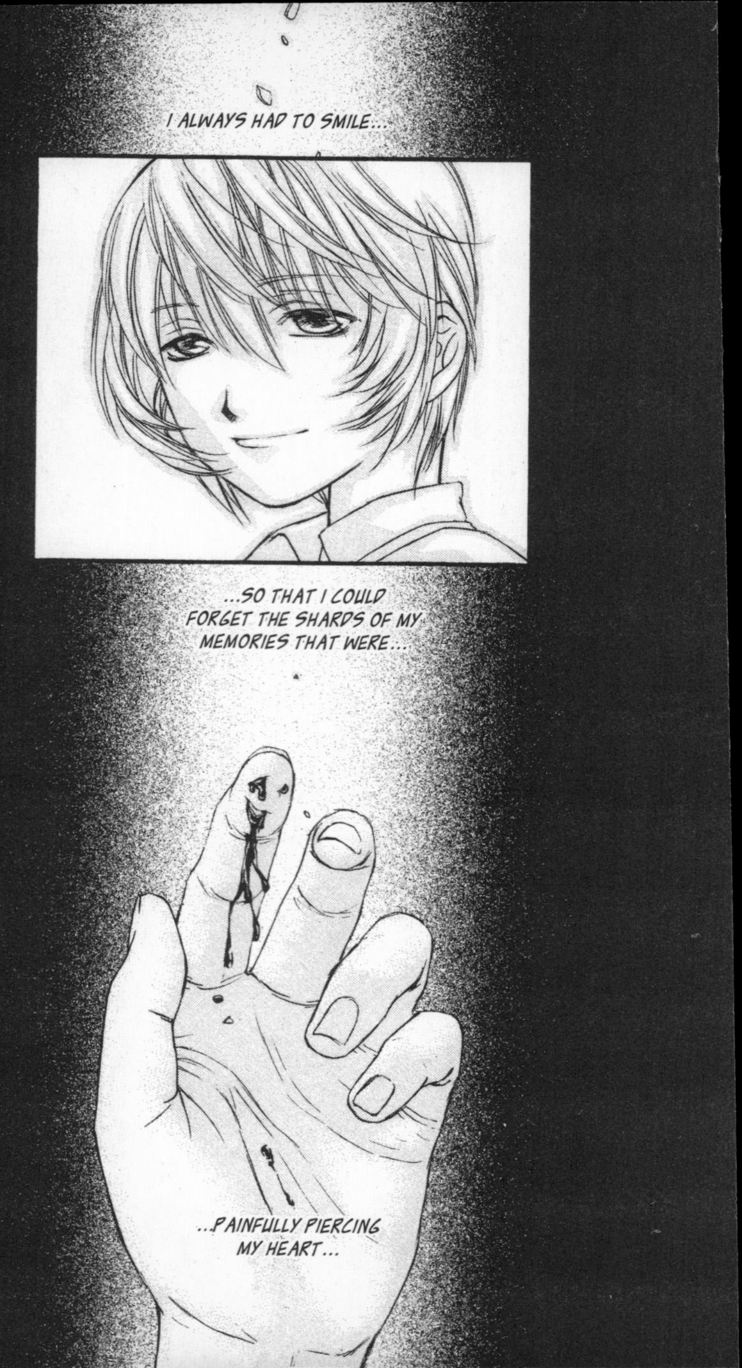
I ALWAYS HAD TO SMILE...
...SO THAT I COULD FORGET THE SHARDS OF MY MEMORIES THAT WERE...
...PAINFULLY PIERCING MY HEART...

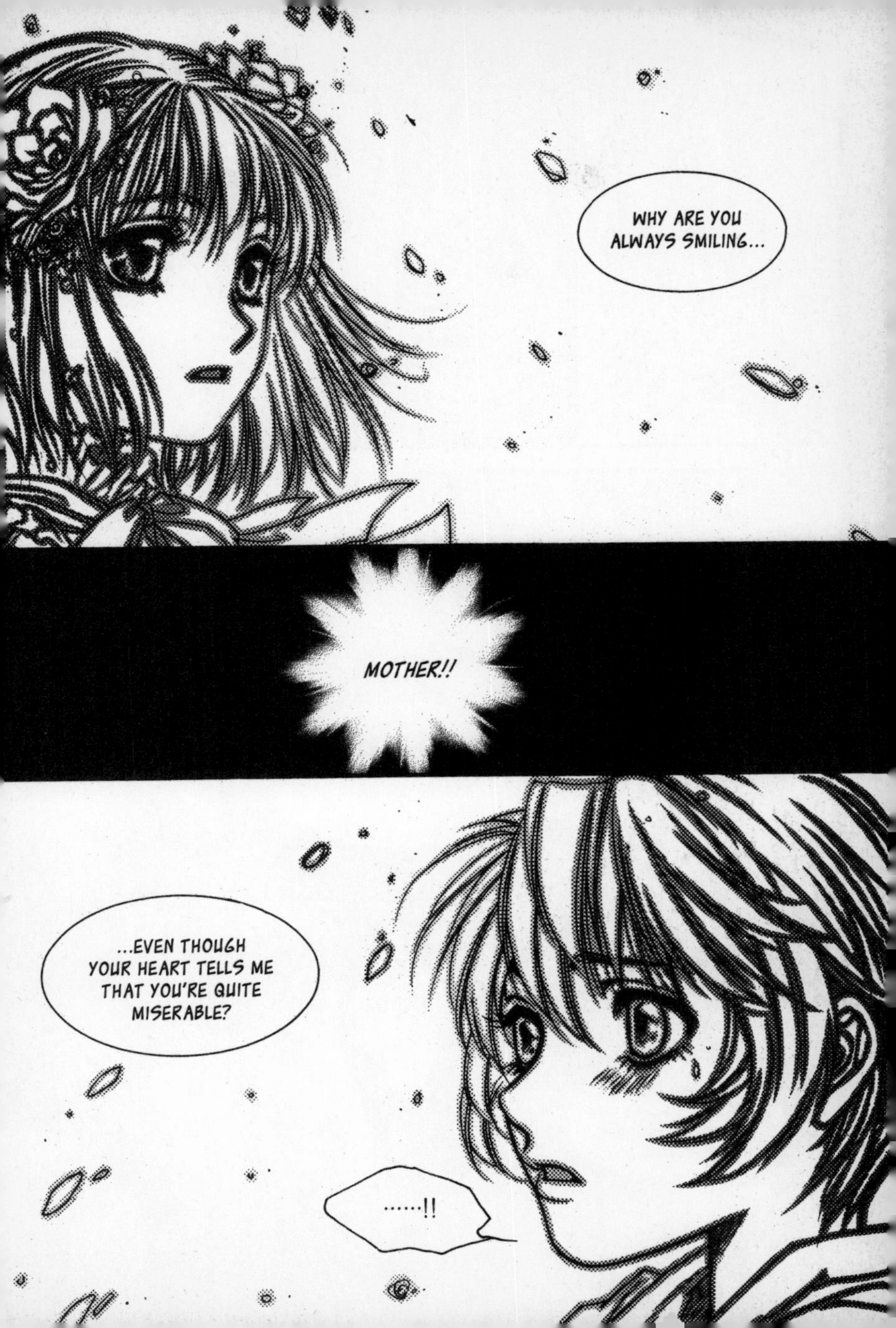
WHY ARE YOU ALWAYS SMILING...
MOTHER!!
...EVEN THOUGH YOUR HEART TELLS ME THAT YOU'RE QUITE MISERABLE?
......!!

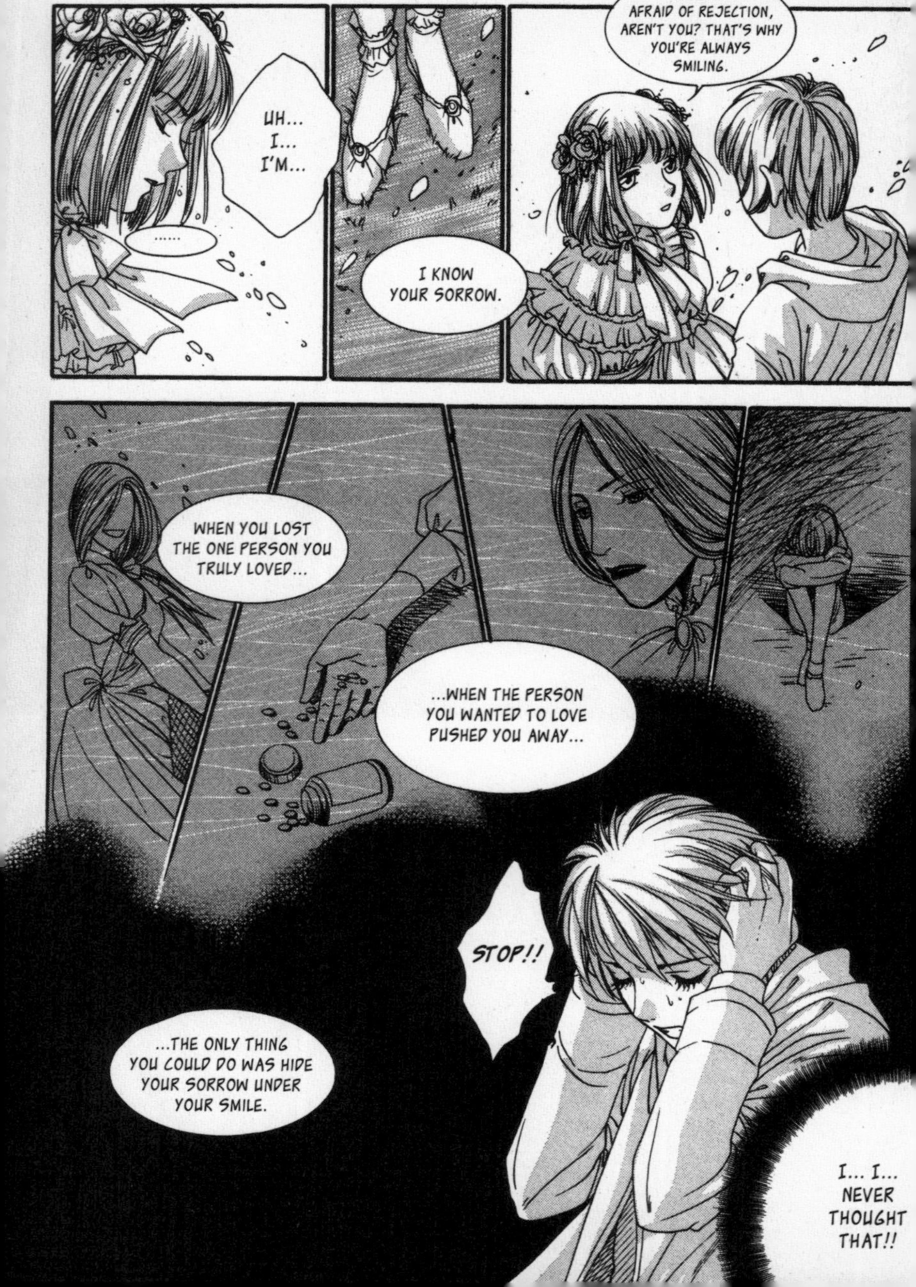
UH... I... I'M...
......
I KNOW YOUR SORROW.
YOU'RE AFRAID OF REJECTION, AREN'T YOU? THAT'S WHY YOU'RE ALWAYS SMILING.
WHEN YOU LOST THE ONE PERSON YOU TRULY LOVED...
...WHEN THE PERSON YOU WANTED TO LOVE PUSHED YOU AWAY...
STOP!!
...THE ONLY THING YOU COULD DO WAS HIDE YOUR SORROW UNDER YOUR SMILE.
I... I... NEVER THOUGHT THAT!!

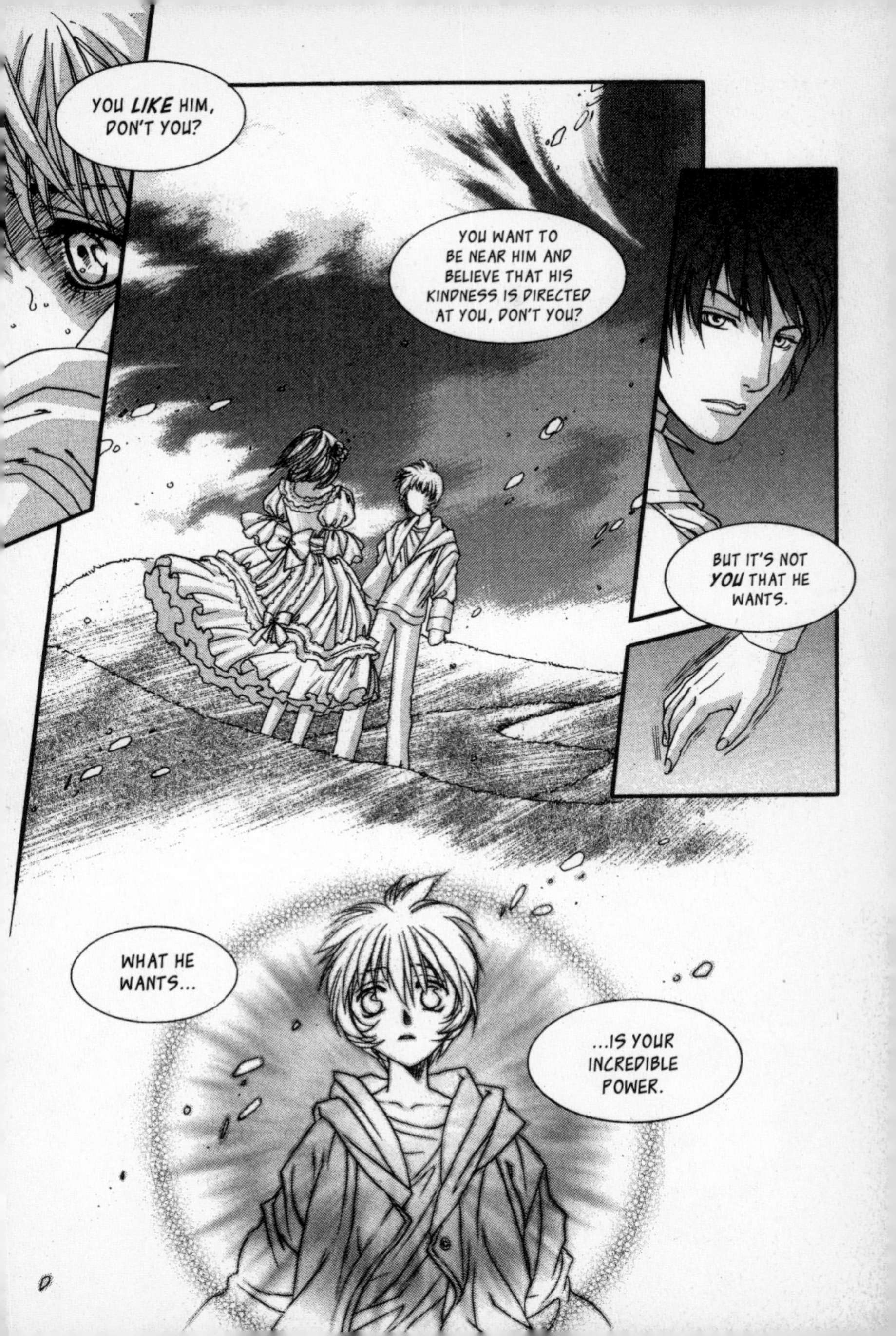
YOU *LIKE* HIM, DON'T YOU?
YOU WANT TO BE NEAR HIM AND BELIEVE THAT HIS KINDNESS IS DIRECTED AT YOU, DON'T YOU?
BUT IT'S NOT *YOU* THAT HE WANTS.
WHAT HE WANTS...
...IS YOUR INCREDIBLE POWER.

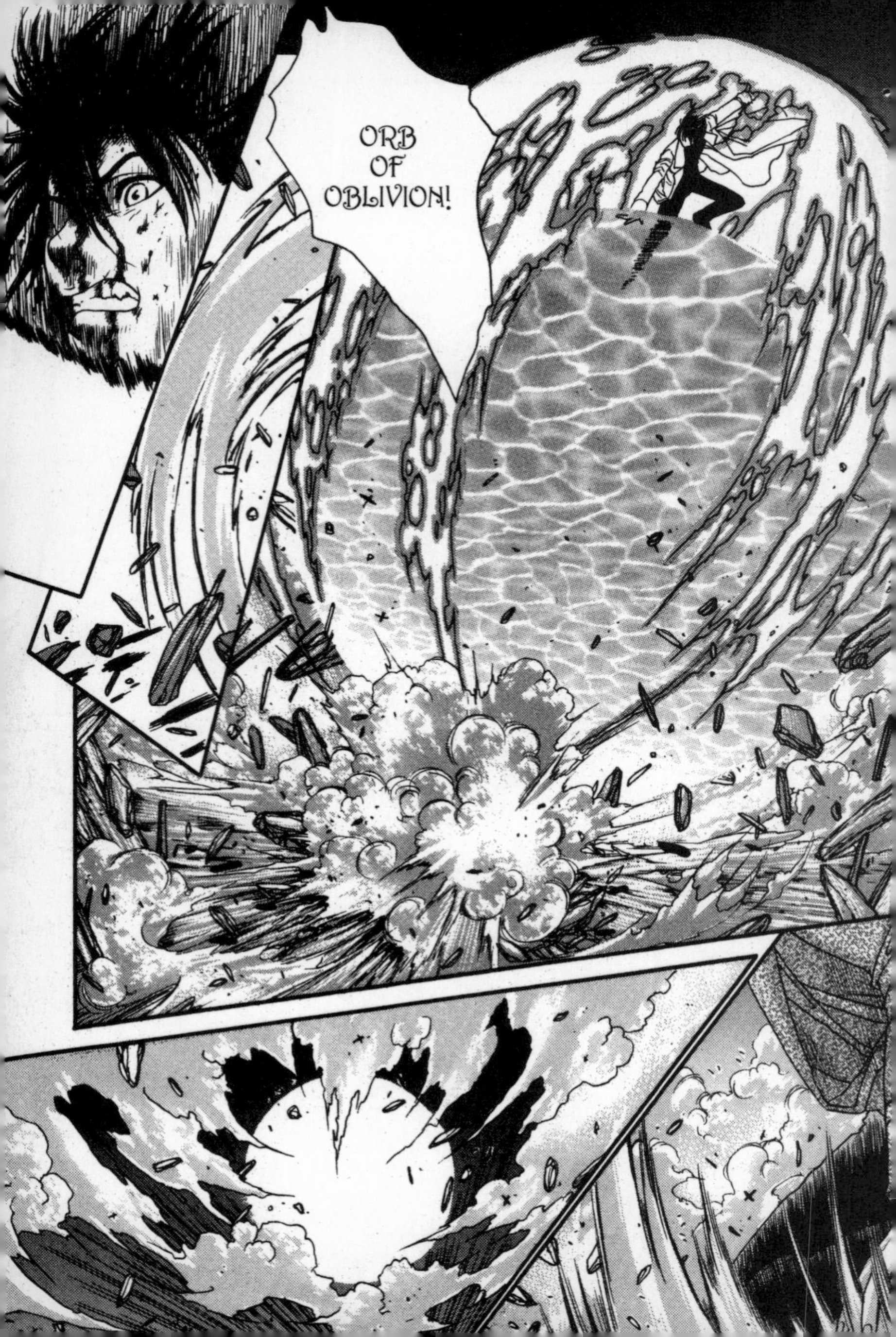
ORB OF OBLIVION!

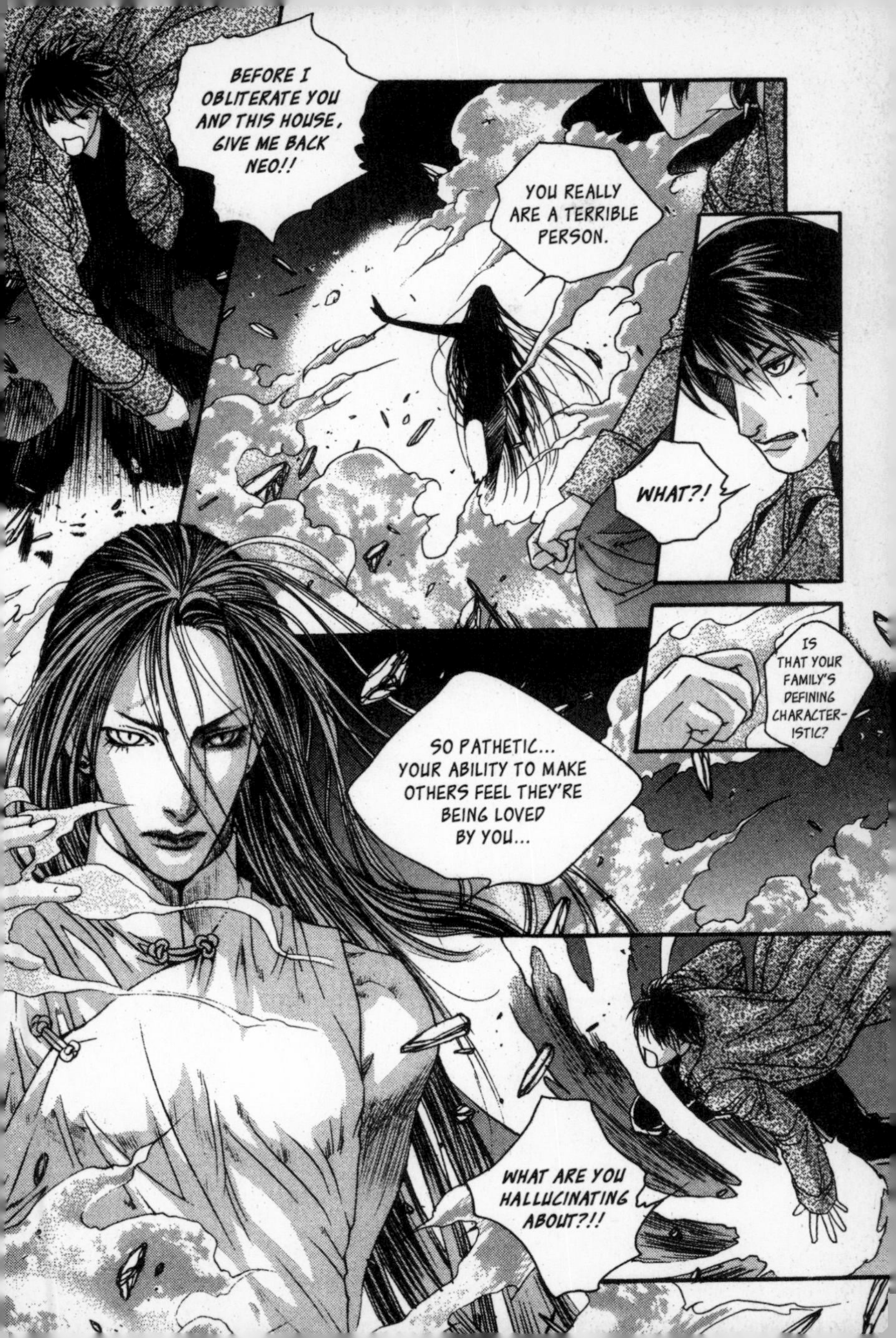
BEFORE I OBLITERATE YOU AND THIS HOUSE, GIVE ME BACK NEO!!
YOU REALLY ARE A TERRIBLE PERSON.
WHAT?!
SO PATHETIC... YOUR ABILITY TO MAKE OTHERS FEEL THEY'RE BEING LOVED BY YOU...
IS THAT YOUR FAMILY'S DEFINING CHARACTER-ISTIC?
WHAT ARE YOU HALLUCINATING ABOUT?!!

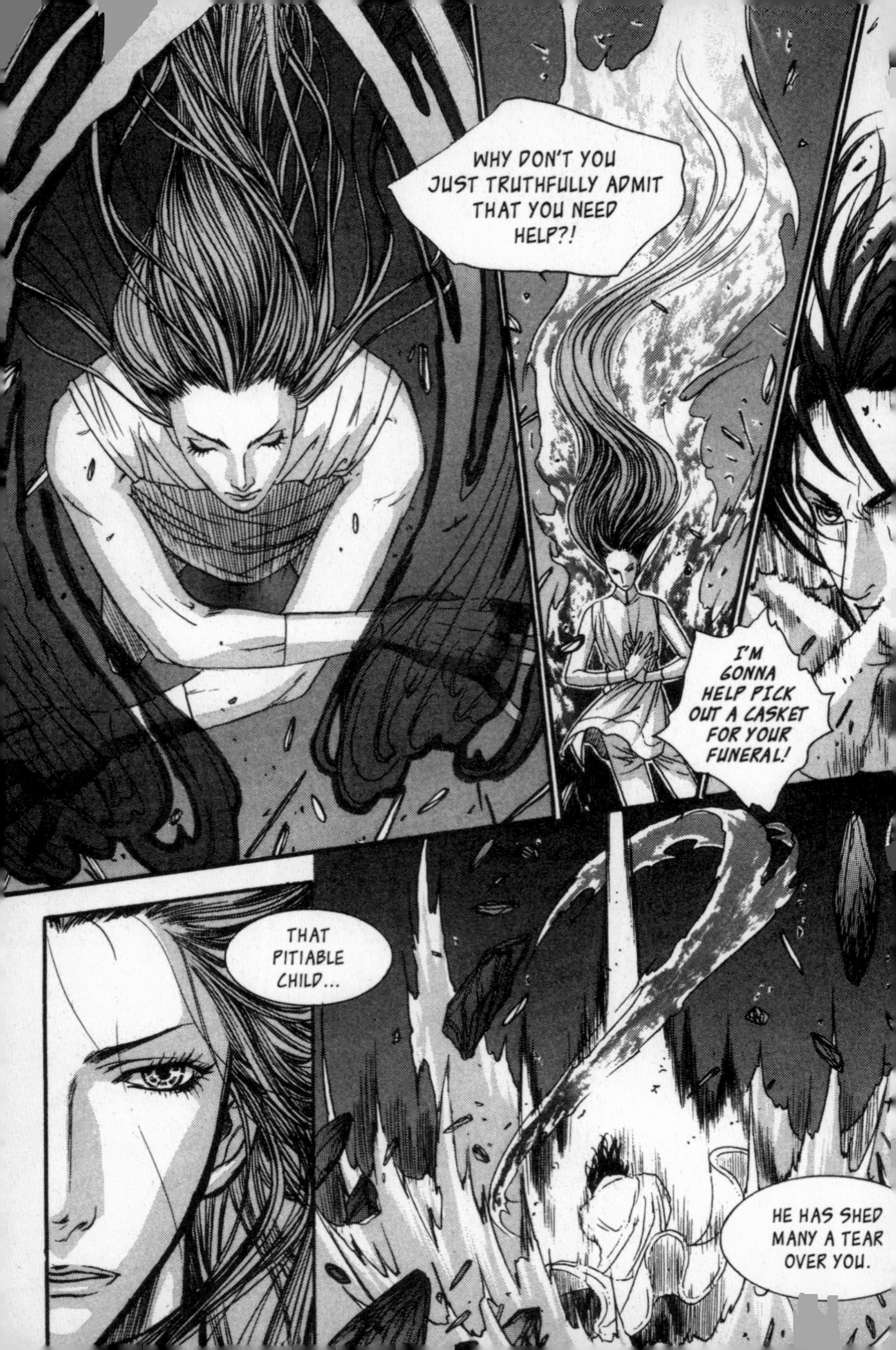
WHY DON'T YOU JUST TRUTHFULLY ADMIT THAT YOU NEED HELP?!
I'M GONNA HELP PICK OUT A CASKET FOR YOUR FUNERAL!
THAT PITIABLE CHILD...
HE HAS SHED MANY A TEAR OVER YOU.

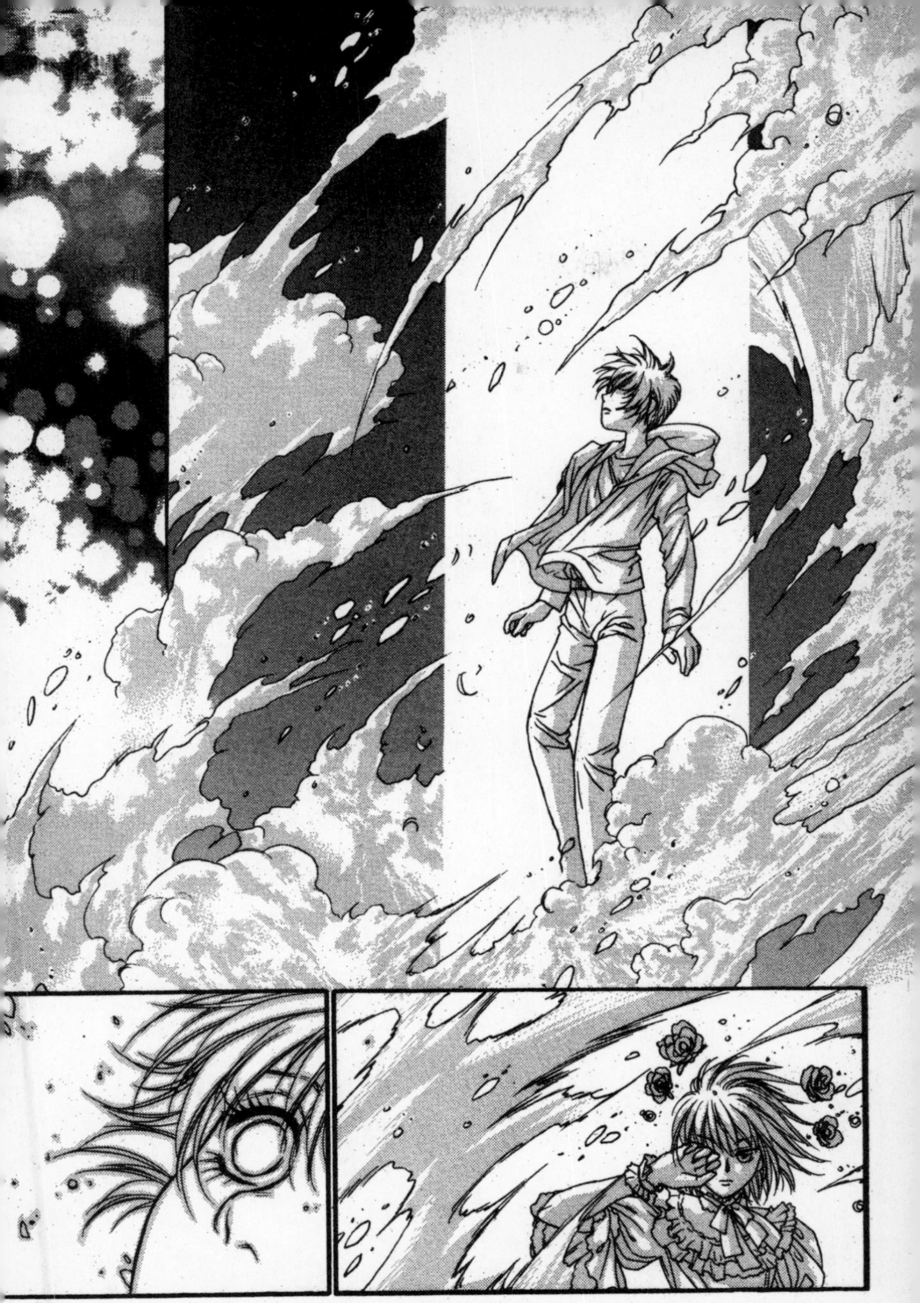

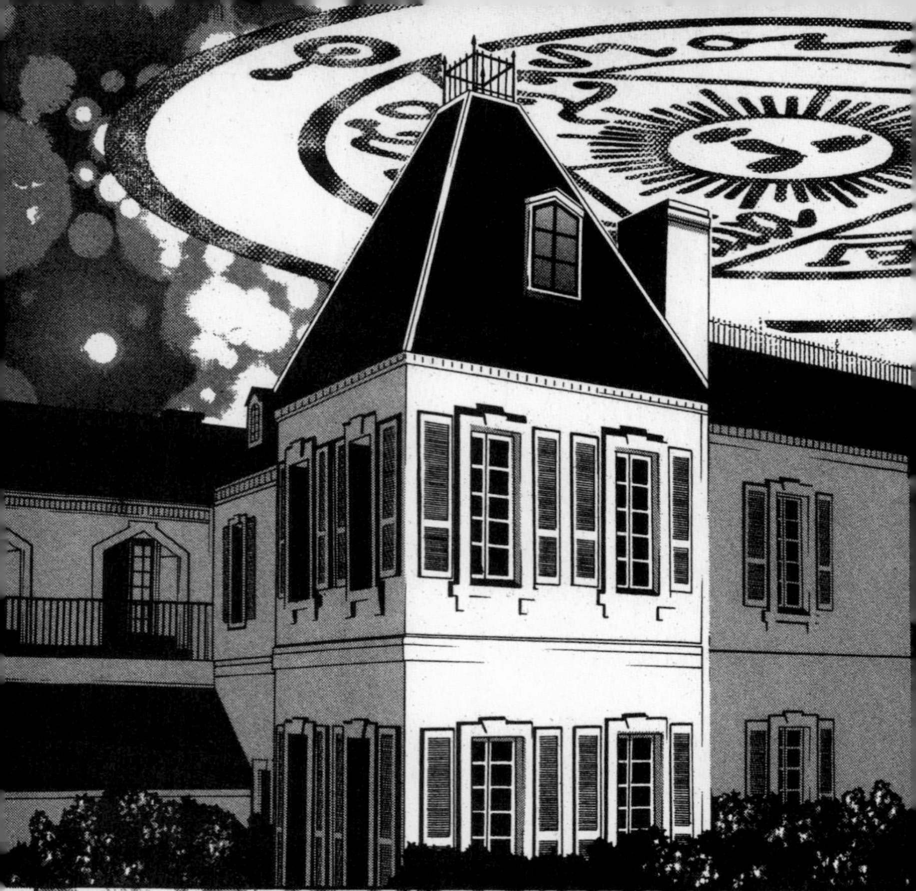
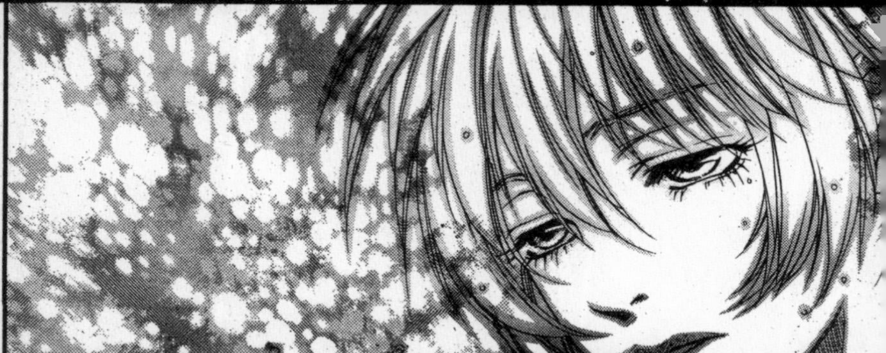

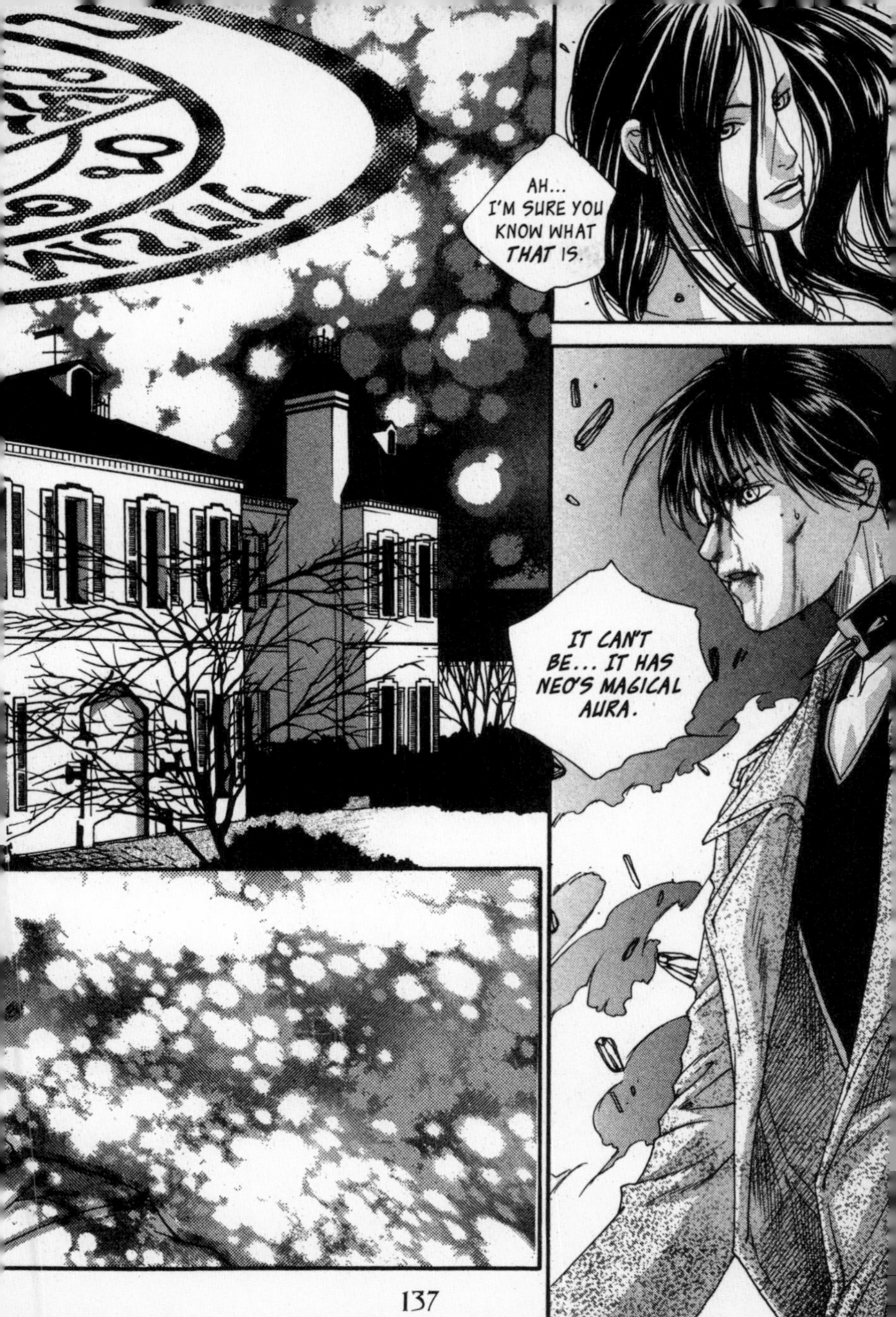
AH... I'M SURE YOU KNOW WHAT THAT IS.
IT CAN'T BE... IT HAS NEO'S MAGICAL AURA.

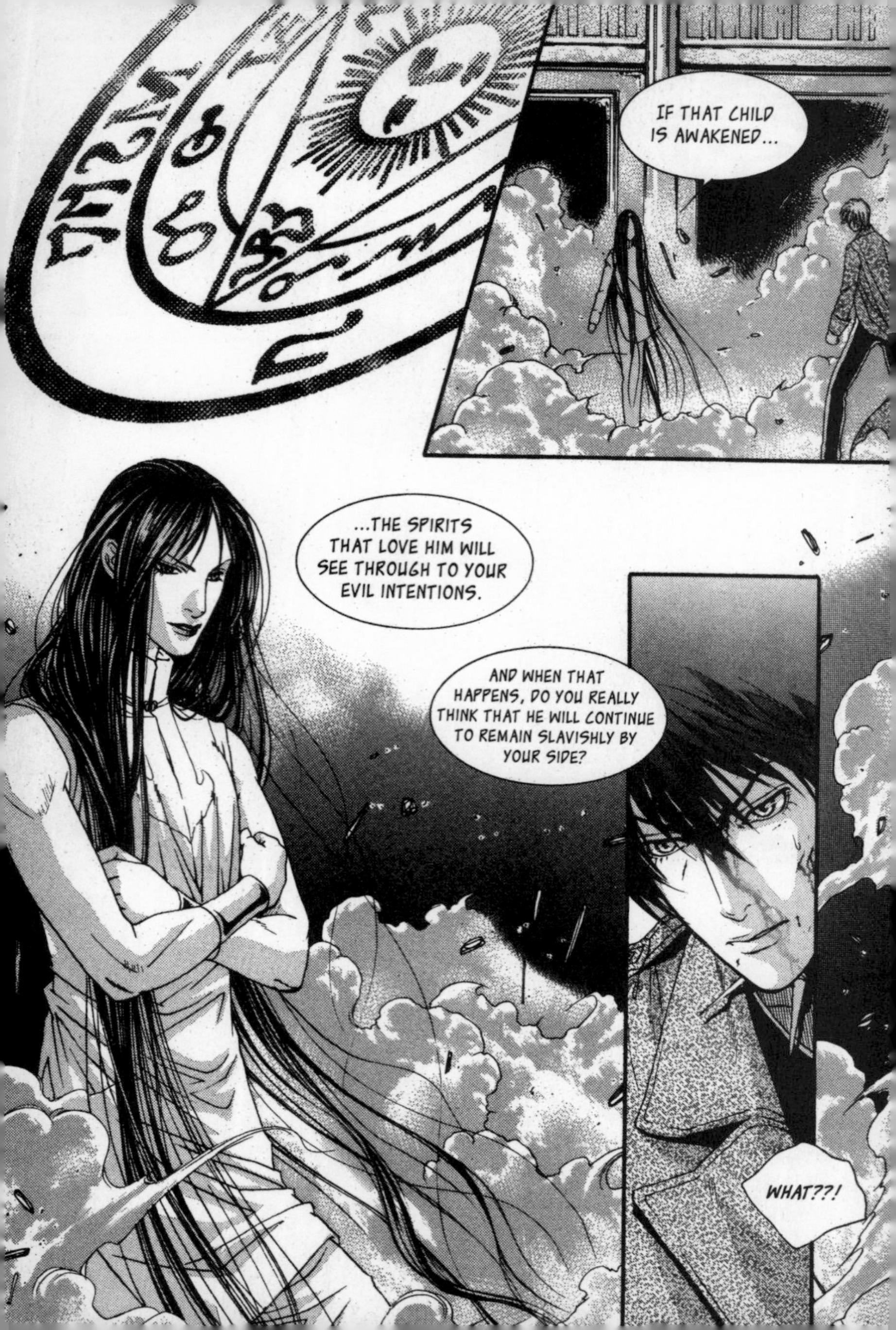
IF THAT CHILD IS AWAKENED...
...THE SPIRITS THAT LOVE HIM WILL SEE THROUGH TO YOUR EVIL INTENTIONS.
AND WHEN THAT HAPPENS, DO YOU REALLY THINK THAT HE WILL CONTINUE TO REMAIN SLAVISHLY BY YOUR SIDE?
WHAT??!

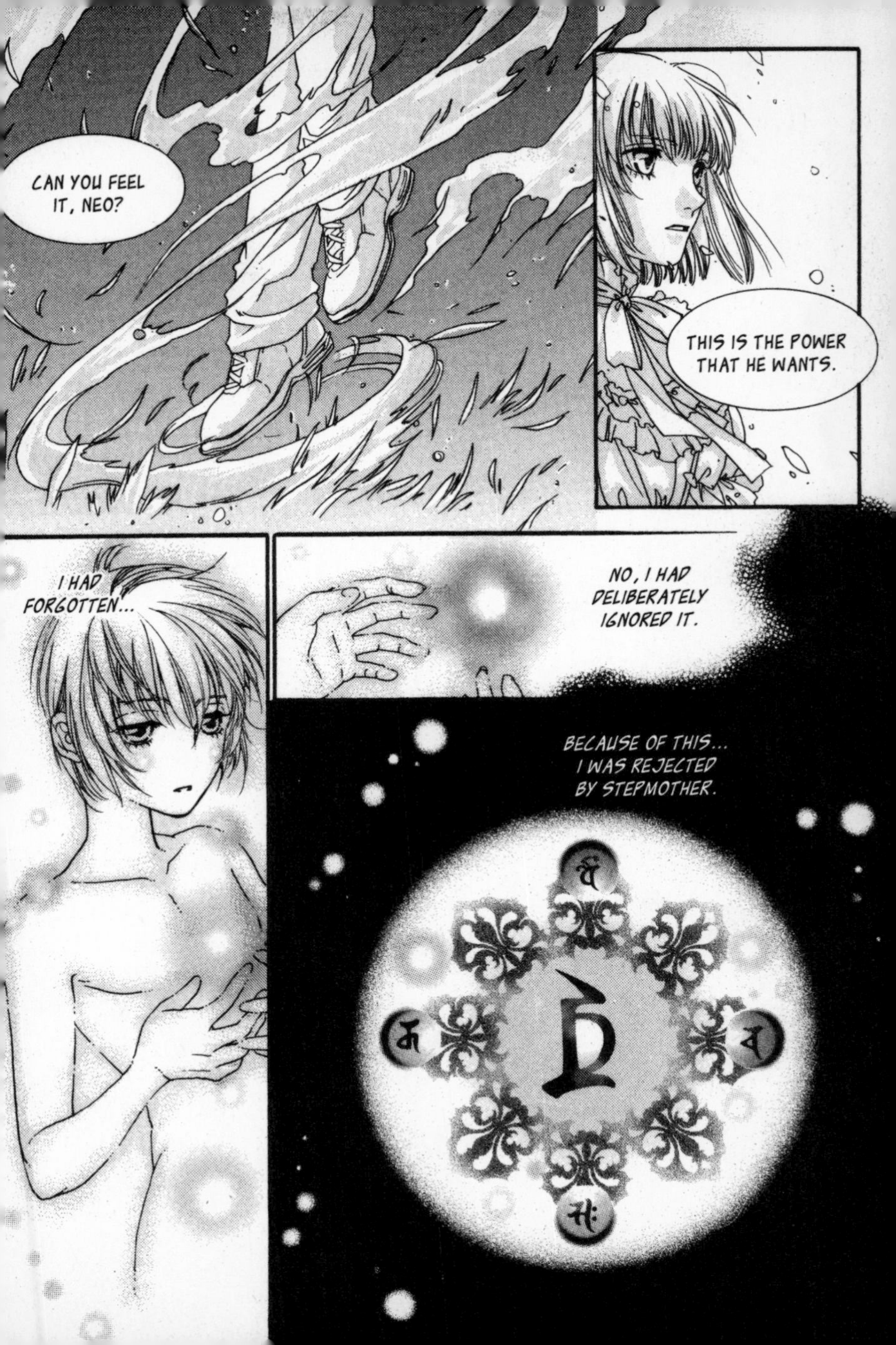
CAN YOU FEEL IT, NEO?
THIS IS THE POWER THAT HE WANTS.
I HAD FORGOTTEN...
NO, I HAD DELIBERATELY IGNORED IT.
BECAUSE OF THIS... I WAS REJECTED BY STEPMOTHER.

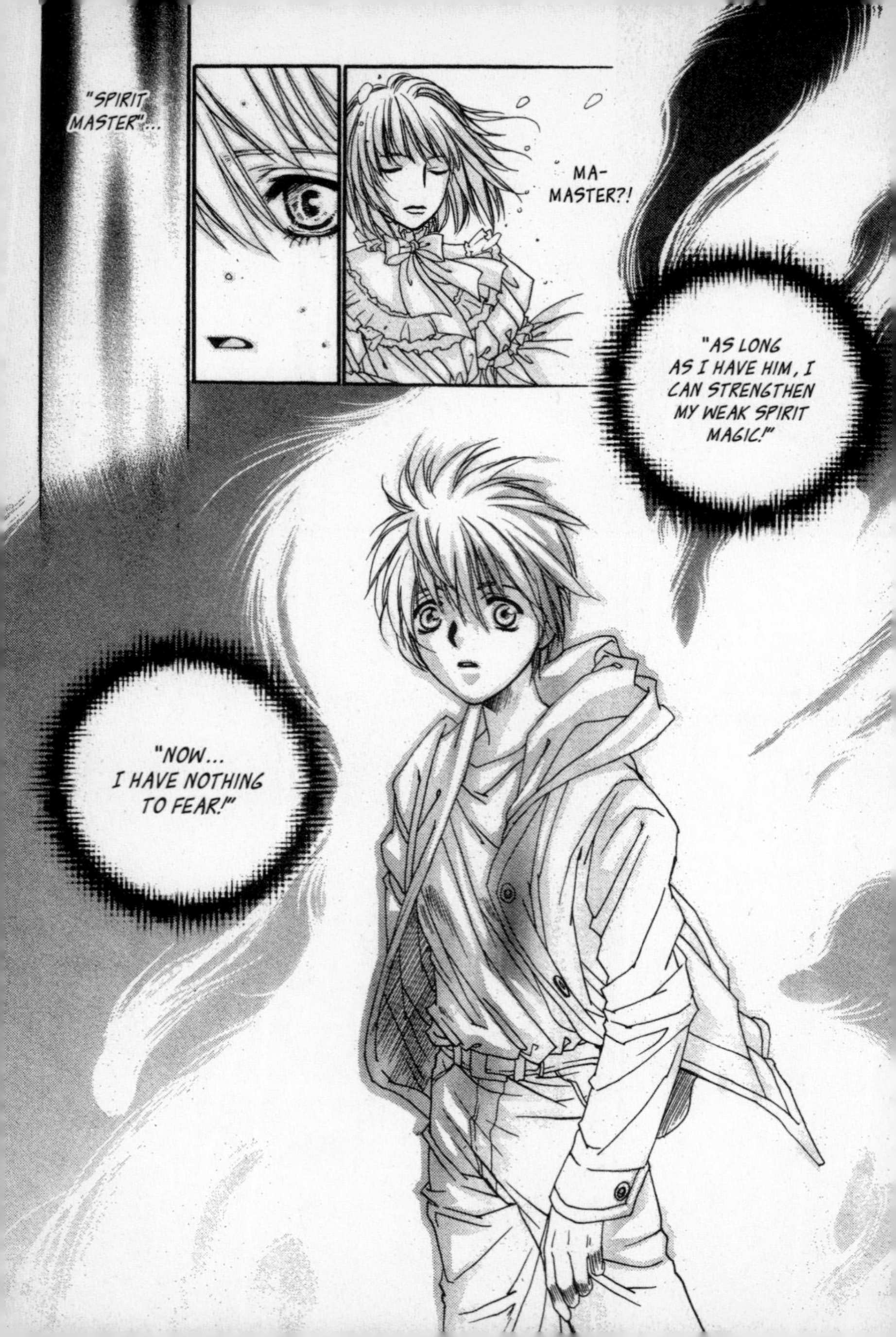
"SPIRIT MASTER"...
MA- MASTER?!
"AS LONG AS I HAVE HIM, I CAN STRENGTHEN MY WEAK SPIRIT MAGIC!"
"NOW... I HAVE NOTHING TO FEAR!"

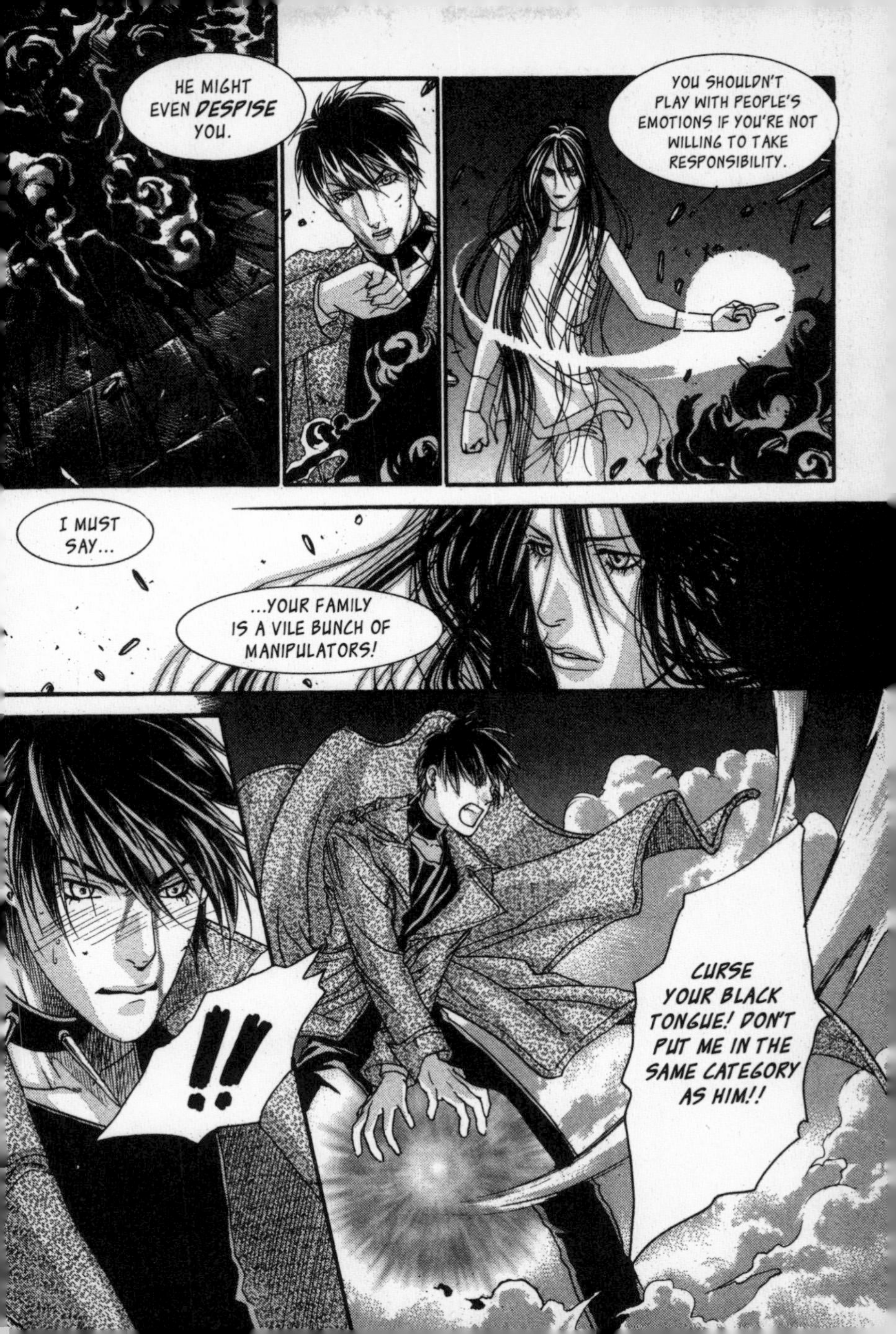
HE MIGHT EVEN DESPISE YOU.
YOU SHOULDN'T PLAY WITH PEOPLE'S EMOTIONS IF YOU'RE NOT WILLING TO TAKE RESPONSIBILITY.
I MUST SAY...
...YOUR FAMILY IS A VILE BUNCH OF MANIPULATORS!
!!
CURSE YOUR BLACK TONGUE! DON'T PUT ME IN THE SAME CATEGORY AS HIM!!

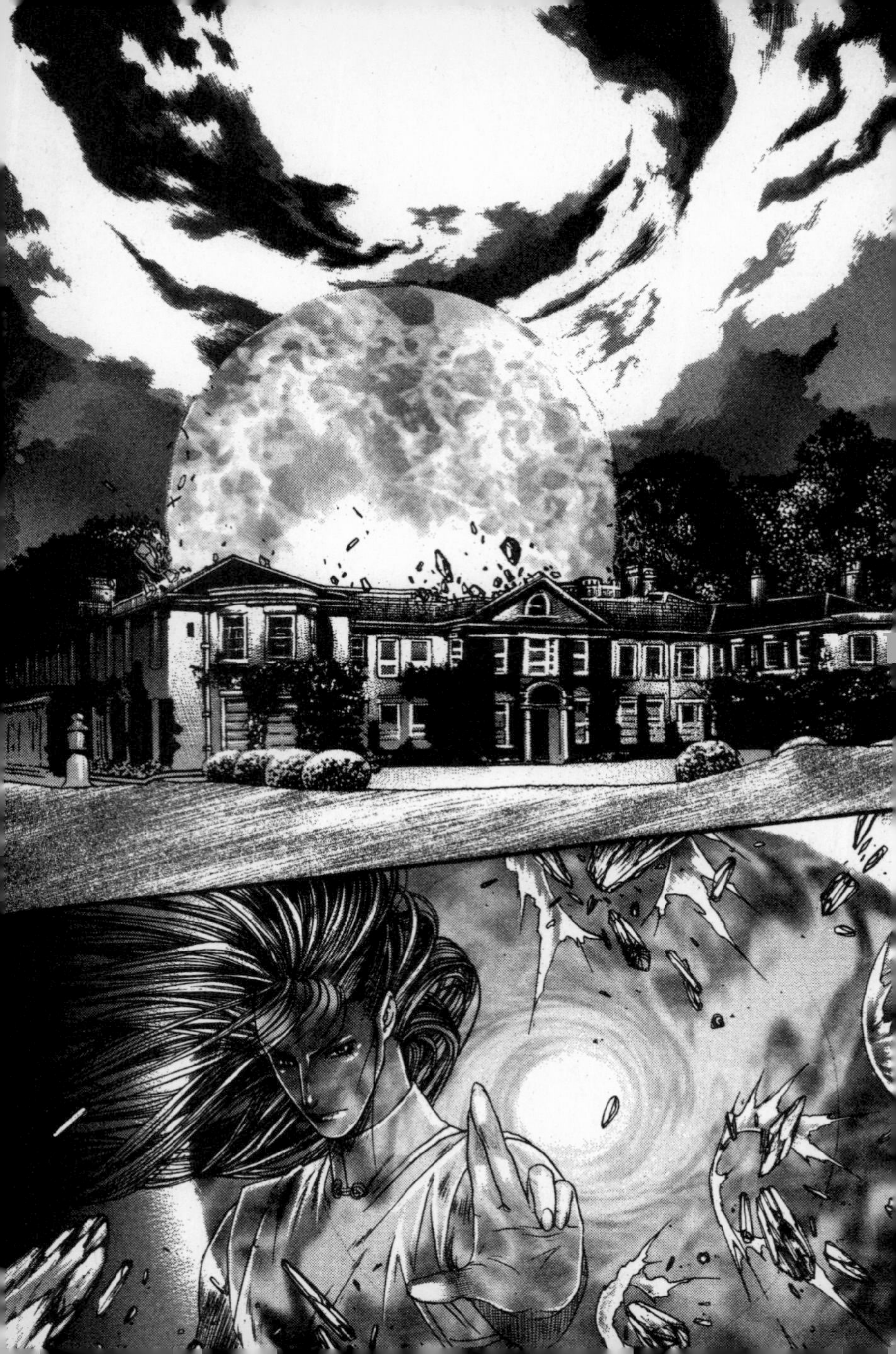

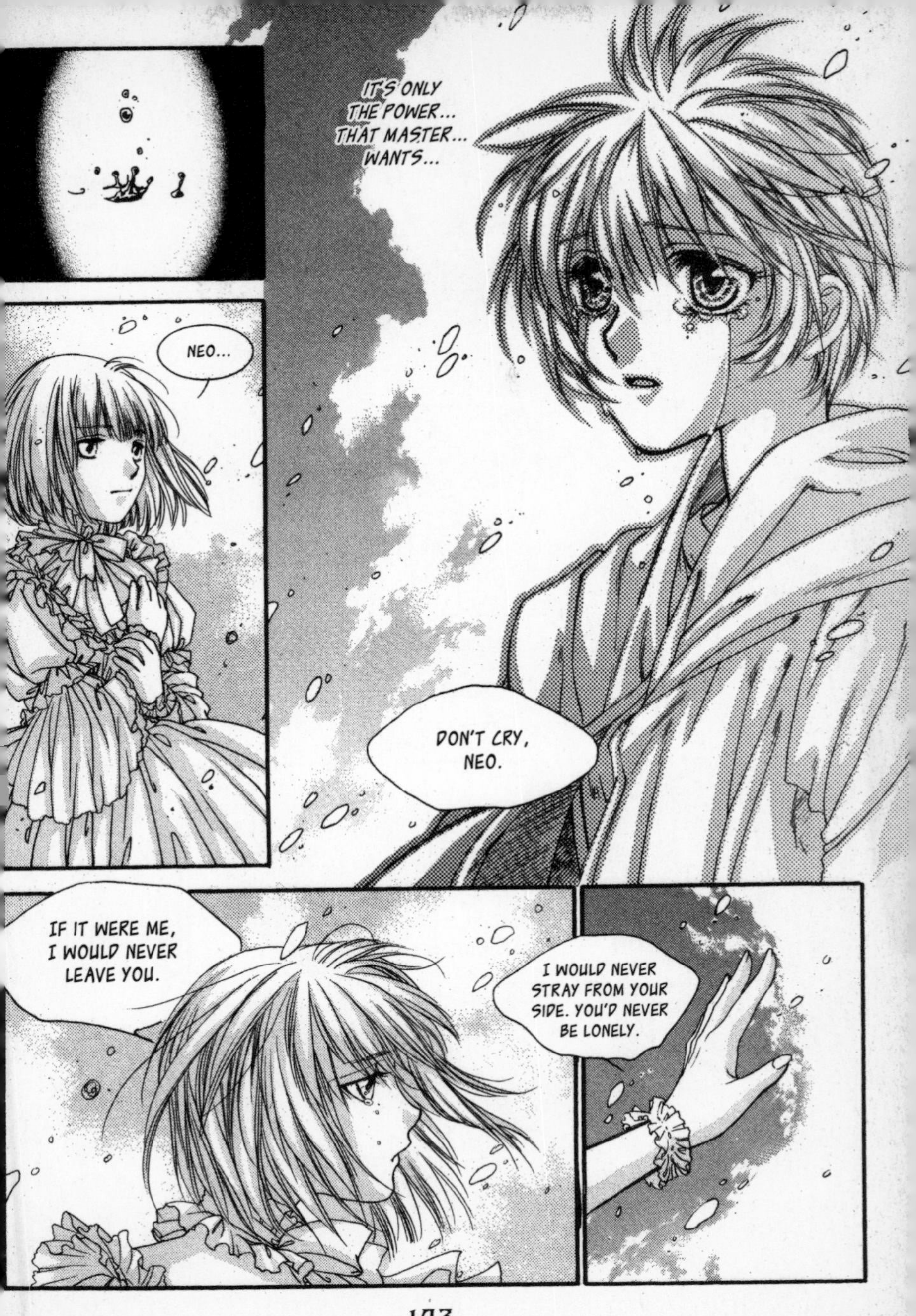
NEO...
IT'S ONLY THE POWER... THAT MASTER... WANTS...
DON'T CRY, NEO.
IF IT WERE ME, I WOULD NEVER LEAVE YOU.
I WOULD NEVER STRAY FROM YOUR SIDE. YOU'D NEVER BE LONELY.

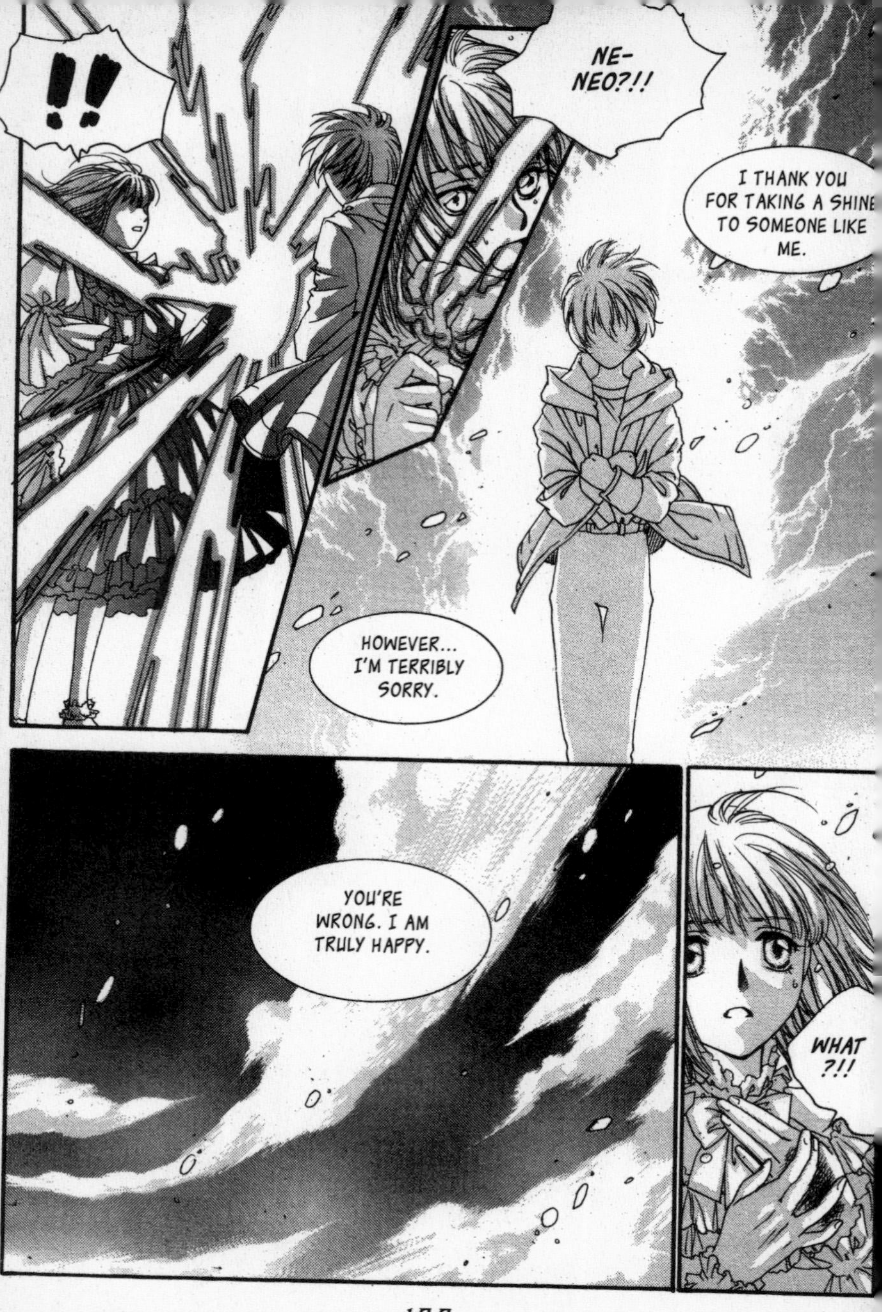

!!
NE-
NEO?!!
I THANK YOU
FOR TAKING A SHINE
TO SOMEONE LIKE
ME.
HOWEVER...
I'M TERRIBLY
SORRY.
YOU'RE
WRONG. I AM
TRULY HAPPY.
WHAT
?!!

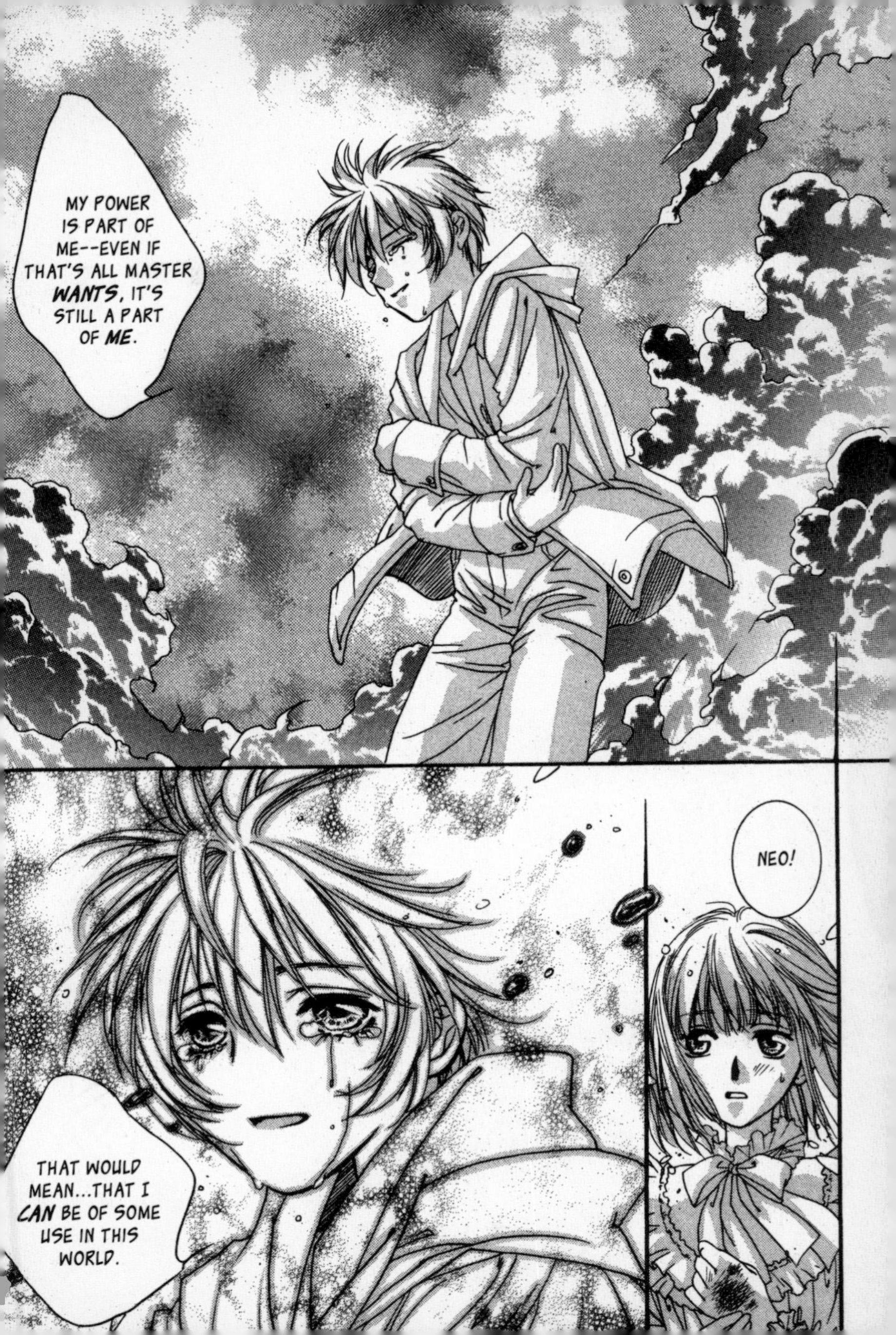
MY POWER IS PART OF ME--EVEN IF THAT'S ALL MASTER WANTS, IT'S STILL A PART OF ME.
NEO!
THAT WOULD MEAN...THAT I CAN BE OF SOME USE IN THIS WORLD.

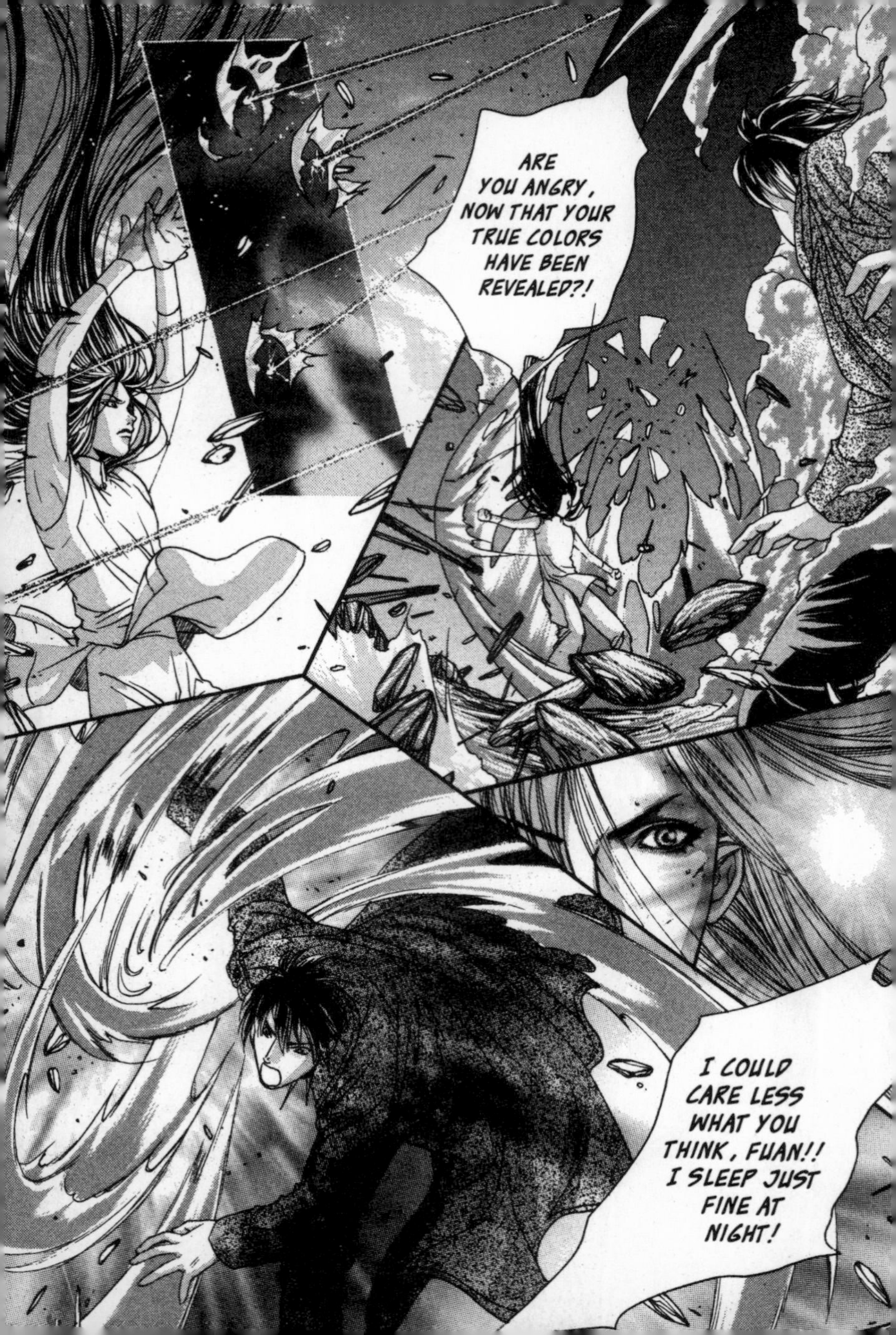
ARE YOU ANGRY, NOW THAT YOUR TRUE COLORS HAVE BEEN REVEALED?!
I COULD CARE LESS WHAT YOU THINK, FUAN!! I SLEEP JUST FINE AT NIGHT!

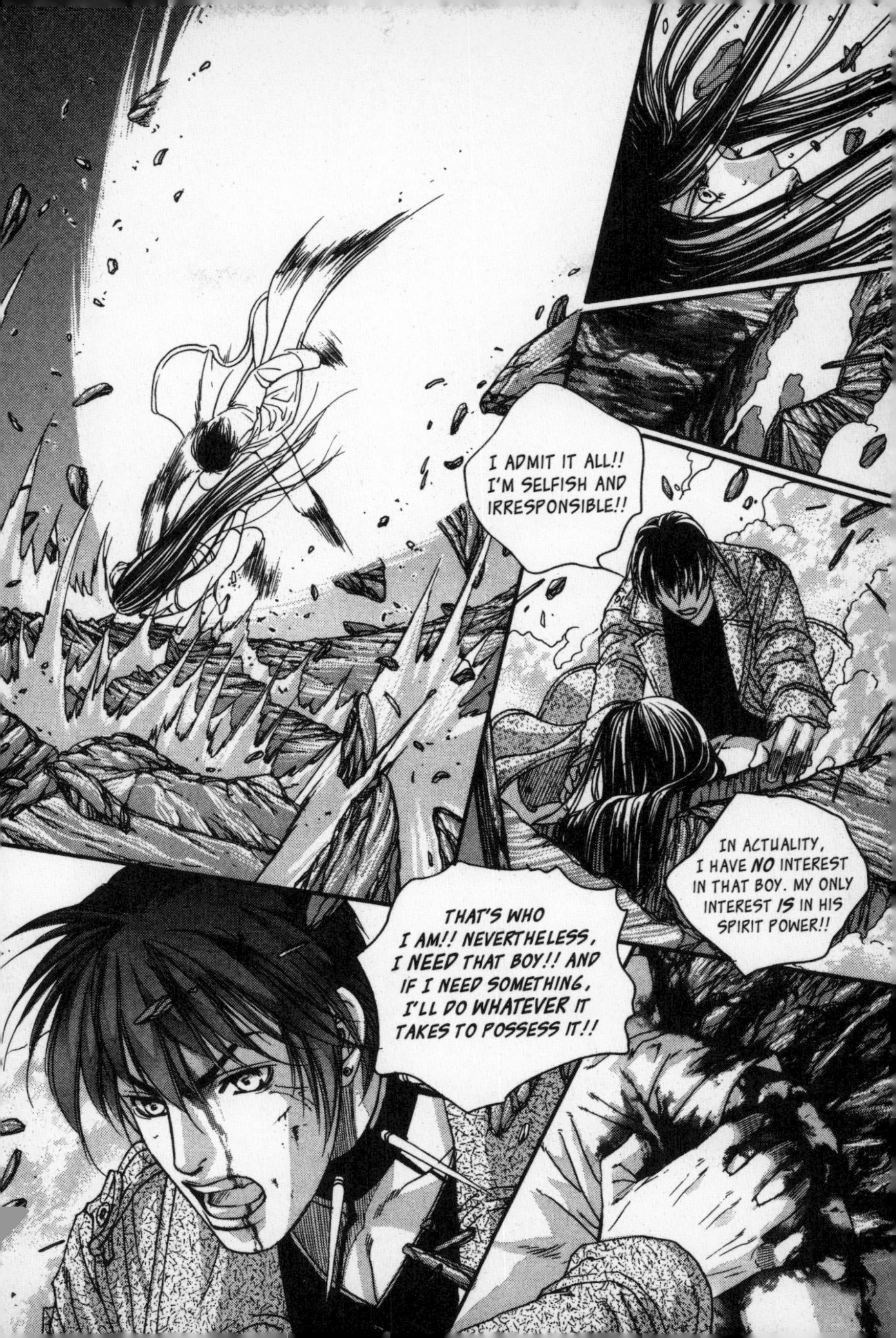
I ADMIT IT ALL!! I'M SELFISH AND IRRESPONSIBLE!!
THAT'S WHO I AM!! NEVERTHELESS, I NEED THAT BOY!!! AND IF I NEED SOMETHING, I'LL DO WHATEVER IT TAKES TO POSSESS IT!!
IN ACTUALITY, I HAVE NO INTEREST IN THAT BOY. MY ONLY INTEREST IS IN HIS SPIRIT POWER!!

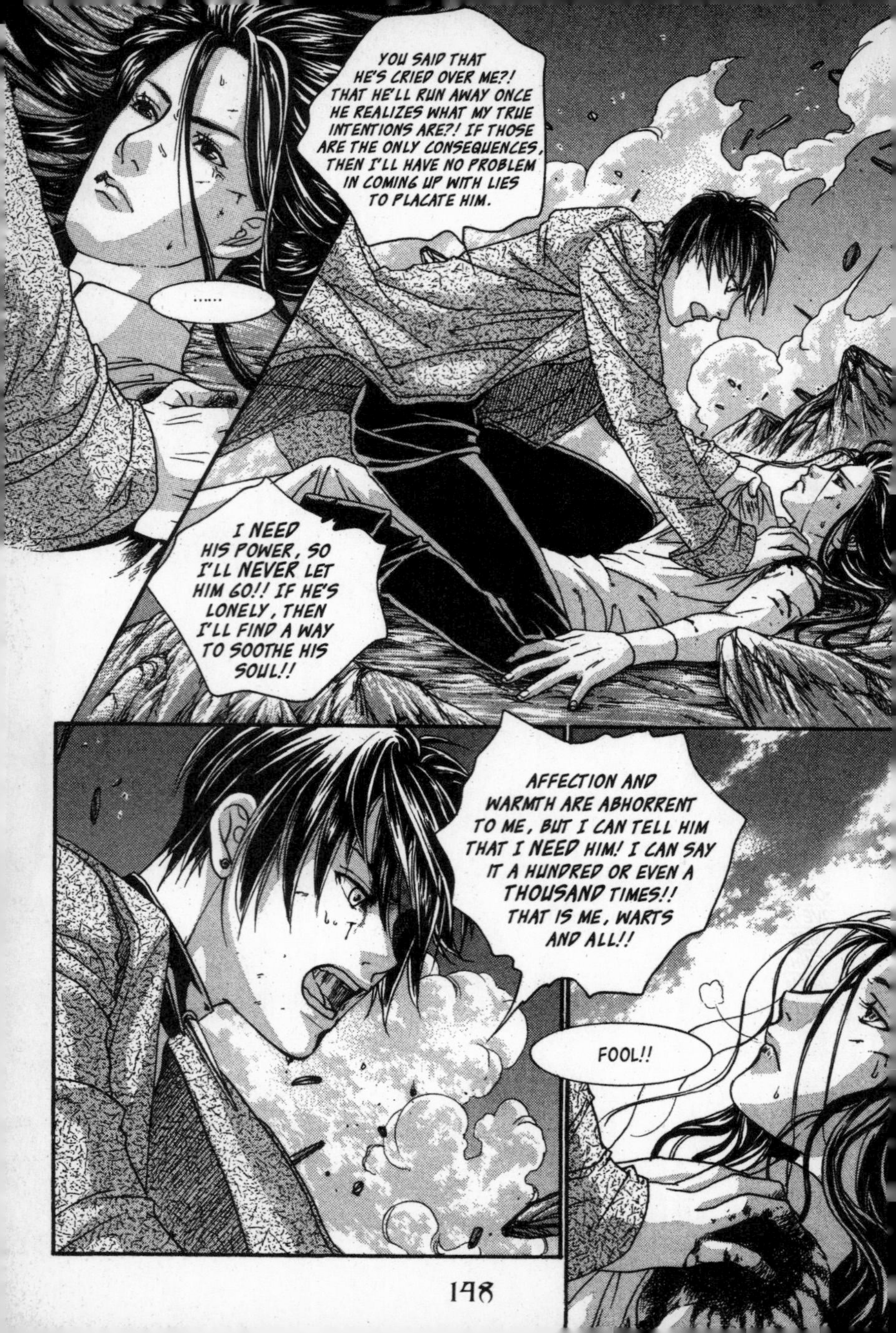
YOU SAID THAT HE'S CRIED OVER ME?! THAT HE'LL RUN AWAY ONCE HE REALIZES WHAT MY TRUE INTENTIONS ARE?! IF THOSE ARE THE ONLY CONSEQUENCES, THEN I'LL HAVE NO PROBLEM IN COMING UP WITH LIES TO PLACATE HIM.
......
I NEED HIS POWER, SO I'LL NEVER LET HIM GO!! IF HE'S LONELY, THEN I'LL FIND A WAY TO SOOTHE HIS SOUL!!
AFFECTION AND WARMTH ARE ABHORRENT TO ME, BUT I CAN TELL HIM THAT I NEED HIM! I CAN SAY IT A HUNDRED OR EVEN A THOUSAND TIMES!! THAT IS ME, WARTS AND ALL!!
FOOL!!

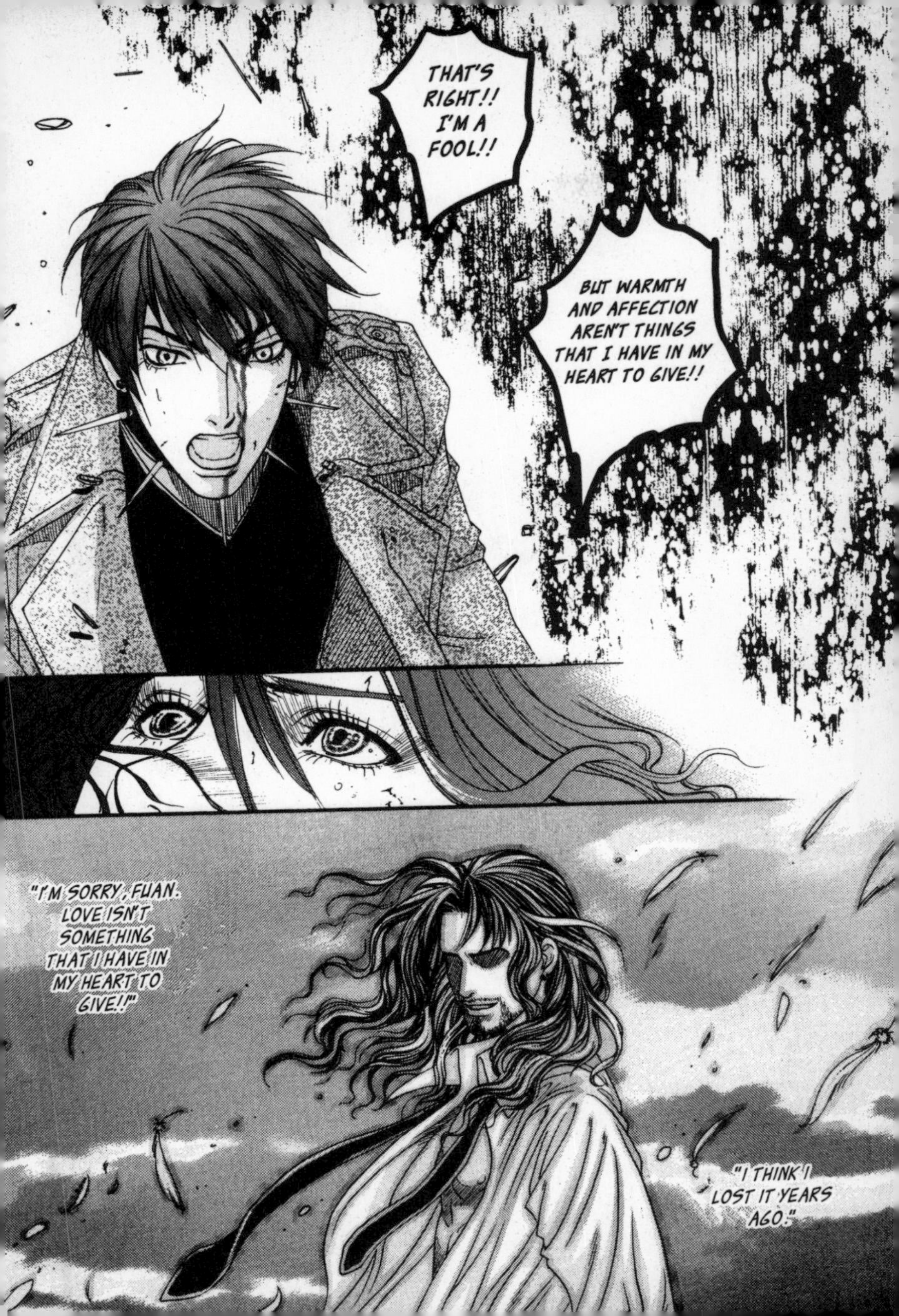
THAT'S RIGHT!! I'M A FOOL!!
BUT WARMTH AND AFFECTION AREN'T THINGS THAT I HAVE IN MY HEART TO GIVE!!
"I'M SORRY, FUAN. LOVE ISN'T SOMETHING THAT I HAVE IN MY HEART TO GIVE!!"
"I THINK I LOST IT YEARS AGO."

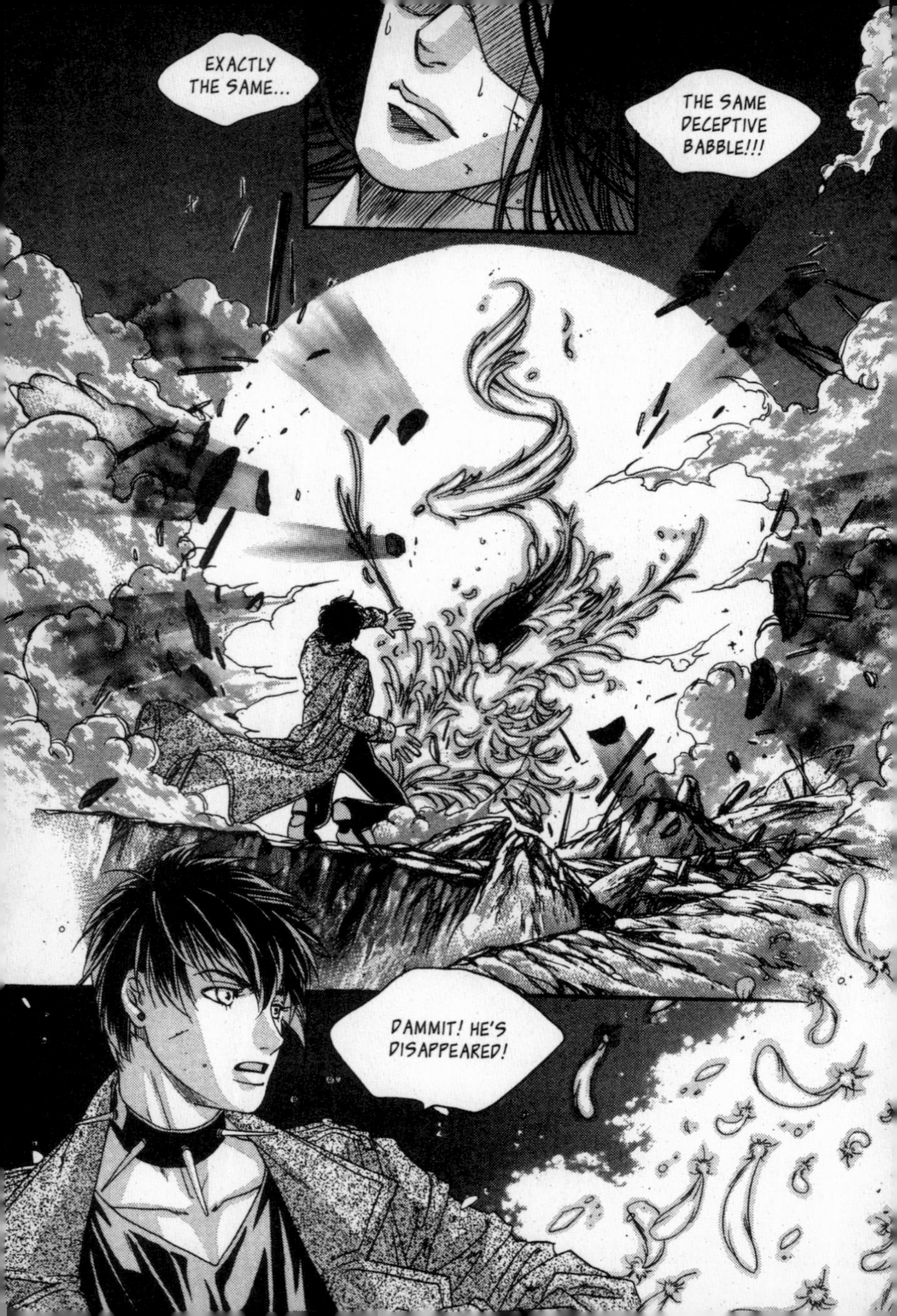
EXACTLY THE SAME...
THE SAME DECEPTIVE BABBLE!!!
DAMMIT! HE'S DISAPPEARED!

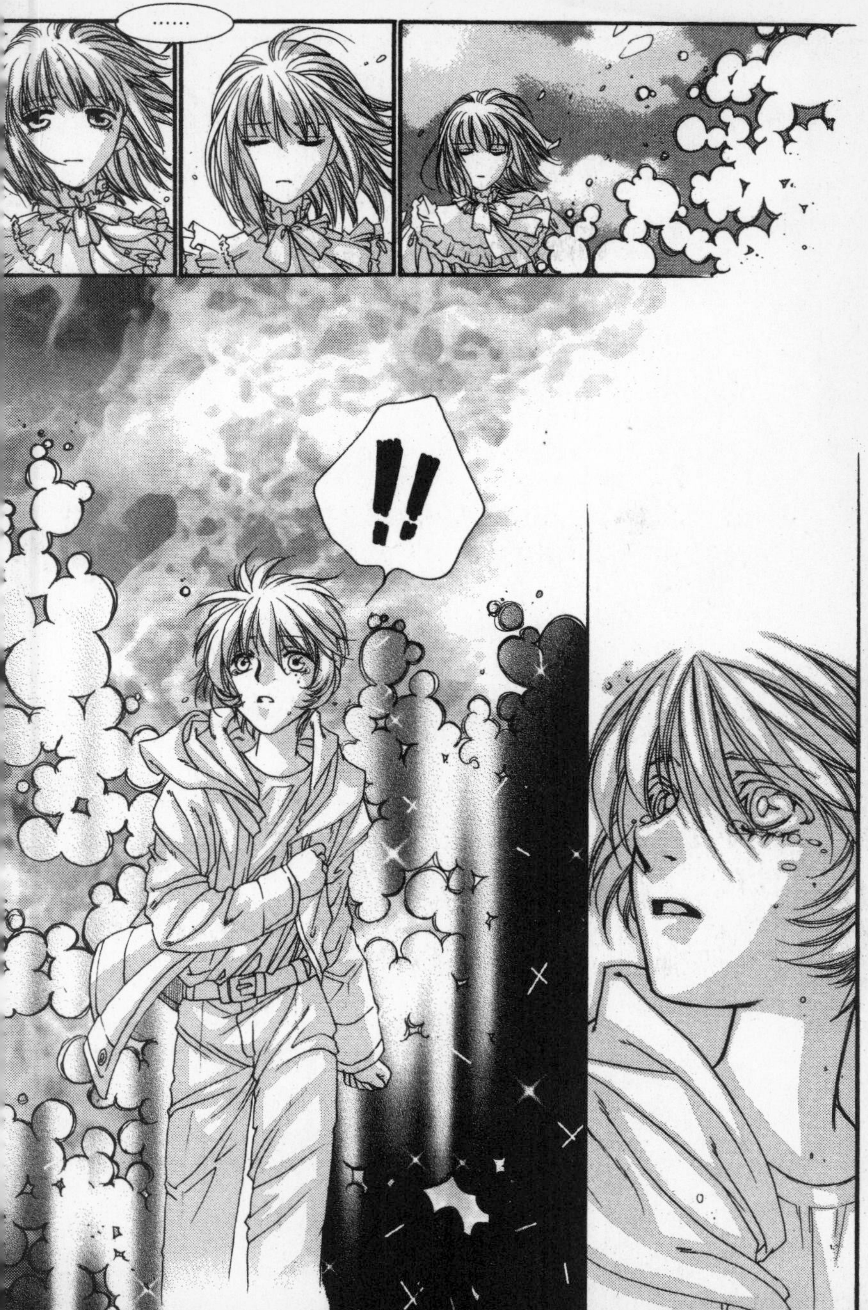
......
!!

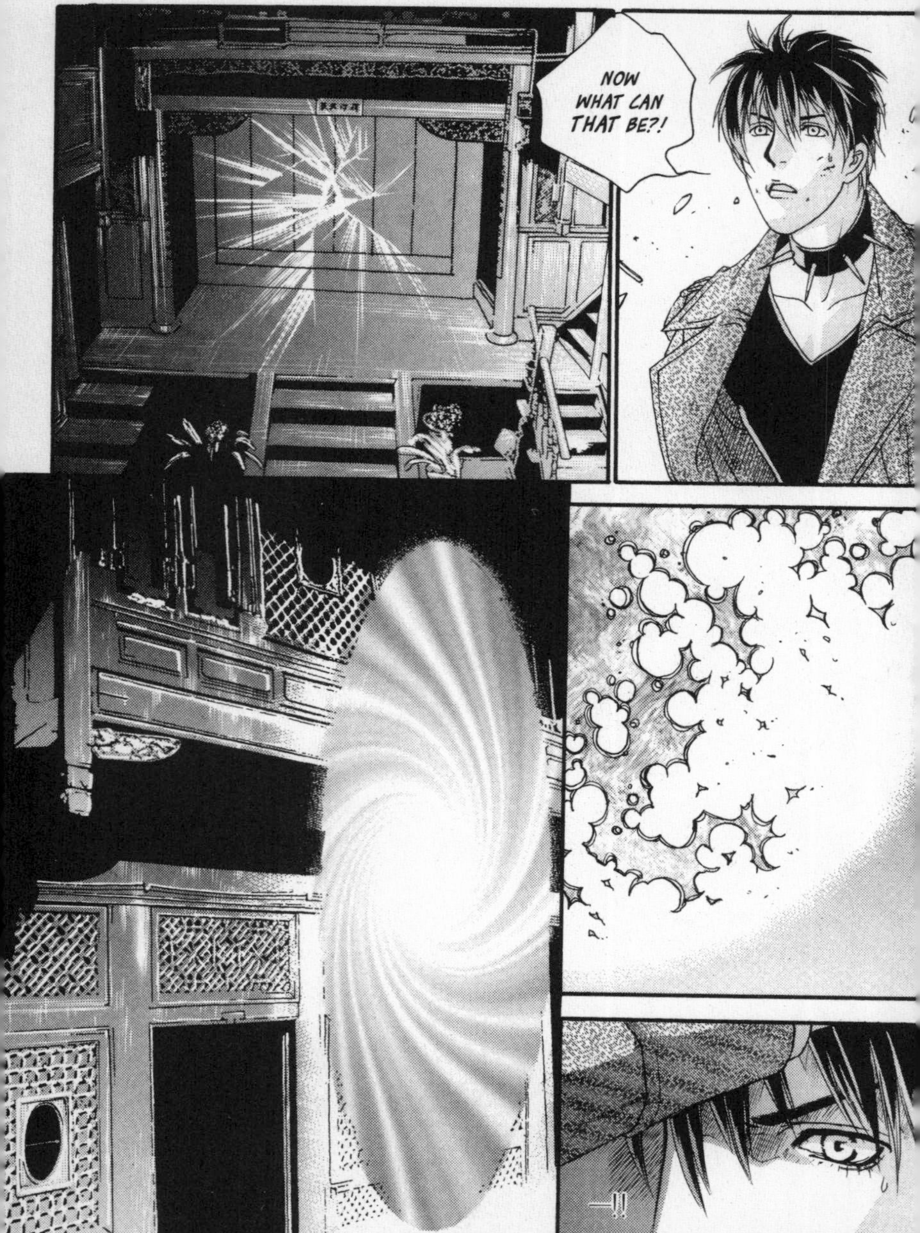
NOW WHAT CAN THAT BE?!
—!!

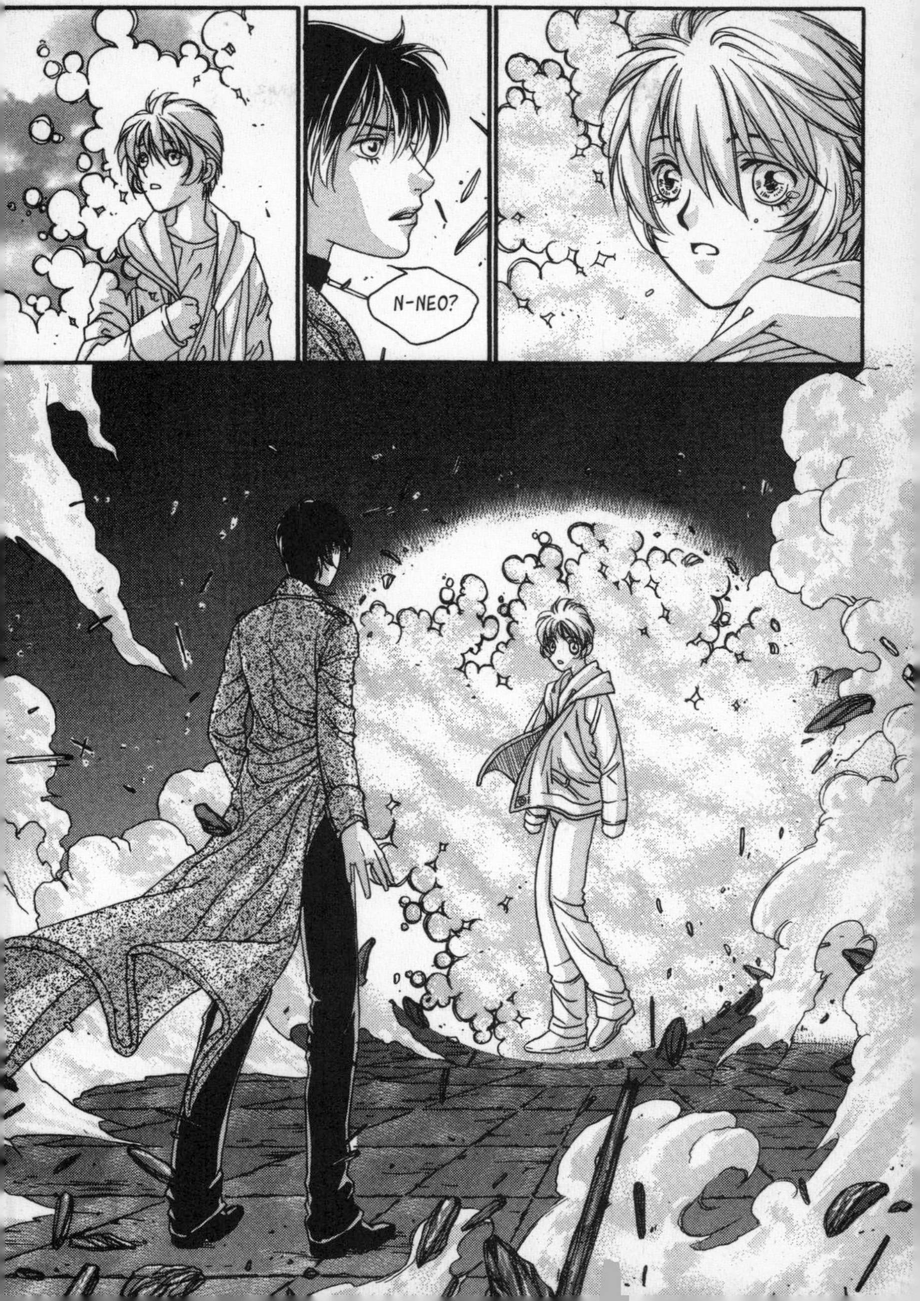
N-NEO?

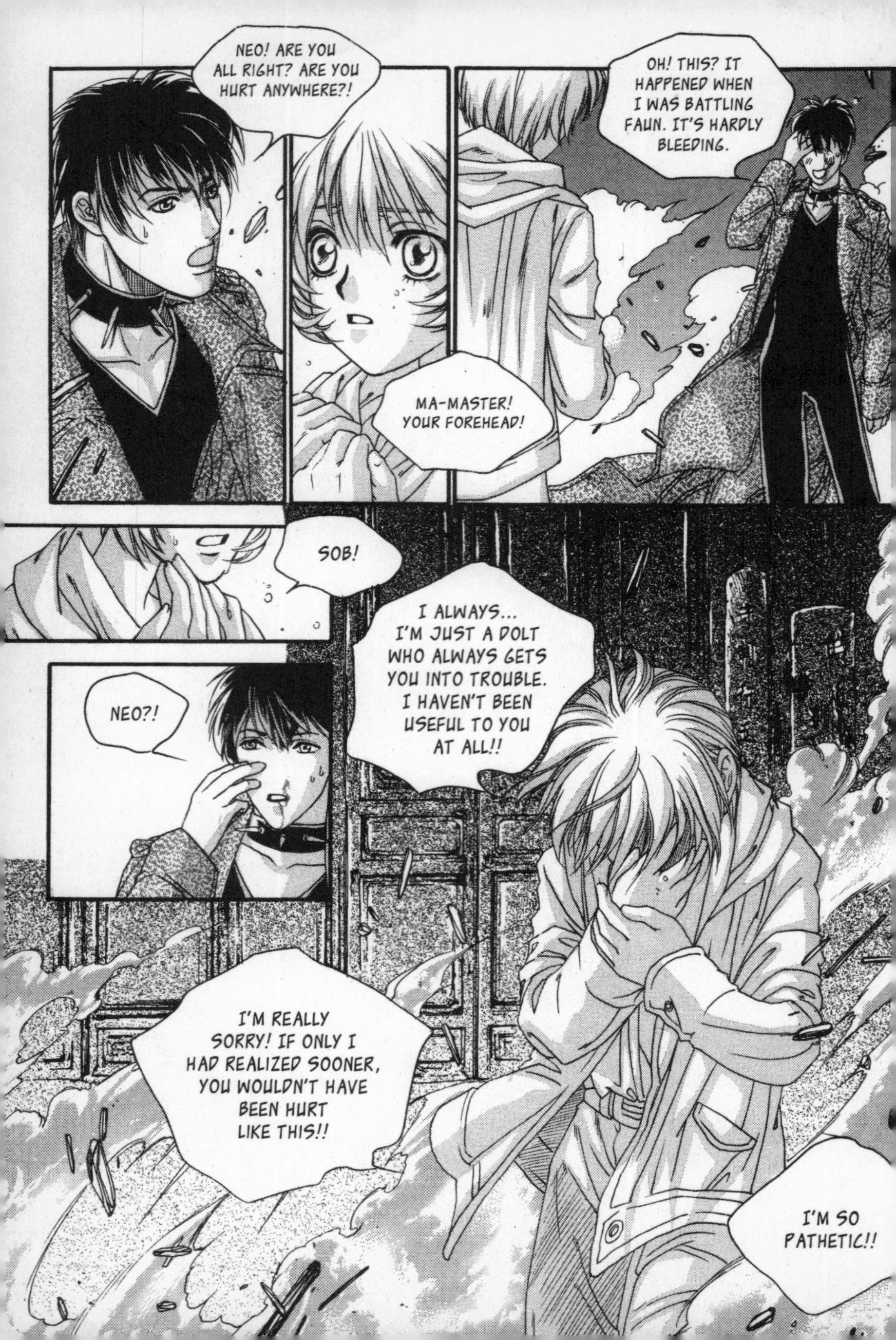
NEO! ARE YOU ALL RIGHT? ARE YOU HURT ANYWHERE?!
MA-MASTER! YOUR FOREHEAD!
OH! THIS? IT HAPPENED WHEN I WAS BATTLING FAUN. IT'S HARDLY BLEEDING.
SOB!
NEO?!
I ALWAYS... I'M JUST A DOLT WHO ALWAYS GETS YOU INTO TROUBLE. I HAVEN'T BEEN USEFUL TO YOU AT ALL!!
I'M REALLY SORRY! IF ONLY I HAD REALIZED SOONER, YOU WOULDN'T HAVE BEEN HURT LIKE THIS!!
I'M SO PATHETIC!!

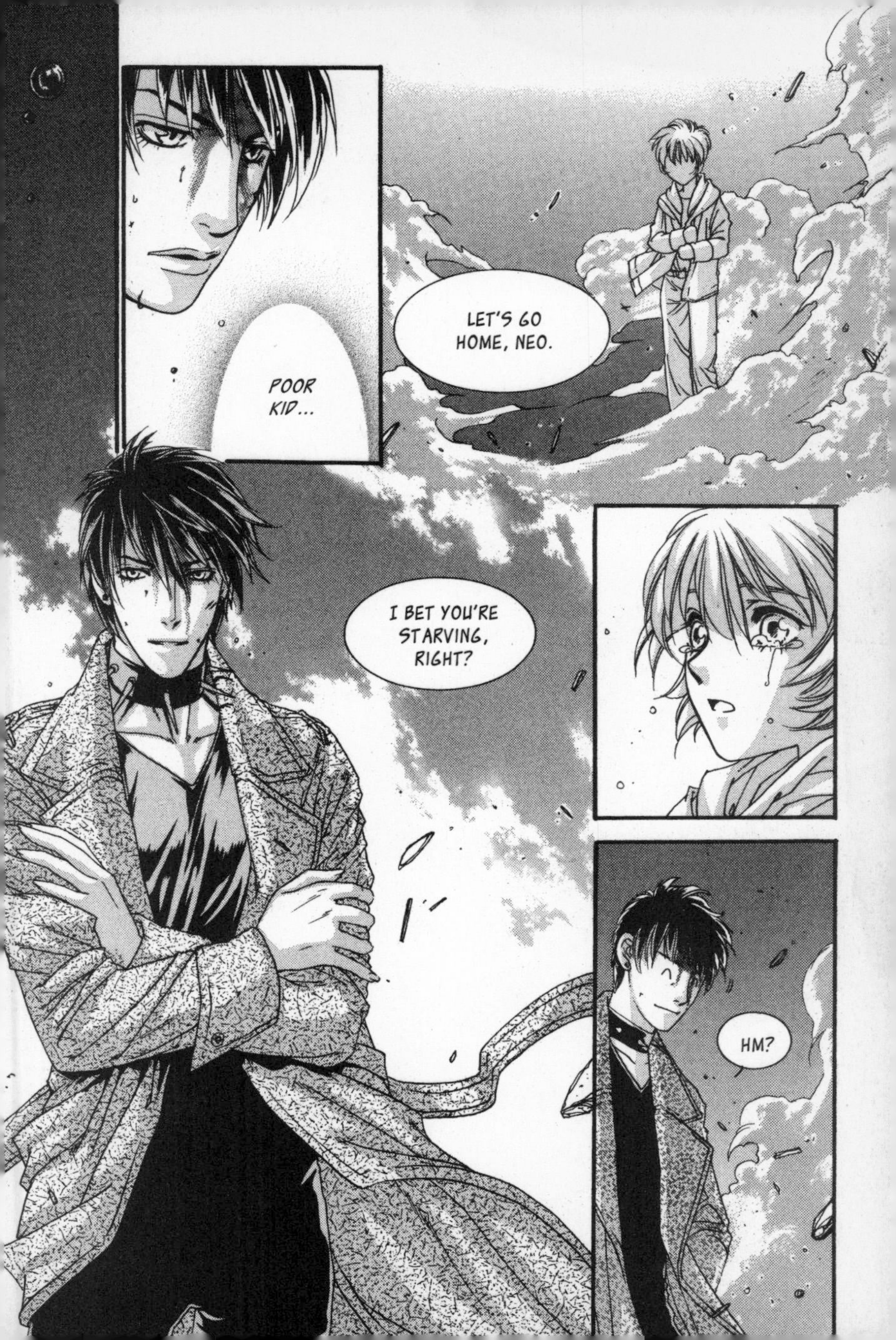
POOR KID...
LET'S GO HOME, NEO.
I BET YOU'RE STARVING, RIGHT?
HM?

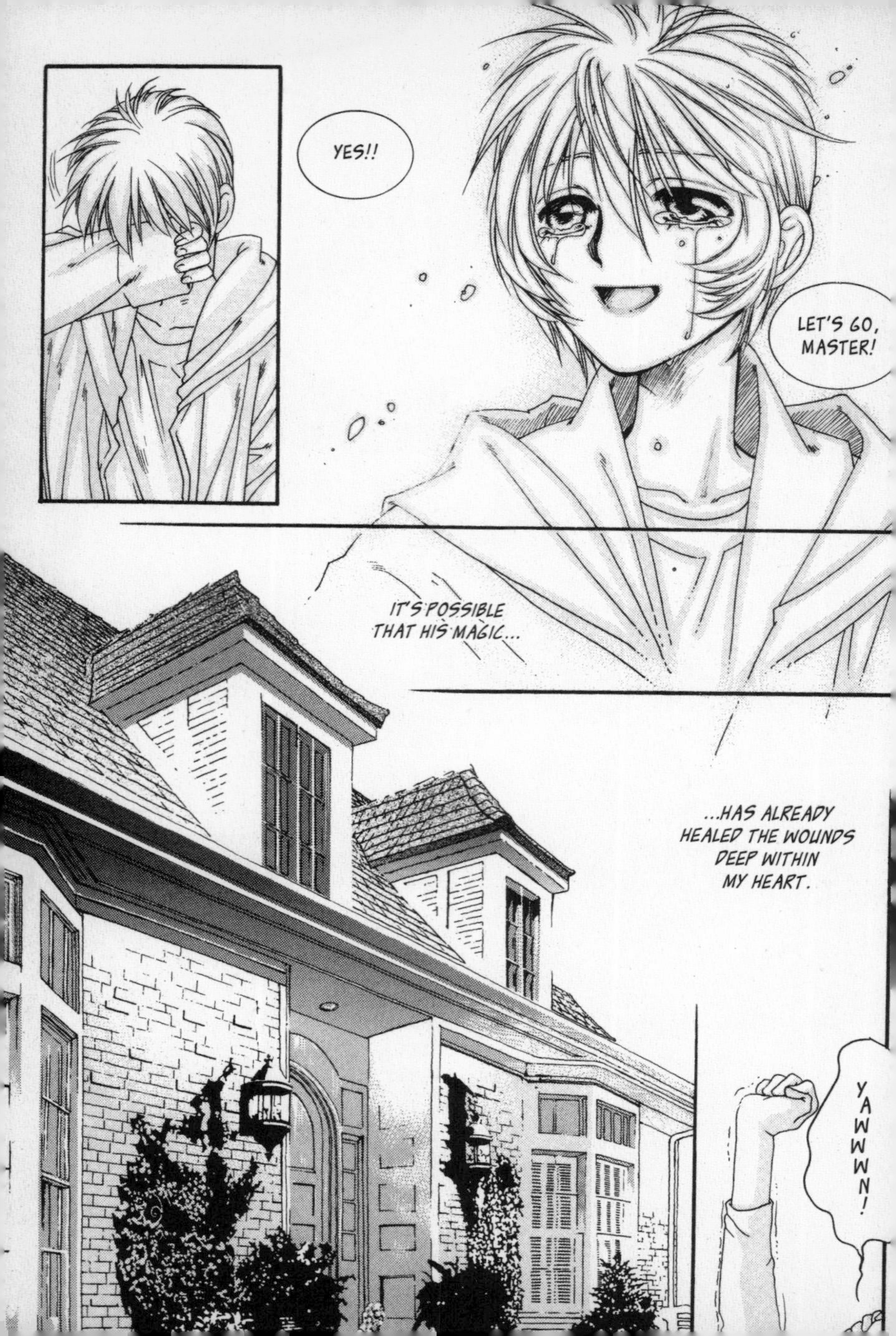
YES!!
LET'S GO, MASTER!
IT'S POSSIBLE THAT HIS MAGIC...
...HAS ALREADY HEALED THE WOUNDS DEEP WITHIN MY HEART.
YAWWWN!

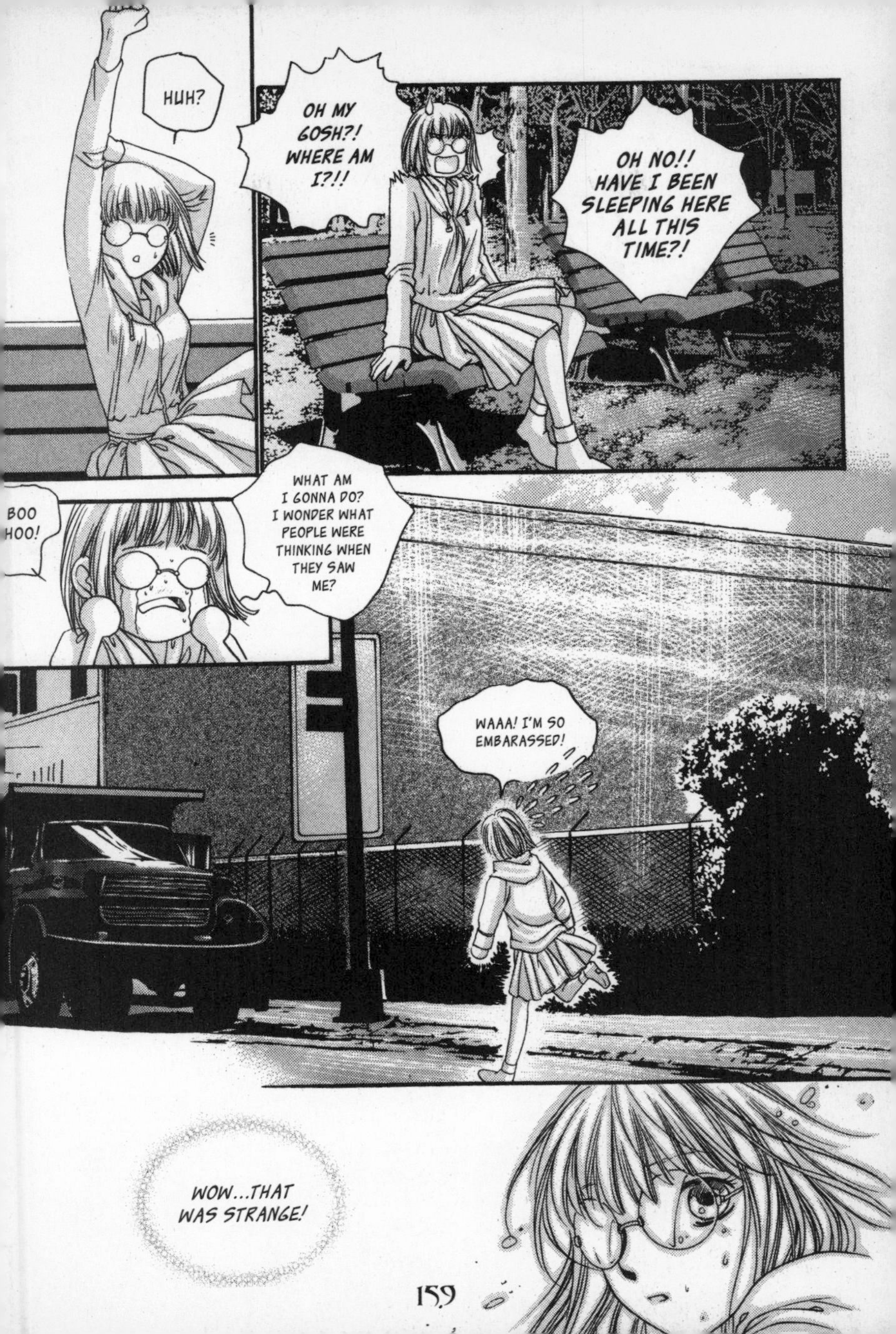
HUH?
OH MY GOSH?! WHERE AM I?!!
OH NO!! HAVE I BEEN SLEEPING HERE ALL THIS TIME?!
BOO HOO!
WHAT AM I GONNA DO? I WONDER WHAT PEOPLE WERE THINKING WHEN THEY SAW ME?
WAAA! I'M SO EMBARASSED!
WOW...THAT WAS STRANGE!

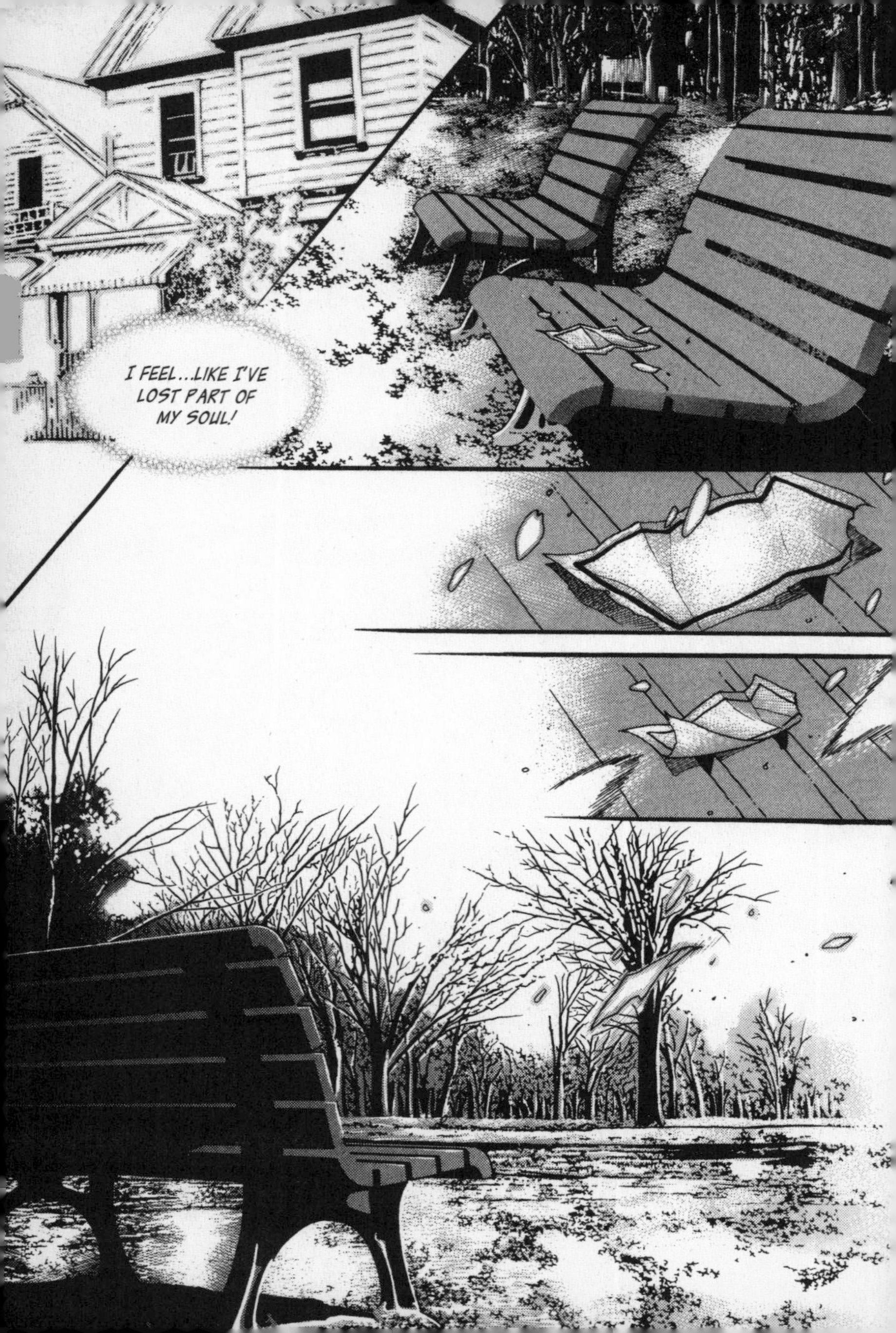
I FEEL...LIKE I'VE LOST PART OF MY SOUL!

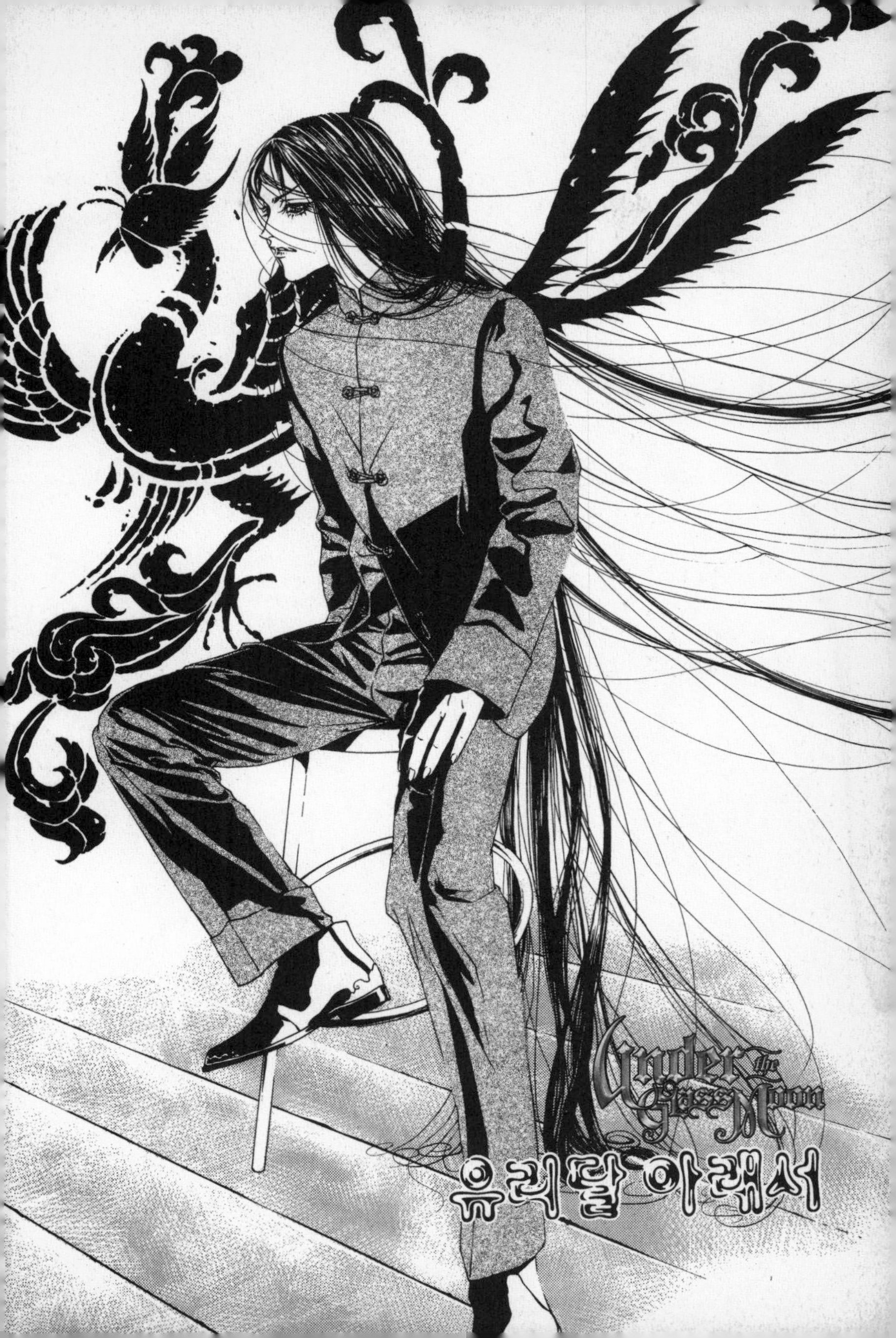
Under the Glass Moon
유리달 아래에서

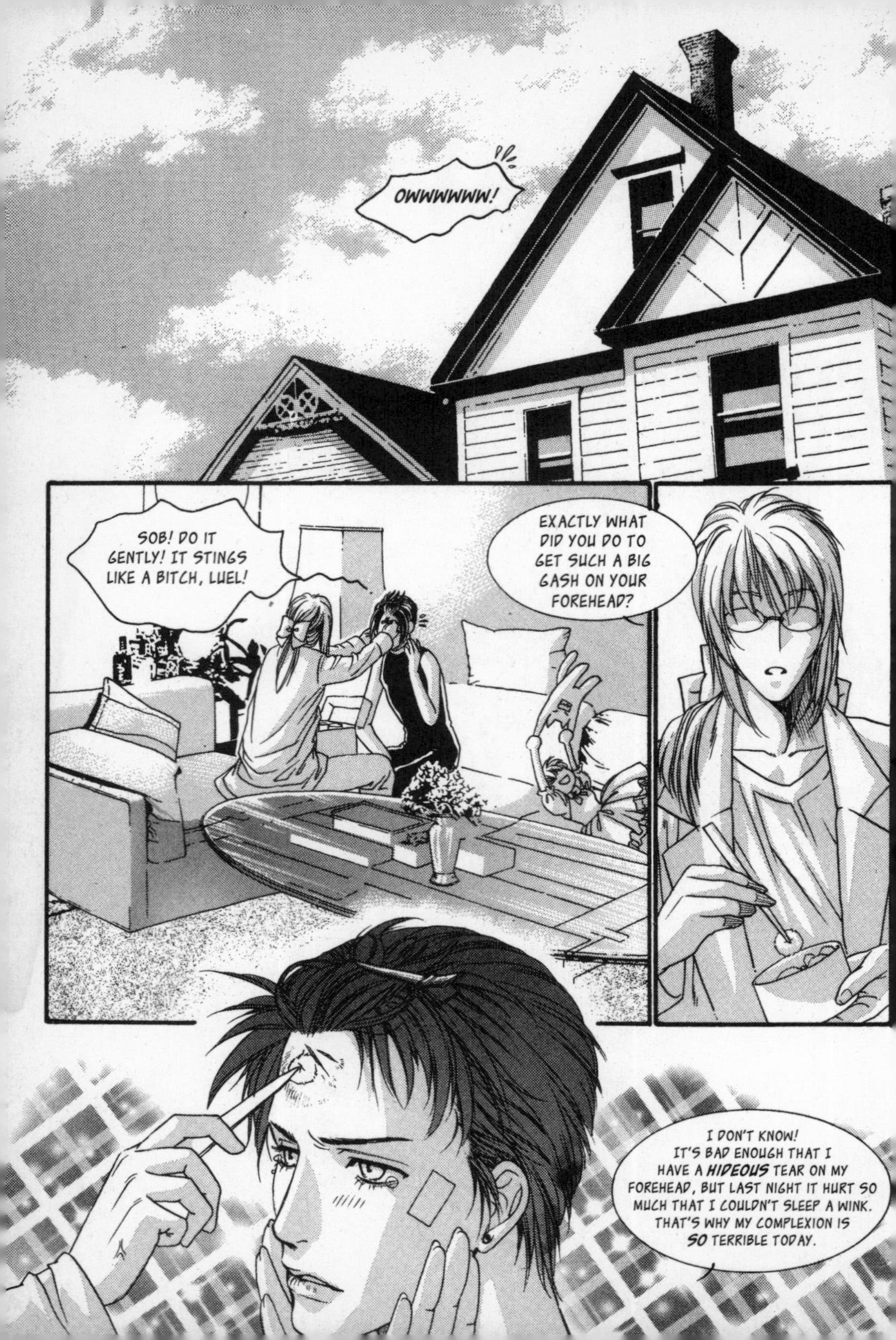
OWWWWWW!
SOB! DO IT GENTLY! IT STINGS LIKE A BITCH, LUEL!
EXACTLY WHAT DID YOU DO TO GET SUCH A BIG GASH ON YOUR FOREHEAD?
I DON'T KNOW! IT'S BAD ENOUGH THAT I HAVE A HIDEOUS TEAR ON MY FOREHEAD, BUT LAST NIGHT IT HURT SO MUCH THAT I COULDN'T SLEEP A WINK. THAT'S WHY MY COMPLEXION IS SO TERRIBLE TODAY.

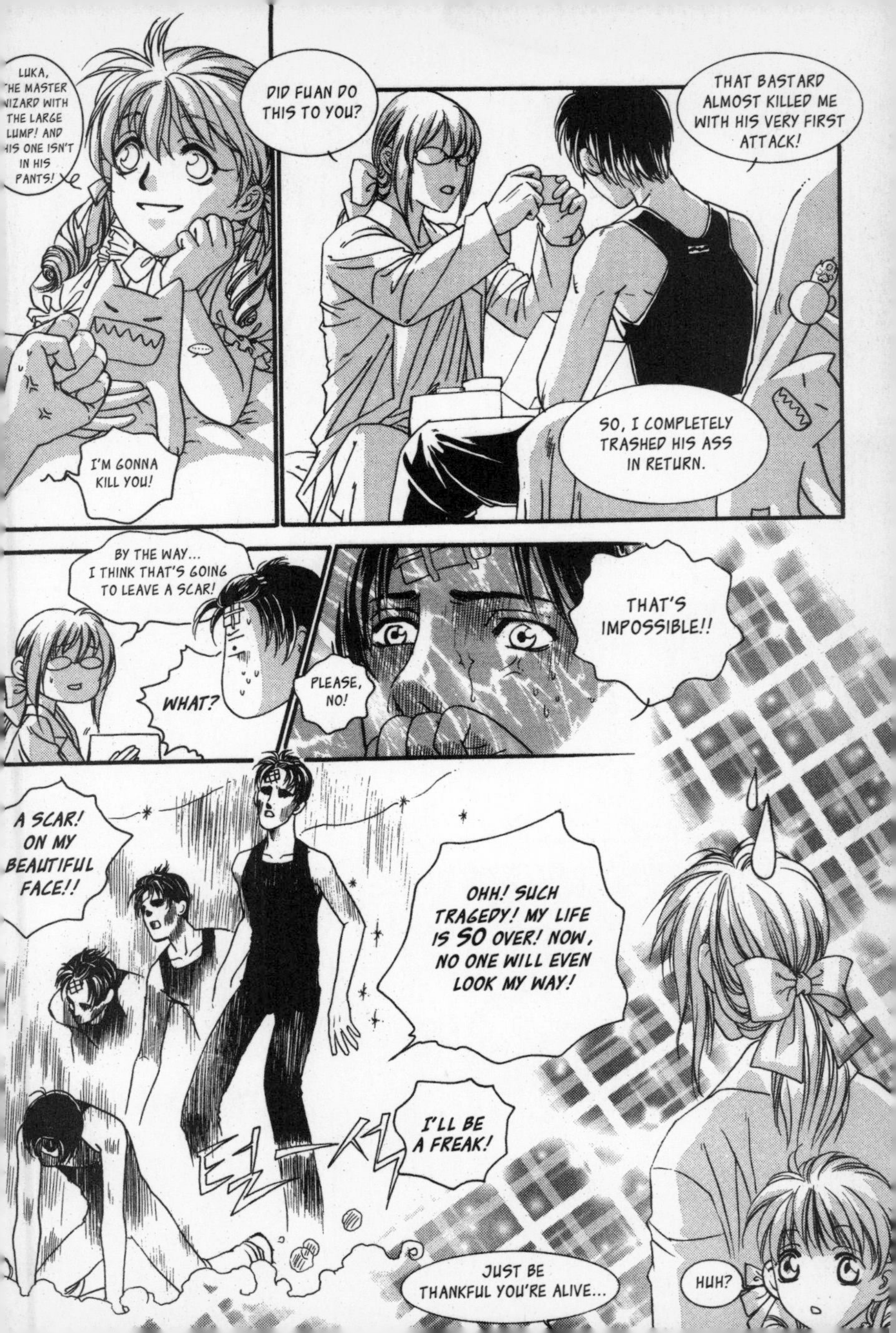
LUKA, THE MASTER WIZARD WITH THE LARGE LUMP! AND THIS ONE ISN'T IN HIS PANTS!
I'M GONNA KILL YOU!
DID FUAN DO THIS TO YOU?
THAT BASTARD ALMOST KILLED ME WITH HIS VERY FIRST ATTACK!
SO, I COMPLETELY TRASHED HIS ASS IN RETURN.
BY THE WAY... I THINK THAT'S GOING TO LEAVE A SCAR!
WHAT?
PLEASE, NO!
THAT'S IMPOSSIBLE!!
A SCAR! ON MY BEAUTIFUL FACE!!
OHH! SUCH TRAGEDY! MY LIFE IS SO OVER! NOW, NO ONE WILL EVEN LOOK MY WAY!
I'LL BE A FREAK!
JUST BE THANKFUL YOU'RE ALIVE...
HUH?

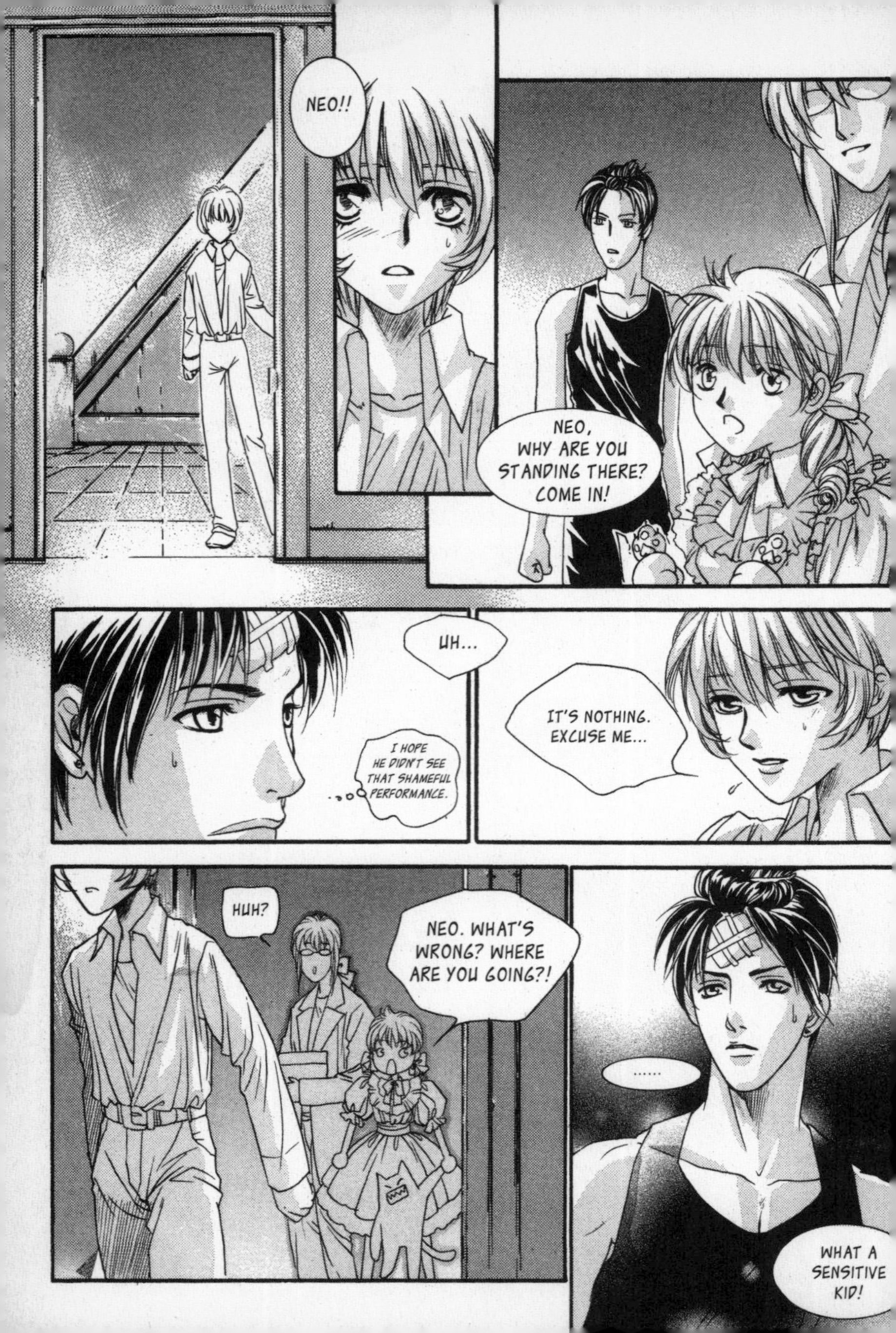
NEO!!
NEO, WHY ARE YOU STANDING THERE? COME IN!
UH...
I HOPE HE DIDN'T SEE THAT SHAMEFUL PERFORMANCE.
IT'S NOTHING. EXCUSE ME...
HUH?
NEO. WHAT'S WRONG? WHERE ARE YOU GOING?!
......
WHAT A SENSITIVE KID!

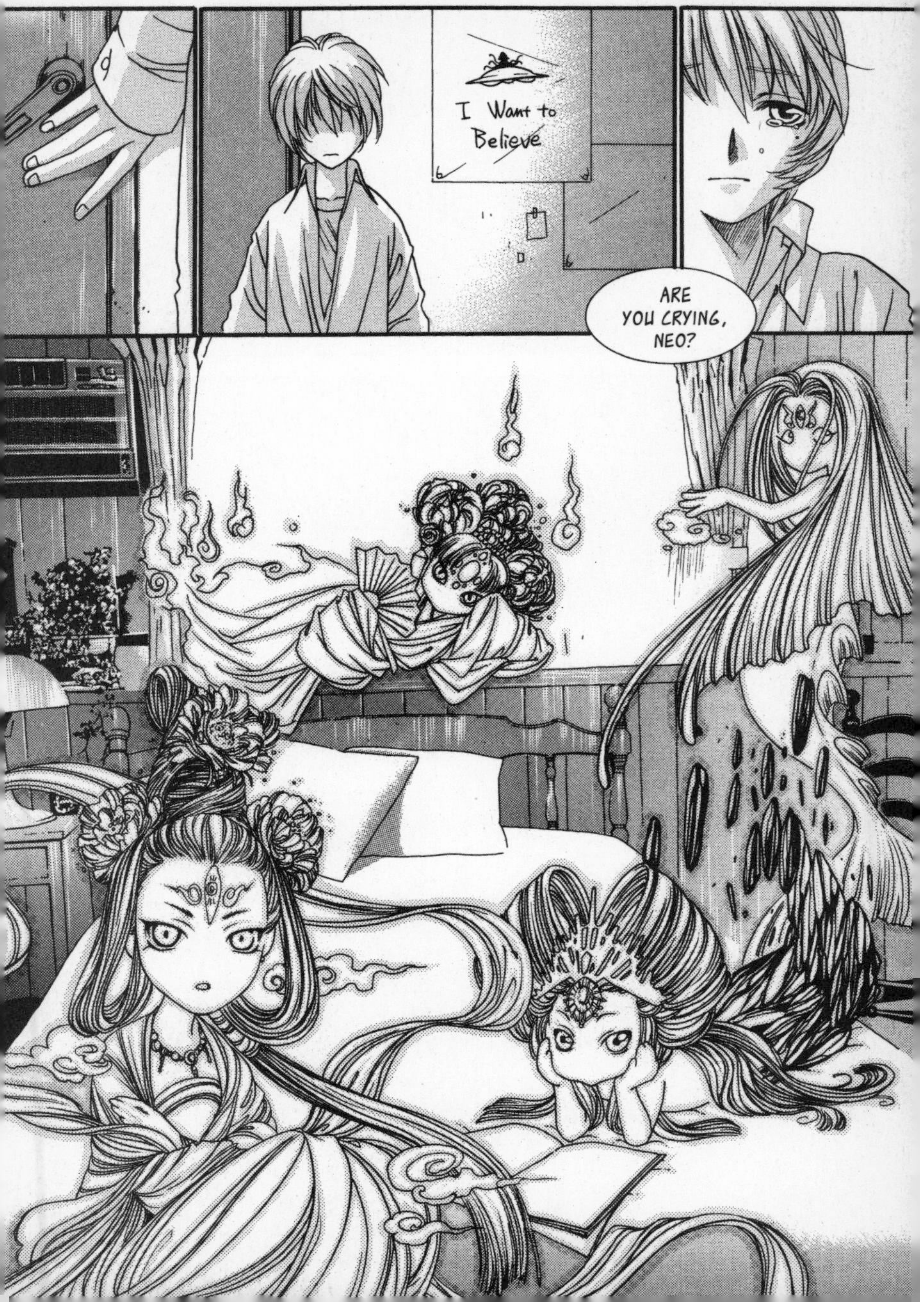
I Want to Believe
ARE YOU CRYING, NEO?

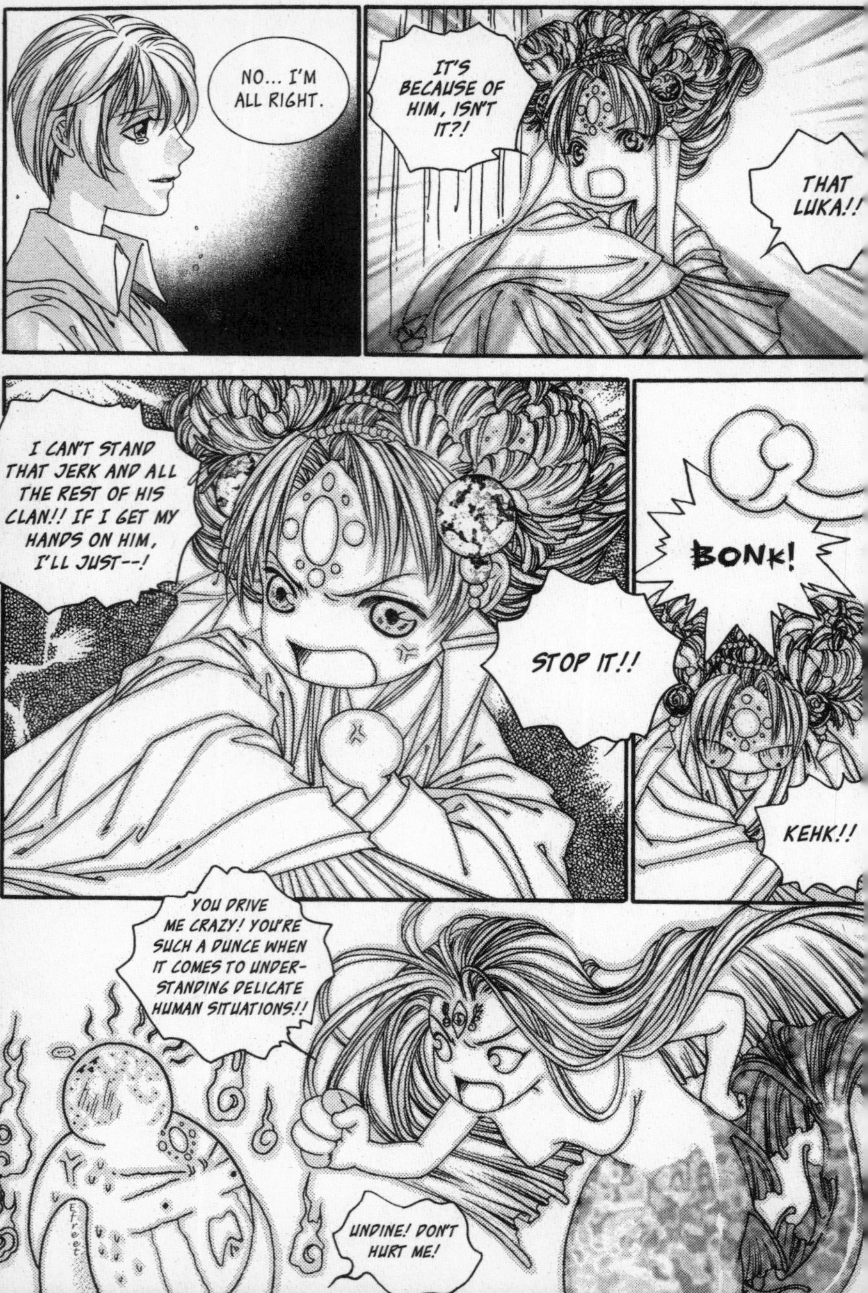
NO... I'M ALL RIGHT.
IT'S BECAUSE OF HIM, ISN'T IT?!
THAT LUKA!!
I CAN'T STAND THAT JERK AND ALL THE REST OF HIS CLAN!! IF I GET MY HANDS ON HIM, I'LL JUST--!
STOP IT!!
BONK!
KEHK!!
YOU DRIVE ME CRAZY! YOU'RE SUCH A DUNCE WHEN IT COMES TO UNDER-STANDING DELICATE HUMAN SITUATIONS!!
Efreet
UNDINE! DON'T HURT ME!

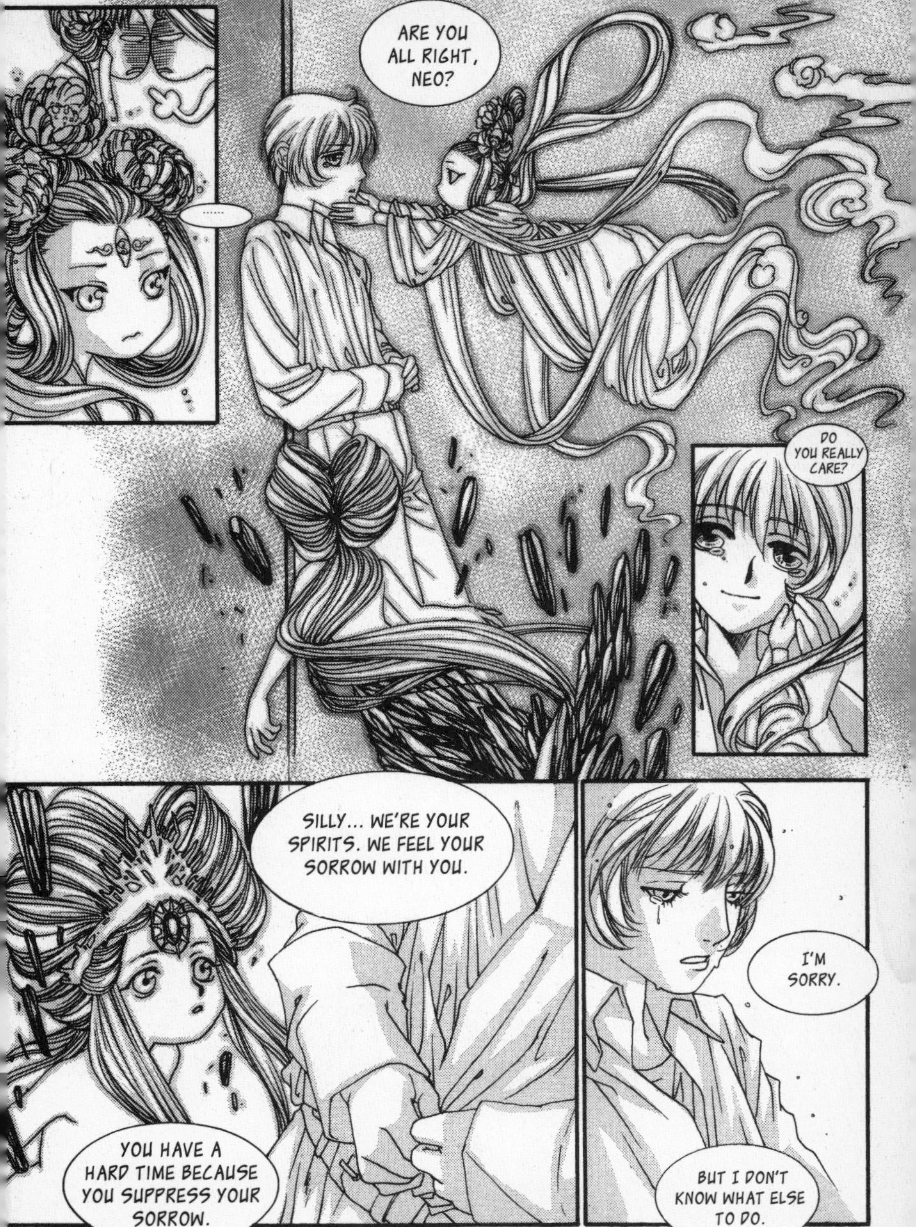
......
ARE YOU ALL RIGHT, NEO?
DO YOU REALLY CARE?
SILLY... WE'RE YOUR SPIRITS. WE FEEL YOUR SORROW WITH YOU.
YOU HAVE A HARD TIME BECAUSE YOU SUPPRESS YOUR SORROW.
I'M SORRY.
BUT I DON'T KNOW WHAT ELSE TO DO.

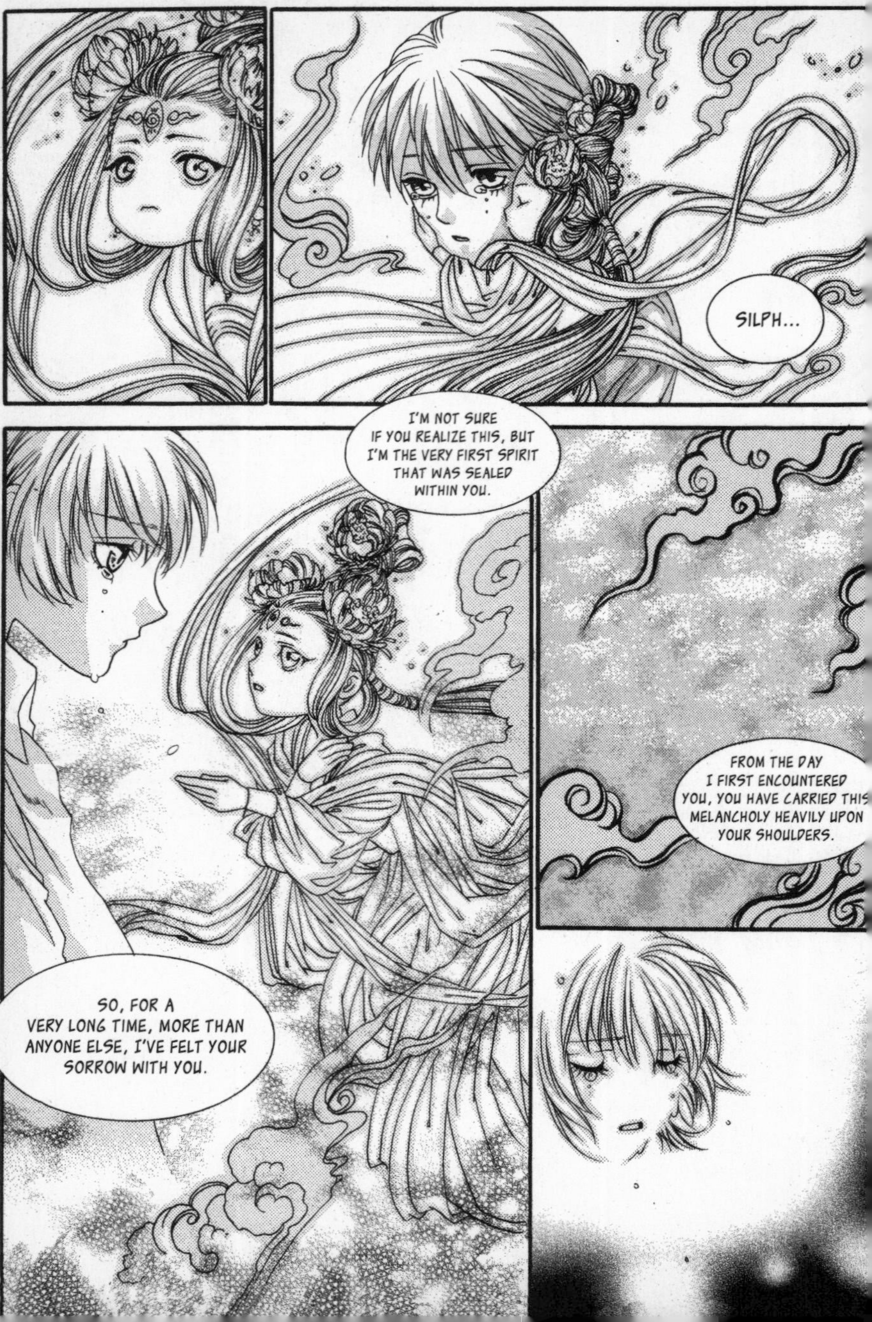
SILPH...
I'M NOT SURE IF YOU REALIZE THIS, BUT I'M THE VERY FIRST SPIRIT THAT WAS SEALED WITHIN YOU.
SO, FOR A VERY LONG TIME, MORE THAN ANYONE ELSE, I'VE FELT YOUR SORROW WITH YOU.
FROM THE DAY I FIRST ENCOUNTERED YOU, YOU HAVE CARRIED THIS MELANCHOLY HEAVILY UPON YOUR SHOULDERS.

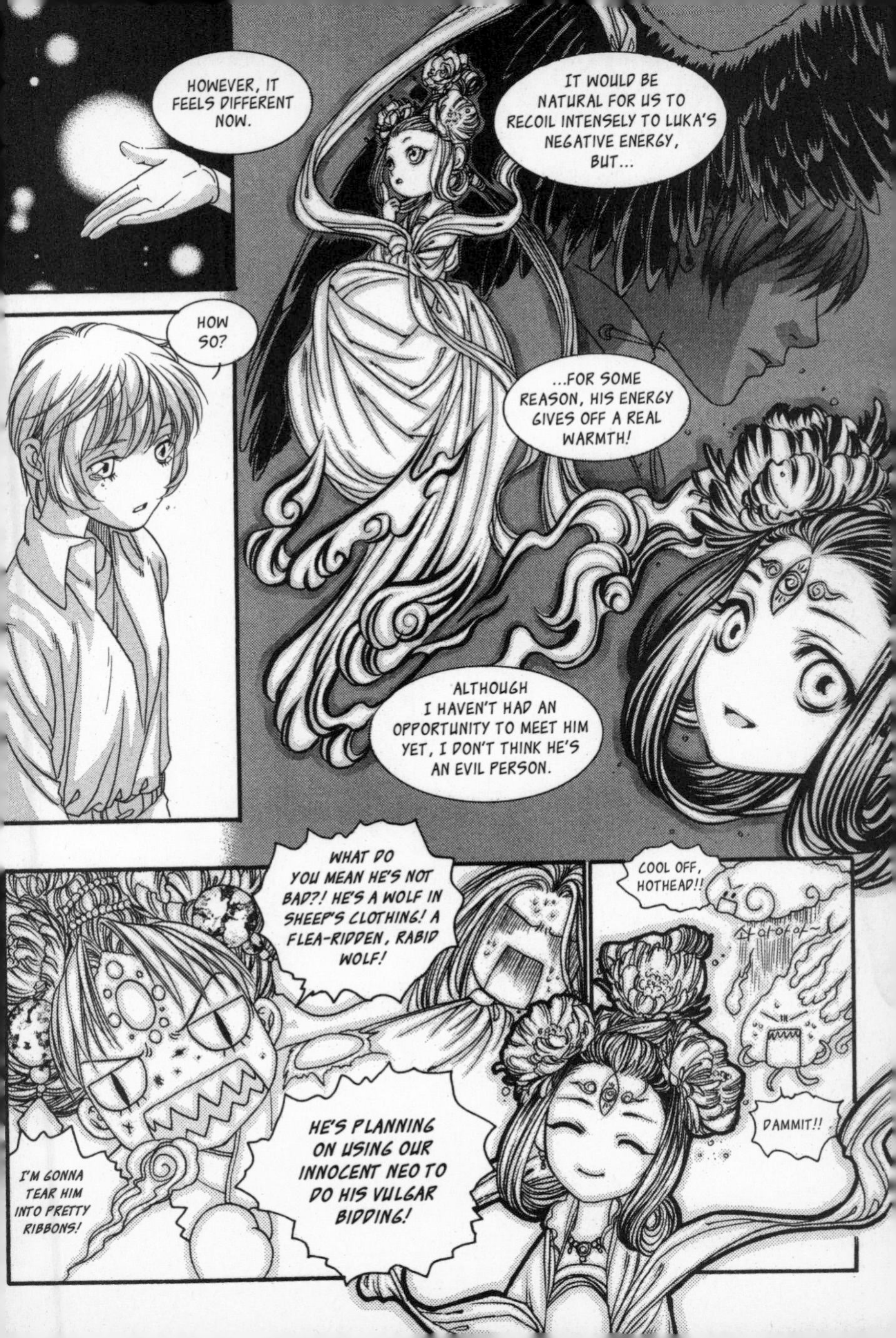
HOWEVER, IT FEELS DIFFERENT NOW.
HOW SO?
IT WOULD BE NATURAL FOR US TO RECOIL INTENSELY TO LUKA'S NEGATIVE ENERGY, BUT...
...FOR SOME REASON, HIS ENERGY GIVES OFF A REAL WARMTH!
ALTHOUGH I HAVEN'T HAD AN OPPORTUNITY TO MEET HIM YET, I DON'T THINK HE'S AN EVIL PERSON.
WHAT DO YOU MEAN HE'S NOT BAD?! HE'S A WOLF IN SHEEP'S CLOTHING! A FLEA-RIDDEN, RABID WOLF!
I'M GONNA TEAR HIM INTO PRETTY RIBBONS!
HE'S PLANNING ON USING OUR INNOCENT NEO TO DO HIS VULGAR BIDDING!
COOL OFF, HOTHEAD!!
DAMMIT!!

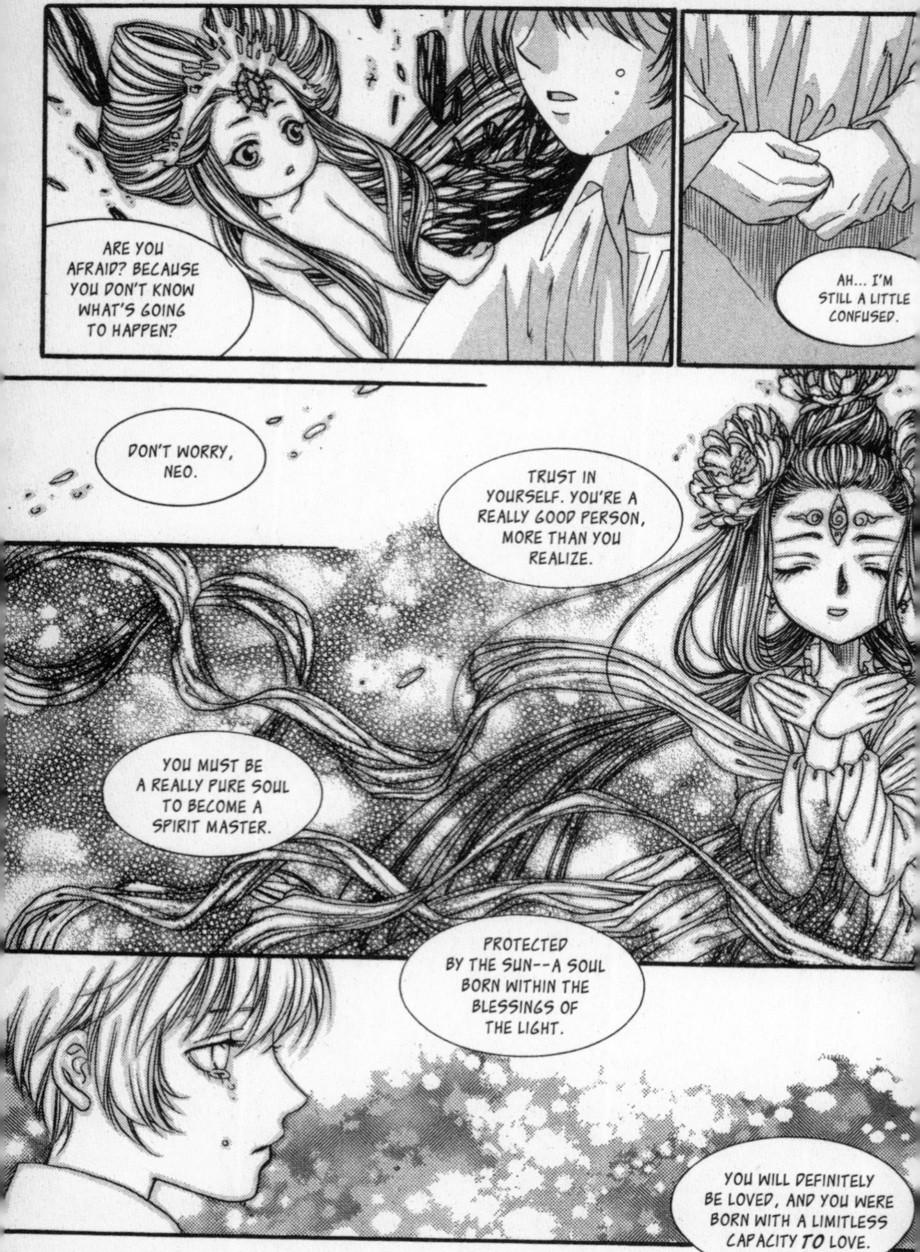
ARE YOU AFRAID? BECAUSE YOU DON'T KNOW WHAT'S GOING TO HAPPEN?
AH... I'M STILL A LITTLE CONFUSED.
DON'T WORRY, NEO.
TRUST IN YOURSELF. YOU'RE A REALLY GOOD PERSON, MORE THAN YOU REALIZE.
YOU MUST BE A REALLY PURE SOUL TO BECOME A SPIRIT MASTER.
PROTECTED BY THE SUN--A SOUL BORN WITHIN THE BLESSINGS OF THE LIGHT.
YOU WILL DEFINITELY BE LOVED, AND YOU WERE BORN WITH A LIMITLESS CAPACITY **TO** LOVE.

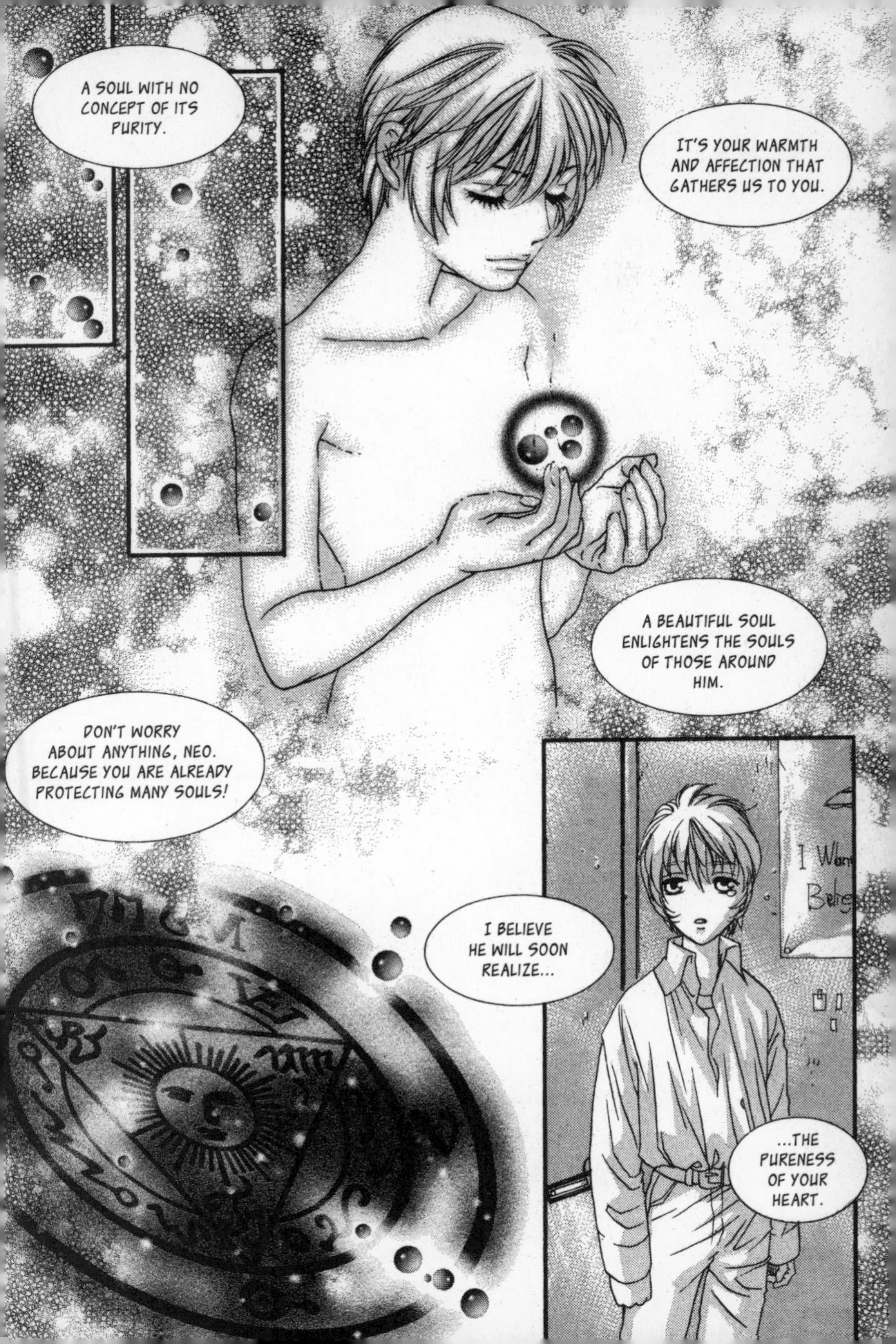
A SOUL WITH NO CONCEPT OF ITS PURITY.
IT'S YOUR WARMTH AND AFFECTION THAT GATHERS US TO YOU.
A BEAUTIFUL SOUL ENLIGHTENS THE SOULS OF THOSE AROUND HIM.
DON'T WORRY ABOUT ANYTHING, NEO. BECAUSE YOU ARE ALREADY PROTECTING MANY SOULS!
I BELIEVE HE WILL SOON REALIZE...
...THE PURENESS OF YOUR HEART.

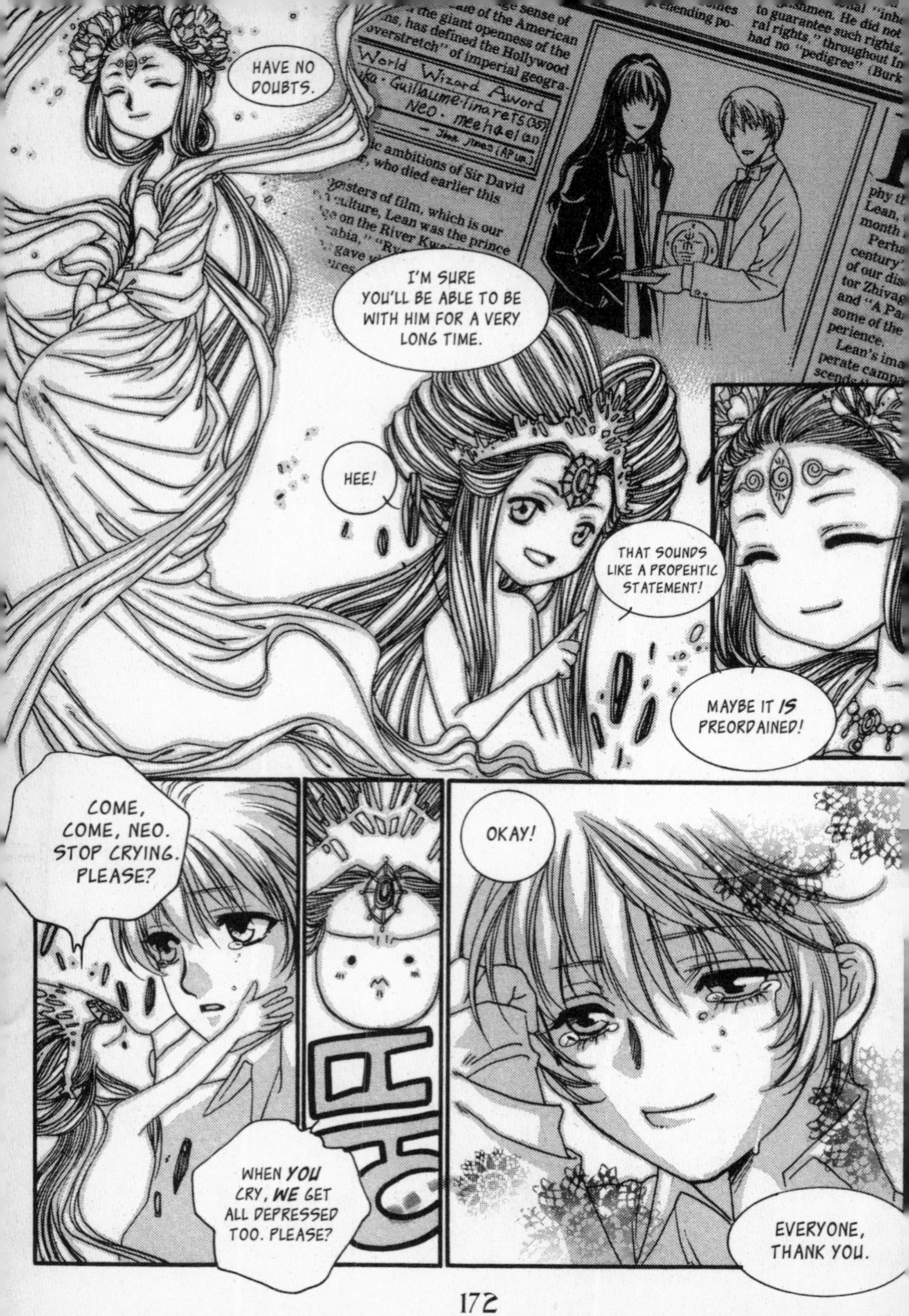
HAVE NO DOUBTS.
World Wizard Award
I'M SURE YOU'LL BE ABLE TO BE WITH HIM FOR A VERY LONG TIME.
HEE!
THAT SOUNDS LIKE A PROPEHTIC STATEMENT!
MAYBE IT *IS* PREORDAINED!
COME, COME, NEO. STOP CRYING. PLEASE?
WHEN *YOU* CRY, *WE* GET ALL DEPRESSED TOO. PLEASE?
OKAY!
EVERYONE, THANK YOU.

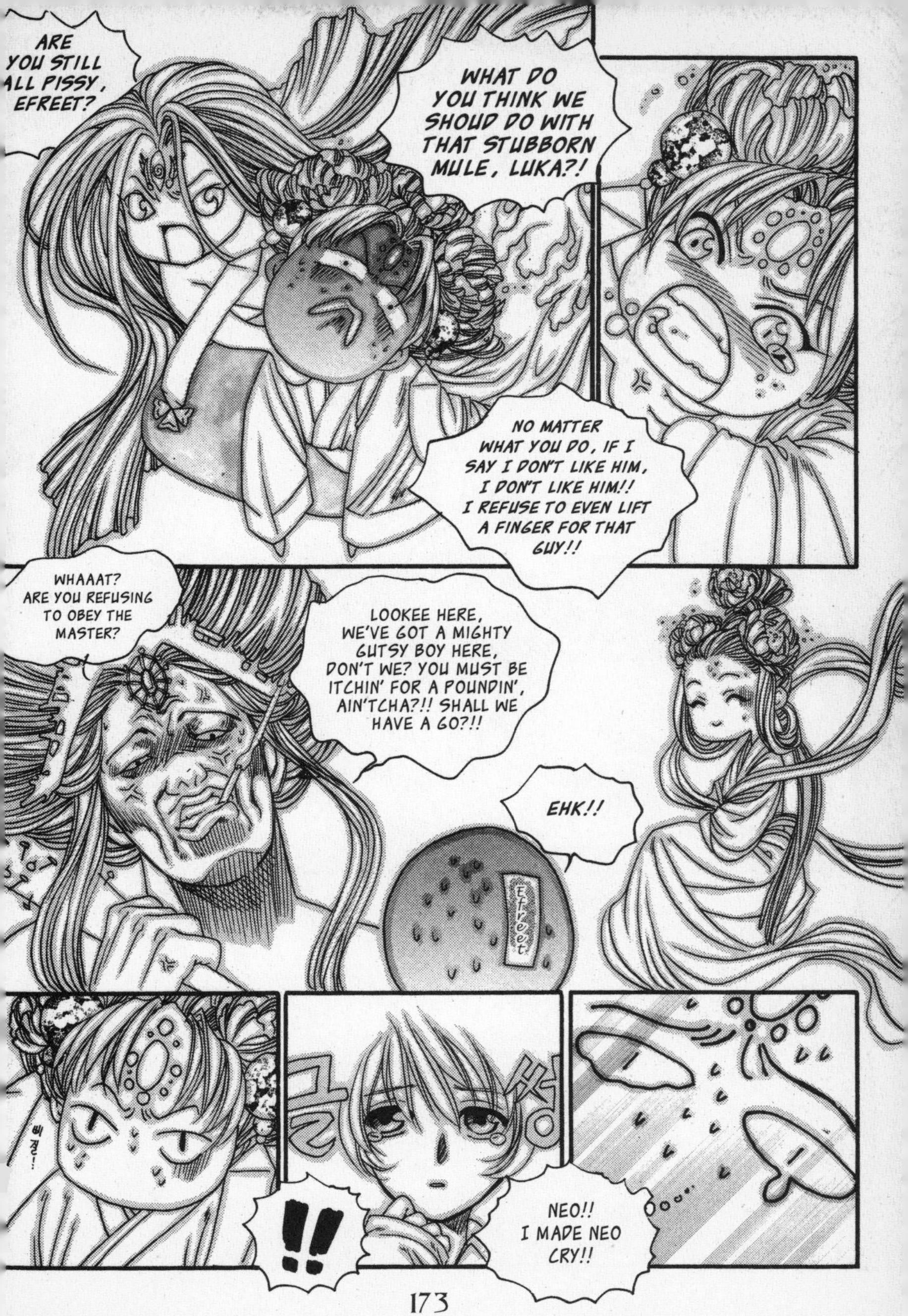
ARE YOU STILL ALL PISSY, EFREET?
WHAT DO YOU THINK WE SHOUD DO WITH THAT STUBBORN MULE, LUKA?!
NO MATTER WHAT YOU DO, IF I SAY I DON'T LIKE HIM, I DON'T LIKE HIM!! I REFUSE TO EVEN LIFT A FINGER FOR THAT GUY!!
WHAAAT? ARE YOU REFUSING TO OBEY THE MASTER?
LOOKEE HERE, WE'VE GOT A MIGHTY GUTSY BOY HERE, DON'T WE? YOU MUST BE ITCHIN' FOR A POUNDIN', AIN'TCHA?!! SHALL WE HAVE A GO?!!
EHK!!
Efreet
!!
NEO!! I MADE NEO CRY!!

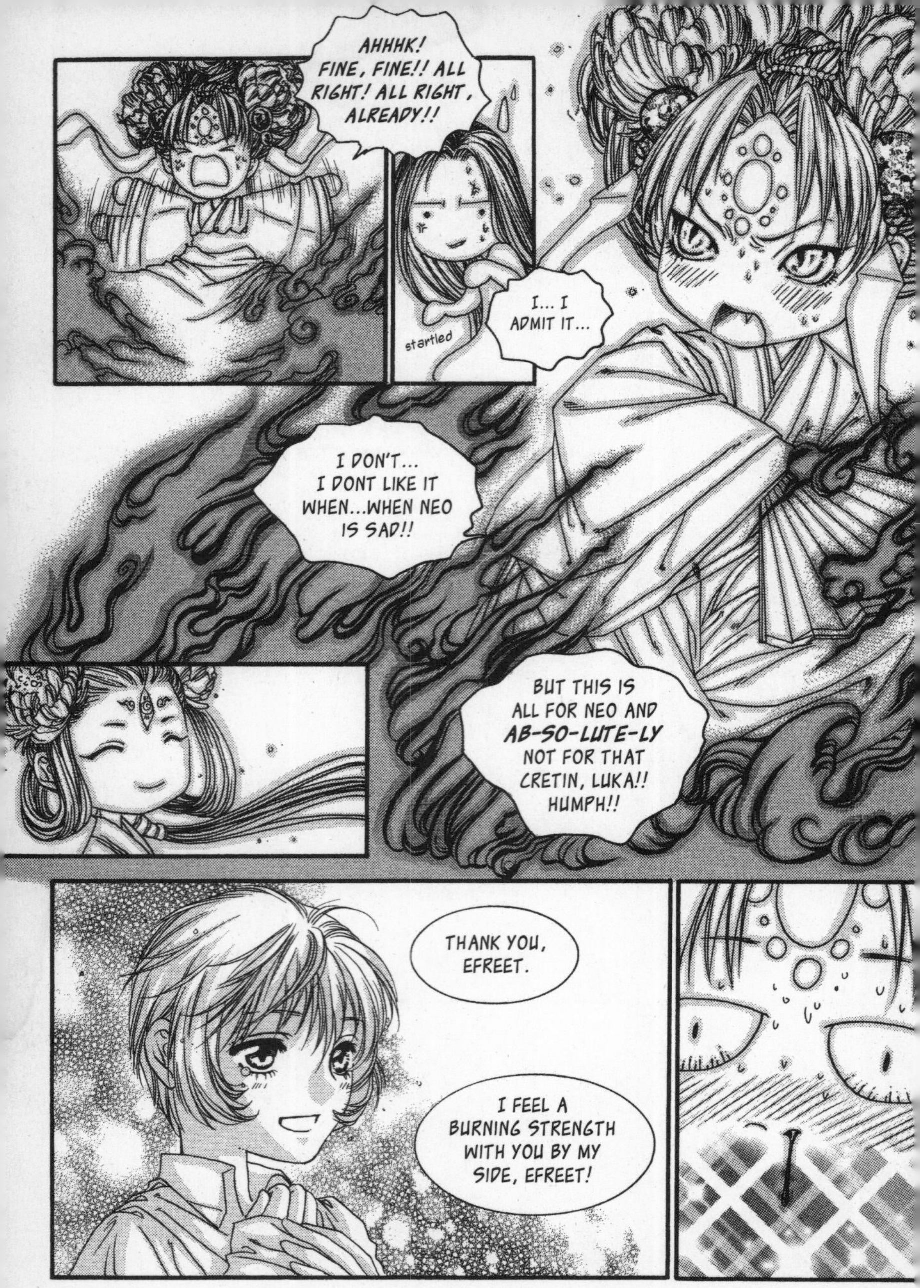
AHHHK! FINE, FINE!! ALL RIGHT! ALL RIGHT, ALREADY!!
startled
I... I ADMIT IT...
I DON'T... I DONT LIKE IT WHEN...WHEN NEO IS SAD!!
BUT THIS IS ALL FOR NEO AND AB-SO-LUTE-LY NOT FOR THAT CRETIN, LUKA!! HUMPH!!
THANK YOU, EFREET.
I FEEL A BURNING STRENGTH WITH YOU BY MY SIDE, EFREET!

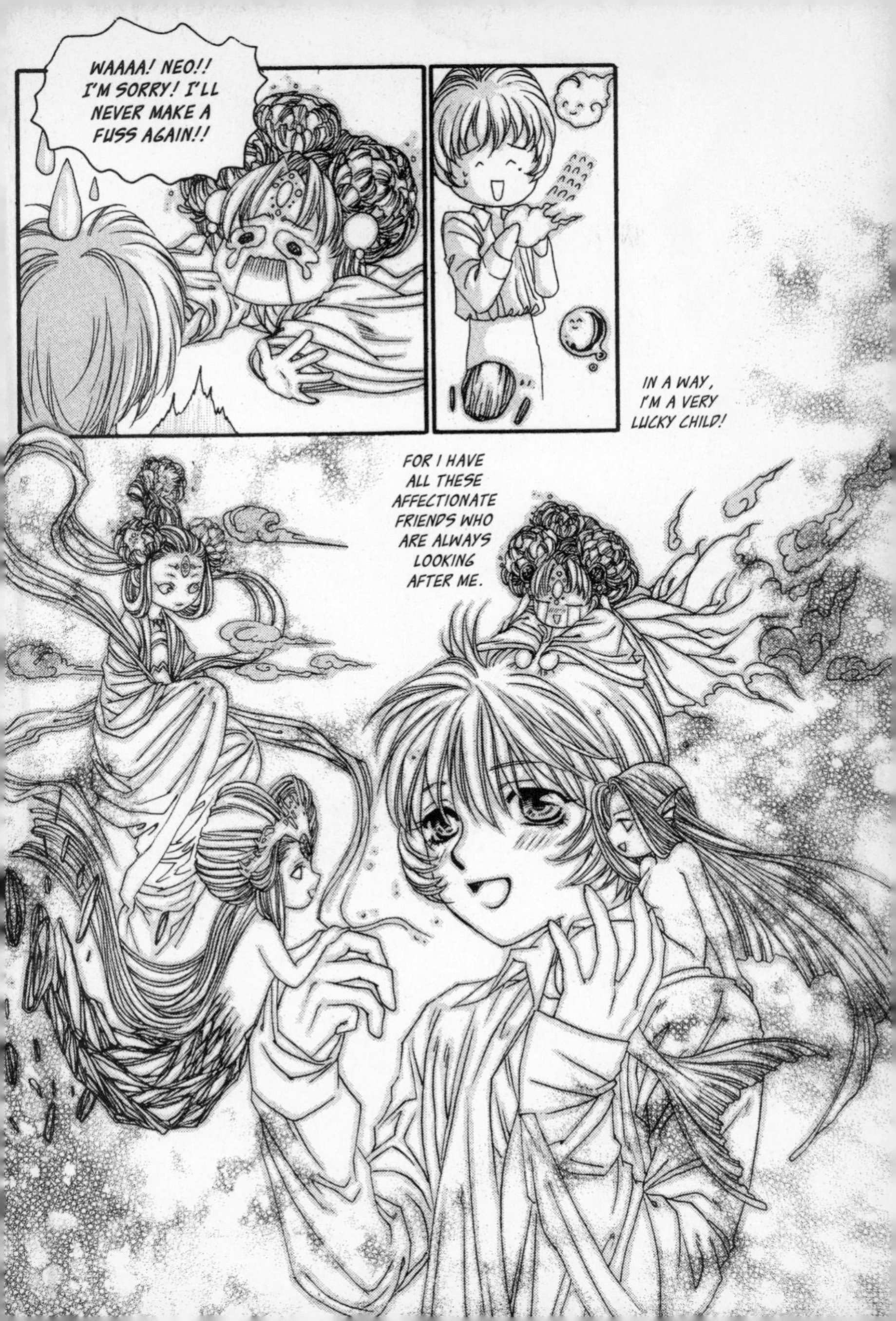
WAAAA! NEO!! I'M SORRY! I'LL NEVER MAKE A FUSS AGAIN!!
IN A WAY, I'M A VERY LUCKY CHILD!
FOR I HAVE ALL THESE AFFECTIONATE FRIENDS WHO ARE ALWAYS LOOKING AFTER ME.

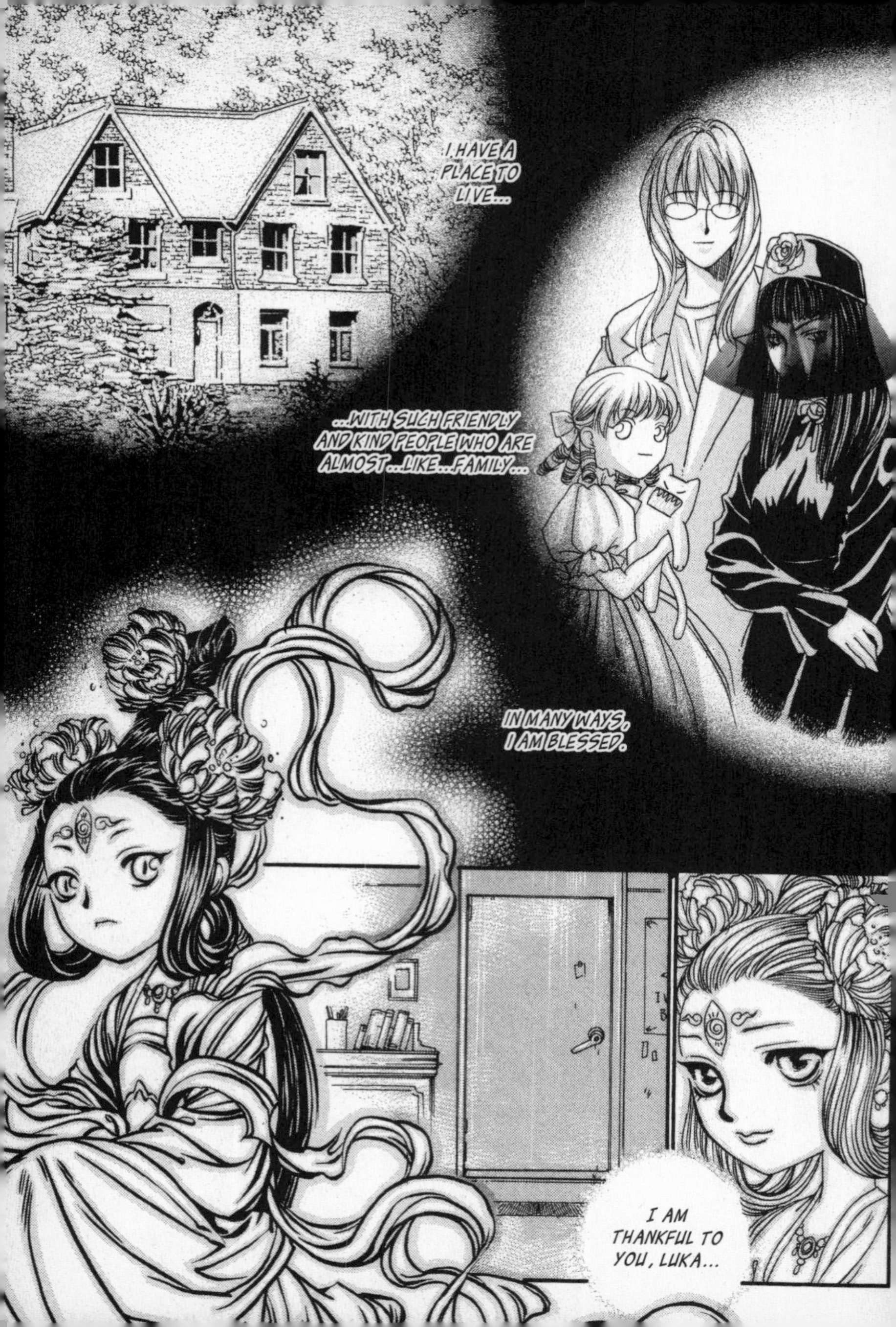
I HAVE A PLACE TO LIVE...
...WITH SUCH FRIENDLY AND KIND PEOPLE WHO ARE ALMOST ...LIKE... FAMILY...
IN MANY WAYS, I AM BLESSED.
I AM THANKFUL TO YOU, LUKA...

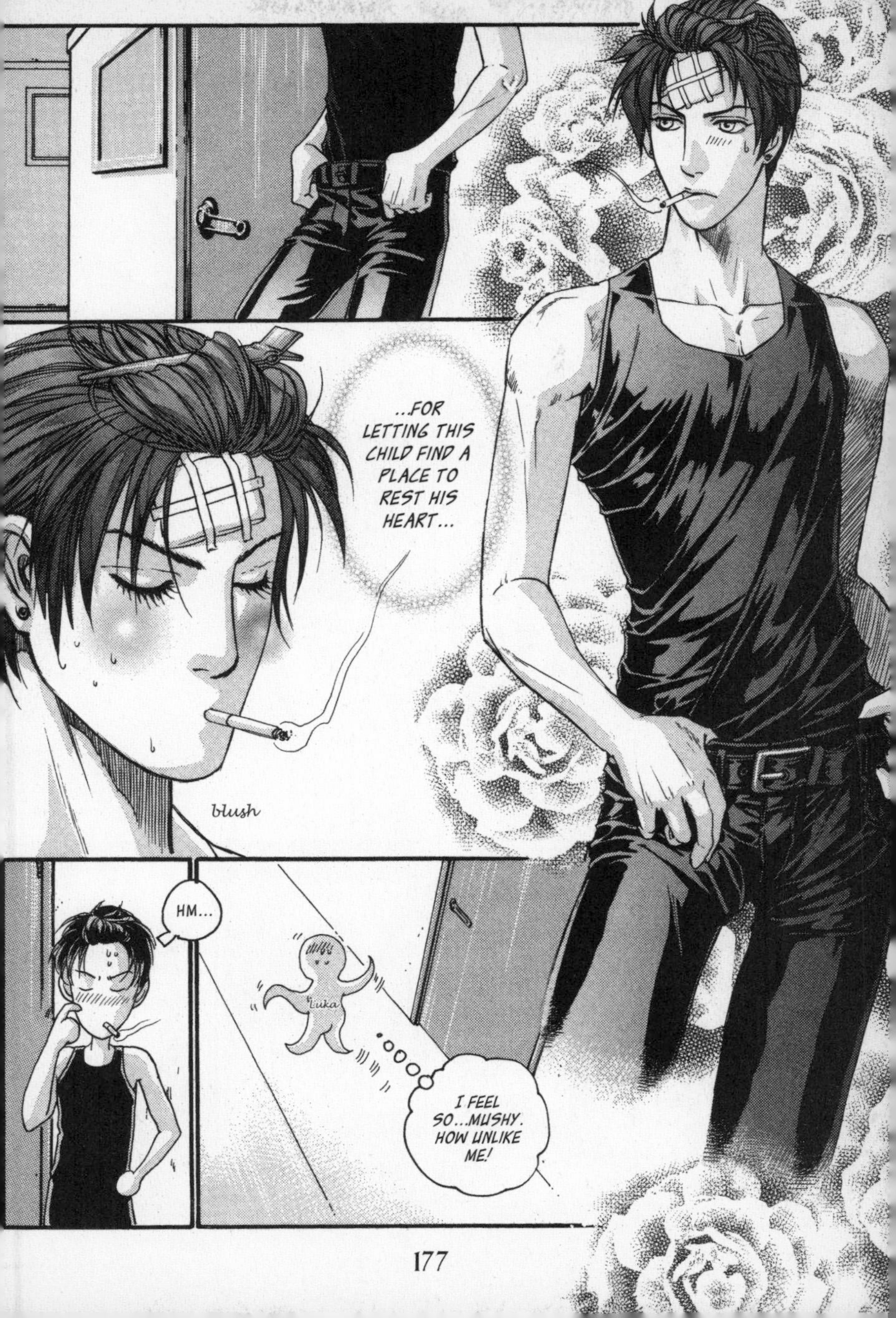
...FOR LETTING THIS CHILD FIND A PLACE TO REST HIS HEART...
blush
HM...
Luka
I FEEL SO...MUSHY. HOW UNLIKE ME!

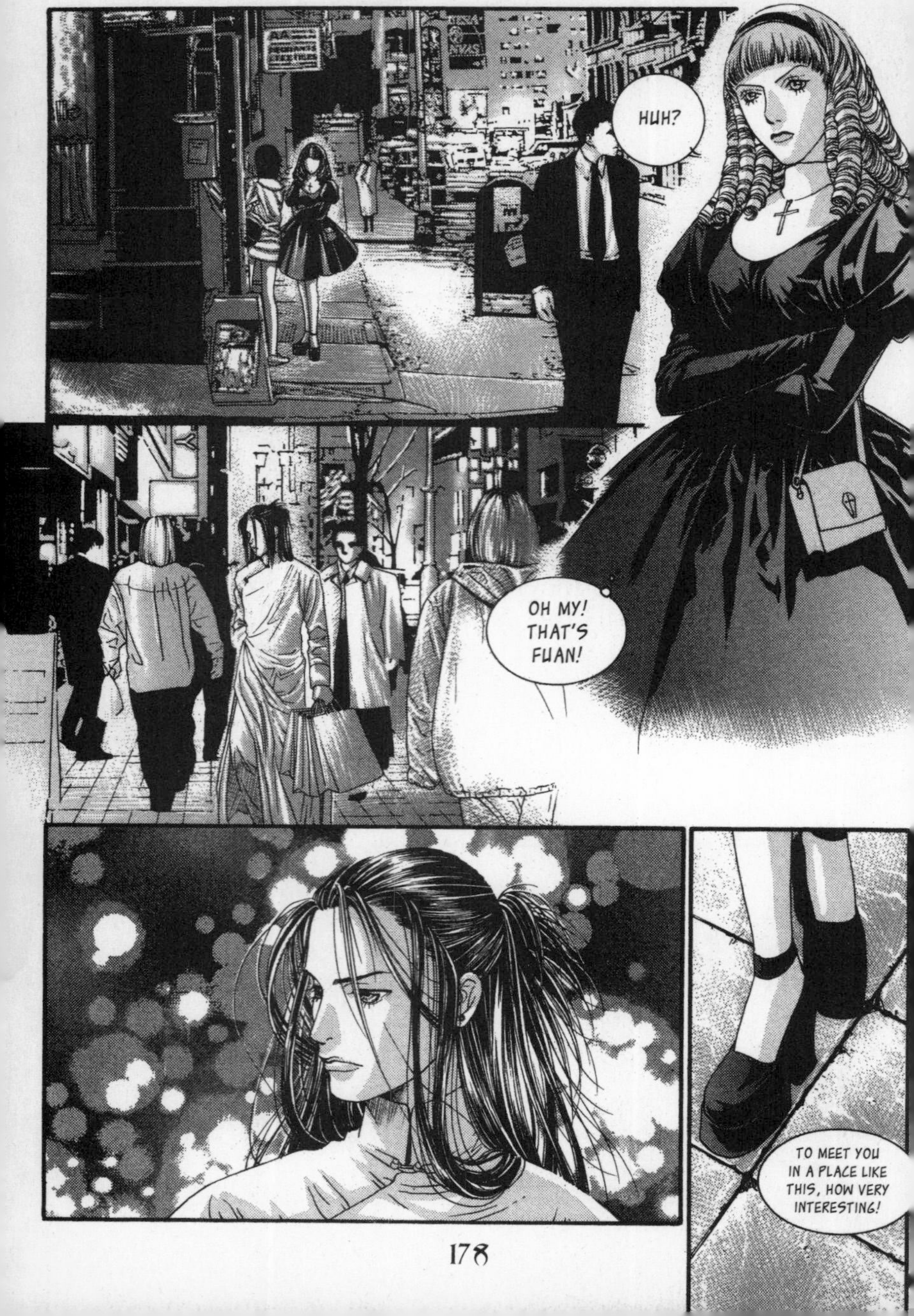
HUH?
OH MY! THAT'S FUAN!
TO MEET YOU IN A PLACE LIKE THIS, HOW VERY INTERESTING!

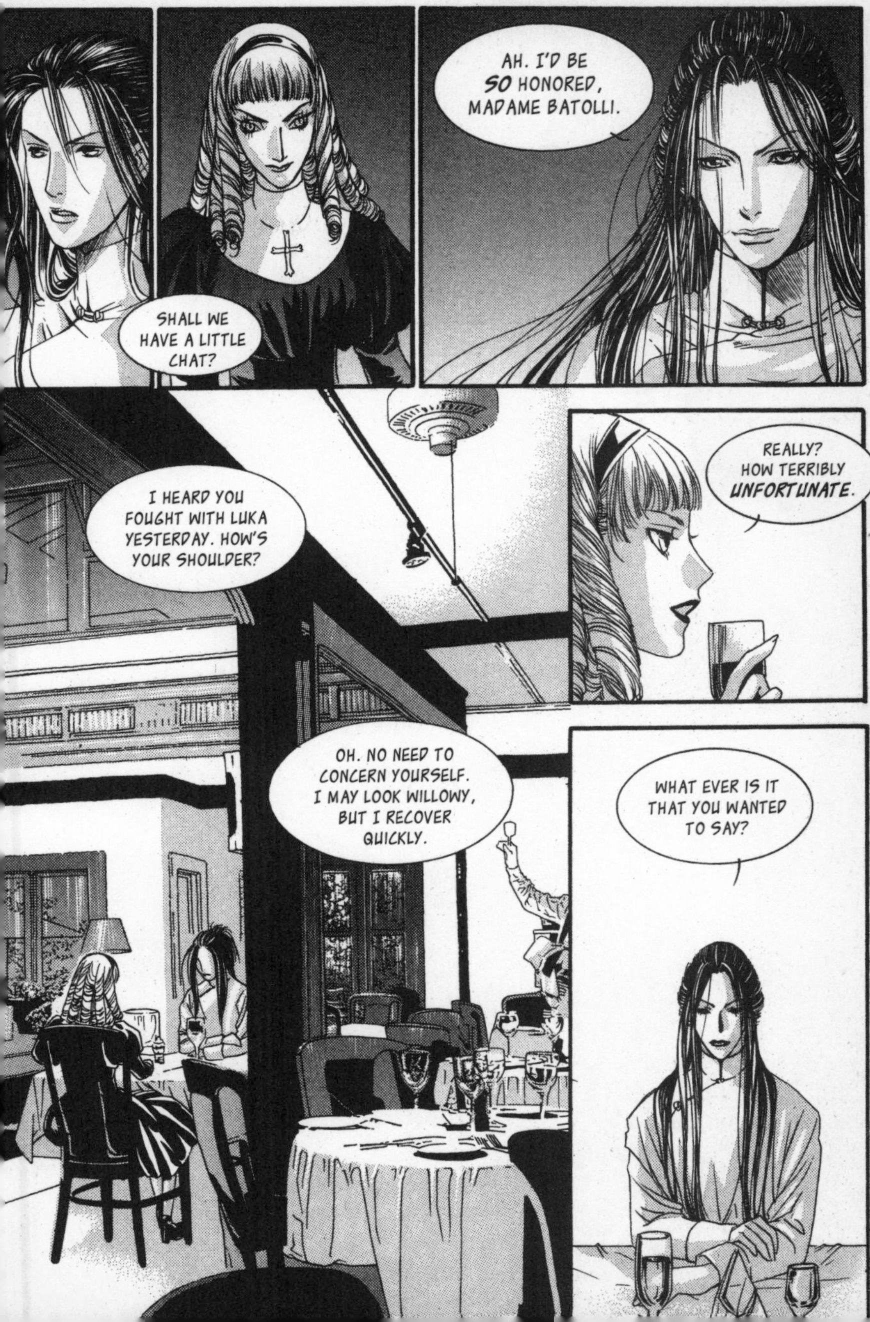
SHALL WE HAVE A LITTLE CHAT?
AH. I'D BE SO HONORED, MADAME BATOLLI.
I HEARD YOU FOUGHT WITH LUKA YESTERDAY. HOW'S YOUR SHOULDER?
REALLY? HOW TERRIBLY UNFORTUNATE.
OH. NO NEED TO CONCERN YOURSELF. I MAY LOOK WILLOWY, BUT I RECOVER QUICKLY.
WHAT EVER IS IT THAT YOU WANTED TO SAY?

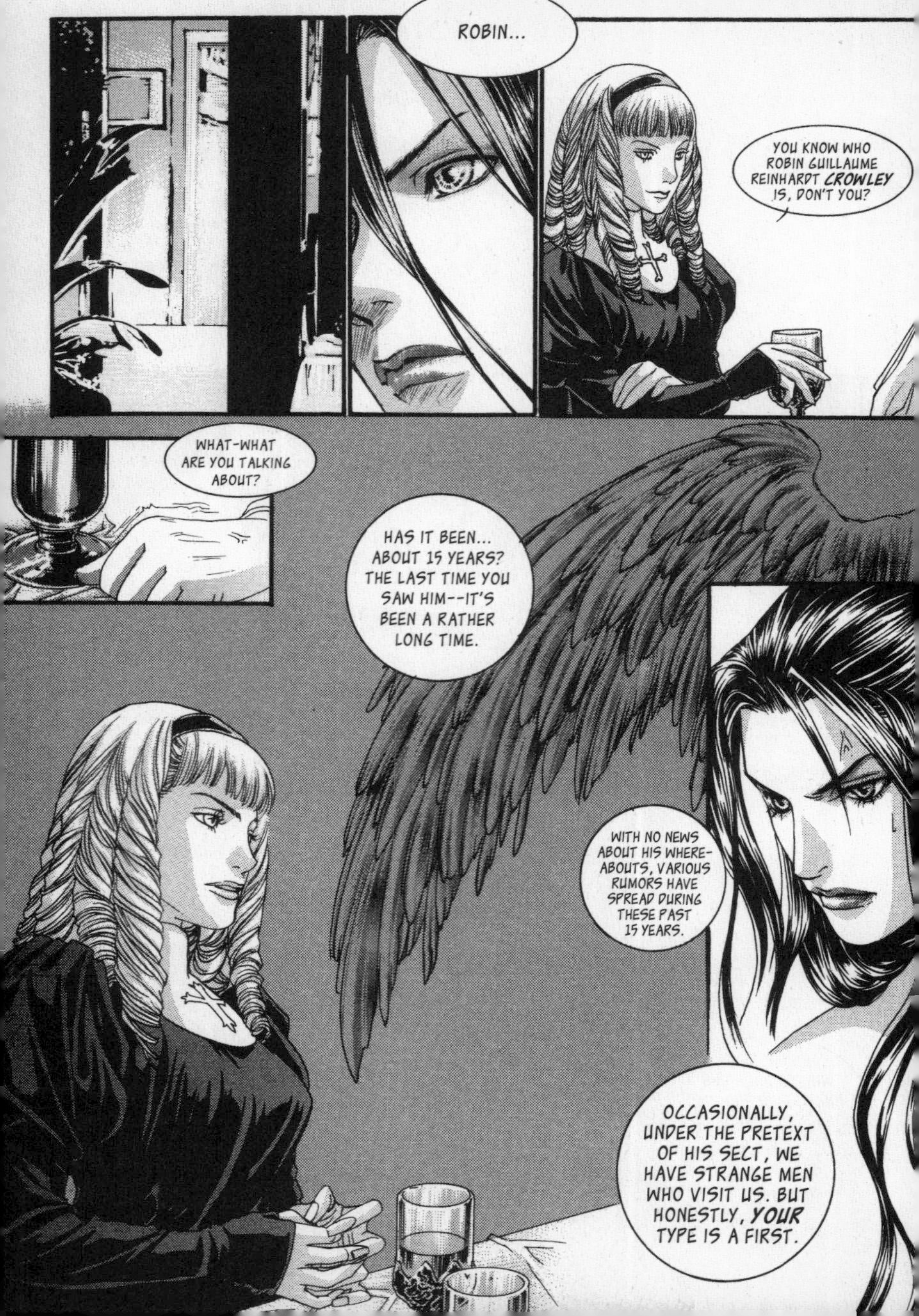
ROBIN...
YOU KNOW WHO ROBIN GUILLAUME REINHARDT CROWLEY IS, DON'T YOU?
WHAT-WHAT ARE YOU TALKING ABOUT?
HAS IT BEEN... ABOUT 15 YEARS? THE LAST TIME YOU SAW HIM--IT'S BEEN A RATHER LONG TIME.
WITH NO NEWS ABOUT HIS WHERE-ABOUTS, VARIOUS RUMORS HAVE SPREAD DURING THESE PAST 15 YEARS.
OCCASIONALLY, UNDER THE PRETEXT OF HIS SECT, WE HAVE STRANGE MEN WHO VISIT US. BUT HONESTLY, YOUR TYPE IS A FIRST.

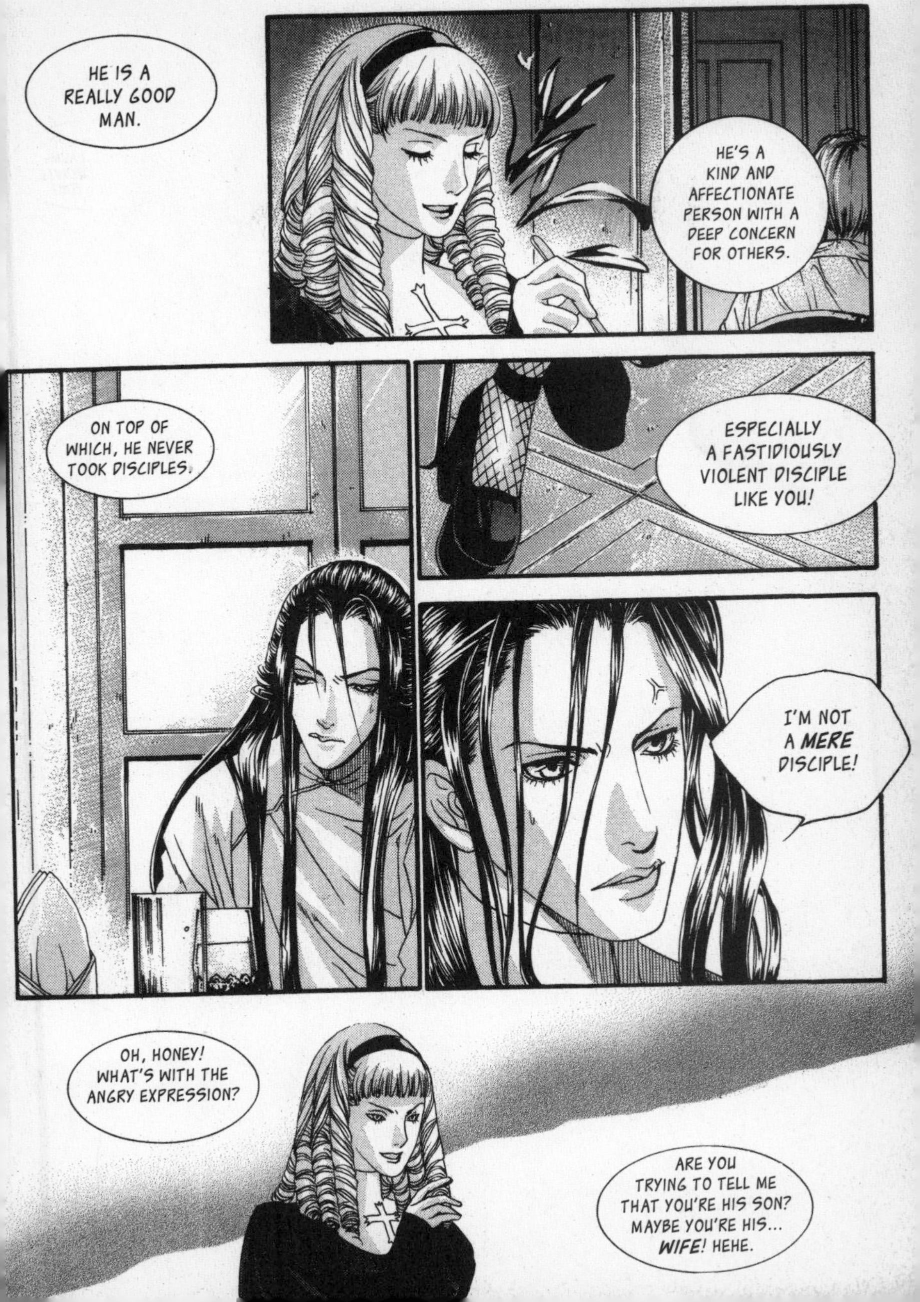
HE IS A REALLY GOOD MAN.
HE'S A KIND AND AFFECTIONATE PERSON WITH A DEEP CONCERN FOR OTHERS.
ON TOP OF WHICH, HE NEVER TOOK DISCIPLES.
ESPECIALLY A FASTIDIOUSLY VIOLENT DISCIPLE LIKE YOU!
I'M NOT A *MERE* DISCIPLE!
OH, HONEY! WHAT'S WITH THE ANGRY EXPRESSION?
ARE YOU TRYING TO TELL ME THAT YOU'RE HIS SON? MAYBE YOU'RE HIS... *WIFE*! HEHE.

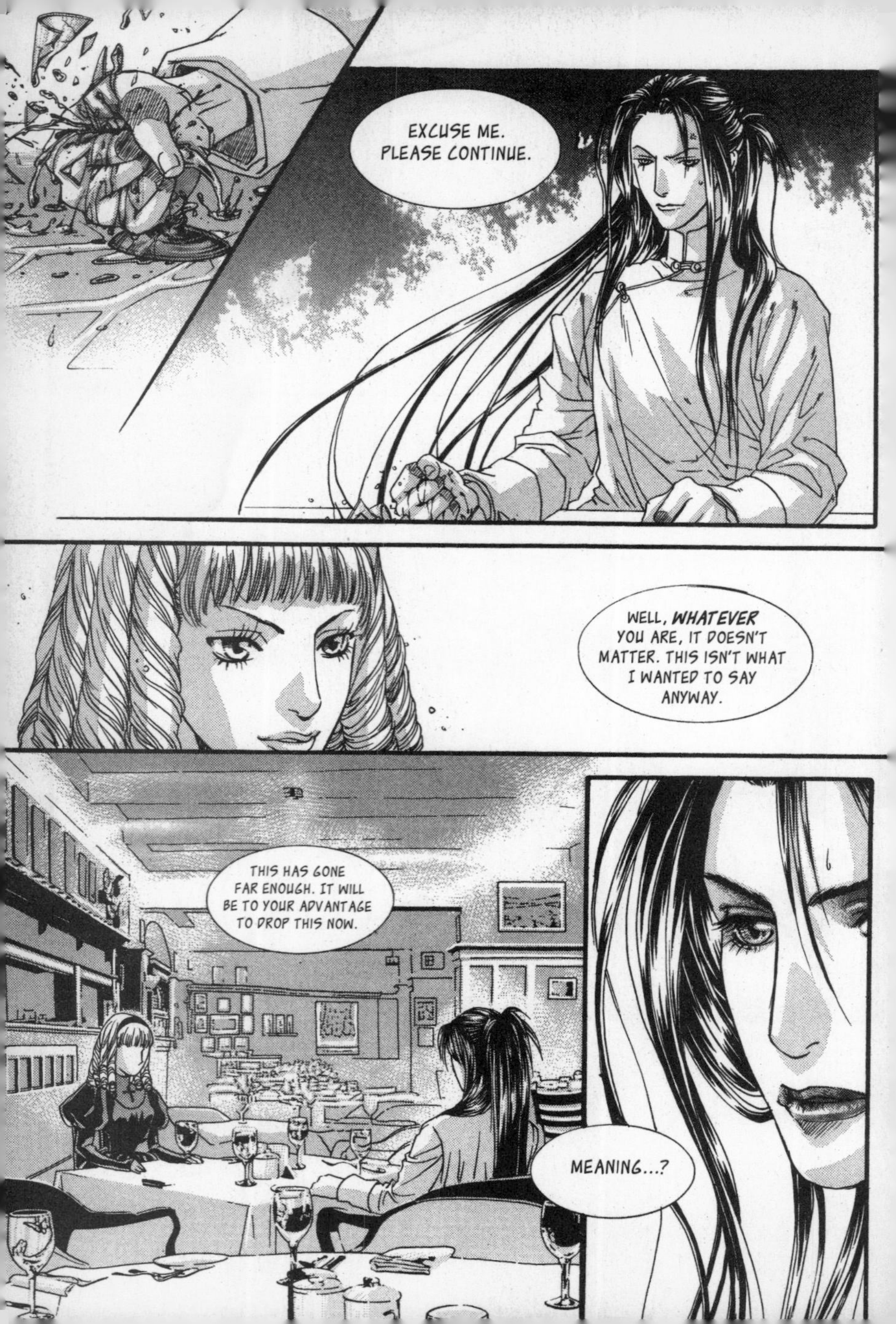
EXCUSE ME. PLEASE CONTINUE.
WELL, ***WHATEVER*** YOU ARE, IT DOESN'T MATTER. THIS ISN'T WHAT I WANTED TO SAY ANYWAY.
THIS HAS GONE FAR ENOUGH. IT WILL BE TO YOUR ADVANTAGE TO DROP THIS NOW.
MEANING...?

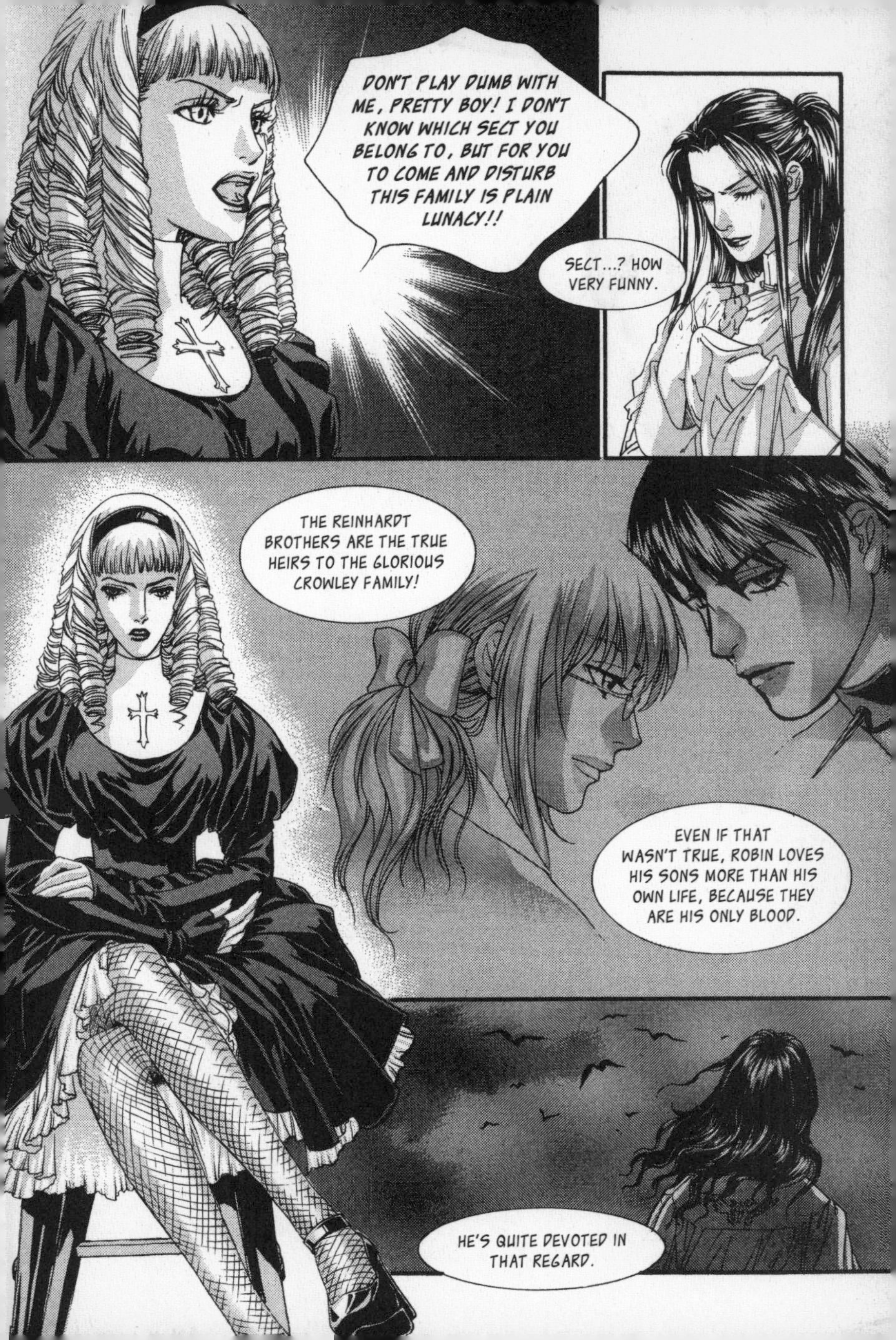
DON'T PLAY DUMB WITH ME, PRETTY BOY! I DON'T KNOW WHICH SECT YOU BELONG TO, BUT FOR YOU TO COME AND DISTURB THIS FAMILY IS PLAIN LUNACY!!
SECT...? HOW VERY FUNNY.
THE REINHARDT BROTHERS ARE THE TRUE HEIRS TO THE GLORIOUS CROWLEY FAMILY!
EVEN IF THAT WASN'T TRUE, ROBIN LOVES HIS SONS MORE THAN HIS OWN LIFE, BECAUSE THEY ARE HIS ONLY BLOOD.
HE'S QUITE DEVOTED IN THAT REGARD.

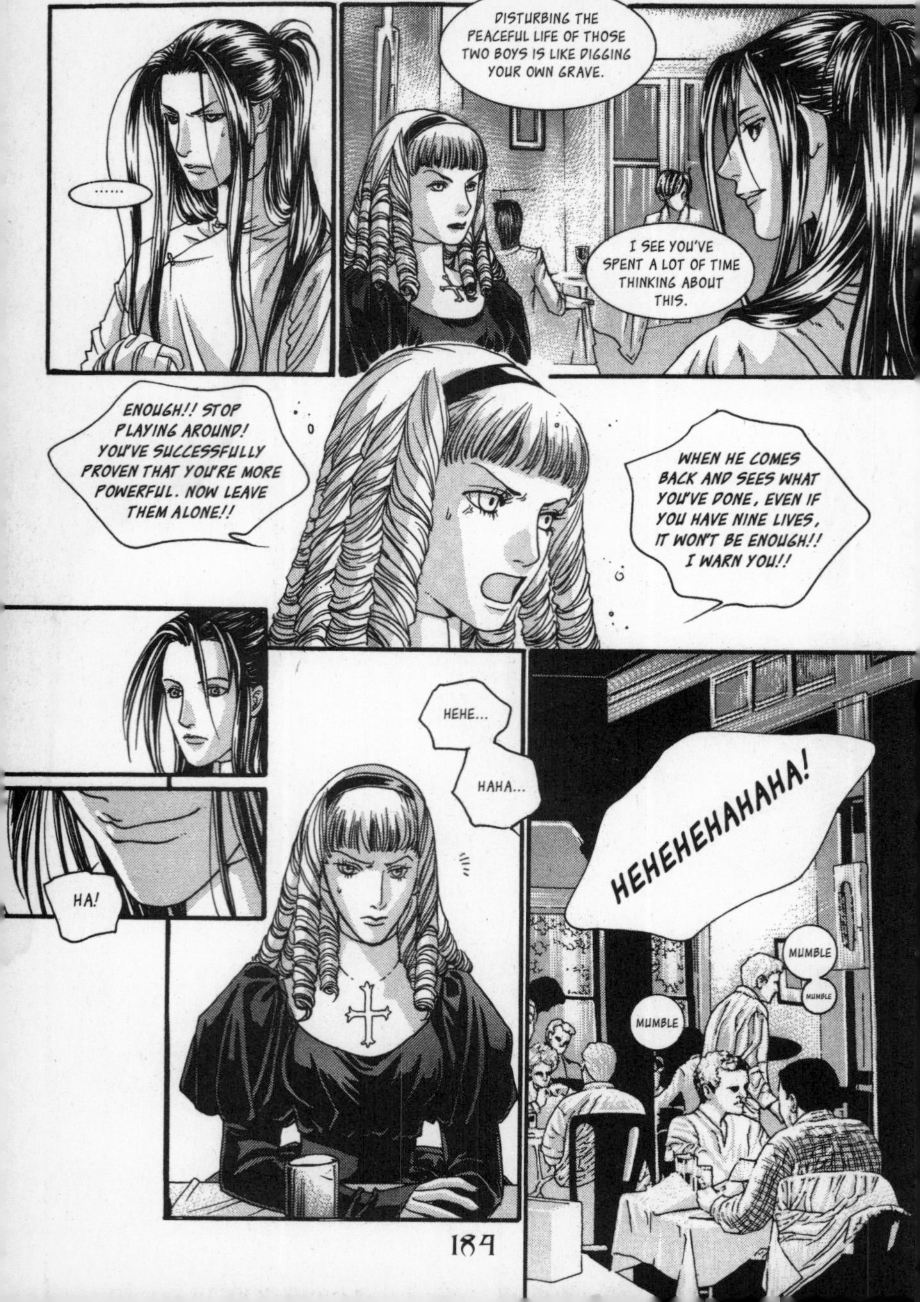
......
DISTURBING THE PEACEFUL LIFE OF THOSE TWO BOYS IS LIKE DIGGING YOUR OWN GRAVE.
I SEE YOU'VE SPENT A LOT OF TIME THINKING ABOUT THIS.
ENOUGH!! STOP PLAYING AROUND! YOU'VE SUCCESSFULLY PROVEN THAT YOU'RE MORE POWERFUL. NOW LEAVE THEM ALONE!!
WHEN HE COMES BACK AND SEES WHAT YOU'VE DONE, EVEN IF YOU HAVE NINE LIVES, IT WON'T BE ENOUGH!! I WARN YOU!!
HA!
HEHE...
HAHA...
HEHEHEHAHAHA!
MUMBLE
MUMBLE
MUMBLE

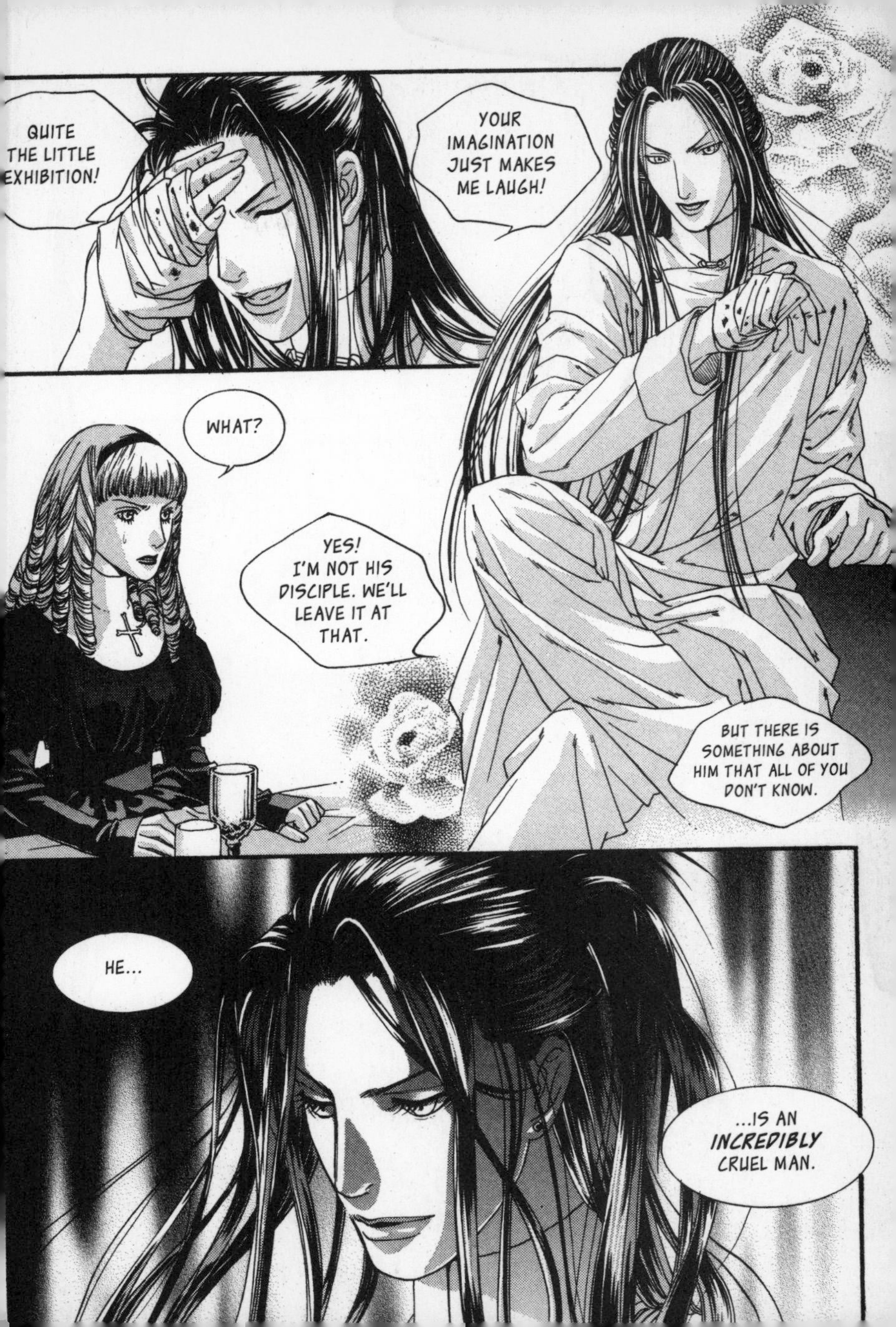
QUITE THE LITTLE EXHIBITION!
YOUR IMAGINATION JUST MAKES ME LAUGH!
WHAT?
YES! I'M NOT HIS DISCIPLE. WE'LL LEAVE IT AT THAT.
BUT THERE IS SOMETHING ABOUT HIM THAT ALL OF YOU DON'T KNOW.
HE...
...IS AN *INCREDIBLY* CRUEL MAN.

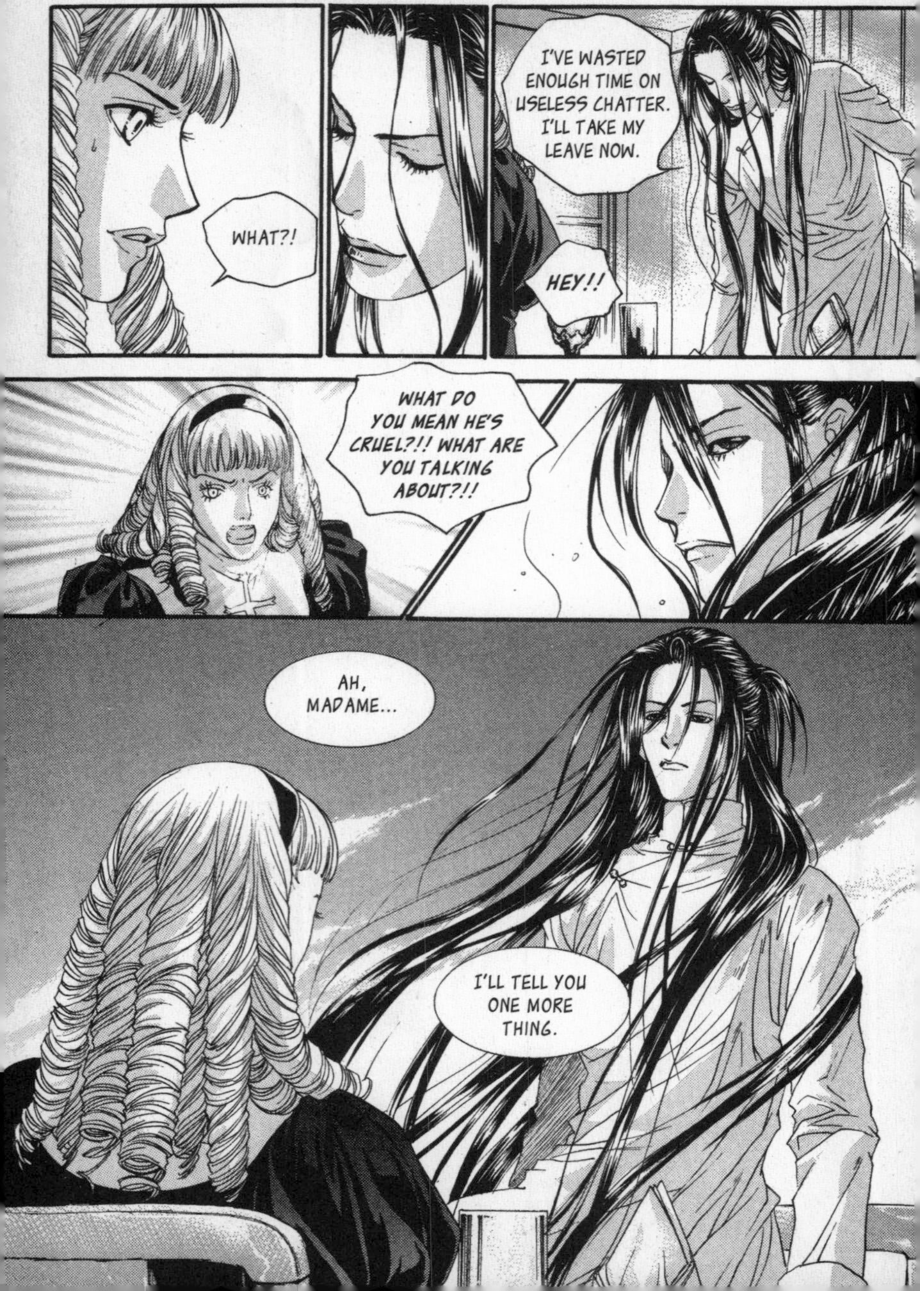
WHAT?!
I'VE WASTED ENOUGH TIME ON USELESS CHATTER. I'LL TAKE MY LEAVE NOW.
HEY!!
WHAT DO YOU MEAN HE'S CRUEL?!! WHAT ARE YOU TALKING ABOUT?!!
AH, MADAME...
I'LL TELL YOU ONE MORE THING.

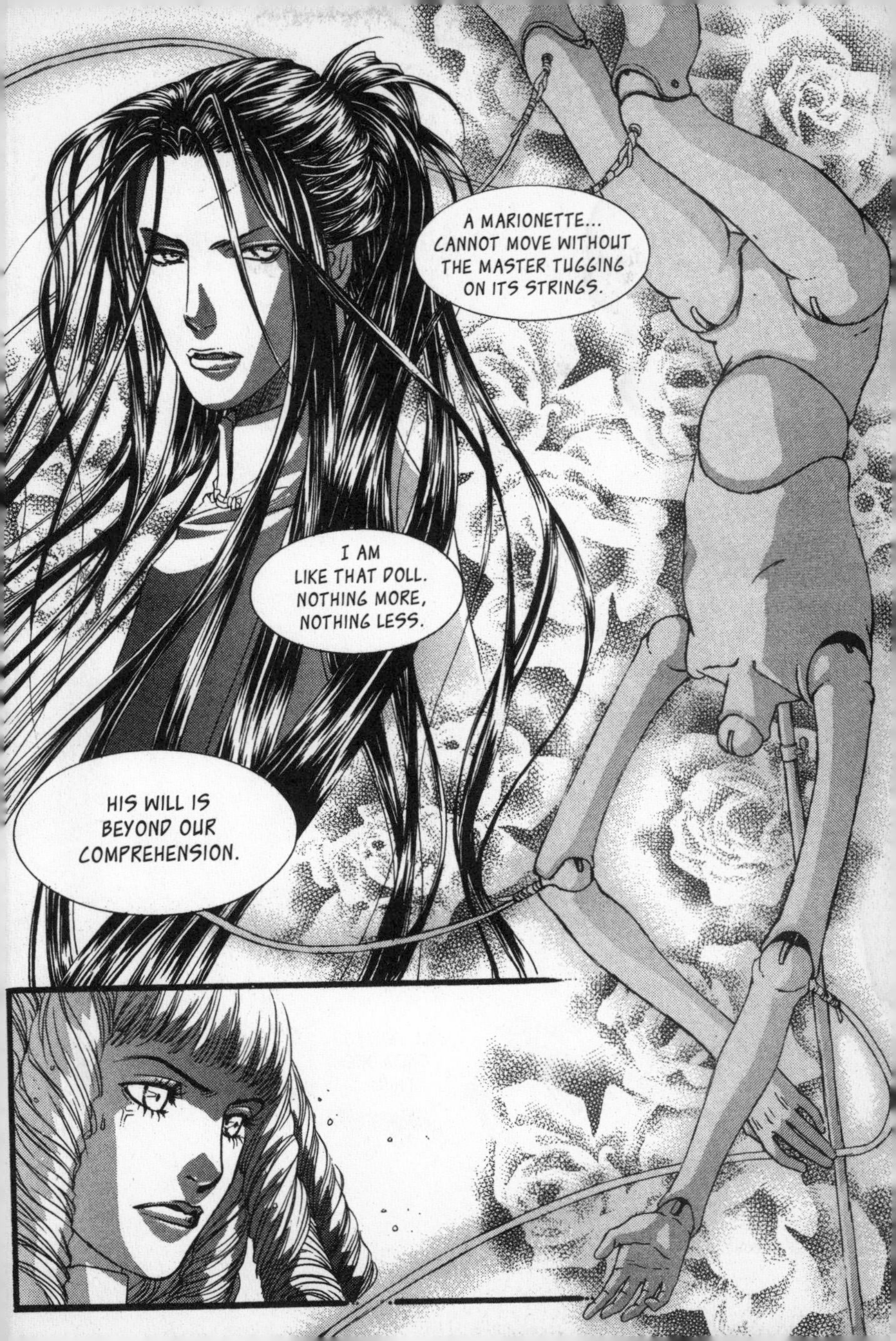
A MARIONETTE... CANNOT MOVE WITHOUT THE MASTER TUGGING ON ITS STRINGS.
I AM LIKE THAT DOLL. NOTHING MORE, NOTHING LESS.
HIS WILL IS BEYOND OUR COMPREHENSION.

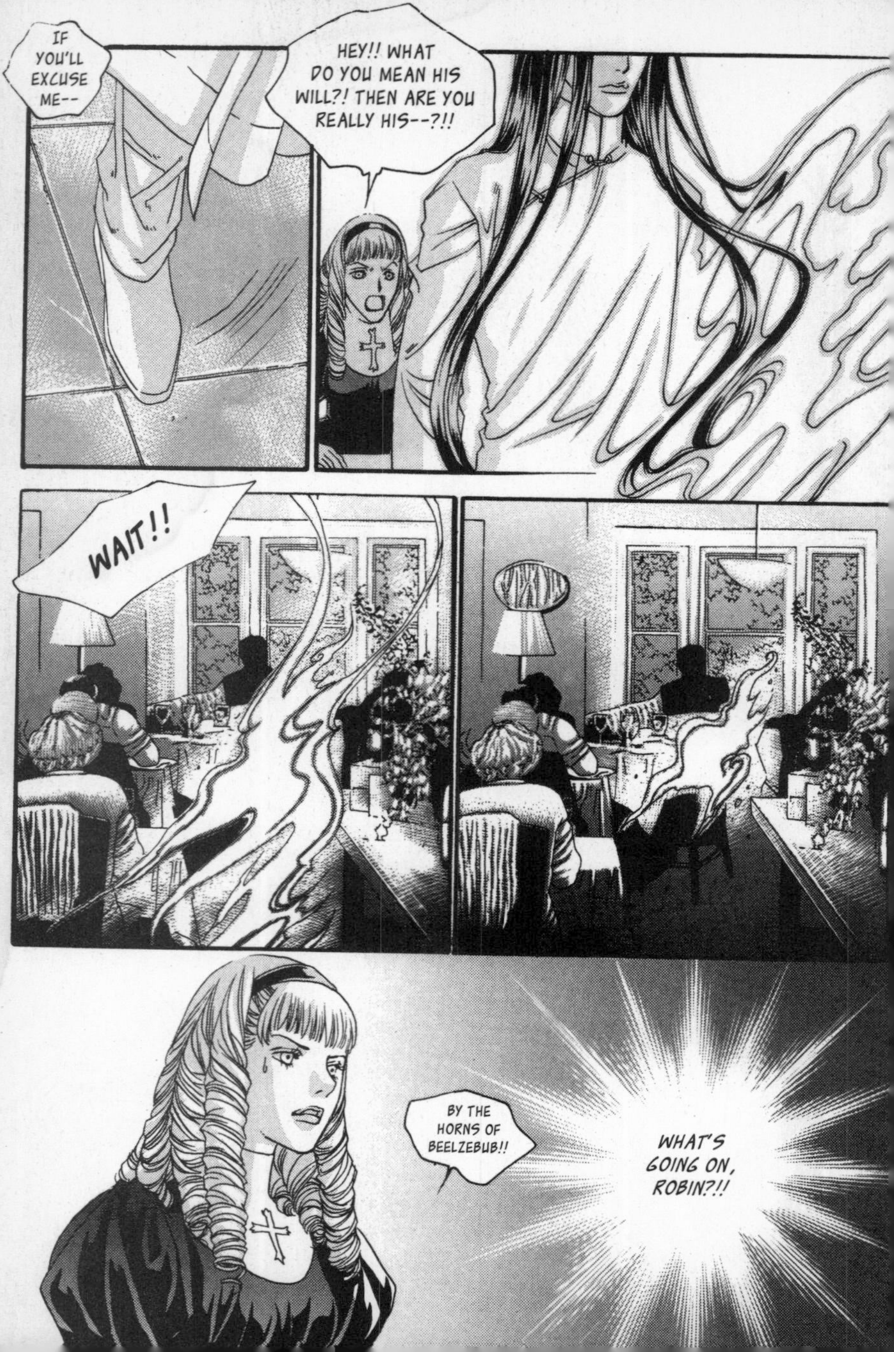
IF YOU'LL EXCUSE ME--
HEY!! WHAT DO YOU MEAN HIS WILL?! THEN ARE YOU REALLY HIS--?!!
WAIT!!
BY THE HORNS OF BEELZEBUB!!
WHAT'S GOING ON, ROBIN?!!

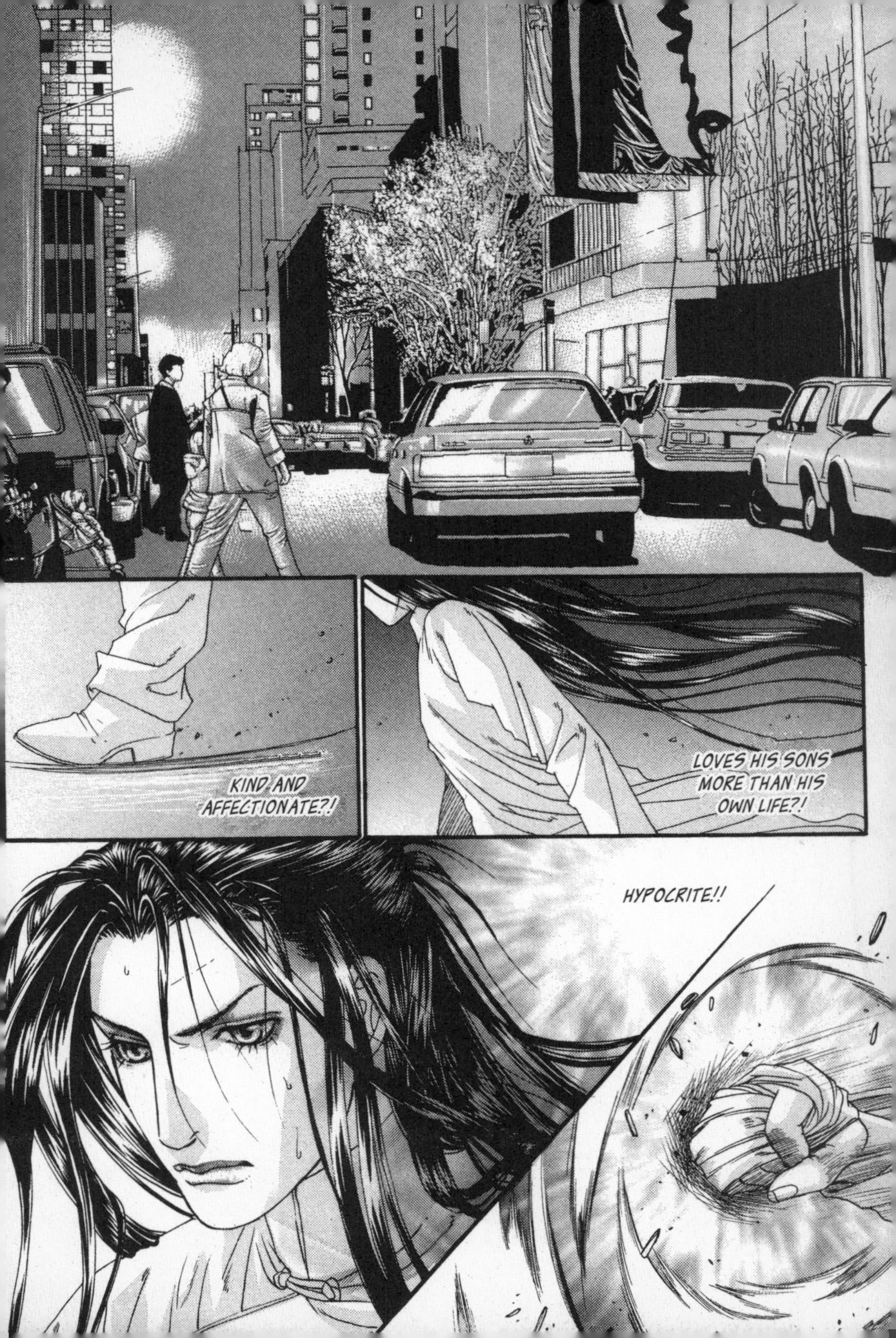
KIND AND AFFECTIONATE?!
LOVES HIS SONS MORE THAN HIS OWN LIFE?!
HYPOCRITE!!

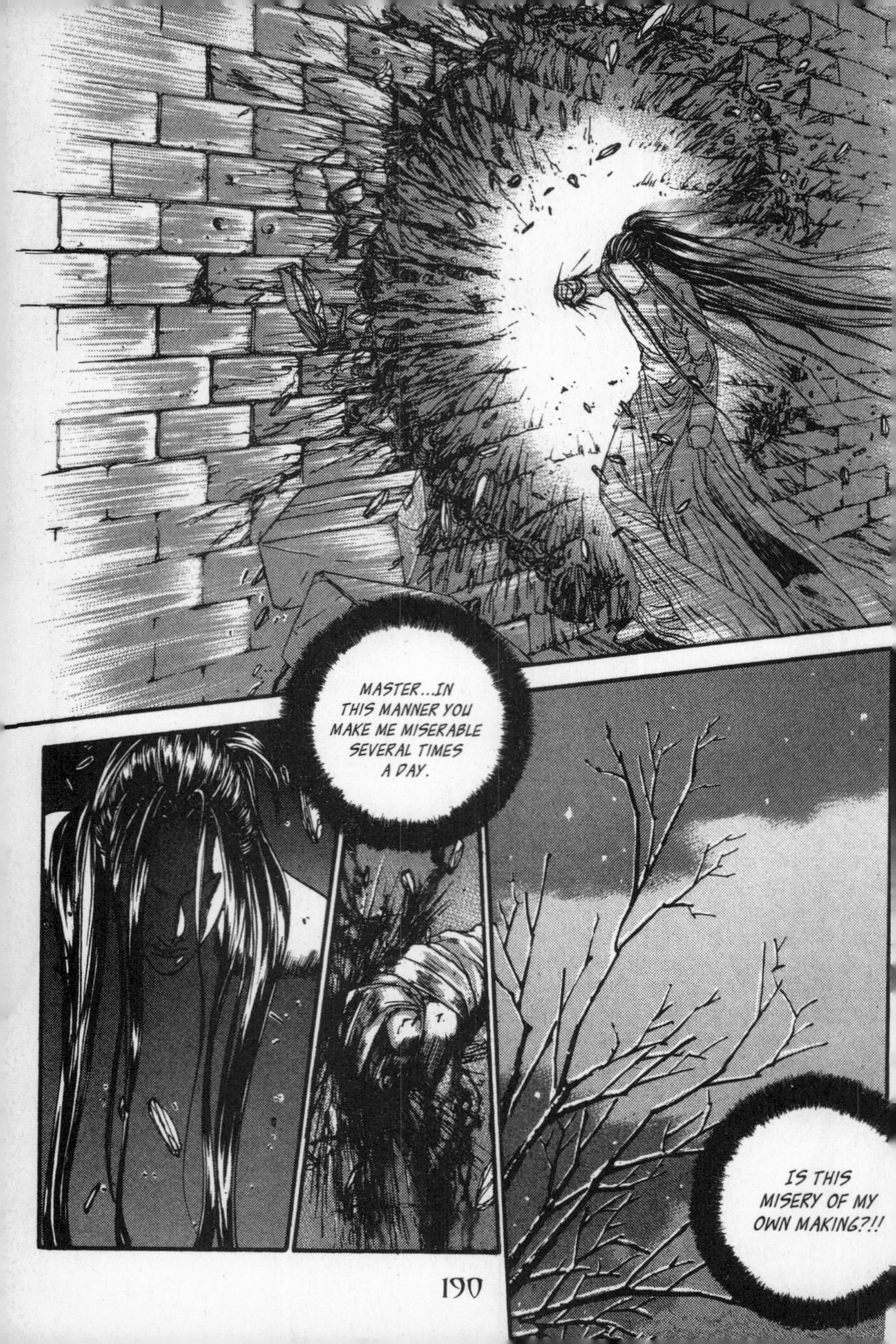
MASTER...IN THIS MANNER YOU MAKE ME MISERABLE SEVERAL TIMES A DAY.
IS THIS MISERY OF MY OWN MAKING?!!

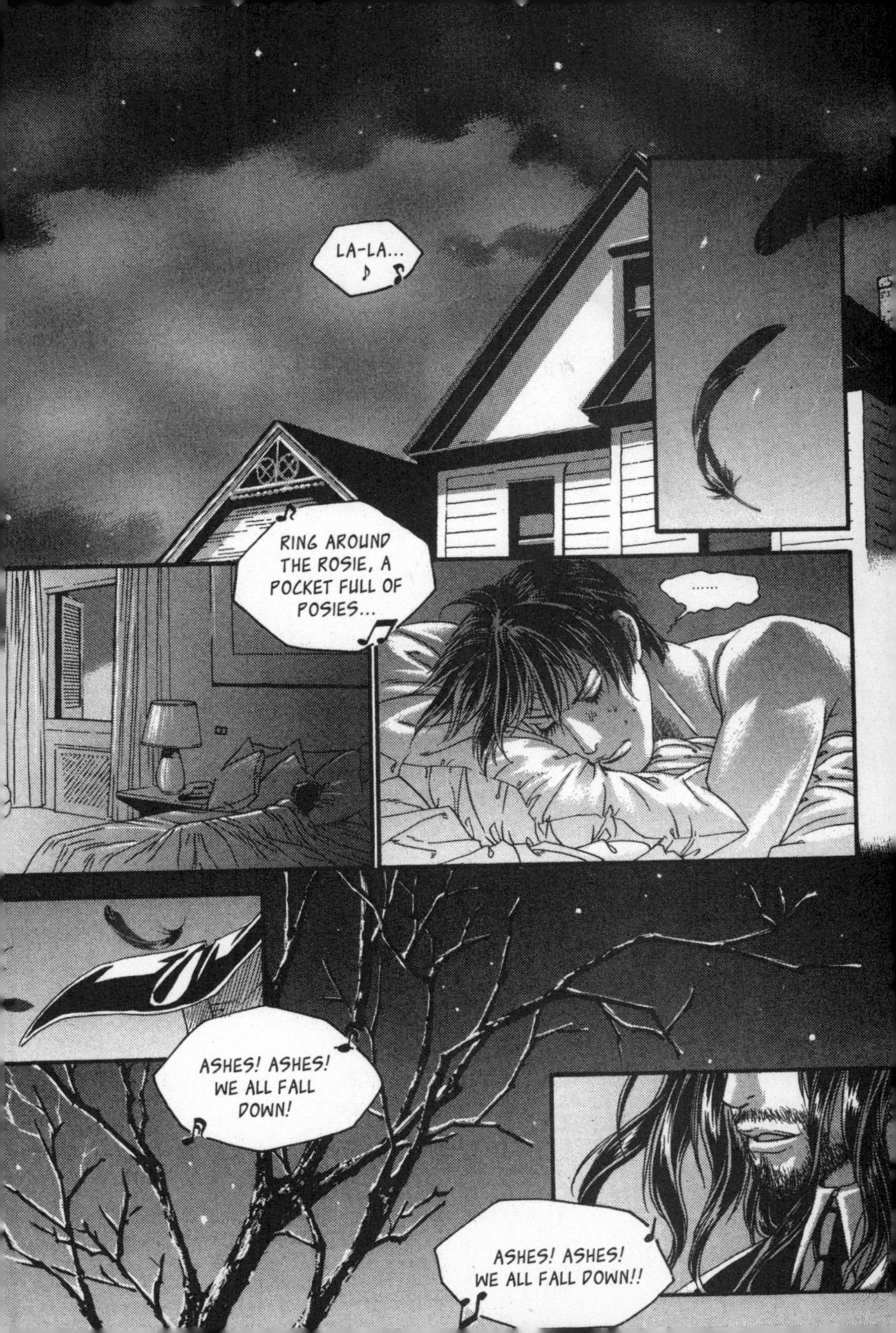
LA-LA... ♪
RING AROUND THE ROSIE, A POCKET FULL OF POSIES...
......
ASHES! ASHES! WE ALL FALL DOWN!
ASHES! ASHES! WE ALL FALL DOWN!!

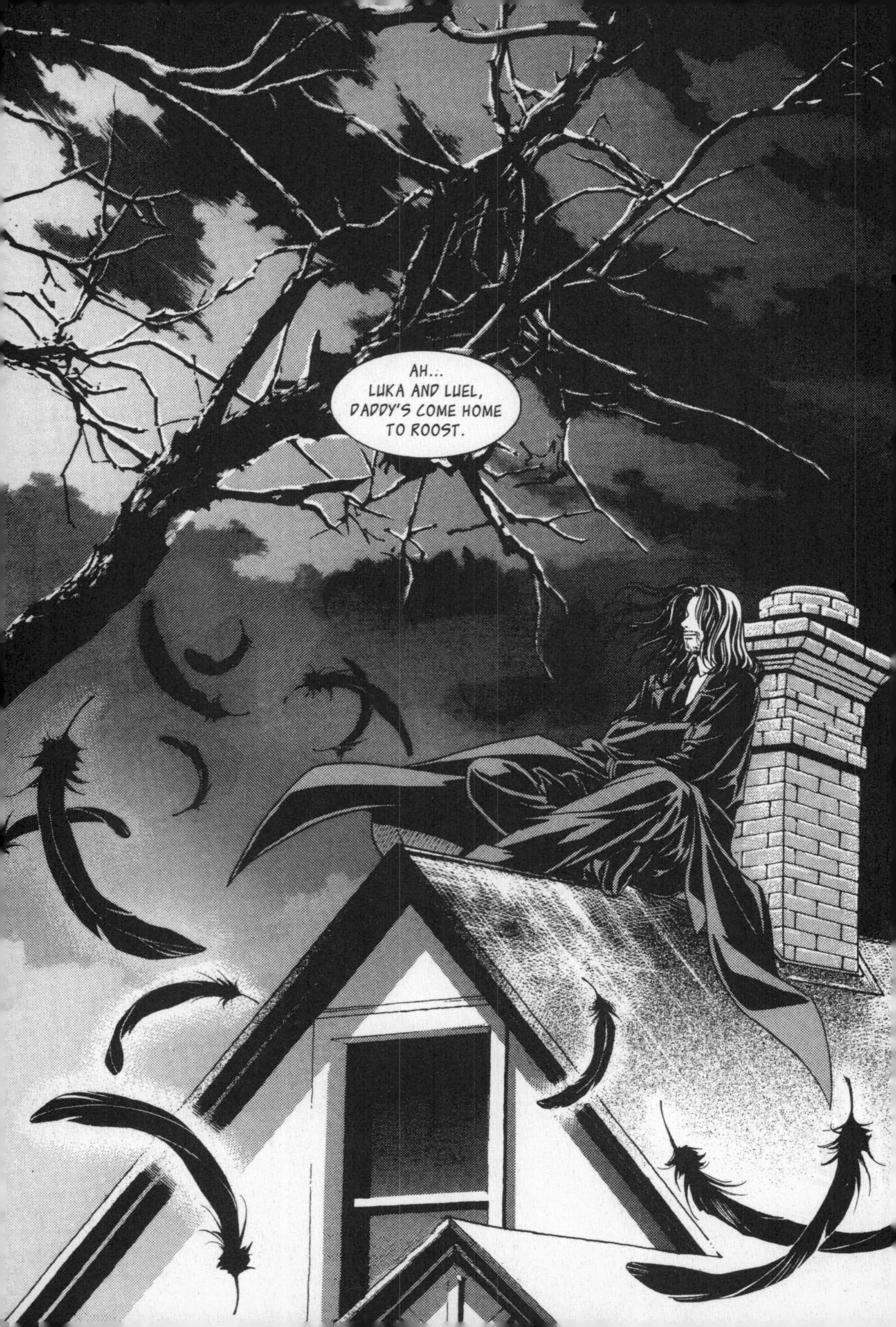
AH... LUKA AND LUEL, DADDY'S COME HOME TO ROOST.

Under the Glass Moon

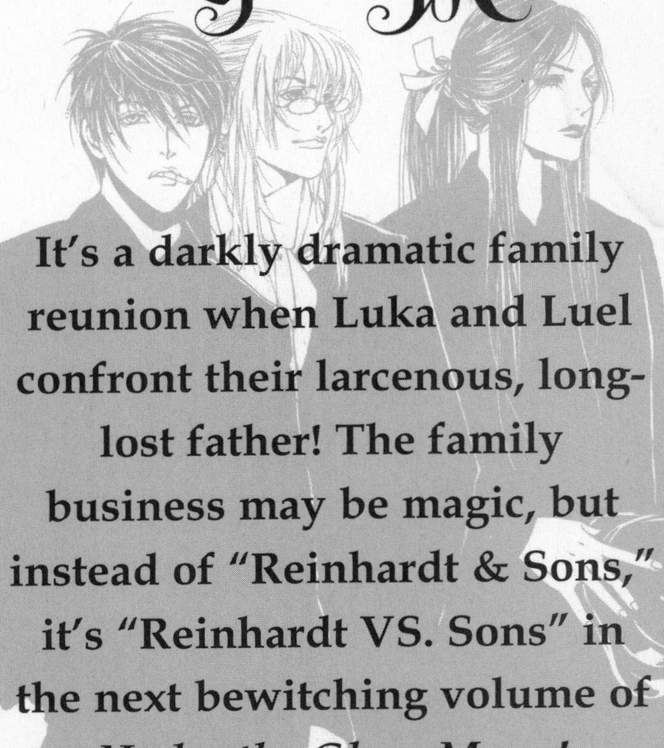

It's a darkly dramatic family reunion when Luka and Luel confront their larcenous, long-lost father! The family business may be magic, but instead of "Reinhardt & Sons," it's "Reinhardt VS. Sons" in the next bewitching volume of *Under the Glass Moon!*

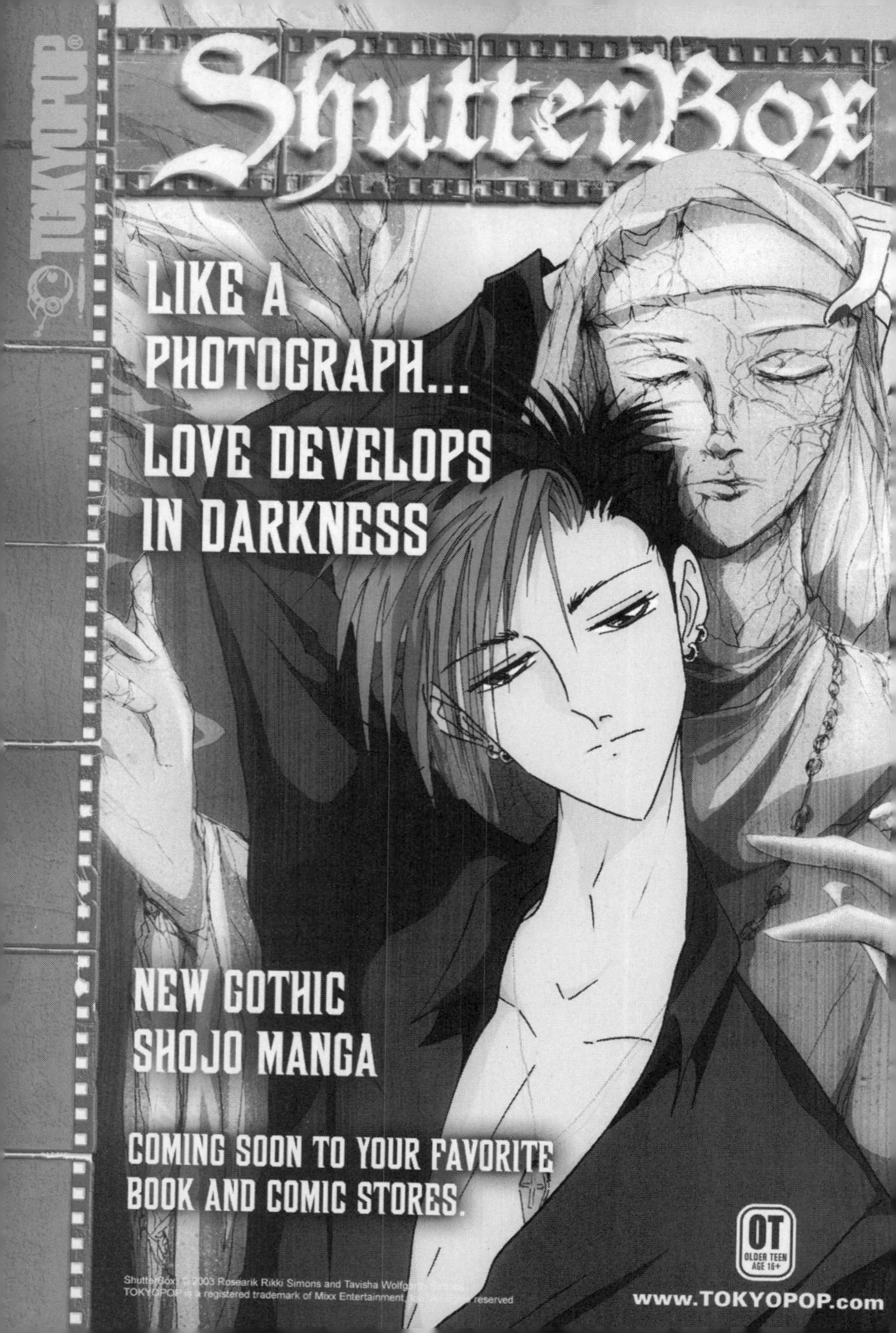
TOKYOPOP
ShutterBox
LIKE A PHOTOGRAPH...
LOVE DEVELOPS IN DARKNESS
NEW GOTHIC SHOJO MANGA
COMING SOON TO YOUR FAVORITE BOOK AND COMIC STORES.
OT OLDER TEEN AGE 16+
ShutterBox © 2003 Rosearik Rikki Simons and Tavisha Wolf
TOKYOPOP is a registered trademark of Mixx Entertainment reserved
www.TOKYOPOP.com

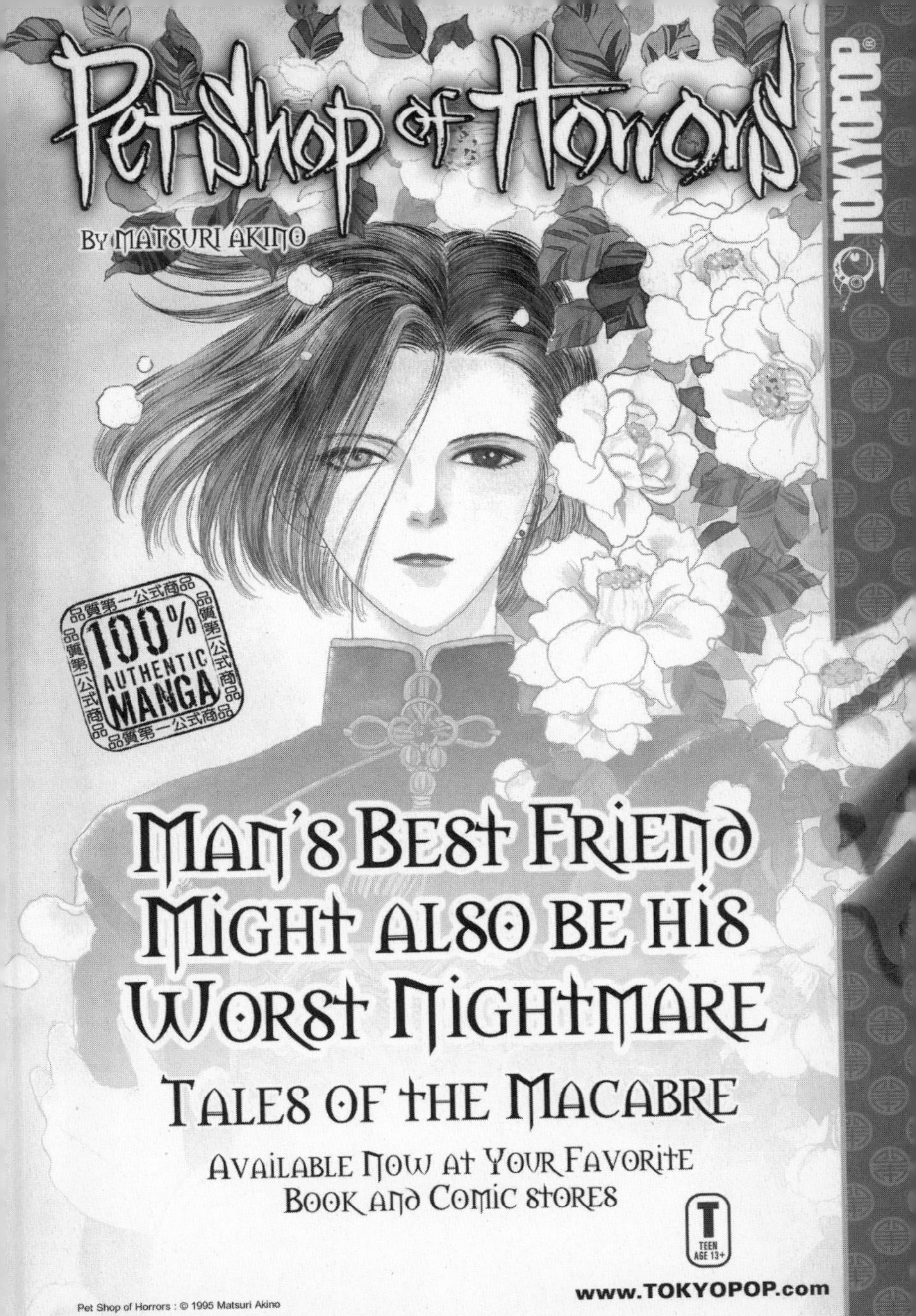
Pet Shop of Horrors
BY MATSURI AKINO
TOKYOPOP
品質第一公式商品
100% AUTHENTIC MANGA
MAN'S BEST FRIEND MIGHT ALSO BE HIS WORST NIGHTMARE
TALES OF THE MACABRE
AVAILABLE NOW AT YOUR FAVORITE BOOK AND COMIC STORES
T TEEN AGE 13+
www.TOKYOPOP.com

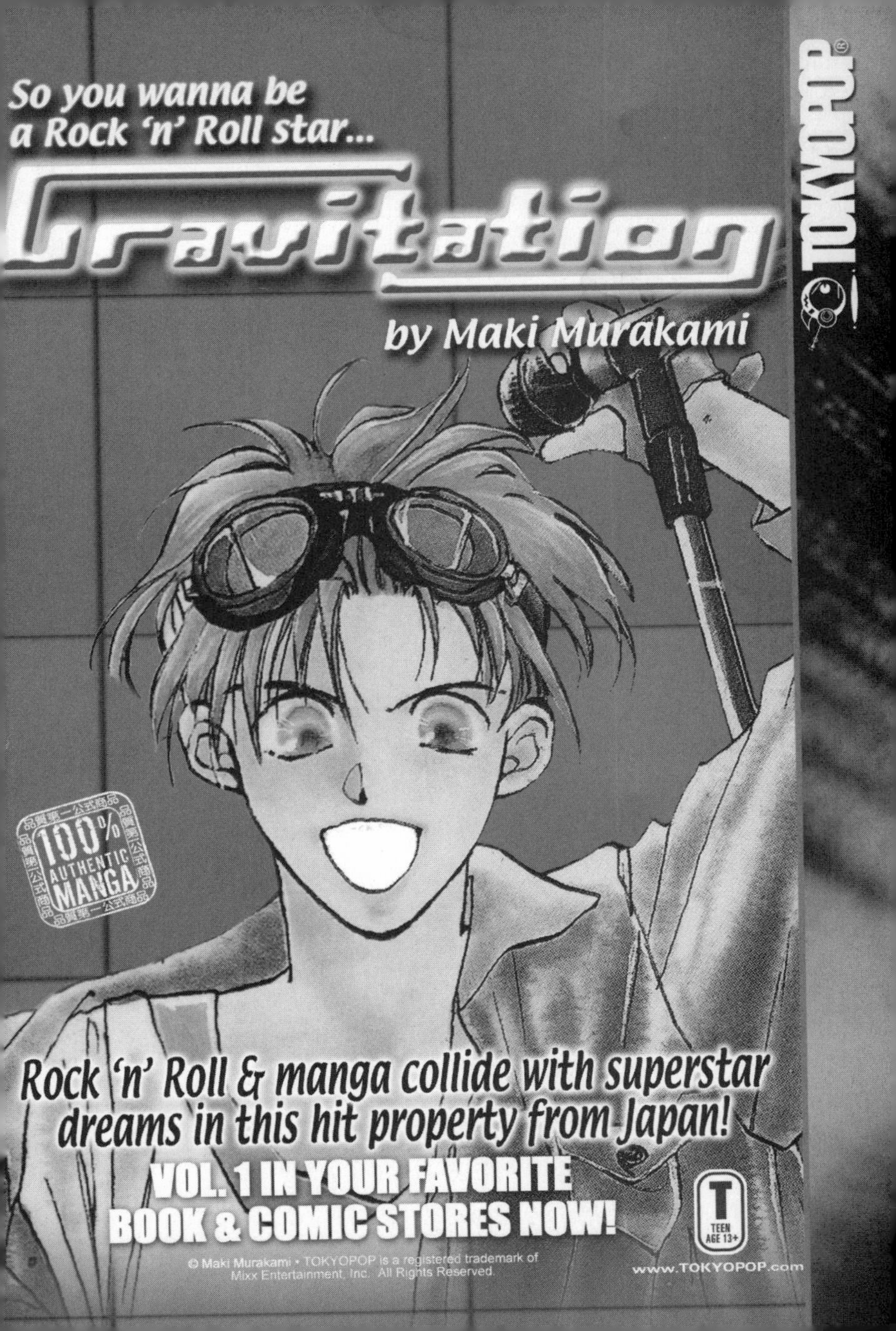
So you wanna be
a Rock 'n' Roll star...
Gravitation
by Maki Murakami
TOKYOPOP
100% AUTHENTIC MANGA
Rock 'n' Roll & manga collide with superstar
dreams in this hit property from Japan!
VOL. 1 IN YOUR FAVORITE
BOOK & COMIC STORES NOW!
T TEEN AGE 13+
© Maki Murakami • TOKYOPOP is a registered trademark of
Mixx Entertainment, Inc. All Rights Reserved.
www.TOKYOPOP.com

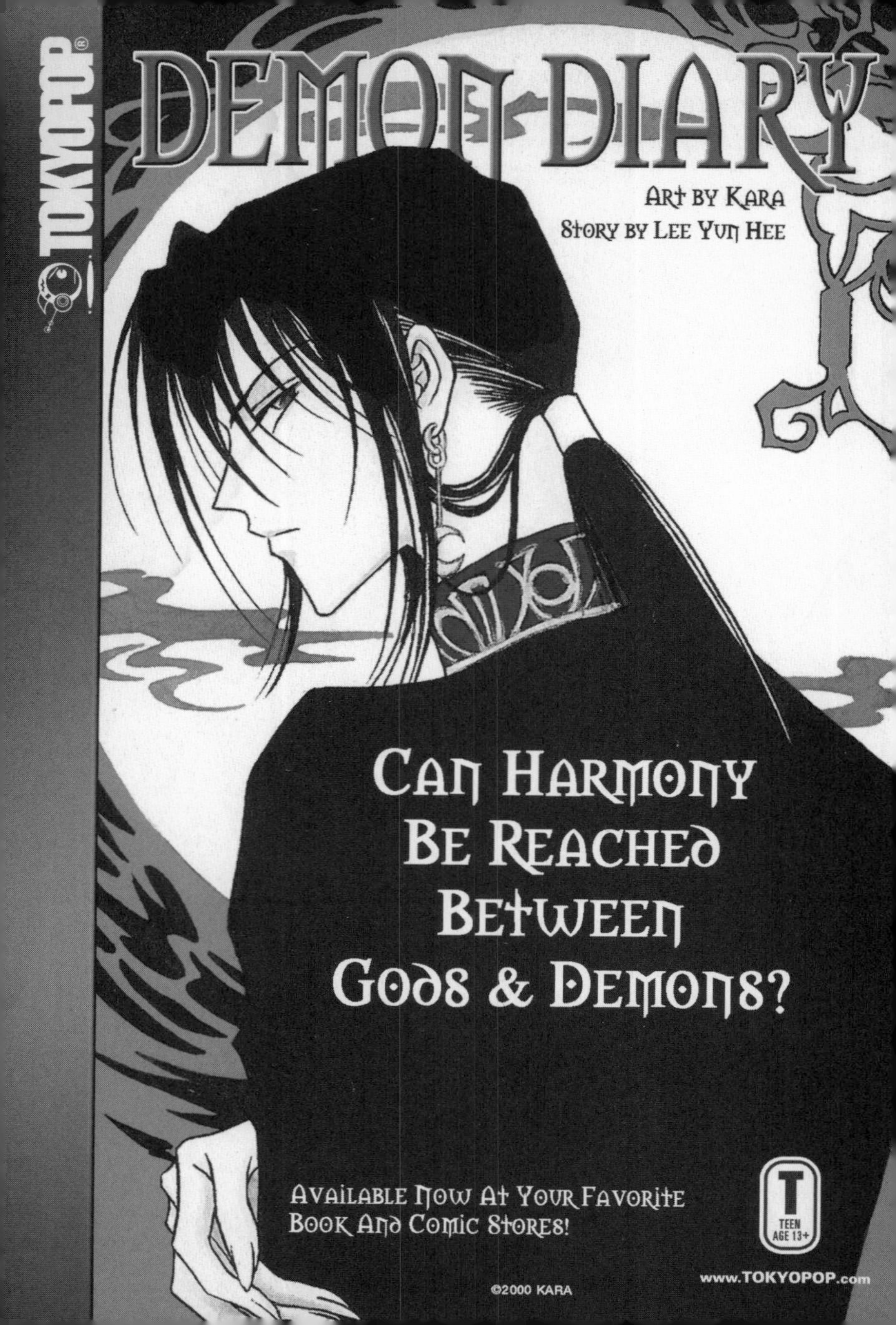
TOKYOPOP®
DEMON DIARY
ART BY KARA
STORY BY LEE YUN HEE
CAN HARMONY BE REACHED BETWEEN GODS & DEMONS?
AVAILABLE NOW AT YOUR FAVORITE BOOK AND COMIC STORES!
T
TEEN
AGE 13+
www.TOKYOPOP.com
©2000 KARA

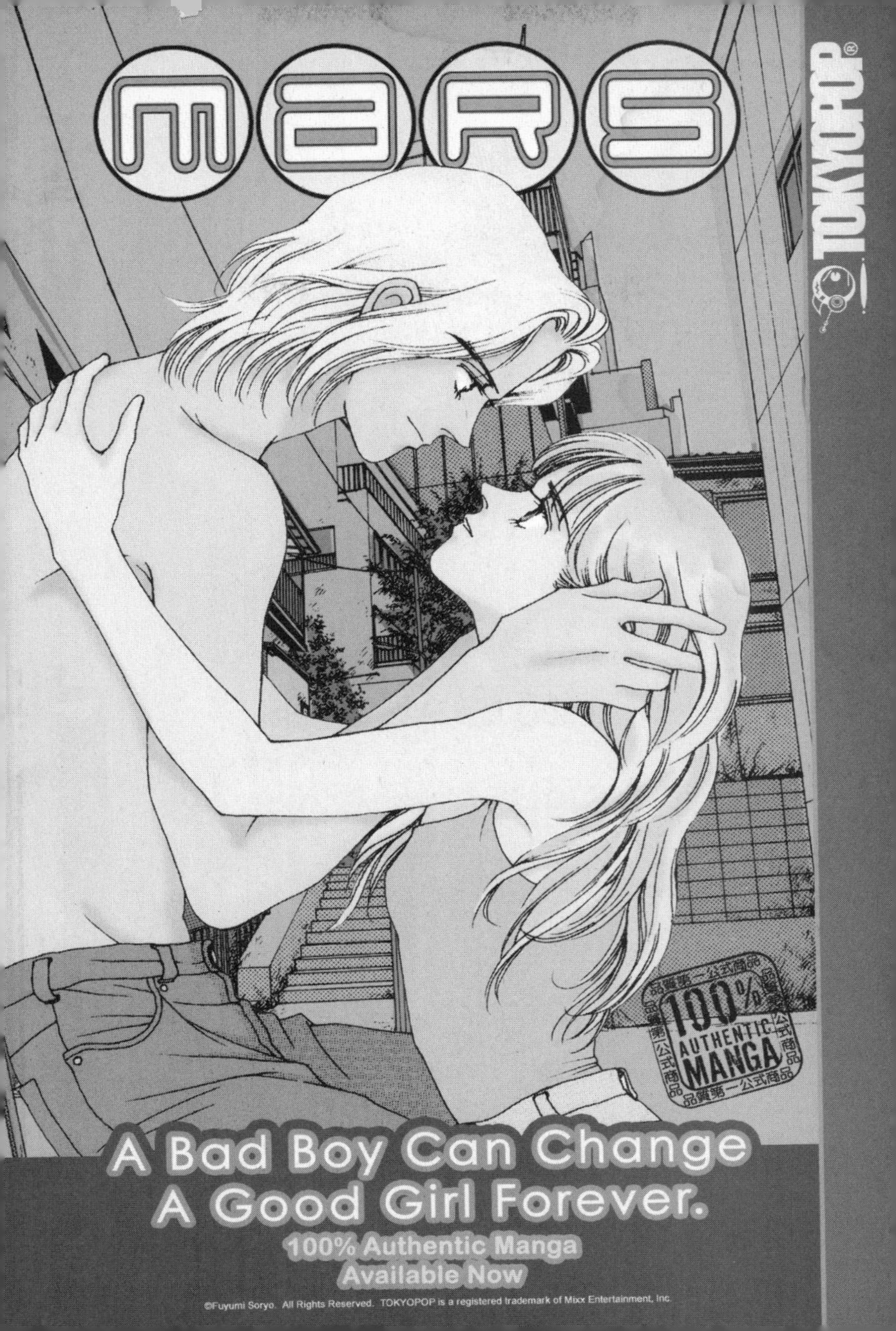
MARS
TOKYOPOP
100% AUTHENTIC MANGA
品質第一公式商品
A Bad Boy Can Change
A Good Girl Forever.
100% Authentic Manga
Available Now
©Fuyumi Soryo. All Rights Reserved. TOKYOPOP is a registered trademark of Mixx Entertainment, Inc.

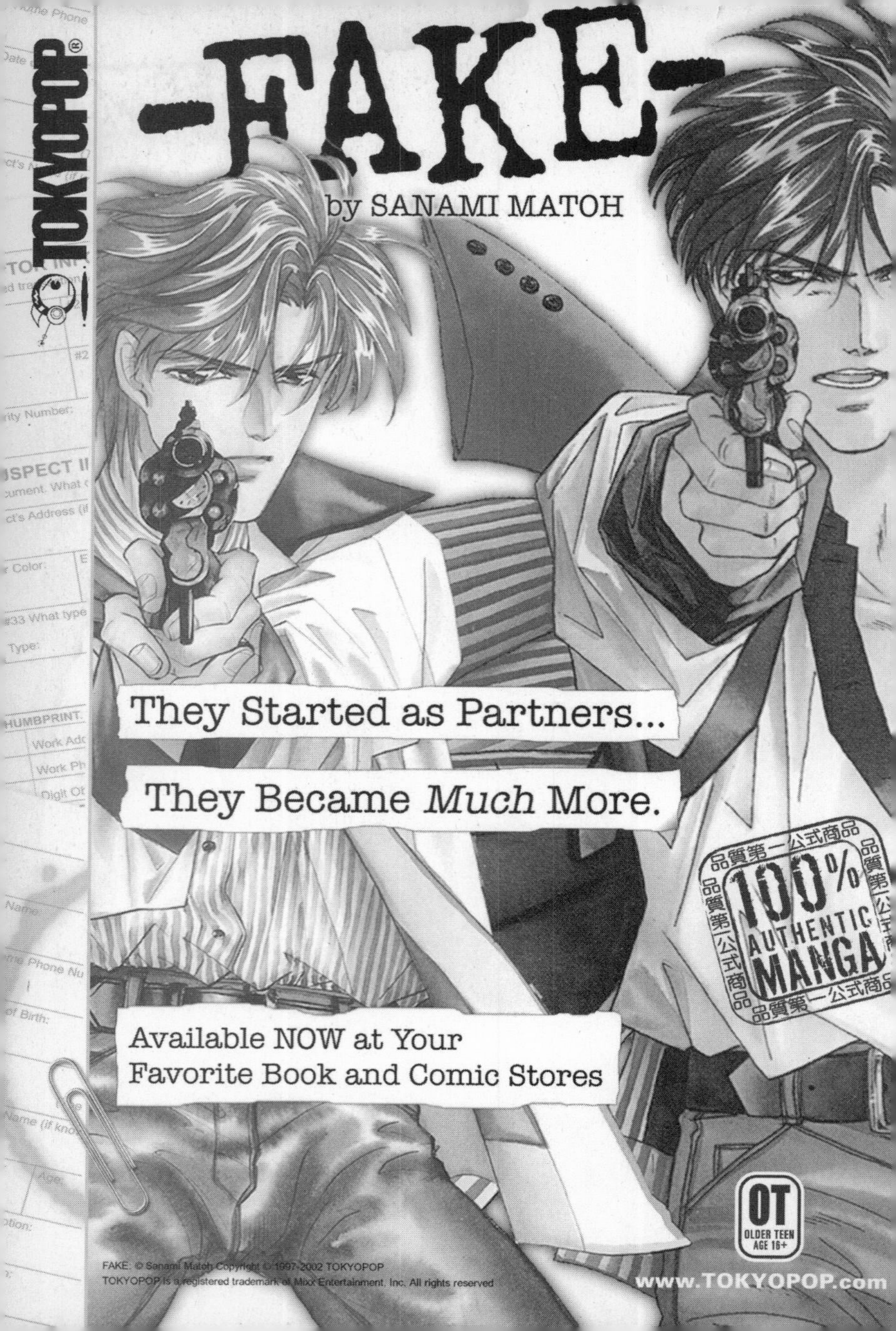

TOKYOPOP®
-FAKE-
by SANAMI MATOH
They Started as Partners...
They Became *Much* More.
品質第一公式商品
100% AUTHENTIC MANGA
Available NOW at Your
Favorite Book and Comic Stores
OT
OLDER TEEN AGE 16+
FAKE: © Sanami Matoh Copyright © 1997-2002 TOKYOPOP
TOKYOPOP is a registered trademark of Mixx Entertainment, Inc. All rights reserved
www.TOKYOPOP.com